"PANENTHEISM (Gk. πας, 'everything'; εν, 'in'; θεος, 'God'). The belief that the Being of God includes and penetrates the whole universe, so that every part of it exists in Him, but (as against Pantheism) that His Being is more than, and is not exhausted by, the universe."

Oxford Dictionary of the Christian Church

"La gloria di colui che tutto move
per l'Universo penetra, e risplede
in una parte più e meno altrove"

"His glory, in whose being all things move,
pervades Creation and, here more there less
resplendent, shines in every part thereof"

Dante: *Paradiso*, Canto I, ll. 1-3

"He who sees Me everywhere and sees all in Me;
I am not lost to him nor is he lost to Me."

The Bhagavadgita, Ch. VI (30)

IN WHOM WE LIVE AND MOVE AND HAVE OUR BEING

Panentheistic Reflections on
God's Presence in a Scientific World

Edited by

Philip Clayton and Arthur Peacocke

WILLIAM B. EERDMANS PUBLISHING COMPANY
GRAND RAPIDS, MICHIGAN / CAMBRIDGE, U.K.

Wm. B. Eerdmans Publishing Co.
255 Jefferson Ave. S.E., Grand Rapids, Michigan 49503 /
P.O. Box 163, Cambridge CB3 9PU U.K.
www.eerdmans.com

Printed in the United States of America

08 07 06 05 04   7 6 5 4 3 2 1

Library of Congress Cataloging-in-Publication Data

In whom we live and move and have our being: panentheistic reflections on God's
    presence in a scientific world / edited by Philip Clayton and Arthur Peacocke.
        p.   cm.
    Includes bibliographical references and index.
    ISBN-10: 0-8028-0978-2 / ISBN-13: 978-0-8028-0978-0 (pbk.: alk. paper)
        1. Panentheism — Congresses.   I. Clayton, Philip, 1956-
    II. Peacocke, A. R. (Arthur Robert)

    BT 113.I5   2004
    211'.2 — dc22

                                                            2003066062

THE EPIGRAPHS

(*Oxford Dictionary of the Christian Church,* ed. F. L. Cross and E. A. Livingstone, 2nd ed.
[Oxford: Oxford University Press, 1985], p. 1027)

Dante: *Paradiso,* Canto I, ll. 1-3 (trans. Geoffrey L. Bickersteth [Oxford: Blackwell, Shakespeare Head, 1965], p. 517)

The Bhagavadgita, Ch. VI (30) (Edition of S. Radhakrishnan [Bombay: Blackie, 1970],
p. 204)

Contents

Contents

Foreword

The present book about God's relationship to the created world grew out of a symposium sponsored by the John Templeton Foundation under the aegis of its Humble Approach Initiative. The initiative is inherently interdisciplinary and sensitive to nuance, is biased in favor of building linkages and connections, and promotes risk-taking discussion that leads to the generation of new ideas for writing, teaching, and research. It assumes a willingness to experiment on the part of all participants. Sir John Templeton has said that "humility is a gateway to greater understanding and open[s] the doors to progress" in all endeavors.[1] He believes that in their quest to comprehend ultimate reality, scientists, philosophers, and theologians have much to learn about and from one another. That those who gathered within the walls of Windsor Castle on 6, 7, and 8 December 2001 did so in very considerable measure is indicated by the essays in this volume.

Their spirited conversation, chaired by Philip Clayton and Arthur Peacocke, took place in St. George's House, which is an integral part of the College of St. George, a community of clergy and laypeople established in 1348 by King Edward III as a spiritual complement to the Knights of the Garter, England's most ancient order of chivalry.

The director of St. George's House, Canon Barry Thompson; the Right Reverend David Conner, Dean of Windsor; and Bishop Basil of Sergievo, along with Thomas Jay Oord, professor and chair of philosophy at Western Nazarene College, were engaged observers for much of the discussion. We are grateful to Dean Conner and his wife for entertaining us in their home at the close of our three-day conversation. It was a festive finale to a probing and provocative exchange of research findings, ideas, and opinions.

In Whom We Live and Move and Have Our Being contains essays written by all the symposium participants plus Michael Brierley, who was specially commissioned after the meeting to contribute a survey of panentheism in modern theology, and our colleague Paul Davies, who had planned to join us in Windsor but, in the end, was unable to do so. While some of the writers place the discussion in a present-day scientific setting and others look to the wisdom of past sages in the East as well as the West, all of them consider issues related to the mystery of divine agency that are at once fundamental and profoundly contemporary. My colleagues and I at the Templeton Foundation appreciate the willingness of each contributor to undertake a quest that must remain forever open-ended and subject to revision. We thank Dr. Clayton and Dr. Peacocke for their help in shaping a dynamic symposium and for their thoughtful and patient editing of this volume. The editors and I gratefully acknowledge the work of Andrea Zimmerman, a graduate student at the Claremont School of Theology, who compiled the book's index. All of us connected with the venture are grateful to Sir John, whose vision inspired our efforts.

MARY ANN MEYERS

Summaries of the Contributions to This Volume

After the introduction by one of the editors, **Arthur Peacocke**, the volume opens with an overview by **Michael W. Brierley**, who was not present at Windsor and was asked to survey both the past and present advocacy of a panentheistic perspective. His paper, drawn from Ph.D. research into the rise of panentheism in twentieth-century British theology, surveys it in modern theological literature. It names the dramatis personae of what Philip Clayton has called the "panentheistic turn" in modern theology by listing some of the theologians who have identified themselves as panentheists, and some more whom others have identified as such. Then, with reference to key authors who give panentheism extended treatment, he names eight characteristics of the doctrine, which are logically connected to each other and are generally (but not in every case universally) held by panentheists. They are: (i) the cosmos as God's body; (ii) language of "in and through"; (iii) the cosmos as sacrament; (iv) language of inextricable intertwining; (v) God's dependence on the cosmos; (vi) the intrinsic, positive value of the cosmos; (vii) passibility; (viii) degree Christology. The chapter concludes with some observations about the rise of panentheism and the importance of the "naming" task.

Part I consists of historical and contemporary panentheistic interpretations of the God-world relation. **Niels Henrik Gregersen** argues that the concept of panentheism, attractive as it is, is far from stable. That God is present everywhere in the world, and that the world is somehow present "in God," was already made explicit by the substance theist Thomas Aquinas and the pantheist Spinoza. Against this background he develops a generic concept of panentheism according to which panentheism contends that (1) the world is somehow contained by God and (2) the world affects God and returns to

God. Against this background he proposes a typology that discriminates between three distinct types of panentheisms in Western thought. He argues that in classic trinitarian thought, dating back to the fourth century, there are resources for what might be dubbed a *soteriological panentheism*. In the context of nineteenth-century romanticism, especially in Hegel, there is to be found a universalized *expressivist panentheism*, and finally, in the twentieth century, Charles Hartshorne developed a *dipolar panentheism* in continuation of Whitehead's process philosophy. He concludes that dipolar panentheism is not compatible with the two other forms of panentheism, and that a metaphysical choice has to be made between them.

David Ray Griffin discusses process panentheism, based on the process philosophies of A. N. Whitehead and C. Hartshorne, and argues that it is a postmodern revelation that most fully embodies the distinctive features of panentheism as an alternative to atheism, pantheism, and traditional theism. Like the sensationist-atheist-materialist naturalism (naturalism$_{sam}$) that has dominated the worldview of the late modern period since the middle of the nineteenth century, the naturalism of process panentheism is nonsupernaturalist, and so is in concord with the basic ontological conviction of modern science. But because it is a prehensive–panentheist–pan-experientialist naturalism (naturalism$_{ppp}$), it can nevertheless explain why moral, mathematical, and logical principles exist and why the world supports creatures capable of instantiating values and of having religious experiences. Process panentheism, he urges, also provides a far stronger basis than traditional theism for a natural theology in the sense of arguments for the existence of God.

Christopher C. Knight sees a modern theistic naturalism and a traditional Logos Christology as providing complementary perspectives for the development of panentheism, in the form of a "pan-sacramental panentheism." His approach, while it has radical pluralistic implications for a Christian understanding of revelation, is rooted in traditional notions of the incarnation and of the sacramentality of the created order, especially as espoused in Byzantine and modern Orthodox theology. The resulting pansacramental panentheism is distinct from some other forms in being dynamic in its concepts, pluralist in its implications, and naturalist in its understanding of divine action.

Keith Ward argues that rather than being a recent Western invention, panentheism has a long and venerable history in India, though not under that name. One of its chief exponents in Indian philosophical history was the twelfth-century philosopher and religious teacher Ramanuja, best known for his distinctive doctrine that the universe is the body of God. This is a panentheistic view insofar as it holds that the universe is part of the Supreme

Lord, just as a human body is part of a human person, though the Lord is infinitely greater than the universe, as the self is greater than the body.

Ward outlines Ramanuja's view of God, comparing it with the views of three major Western philosophers, Aquinas, Hegel, and Whitehead. He suggests that Ramanuja's view is very like that of Hegel, though it seems to contrast sharply with Aquinas's belief that the being of God totally excludes the finite universe. The panentheistic philosophy of Whitehead, though it may seem to suggest the metaphor of the universe being the body of God, assumes a very different view of the relation of body to embodied self, and its characterization of the relation of God and the universe is almost the opposite of Ramanuja's.

In conclusion Ward outlines what he considers the main theological questions raised by Ramanuja's account, and proposes that while there are good reasons for rejecting a panentheistic view of the present cosmos, Christianity does deploy the metaphor of the body of the Lord as pointing to a future form of relationship between God and the cosmos. Panentheism is not true yet, but it may yet become true.

Philip Clayton argues that the debate over panentheism has suffered from confusion about what criteria might be used in resolving the dispute — a confusion that stems, in turn, from uncertainty about what are the questions to which panentheism is meant to be a response. After an introduction that addresses this uncertainty, his chapter focuses on two major lines of argument that militate in favor of panentheism.

The first is metaphysical. Most of classical philosophical theology was developed in the context of a metaphysics of substance. But, the chapter argues, that metaphysics was superseded in the modern era by a metaphysics of the subject. Subjects are not isolated but exist essentially in relation. This would mean that God could not be understood as separate from the world but only as existing in interdependent relationship with it. The chapter then sketches the major steps in this emergent philosophical theology from Descartes and Spinoza through Kant, Fichte, Schelling, and Hegel, finding in their work both the historical antecedents of, and the most compelling arguments for, contemporary panentheism. The strengths and weaknesses of the "panentheistic analogy," which is central to the resulting position, are considered.

The second major argument is scientific and is drawn from the concept of emergence. Beginning with evolutionary biology, science in the last decades has moved from reductionistic or downward-directed approaches to emergentist or upward-directed approaches. The paper concludes with a constructive reflection on *emergentist panentheism*, exploring how far God can be understood as the culmination of emergence in history and to what extent

God must be seen also as prior to, and as the cause of, the hierarchy of emergence. To assert *both* the antecedent dimension of the divine and the emerging or consequent side of God, as it appears we must, is to espouse some form of dipolar theism.

Part II consists of scientific perspectives on the God-world relation. **Paul Davies** affirms that the concept of purpose or teleology was eliminated from physics by Newton and from biology by Darwin, yet the idea will not go away completely. Biologists concede that life behaves *as if* it is the product of purposeful design, while physicists and cosmologists glimpse a grand plan or coherent scheme in the way the universe progressively unfolds rich complexity from simple beginnings. Davies argues that careful examination of the laws of nature suggests that an implicit teleology is built in at the fundamental level. Though future states of physical systems are normally open, and subject to the vagaries of chance, the general trend of cosmological and biological evolution from simple to complex bestows on nature an effective broad-brush teleology. He explores resonances between this worldview and panentheism.

Russell Stannard introduces his paper by discussing our current understanding of time, as revealed by Einstein's theory of relativity. A common interpretation of the findings holds that all of physical time — past, present, and future — in a sense exists. This would appear to have a bearing on the traditional view that God is not only to be found immanently within space and time but also transcendentally beyond them. It is argued that this "block universe" idea renders more plausible the notion that God might possess knowledge of that existent future. He goes on to note that, according to modern cosmology, there was no time before the instant of the big bang, and hence no preexistent cause of that event. This prompts him to examine what we mean when we speak of God as the creator of the world.

Robert L. Herrmann suggests that the remarkable continuity throughout evolution seemingly leaves no place for specific acts of the Creator, with God's activity better seen perhaps as working in and through the creation and as intimately involved in what may be seen as free and natural processes. The later stages of evolution reach a level of complexity allowing for the emergence of uniquely new entities. The most recent among these is *Homo sapiens,* who first appeared some one hundred thousand years ago displaying remarkable properties of consciousness and spirit. A model of God's activity that embraces these ideas is the panentheistic analogy in which the Creator includes and penetrates the whole yet is infinitely more. This model, for which it is critical that mind or consciousness is irreducible, can visualize God's activity in the world as analogous to the relation of the human mind to body.

Harold J. Morowitz thinks modern ideas of emergence permit the development of a hierarchy in the opposite direction from that constructed reductionistically through scientific disciplines viewing the world from the observed to the most primitive accessible level of knowledge. The pruning rules that allow the generation of the upper hierarchical levels from the combinatorial explosion of possibilities are the least understood feature of the developing science of emergence. He explores the new dialogue that this opens between scientists and theologians, focusing on immanence, emergence (how the immanent became flesh), and transcendence (how the human mind emerged). Within this context the "something more" of panentheism is humanity and its ability to act for good or evil.

Arthur Peacocke recapitulates those developments in the scientific understanding of the world that have prompted a reconsideration of how to conceive of God's presence in the world. These include the unification on one mathematical framework of space-time-matter-energy; the monistic (constitutionally reductionist) recognition that everything is made out of the same basic physical units; the application of the developing science of complexity to the hierarchy of complexity of the world's systems; the abandonment of dualistic accounts of the human person; the "epic of evolution," both cosmic and biological; and the concomitant widespread awareness that the nexus of causality is unbroken in naturally creative events and processes. He proposes a theological reconstruction that gives prominence to: an intensification of the immanence of God in a theistic naturalism that affirms God as "in, with, and under" natural processes; a panentheism that prescinds from any suggestion of the world as "a part of God" or as "God's body"; and the universe as sacramental, being the milieu of God as Wisdom and as Logos.

Part III consists of theological perspectives on the God-world relation, and has two subparts, one from Eastern Orthodox writers, the other from Western writers. From the former, **Kallistos Ware** stresses that the three great "Abrahamic" religions share the conviction that God is both transcendent and immanent. He points out that in the Greek patristic tradition this antinomy of transcendence/immanence is expressed chiefly in two ways: Maximus the Confessor speaks of the divine Logos implanting indwelling logoi in all created things, while Gregory Palamas, developing the standpoint of the Cappadocians, distinguishes between the essence and the energies of God. These energies, according to Palamas, are not an intermediary between God and humankind, but God himself in action; and they are not a part or division of God, but God in his entirety. In this way the essence-energies distinction does not impair the divine simplicity. Palamas may be styled a "panentheist," but in a weak rather than a strong sense; for while he believes that the being of God embraces and penetrates the universe, he also believes that the divine being is in no way exhausted by the universe, for God remains utterly transcendent in his imparticipable essence. More specifically, Palamas may be termed a "soteriological" panentheist, and also — with certain qualifications — an "expressionist" panentheist; but he is not precisely a "bipolar" panentheist in Whitehead's sense, for while he maintains that God is necessary to the world, he does not consider that the world is necessary to God. Nevertheless, creation is in no way an arbitrary or external act so far as God is concerned, but it expresses his true nature as self-diffusive love. The Palamite energies are nothing else than the personal love of God.

Alexei V. Nesteruk discusses the sense in which the notion of panentheism can be understood within the Orthodox Christian position. He argues that the nonontological presence of God in the universe can be expressed as the subsistence or inherence of the universe in the hypostasis (person) of the Logos of God. Then the claim of panentheism that the world is "in" God can be interpreted as an affirmation about the articulation of impersonal nature in the personhood of the Logos. Human beings as microcosm articulate further the hypostatic and intelligible features of the universe, thereby revealing that the universe subsists in the person of the Logos. Through this articulation the universe itself acquires a microcosmic, hypostatic dimension, and its relation to God can be described as "microcosmic panentheism." An "ecclesial" dimension is thereby added to panentheism since human beings build the universal church which recapitulates the universe as the incarnate Logos-Christ recapitulated: the church is held hypostatically by Christ and the whole universe is held hypostatically by the Logos of God, who is the head of the universe understood as Church.

Andrew Louth outlines Maximos's vision of the cosmos, partly to suggest that the Byzantine Fathers preserved a cosmic theological outlook that was largely lost in Western theology, one that might have something to offer modern attempts to articulate a cosmic understanding that draws on the insights of modern science. A central doctrine of Maximos's vision — that of the logoi of creation — expresses the idea that the cosmos, as a whole and in each of its parts, expresses the meaning that God intended in creation through his Word or Logos. These meanings, logoi, form an interlocking whole in the creative Logos of God. For Maximos, as for most ancient philosophers, the human was a microcosm: expressing in itself the interrelated reality of the cosmos, indeed more perfectly than in the cosmos itself. For the human person, by being created in God's image, is capable of understanding (or beginning to do so) the coinherence expressed by the logoi. The significance of this is integrated with Maximos's doctrine of the division of nature. Louth suggests that the wholeness of his concepts may have something to offer to the fragmented state of modern scientific knowledge. But this latter points to a universe quite different from the geocentric one of Maximos, and Louth concludes by attempting to sketch briefly how Maximos's cosmic vision might be restated by drawing on the insights of Pascal and of the so-called anthropic principle.

The essays in the second section of part III, from writers with a Western Christian viewpoint, are introduced by **Denis Edwards,** who begins by attempting to specify a trinitarian form of panentheism, in which the dynamic divine communion is thought of as the "place" of the unfolding of the universe. In this kind of theology the Spirit can be thought of as "making space" within the dynamism of the divine shared life for a world of creatures. He goes on to propose that contemporary science puts before us an interrelational world in which individual entities have their own integrity and which is evolving at all levels. He affirms that the contemporary retrieval of a trinitarian understanding of God offers a view of God as communion that is characterized by relational unity and diversity. It points to the understanding of God in recent eschatological theology as absolute future. By bringing these insights from science and theology into mutual dialogue, Edwards goes on to develop a view of reality in which the entities that make up the universe can be understood as *interrelational, integral,* and *evolving* within the dynamism of the divine life.

Joseph A. Bracken, S.J., proposes a panentheistic understanding of the God-world relation based on a rethinking of the process-relational metaphysics of Whitehead in which the basic category of "society" is regarded as a structured field of activity for its constituent "actual occasions" or momentary subjects of experience. Within this context the three divine persons of the Christian doctrine of the Trinity can then be said to co-constitute an all-inclusive divine field of activity which simultaneously serves as the "matrix" or womb of creation. Within this divine matrix, creation has gradually taken shape as an extremely complex, hierarchically ordered set of fields for Whiteheadian actual occasions with varying degrees of complexity. Furthermore, using this field-oriented model for the God-world relationship, Bracken argues that he can philosophically justify belief in God as triune rather than simply unipersonal and also belief in creation out of nothing (apart from God).

Ruth Page considers panentheism to be a valuable contribution to theological thought but thinks its application may lead to difficulties, for it sometimes expresses the human ascent to complexity and consciousness as an unambiguous good from God's hand. However, much has been surrendered on the way to human complexity, while consciousness may breed regret for the past and fear for the future. Both are in that sense ambiguous. A further objection arises from the massive extinctions on the way to humanity, if that is thought to come from divine purpose. These emphases are both anthropocentric and a dubious attribution to the God of love. Instead she proposes that God gave freedom and a framework of possibility to all creatures from the beginning, so that natural evil is the outcome of the clash of finite freedoms. Having given freedom, God then companions creation ("pansyntheism"), delighting at each creature's use of possibility, a powerful presence when attended to.

Celia E. Deane-Drummond argues that in defining the relationship between God and the world, due consideration needs to be given to the radical claim of Christianity that Christ is incarnate in the world as Logos/Wisdom. Wisdom Christology was implicit in the earliest Christian traditions, but alternative Christologies gradually replaced it. Wisdom is particularly significant since it is a relational category and thus opens up a wider cosmological reference to the meaning of Christology. Deane-Drummond distinguishes between Logos and Wisdom/Sophia inasmuch as Wisdom is trinitarian rather than purely christological. Wisdom is significant in that not only does she become a way of interpreting panentheism in an age of scientific discovery, but also because she takes due account of the suffering of creation and allows an empathetic friendship between God and creatures to emerge while retaining the distinction between them. Hence Wisdom invites participation in both the suffering and the joys/creativity of creation. Furthermore, the concept of wisdom points toward humanity's vocational praxis, in other words, ethics.

The volume concludes with an overview of the contributions by the other editor, **Philip Clayton.**

Introduction:
"*In* whom we live and move and have our being?"[1]

ARTHUR PEACOCKE

The conviction that God is, in principle and by definition, ineffable, beyond all explicit description, greater than we can ever conceive, has in practice not inhibited human beings over the centuries from speculation — and often dogmatic assertion — concerning that same God's relation to the world. Since "theology" may be described as the investigation of all things in relation to God, it is not surprising that recent decades have witnessed intense activity directed at how to conceive of that relation in the light of rapidly developing new perspectives on human nature and the natural world.[2] Thus it is that many supposed features of what was thought to be a widely accepted, classical philosophical theism have come to be called in question, inter alia — God as external to the world, that the world does not affect God (God's impassibility), and God's ability to intervene in God-created natural sequences of events to effect God's purposes (e.g., by "miracles"). One consequence of these discussions has been the reemergence into interdisciplinary discourse, especially that between theologians and scientists, of the admittedly inelegant term "pan*en*theism" to represent what now needs to be emphasized in a contemporary, defensible understanding of the God-world relation.

"Panentheism" has been defined in the *Oxford Dictionary of the Christian Church* as "The belief that the Being of God includes and penetrates the whole universe, so that every part of it exists in Him, but (as against Pantheism) that His Being is more than, and is not exhausted by, the universe,"[3] a definition not without its critics, as will transpire. John Cobb, the process theologian, has expounded panentheism as

> The doctrine that all is in God. It is distinguished from pantheism, which identifies God with the totality or as the unity of the totality, for it holds that God's inclusion of the world does not exhaust the reality of God. Panentheism understands itself as a form of theism. . . .
>
> . . . what happens in the world contributes to the divine experience which in its unity transcends qualitatively and quantitatively the contribution of the world.[4]

The resuscitation of this term, whose very definition is still under discussion, has been indeed — as Michael Brierley describes in the next chapter — "a quiet revolution" during twentieth-century and early-twenty-first-century theology. Like all such revolutions, however, the usefulness and applicability of the term have not been without controversy, whether in proposing that the created world is a "part of God" or is "God's body."[5] Such proposals inevitably stress that the language used is metaphorical, but there remains the suspicion that the term is altogether too imprecise and so ambiguous. The fate of a particular term is, of course, much less important than the cluster of ideas to which it points, and these constitute the concern of this volume. A retrospective review of the nuances of the term is given by Philip Clayton, my coeditor, and readers will be able to make their own judgment as to its usefulness in the light of the variety of approaches we have been able to assemble.

The factors which have together provoked the current revival of the term "panentheism" are in fact extremely significant for our understanding of God's relation to the world, including humanity. Broadly they all point to the need to accentuate, in the light of contemporary knowledge of the world and of humanity, a much stronger sense than in the past of the immanence of God as in some sense "in" the world — without, for most of our authors, demeaning from or qualifying God's ultimate transcendence, God's ontological ultimate "otherness." How this is to be achieved turns crucially in the meaning to be attached to the *en* of "pan*en*theism," the "in" of the definitions above. This in its turn depends on prior metaphysical and theological interpretations of the world "in" which God is deemed to be present. Not surprisingly, a rich variety of approaches is expounded in the chapters by different authors. However, the pressures moving many of them to espouse the term in some form or other are broadly common, and to these we now turn.

A notable aspect of the scientific account of the natural world, both cosmological and terrestrial, that has been consolidated during the twentieth century is the seamless character of the web that has been spun on the loom of time: at no point do modern natural scientists have to invoke any nonnatural causes to explain their observations and inferences about the past. This intelligible and all-pervasive continuity, amplified more recently by an understanding through chaos theory of how even catastrophic changes of pattern and regime can be understood, has rendered it increasingly problematic to conceive of God's action in the world as intervening in any way that involves an abrogation of the very regularities with which God's own self is regarded, by theists, as having endowed the world. Even though in principle a creator God might consistently be thought to be able to set aside those regularities, this recognition of lawful continuity and regularity has so raised the threshold of minimum historical evidence needed to establish such interventions that it has become imperative to consider more coherent and plausible ways of relating God to natural events — even those expressing particular divine intentions. How this might be possible has been the subject of intense and (one must admit) inconclusive study.[6] It is enough to note here that all the proposals addressing this issue require a much more intimate involvement of God in the actual processes of the world as described by science than has hitherto been commonly proposed.

Moreover, the past and present processes of the natural world are characterized by "emergence," for there appear in the course of time new forms of matter, often articulated in a hierarchical manner. The world may be said to be an evolving system of systems. New kinds of realities come into existence, often by processes involving the *self*-organization of natural systems in ways explicable by the relevant sciences. This has provoked a renewed emphasis on the *immanence* of God as creator "in, with, and under" the creative, natural processes of the world unveiled by the sciences.

Indeed, the scientific perspective of the world, especially the living world, inexorably impresses upon us a *dynamic* picture of the world of entities, structures, and processes involved in continuous and incessant change and in process without ceasing. This has impelled many to reintroduce a dynamic element into their understanding of God's creative relation to the world. This was always implicit in the Hebrew conception of a "living God," dynamic in action, but has been obscured by the tendency to think of "creation" as an event in the past. God has again to be conceived of as continuously creating, continuously giving existence to, what is new. God is thus creating at every moment of the world's existence in and through the perpetually endowed creativity of the very stuff of the world. All this has reinforced the need to reaffirm more strongly than ever before in the Christian (and Jewish and Islamic?) tradition that in a very strong sense God is the immanent creator creating in and through the processes of the natural order.

Hence it is that many thinkers, reflecting on these new perspectives of the sciences on the evolving natural and human worlds, have resorted to affirming that, in some sense or other, both the world is "in" God and God is "in" the world.

Along with these dominant and compelling new perspectives on the natural world, including the world of humanity as an evolved creature of nature, there has also been correspondingly a marked diminution in the need to postulate a "supernatural" dimension to reality as a kind of middle term between God and the world, as a postulated milieu through which the divine may be thought to operate in the world. The only dualism that seems to be theologically supportable is simply the distinction between the ultimate ontology of God and that of everything else, the "creation." Inevitably this raises acutely the question of how best to conceive of, what models and metaphors to adopt for, this intensified intimacy of the creator God with the world processes that we have seen is stimulated by our awareness of their continuous creativity.

Furthermore, the entirely justified abandonment by philosophers and cognitive scientists of any dualistic account of human nature — in the past usually in terms of mind/body or mind/brain — has inevitably reflected upon the use of traditional models of God's relation to the world in terms of personal agency. In these models God's action on the world was analogous to a person's intentions being implemented in bodily actions. Actually this typically biblical model should not have presupposed a dualist account of human nature, for such an account is absent from the biblical corpus, which thinks rather of the human being as a psychosomatic unity. In spite of this, much traditional theology has implicitly been based on dualistic models. The rejection of these in philosophy, science, and theology means that if a model of personal agency for God's action in the world continues to be adopted by theologians (and there is a warranted investment in the continued use of personal terms in this context), questions arise about how to conceive of God's relation to the processes of the world. How can the model of a person's intentions being implemented in bodily actions illuminate that relation? Can the notion of panentheism help fill out this model? Much turns on the sense of the *en*/"in" of pan*en*theism, and this will emerge in the papers that follow.

One of the distinctive features of twentieth-century theology has been the denial of the traditional doctrine of the impassibility of God and correspondingly the affirmation that God in God's own self experiences in some sense "from within" the suffering of the world's sentient creatures, including human suffering. Creation is deemed as costly to God not only as a divine self-emptying to give existence to Another (the world), but continuously as

God experiences the negative events of that world from its inside. A panentheist could reasonably affirm that such proposals generate a strong pressure to assert that the events of the world are sufficiently "in" God for God to be affected by them — but again, in *what* sense "in"? It is noteworthy that a wide range of theological terms in Judeo-Christian discourse has been used in various implicitly, and sometimes explicitly, panentheistic proposals to respond to this question, and not only in the context of the affirmation of divine passibility. As we shall see in the contributions that follow, these include reference to God conceived as Holy Wisdom, to the world as sacrament, to the uncreated energies of God, as well as trinitarian interpretations and the whole project of process theology.

The very use by many contemporary authors of what Philip Clayton has called the "panentheistic analogy"[7] indicates the pressing need for a reconsideration in depth of the perennial issue of the dialectic involved in affirming both God's transcendence *over* and God's immanence *in* the world. This volume is offered as a substantial contribution to that enterprise.

Naming a Quiet Revolution:
The Panentheistic Turn in Modern Theology

MICHAEL W. BRIERLEY

[The three-decker universe] has been discarded by nearly all. What are we to put in its place? Panentheism appears to supply the answer.[1]

Via the constructive employment of the panentheistic model, Christian thought and life are in the process of being revitali[z]ed.[2]

Panentheism is desperately needed by individuals and religious institutions today.[3]

This volume of essays attempts to review to what extent the word "panentheism" should be given a prominent place in contemporary theology. Theologians, scientists, and scientist-theologians each offer their own understanding of the word, or their response to the challenges it represents. Many of them believe, as do I and the authors of the quotations above, that panentheism holds great promise as a doctrinal and spiritual resource in the third millennium. They are conscious of what Philip Clayton has called "the panentheistic turn"

This paper is drawn from ongoing Ph.D. research at the University of Birmingham, and I am grateful to Professor Gareth Jones for his supervision.

in theology of the twentieth century,[4] but they are aware that the word itself needs to be better known, better defined, and better understood if it is to be taken as a serious part of the world's future theological agenda.[5]

Donald Neil, who wrote a doctoral dissertation on panentheism in the 1970s,[6] realized that "the time is ripe for a close study, historical and analytical, of the doctrine of panentheism";[7] the published version of his thesis, *God in Everything*, represents the first volume devoted to the word. The present essay seeks to provide a historical and analytical perspective for the present volume, the first collection of essays around "panentheism," by surveying the use of the word in theological literature: it gives, first, an account of the dramatis personae of the panentheistic turn; second, an account of the patterns into which the use of the term seems to have fallen; and third, some suggestions as to why the "turn" might have occurred. In this way it sets the stage for the variety of responses to the word in the chapters which follow, whether or not they hold that the word is necessary or welcome.

Dramatis Personae of the Panentheistic Turn

The word "panentheism" is less well known than "pantheism," which was coined early in the eighteenth century[8] and came to be used by traditionalists as a term of abuse for any hint of departure from classical theism,[9] especially when the immanence of God came to the fore of theology from the late nineteenth century to the end of the First World War.[10] "Panentheism," as all the standard dictionary articles testify,[11] was coined by Karl Christian Friedrich Krause (1781-1832),[12] the German idealist philosopher[13] and a contemporary of Hegel.[14] Translating Krause in 1900, William Hastie commented, "His enthusiastic disciples claim for him that his system is the truest outcome of modern speculation; that it brings all contemporary knowledge and science into completest harmony; and that the Twentieth Century, understanding and appreciating Krause better than the Nineteenth Century has done, will find the certainty, security, and unity we long for in his profound rational 'Panentheism.'"[15] Philip Clayton suggests that idealist theologians of the early nineteenth century such as Krause developed a basic set of intuitions bequeathed by the eighteenth century,[16] and that these intuitions themselves derived from Nicholas of Cusa's understanding of creation occurring "within" God[17] and Descartes's replacement of the scholastic notion of infinitude with a participatory one.[18]

The first use of the word in English theology appears to be on the eve of the twentieth century, by Dean Inge, in *Christian Mysticism* (1899), where he acknowledges the word's origin in Krause.[19] George Tyrrell and Friedrich von Hügel, the Catholic modernists, both used the word approvingly,[20] and it was taken from Inge by another writer on mysticism, Brigid Herman.[21] The word was made widely known in America through Charles Hartshorne,[22] "the leading twentieth-century advocate of panentheism,"[23] in particular through his reader in the doctrine of God, *Philosophers Speak of God.*[24] The word was reintroduced to Britain by John Robinson,[25] whose book *Exploration into God* (1967) developed the doctrinal suggestions of his controversial best-seller *Honest to God* (1963);[26] and its chief exponent in Britain,[27] though he does not like the term itself,[28] is John Macquarrie.[29] Macquarrie's panentheism derived from the "existential-ontological" position of the first edition of his *Principles of Christian Theology,*[30] which itself evolved from his ontological critique of the existentialists Heidegger and Bultmann.[31]

At every stage of its entry into modern theology, panentheism has represented a middle path between two extremes, and so it has explicitly become one of the three essential types of the most fundamental of doctrines, the doctrine of God. Classical theism, pantheism, and panentheism are recognized as the basic patterns through which the doctrine of God can be analyzed.[32] To be sure, not every doctrine of God can easily be assigned to one of these three,[33] but even in these cases the ambiguity which the categories reveal in theologians' doctrines of God demonstrates the categories' validity as illuminating tools for theological understanding.

Today a whole host of theologians identify themselves as panentheists (in listing some of them here, no claim is made to be exhaustive). Some subscribe to process theism, a subset of panentheism: Hartshorne, Norman Pittenger,[34] Charles Birch,[35] Schubert Ogden,[36] John Cobb,[37] James Will,[38] Jim Garrison,[39] David Pailin,[40] Joseph Bracken,[41] David Griffin,[42] Jay McDaniel,[43] Daniel Dombrowski,[44] and Anna Case-Winters.[45] Others who identify themselves as panentheists include Alan Anderson,[46] Leonardo Boff,[47] Marcus Borg,[48] Philip Clayton,[49] Scott Cowdell,[50] Denis Edwards,[51] Paul Fiddes,[52] Matthew Fox,[53] Donald Gelpi,[54] Peter Hodgson,[55] Christopher Knight,[56] John Macquarrie, Paul Matthews,[57] Sallie McFague,[58] Jürgen Moltmann,[59] Hugh Montefiore,[60] Helen Oppenheimer,[61] Arthur Peacocke,[62] Piet Schoonenberg,[63] Claude Stewart,[64] and Kallistos Ware.[65]

Furthermore, a number of other theologians have been identified as panentheists.[66] These include the twentieth-century figures Nicolay Berdyayev,[67] Peter Berger,[68] James Bethune-Baker,[69] Dietrich Bonhoeffer,[70] Martin Buber,[71] Sergei Bulgakov,[72] Rudolf Bultmann,[73] Martin Heidegger,[74] Karl Heim,[75] William Hocking,[76] Geddes MacGregor,[77] Charles Peirce,[78] Rosemary Radford Ruether,[79] Albert Schweitzer,[80] Pierre Teilhard de

Chardin,[81] Paul Tillich,[82] Ernst Troeltsch,[83] Alan Watts,[84] Paul Weiss,[85] and Alfred North Whitehead;[86] British idealists John and Edward Caird[87] and Andrew Seth Pringle-Pattison;[88] nineteenth-century Germans Schleiermacher,[89] Fichte,[90] Hegel,[91] Schelling,[92] Baur,[93] Fechner,[94] and Pfleiderer;[95] as well as the medieval theologians Nicholas of Cusa[96] and Eckhart;[97] the mystics Mechtild of Magdeburg[98] and Julian of Norwich;[99] and even Luther.[100] In addition, good cases could be made for very many others, not least R. J. Campbell,[101] John Oman,[102] John V. Taylor,[103] and classic Anglican liberals such as Peter Baelz,[104] Geoffrey Lampe, and Maurice Wiles.[105] Whole movements have been claimed for panentheism:[106] Neoplatonism,[107] Orthodox Christianity,[108] mysticism,[109] and English modernism.[110] Panentheism cannot therefore be dismissed as "a somewhat suspect 'fudge' word."[111]

It would be going too far to suggest that "we are all panentheists now":[112] this cannot be sustained in the face of neo-Thomism, the contemporary credence given to such Barthianism as that propounded by Colin Gunton and John Webster,[113] and postmodern "radical orthodoxy."[114] Nevertheless, the list of some adherents demonstrates that panentheism "exerts a substantial influence on contemporary theology."[115] It is claimed that the concept has biblical roots,[116] and indeed is the true "orthodoxy,"[117] and it has been deemed to respond more flexibly than varieties of classical theism to the concerns of feminist,[118] lesbian and gay,[119] ecological,[120] and "economic" liberation theologies;[121] the demands of dialogue between science and religion;[122] and the demands of dialogue between different faiths.[123] Panentheism is thus successful "in addressing a number of issues that have become of considerable importance for twenty-first century theology."[124]

The most adequate way to describe the adoption of panentheism in the past two centuries, and particularly at the current time, is in terms of a doctrinal revolution. Michael Drummy uses this word (though the wrong adjective) when he posits that "particularly in the area of the doctrine of God, the accommodation by many serious Christian scholars to a 'panentheistic' model of the God-world relationship has amounted to a small-scale revolution in contemporary theological circles."[125] The "revolution" is not "small-scale," because panentheism subverts the priorities of classical theism, and thereby undercuts its edifice and structure. It challenges classical theism's imperium, and places the doctrine of God in ferment. The peculiar character of this revolution concerns not so much its far-reaching extent as its recognition. The revolution has been quiet, partly because panentheism has until recently been used by its chief exponents under other names: "dialectical theism" (Macquarrie), "neoclassical theism" (Hartshorne), "naturalistic theism" (Griffin), or the more narrow category "process theism." The "quiet" character of the revolution is therefore like that of the twentieth century's secret revolution in passibility, or the suffering of God, described by Ronald Goetz,[126] and the rise of panentheism as a contemporary force to reckon with classical theism is thus one of the untold stories of twentieth-century theology.

Now that we are seeing the explicit emergence of panentheism as a broad doctrinal category, and the revolution is coming to attention, the questions arise: What is panentheism? What are its distinguishing features?

Some Common Panentheistic Themes

The essays in this volume demonstrate that "panentheism" covers a multitude of descriptions of the relationship between God and cosmos. There is, for example, Ware's patristic panentheism, Bracken's "field panentheism," and Philip Clayton's isolation of the distinctiveness of panentheism in the configuration of finitude and infinitude.[127] Similarly, panentheists outside this volume hold different versions of the doctrine: Charles Hartshorne, for example, gave an early and detailed exposition of the concept as "ETCKW" (God as "Eternal-Temporal Consciousness, Knowing and Including the World");[128] and David Nikkel has identified Tillich as a panentheist through Tillich's distinctive language of "being."[129] Despite authors' individual idiosyncrasies, it is possible to establish common ground shared by the various panentheisms, not least from the vocabulary which recurs in the doctrines of the small number of theologians ("key panentheists") who give the word itself sustained treatment: Clayton, Griffin, Hartshorne, Macquarrie, McDaniel, Pailin, and Peacocke. This common ground falls into eight different themes.

The classic definition of "panentheism" is that provided by the *Oxford Dictionary of the Christian Church:* "the belief that the Being of God includes and penetrates the whole universe, so that every part of it exists in Him."[130] It is a weak definition, because it goes very little beyond the literal meaning of the word. The statement that God "includes" the universe merely states the literal meaning, "all in God," with God as subject, leaving "penetration" as the only gloss on what God's "inclusion" of the universe, or the universe's existence "in" God, might actually mean. The question therefore remains: In what sense does the universe exist in God? It may be that this lack of precision in the meaning of the term "all in God" is responsible for some of the "tantalising ambiguities" which "seem to plague panentheistic discussion."[131]

Certainly the ambiguity of "in" has caused some theologians to distinguish between different types of panentheism.[132] Thus McDaniel differentiates between "emanationist" and "relational" panentheism: in "emanationist" panentheism the cosmos is a direct expression of God's own being, so that the cosmos's creative action is at the same time the creative action of God. "Relational" panentheism, for McDaniel, allows the cosmos creative independence from God, so that humanity has its own creative power. Similarly, Peterson talks of "weak" and "strong" panentheism, where the weak version refers (only) to the presence of God in the cosmos and the strong version involves some identity between them. These options, however, turn out to be superficial choices, in the light of the eight facets of panentheist language which are (largely) common to the key panentheists, and which effectively explicate the "in":[133] the cosmos as God's body; language of "in and through"; the cosmos as sacrament; language of "inextricable intertwining"; the dependence of God on the cosmos; the intrinsic, positive value of the cosmos; possibility; and degree Christology.[134] These features can be applied as a test to theologians to see whether or not they can be described as panentheist.

The Cosmos as God's Body

The first facet is the question of divine embodiment.[135] Some key panentheists are content to describe the cosmos as God's body,[136] while others are more cautious,[137] and some come out against the idea.[138] The concept has some attraction: the relation of mind and body, and correspondingly of God and cosmos, safeguards the distinction of each yet does not (on a psychosomatic anthropology) allow their separation; part of God can be seen and touched (leading to concern for the environment), while part nevertheless exists "beyond"; and the model also appropriately expresses a relationship of asymmetrical interdependence, God and mind each being dependent on cosmos and body, but not in the same way that cosmos and body are in turn dependent on them.

Crude objections can be easily dealt with: the claim that the cosmos is said to exist within God, or be a "part" of God, yet the body does not exist "within," nor is it a "part" of, mind, is a reminder that the comparison should always be made with body and the whole *person*, not body and mind; and the claim that divine embodiment involves the identity of God with all aspects of the world, good and bad, is simply a non sequitur, assuming with Augustine that evil is privative.

There are, however, points where the model breaks down. For example, there are things beyond human bodies, but it is not clear what, if anything, can be said to be "beyond" the cosmos. Another weak point is that the parts of human bodies do not have conscious relations with the person who is their whole, unlike parts of the cosmos and God.[139] Again, whereas it is held that God has perfect knowledge of the cosmos, human beings do not have perfect knowledge of their bodies. These caveats, however, are to be expected, since the model is an analogy: Clayton has rightly styled the model the "panentheistic analogy" (and has indeed shown that the model and the concept lie at the very root of the principle of analogy),[140] and it is inherent in analogy that there are points where the fit between human and divine cannot be made. The original concept may be held, so long as the disanalogies are borne in mind.

Arthur Peacocke in the end comes out against divine embodiment,[141] because he believes that conceiving of the cosmos as a "part" of God makes it of the same ontological order as God.[142] Philip Clayton's work, however, shows how the ontological difference between God and cosmos is preserved in terms of infinitude and finitude, and perfection and imperfection,[143] and therefore it seems right to assert with other key panentheists,[144] as part of the definition of the concept, that the cosmos is to be regarded as God's body.

Language of "In and Through"

Certain language is characteristic of the relation between person and body, and this language, through the analogy with the relationship between God and cosmos, comes to be characteristic of panentheism. For example, people are said to express themselves, or act, "in and through" their bodies: I express myself "in" my smile, or "through" the embrace of my arms. The "in" simply repeats the "in" of panentheism which needs to be explicated, but the "through" implies both the immanence of the actor and also the actor's transcendence, since for something to come, work, or act "through" something else, it needs to come from beyond it. Hence talk of God working or acting "in and through" the cosmos is language characteristic of panentheism.

Of confessed panentheists, Peacocke and Pittenger most notice this distinctive language. Peacocke draws the connection between panentheist use of this language and its use by Luther: "hence my continued need to apply the phrase 'in, with, and under,' which Luther used to refer to the model of the Real Presence of Christ in the Eucharist, to the presence of God in the processes of the world."[145] "In, with, and under" is only a variation on "in and through": it expresses connection between agent and instrument, without their identity. Pittenger also noticed these "celebrated Lutheran prepositions,"[146] claiming that "the basic question which we must face is whether the way in which God is in fact found in that realm of creaturely occasions is of the order which may be described as 'with, in and under' (to use again the appropriate words derived from Lutheran eucharistic theology) his creation, or whether it is of the order which can only be described as the entrance, 'from outside,' of the divine reality into the creation."[147] Again, the use of these prepositions by prominent panentheists indicates their role as a defining characteristic of the position.[148]

The Cosmos as Sacrament

Peacocke's connection of his prepositions with Luther's use of them in discussing the Eucharist is not coincidental, for the prepositions themselves belong to the definition of a "sacrament": a sacrament is a physical thing "under,""in," or "through" which God comes. The prepositions are thus intrinsic to sacramentalism (the idea that the cosmos and what is in it are sacraments), as well as to panentheism. Panentheism and sacramentalism refer to different aspects of the same reality, and sacramentalism becomes another defining characteristic of the panentheist position. In panentheism, by contrast to classical theism, the "sacraments" are not restricted to certain rites of the church: the whole cosmos, for panentheism, is sacramental, for it is something under, in, and through which God comes; and the specific sacraments of the church are simply particular intensifications of the general "sacramental principle," signs, symbols, and reminders that any and every thing has the potential to become a full vehicle of the divine.[149]

The sacramental principle, like the prepositions "in, with, and under," is recognized by Peacocke among those panentheists who define the term in depth.[150] It is also noted in passing by others, including Fiddes, Fox, McFague, Pittenger, and Ware.[151] It may be taken as another defining feature of the term "panentheism."

Language of Inextricable Intertwining

If embodied things are the instruments or vehicles through which and only through which God comes and can be expressed, if embodiment, that is to say, is an intrinsic feature of divinity, as Clayton's panentheistic analogy suggests, then the two, God and cosmos, while distinct from one another, cannot be separate. Subject and object are distinct entities but can never entirely be divorced, one from the other, since they are interdependent. This means not only that they are "inextricably intertwined," but that this inextricable intertwining is also an intrinsic and therefore defining feature of their reality. Once again it is a case of certain language being characteristic of the panentheistic position: the presence of terms such as "distinct but not separate," or "inextricably intertwined," is evidence that the position which underlies them is panentheistic.

So, for example, Macquarrie makes clear that the cosmos is not "separate" from God.[152] His whole scheme of "dialectics," as Hartshorne's doctrine of "dipolarity," is an attempt to express the necessary link (or, in Hartshorne's word, "correlativeness") between sets of distinct poles.[153] Clayton talks of the identification *and* the distinction, the inclusion *and* the separation, of God and cosmos.[154] Boff says God and cosmos are "always intertwined."[155] Pittenger was sufficiently aware of "the difference between distinction and separation, a difference often overlooked by theologians and philosophers," to apply "inextricable intertwining" to a whole range of subjects, including object and subject, event and reception, and fact and interpretation.[156] The use of such language, once again, becomes one of the hallmarks by which panentheism is identified.

God's Dependence on the Cosmos

If embodiment is indeed an intrinsic feature of divinity, and if indeed the interconnections between God and cosmos cannot be completely undone, then this leads to the unorthodox assertion that God is dependent on the cosmos.[157] God *needs* the cosmos for the fulfillment of God's nature of love.

Some panentheists (notably those under the process influence) have urged a careful distinction here: they have suggested that if divine embodiment is indispensable, God needs *a* cosmos but not necessarily *the* cosmos, in the sense of this particular one.[158] In other words, God needs "somebody to love," but the "somebody" could conceivably have been a very different universe. Paul Fiddes is right to be uneasy about this proposal, arguing that particularity is intrinsic to the desire and need of love.[159] God, it could be said, needs and is dependent on the particular cosmos that is in the process of becoming. This can be accepted, as long as it is recognized that this cosmos could have been a very different one.

Panentheists who are less ready than process theists to jettison Christian tradition express a certain hesitancy over the dependency of God on the cosmos. Macquarrie, for example, claims "it is a misuse of language to say that it is necessary for [God] to create," because he feels that the language of "necessity" implies a coercive force external to God. He prefers to state that God freely creates, because on the Augustinian view of freedom to act freely is to act within the constraints of perfect love, and so to act within one's ultimate nature: in God's relationship with the cosmos, freedom and necessity, creation and emanation, will and love, coincide.[160] By Macquarrie's own admission, however, the language of "freedom" is susceptible to the misinterpretation that God could have acted otherwise. Given, therefore, that the language of "freedom" and the language of "necessity" are both open to misinterpretation, there does not seem to be any reason why the language of necessity may not be used, with the proviso that this does not mean that God is under some kind of external compulsion.[161]

Just as one key panentheist, Peacocke, resisted the notion of divine embodiment, so another key panentheist (other than Macquarrie), Clayton, resists the notion of a necessary divine dependence on the world. Whereas Fiddes is keen to keep divine will and divine nature free from subordination to each other, Clayton, under the influence of Schelling, is content to subordinate God's nature of love to God's freedom or will: hence the cosmos represents the preexistent God's free choice to create, and God, who can exist without a cosmos, is only dependent on it after this free decision.[162] Clayton states that "the reason [for this position] is a logical one: the claim that 'a contingent world must of necessity exist' is, I think, incoherent."[163] But it may be precisely that God, through love, needs a world that (by nature) is radically dependent on God. Some such association of necessity and dependence would therefore be entailed by God's love. Clayton again: "one can't use the difference in natures between God and world (necessary vs. contingent) to defend use of the panentheistic analogy . . . and at the same time maintain that it was eternally necessary that God create a world."[164] But if divine love qualifies necessity and contingency as qualities which distinguish between God and cosmos, then other qualities for distinguishing between the natures remain: infinitude and finitude, perfection and imperfection. Love demands that God and cosmos are both in some way dependent on, and necessary to, the other; but the difference in natures demands that they are not dependent on, and necessary to, the other *in the same way*. This would seem to be consistent with Clayton's insistence that divine embodiment is indispensable,[165] and Clayton's position would therefore be more secure if his interpretation of freedom followed more Augustinian lines, as for Macquarrie and Moltmann, so that God was indeed freely dependent on the cosmos, with no other option and without any outside force.

The Intrinsic, Positive Value of the Cosmos

Another corollary of panentheism is that as God is good, so God's body is good: the physical material "in and through" which God operates is fundamentally positive. That which is a part of God shares the same basic value as God's self. In this, panentheism breaks the long suspicion of Christian tradition, under the influence of classical theism, of all things physical.

It is possible for panentheism not to go this far. Clayton, for example, implies that the world created by God is neutral, and that no judgments about its intrinsic value can be made.[166] Similarly, panentheisms which do not hold evil to be privative might understand the evil of the cosmos to be "in" God and a part of God, just as much as the good. Clayton rightly notes that on this type of reading, panentheism offers no assistance with theodicy, since God remains ultimately responsible for evil, as in classical theism; it does not ease the problem of evil, but neither does it make it worse.[167] Most panentheisms, however, would subscribe, after Augustine, to a privative view of evil.[168] On this view evil is a lack of good, a negation which plagues and infects the cosmos: God works in and through the good of the cosmos to eliminate this blight, and bring the cosmos to the fullness of glory. The intrinsic, positive value to the cosmos can therefore be taken as a defining characteristic of the doctrine.

Passibility

God and the cosmos have an unusual relationship in that they do not simply relate as two personal lovers, but the latter is also the body of the former. Both facets — the nature of the relationship as love, and divine embodiment — imply that God suffers: the former because it is in the nature of authentic love to suffer the response of the beloved, and the latter because when a body suffers, the corresponding person suffers. These arguments are respectively the ontological and the immanentist arguments for passibility, the doctrine that God suffers.[169] Because these arguments for passibility stem from panentheistic principles, panentheism entails passibility. There are other grounds for holding that God is passible, so panentheism does not lie behind every instance of passibility; but because of the connections between the two, passibility, in the course of its twentieth-century rise,[170] has often led to panentheism.[171]

The recognized rise of passibility means that it is one of the most common marks of panentheism when panentheism is discussed. Passibility is held by Fiddes,[172] Griffin,[173] Hartshorne,[174] Macquarrie,[175] McDaniel,[176] McFague,[177] Moltmann,[178] Pailin,[179] Peacocke,[180] and Pittenger,[181] among others.[182]

Degree Christology

Panentheists make natural "degree christologians." That is to say, those who hold a panentheistic model of God tend to think of Christ as different from other persons by degree rather than kind. This is because if God is somehow "in" the cosmos generally, then God's work in Christ needs to be related with some continuity to that cosmic work, and not isolated from it; else there is an unpanentheistic dichotomy between God in Christ and the rest of the cosmos.[183] Because such a Christology issues from a panentheistic position, the identification of a person's Christology as a "degree Christology" is good evidence that the person holds to a panentheistic doctrine of God.[184]

Not many panentheists have made this connection. Degree Christology is, however, explicitly claimed by John Robinson[185] and Macquarrie,[186] and the work of Griffin strongly implies a Christology where the mode of divine presence or agency in Christ does not differ metaphysically from its operation in others.[187] Similarly, Peacocke gives a Christology that while not named as such, is clearly in the "degree" mold,[188] and McFague argues that "Jesus is not ontologically different from other paradigmatic figures either in our tradition or in other religious traditions who manifest in word and deed the love of God for the world."[189] The panentheist who subscribes most explicitly to a degree Christology is Norman Pittenger, who advocated the doctrine early in his career,[190] gave it sustained treatment in an essay of 1956,[191] and maintained the position in his two works on Christology, the first of which was one of the earliest applications of process thought to Christology, and widely respected.[192]

Conclusion

> What is needed, perhaps, is not an abandonment of panentheism but the reconsideration of existing metaphors as well as the development of new ones.[193]

The eight features above, largely common to key panentheists, yield a definition of panentheism which can be taken not only as a summary of the doctrine as it has emerged thus far but also as a yardstick for measuring individual varieties and strains of the doctrine, not least those espoused by the contributors to this volume. That is to say, panentheism can be defined as the doctrine of the cosmos being the good (against Clayton) "body" (against Peacocke), or "sacrament," needed by God (against Clayton), with which God is inextricably intertwined, and "in and through" which God works and suffers. The doctrine involves a degree Christology.[194] It is necessary to emphasize again that not of all these features will be explicit in the work of every panentheist, but the presence of a good proportion will indicate to which of the three basic doctrines of God a given theologian's ideas can be assigned.

Why, then, has the doctrine emerged? What historically are the pressures which have led to its adoption? It cannot be coincidence that the earliest conceptions of the doctrine, both implicit and explicit, came from the idealists of the nineteenth century. The rise of panentheism mirrors the rise of passibility, in that both were developed in Britain and the States under the influence of the German idealists.[195] Moreover, the panentheist revolution mirrors the passibilist revolution in being driven forward by experiences of suffering: just as the First and Second World Wars gave additional impetus to passibilism, so it can be no coincidence that panentheism gained popularity in a century which sought to reinterpret the love of God in the face of worldwide suffering.[196]

Insofar as idealism represented theology's assimilation of evolutionary values, it is possible to see panentheism as the theological response to science and the Enlightenment. It might be rash, however, to deduce that science was the ultimate historical pressure for the panentheist revolution. For rationalism itself, like mysticism, is a way of ordering human experience, and mysticism testifies to the panentheistic character of the deepest human religious experience. This suggests that the outworking of panentheism in doctrinal terms, like evolutionary science, was a reaction against the static resonances, either inherent or perceived, which emanated from the prevailing classical, "substance" ways of thinking, in line with the relationality of humanity's deepest experience. That is to say, the changes both scientifically and theologically may have resulted from a fundamental shift in ontology, from a "substance ontology," to a "relational ontology."[197] Classical theism tended to conceive of God and the world as substances, which would always make it difficult to relate the two, since substances are essentially spatial and cannot overlap. Panentheism is the result of conceiving "being" in terms of relationship or relatedness.[198] This is why process theism is a type of panentheism, for "process" asserts that "entities" are inseparably interrelated, and thus that relationship, rather than substance, is "of the essence."[199]

This is not to say that classical theism is not capable of refining itself in subtle and sophisticated ways which make dynamism more central to its system.[200] The ultimate question is whether it is better to state with qualifications that the cosmos is in God or with qualifications that the cosmos is not in God. It has been argued that the former option is to be preferred on three grounds: first, that even though classical theism has on occasion been made into a target of straw by panentheists,[201] just as panentheism has been by classical theists,[202] nevertheless the caricature of classical theism does tend to represent what the classical view has conveyed to the popular mind, and therefore the picture of God that people seem generally to have believed;[203] second, that despite the caricature of classical theism that seems to have been widely assimilated, the panentheistic model in fact more accurately expresses than classical theism the basic religious conviction of humanity;[204] and third, that the panentheistic way of expressing things has greater moral potential for the world.[205]

This moral potential of panentheism is seen in its affinity with liberation theologies, which insist on replacing relationships of domination with ones of genuine reciprocity. Panentheism is the result of process, mutuality, reciprocity or love, being made foundational to "being." This is why "love," as a term expressing relation, is such an important concept for process theologians, and why attention to love has been the cause of much doctrinal revisionism.[206] There is some asymmetry in the relation between God and cosmos, because the infinite is not dependent on the finite in the same way that the finite is dependent on the infinite.[207] Nevertheless, the mutuality in the relationship under panentheism is genuine. Again, classical theism would also claim that "love" is at the center of its doctrine of God. Yet this love is *agapē* — pure beneficence, needing no love in return — whereas panentheism would conceive of love as an inextricable mix of *agapē* and *erōs,* as the interdependence of giving and receiving. Thus the difference between classical theism and panentheism comes back to a difference of human experience, namely, which of these loves experienced by humanity, *agapē* or *agapē-erōs,* is the deeper symbol of the love of God;[208] and this confirms human experience as the prompt for the rise in panentheistic doctrine.

One of the features of panentheism that has received no recognition is its particular strain of ecclesiology, and it is ecclesiology that holds the clue to the whole purpose in naming the panentheist revolution. The ecclesiology distinctive to panentheism is the doctrine of the church as that which *names* God and God's activity.[209] On a classical model the church is the "ark of salvation": those who clamber on board out of the evil world will arrive at God's goodness in heaven. If, however, as panentheism maintains, God's goodness is at work more diffusively in the world, then the church can have no monopoly on goodness or salvation. What makes the church distinctive, therefore, is its task in relation to the mixture of good and evil to be found throughout both itself and the world: and that task is to realize more goodness through its own inheritance of faith and worship; that is to say, its tradition and language are to be used to increase salvation in the world. Thus the application of its language and tradition to the world is what the church distinctively has to offer; hence the concept of the church as that which "names," in its distinctive language, what is going on in the world.

The naming activity is a vital one, because consciousness and awareness of something can aid its delivery and furtherance; the implicit needs the explicit as much as the explicit needs the implicit.[210] If panentheism, being based on genuine reciprocity or love, is able to bring moral benefits to the cosmos, then, on the basis of its own ecclesiology, its identification and naming as a doctrine can aid the world's salvation. In other words, the identification and naming of panentheism which this volume attempts is not simply an exercise in historical theology, or even philosophical theology, if the latter is simply the enterprise of establishing a viable concept of God: it is part of the ecclesiological, or churchly, task: to name the things of God in order that love and justice in the cosmos might be more fulfilled. The naming of panentheism assists the world's redemption.

I Panentheistic Interpretations of the God-World Relationship

Three Varieties of Panentheism

NIELS HENRIK GREGERSEN

Willst du ins Unendliche schreiten, geh im Endlichen und
schaue nach allen Seiten.

J. W. Goethe, letter to Herder, 1787

Literally, pan-en-theism means that "all" (Gk. *pan*) is "in" God (Gk. *theos*),
but God is not exhausted by the world as a whole (G > W). As such panentheism attempts to steer a middle course between an acosmic theism, which
separates God and world (G / W), and a pantheism which identifies God with
the universe as a whole (G = W). Positively speaking, panentheists want to
balance divine transcendence and immanence by preserving aspects of the
former's claim of God's self-identity while embracing the latter's intimacy between God and universe.

So far it seems to me that panentheism offers a general direction of
thought that should be welcomed by Christian theology. The problem is,
however, that the concept of panentheism is not stable in itself. The little
word "in" is the hinge of it all. There may be as many panentheisms as there
are ways of qualifying the world's being "in God." The idea of panentheism
therefore needs specification, and this can be offered only by the interpretative frameworks of specific philosophical or religious doctrines of God. In
what follows I shall thus propose a typology of three versions of panentheism
within Western tradition. (I suspect that more varieties could be identified in
Eastern religion and philosophy, but I shall not attempt an exhaustive taxonomy here.)

I further argue that the philosophical and theological viability of panentheism depends on the particular version of panentheism appealed to, and on the status that one will accord the panentheistic imagery. Let me begin by pointing to two caveats. First, does God literally "contain" the universe in a spacelike manner? From the perspective of a Christian doctrine of creation the answer would be negative, for in this case the transcendence of God would be understood as a mere extension of the world's space. But "God is His own space," as an old principle says (formulated by John of Damascus in *On the Orthodox Faith* 13.11). The point here is that the Creator's "space" is not based on the created time-space continuum; rather the world's spatial-temporal existence is opened by and embraced by God's unimaginable "roominess." In this sense God's embrace of the world of nature is fully affirmed, but the container metaphor should not be taken to suggest a spatial continuum from the world to God. Similarly with the claim that God "has" a body, and that the world is therefore "God's body." This metaphor should in my view be used with even more care. While the soul in antiquity was seen as the life-supporting part of the human person, "mind" is, in today's anthropology, generally viewed as a "supervening" reality based on the "subvenient" causal basis of the human body.[1] Attractive as the soul-body metaphor may have been in the past, it no longer commends itself as an adequate contemporary model for the God-world relationship. God would appear as an emergent reality arising out of natural processes rather than the other way around.

There is, however, an important ontological position, which is more or less shared by all versions of panentheism, and which I find theologically central. This is the claim that there exists a real two-way interaction between God and world, so that (1) the world is somehow "contained in God" and (2) there will be some "return" of the world into the life of God. The idea of bilateral relations between God and world may even be said to be distinctive for panentheism. At least the idea that the world affects God differs markedly from the monism of pantheism, which does not allow for any God-world interactionism, and from classic philosophical theism, which has traditionally claimed that God remains unaffected by the fates and fortunes of the world.

Three Varieties of Panentheism

Setting up a *typology* means proposing a map of viable options within a more general landscape of intellectual pathways, but not a comprehensive map of the whole territory. In contrast to a taxonomy, a typology does not necessarily operate with either-or alternatives. But even if there are overlaps between, say, type 1 and type 2, and between type 2 and type 3, there need not necessarily be a common substrate between types 1, 2, and 3. Often we are dealing with what Wittgenstein called "family resemblances" beyond identifiable essences. The only generic elements I presuppose is the claim of a two-way traffic between God and world.

The first version I call a *soteriological panentheism* because the world's being "in God" is not taken as a given, but as a gift. It is only by the redeeming grace of God that the world can dwell in God; not everything shares automatically in divine life. Wickedness and sin, for example, have no place in the reign of God. Thus in a classic Christian perspective the world's being "in God" does not so much state a general matter of fact, but is predicated only about those aspects of created reality that have become godlike, while they still remain a created reality. Only in the eschatological consummation of creation shall God finally be "all in all" (1 Cor. 15:28).

Another form of panentheism I call a revelational or *expressivist panentheism*. This idea came up in the context of early-nineteenth-century German idealism in order to overcome a purely anthropocentric concept of God.[2] The point here is that the divine Spirit expresses itself in the world by going out of God and returning to God, enriched by the experiences of world history. This kind of theology can be seen as a universalized but also as a secularized version of the received Christian view. In fact, the term "panentheism" emerged in the context of post-Hegelian philosophical theology.

Finally, we have the *dipolar panentheism* of Whiteheadian process theology. Here God is assumed to be in some aspects timeless, beyond space and self-identical, while in other aspects temporal, spatial, and affected by the world. While dipolar process theism is conceptually worked out in terms of panentheism, the two aforementioned models of thought can be termed panentheistic only in a restricted sense. The soteriological model would say that the self-revelation of divine love is not found everywhere in a world, but only here and there. In this sense the "all" of *pan*-en-theism is qualified: while truth, love, and beauty certainly "exist in God," evil cannot be said to exist in God in the same manner. The expressivist model would add that only when the history of the world has been completed and sublated in God will the circle of divine self-expression and self-return be closed. In this sense also the "in" of pan-*en*-theism is called into question. By implication it seems that a full-blown panentheism risks the twofold danger of not fully preserving the identity of God while at the same time giving evil an ontological status not accorded it in the three Abrahamic traditions of Judaism, Christianity, and Islam. Whether or not these dangers can be circumvented remains to be seen.

Generic, Strict, and Qualified Panentheism

With these distinctions in mind, we may ask: What constitutes the common aspiration of the three versions of panentheism? I suggest that they all *share the intuition of a living two-way relation between God and world, within the inclusive reality of God.* Accordingly there are both active and responsive aspects of divinity vis-à-vis the world. Thus understood, a broad or general notion of panentheism seems to include at least two elements:

Generic Panentheism, Defined
1. God contains the world, yet is also more than the world. Accordingly, the world is (in some sense) "in God."
2. As contained "in God," the world not only derives its existence from God but also returns to God, while preserving the characteristics of being a creature. Accordingly, the relations between God and world are (in some sense) bilateral.

As is evident, the difficulty in both (1) and (2) is to determine the "in some sense." A panentheism in the strong sense holds that there is a *necessary* interdependence between God and world so that the world contributes to God as much as God contributes to the world. This view is unreservedly expressed by Alfred North Whitehead,

> It is as true to say that God is permanent and the World fluent, as that the World is permanent and God is fluent.
> It is as true to say that God is one and the World many, as that the World is one and God many. . . .
> It is as true to say that God transcends the World, as that the World transcends God.
> It is as true to say that God creates the World, as that the World creates God.[3]

This symmetrical view of the God-world relation was further developed by Charles Hartshorne into the concept of process panentheism or "surrelativism."[4] On this account, God is metaphysically limited by the world, since God cannot exist without a world, though God could coexist with another world than our present cosmos. Furthermore, even though God's actual being is affected by the indelible freedom of natural events, God is surpassing the world by God's eternal envisioning of all potentialities. These tenets of process theism differ not only from a classical substance theism, but also from the relational theism of Christian trinitarianism (panentheism 1) as well as from the romantic expressivism (panentheism 2). The differences may be stated as follows.

Strict (Dipolar) Panentheism, Defined

1. God cannot exist without generating a world, analogous to the way a soul cannot exist without a body; however, God can exist by embodying other worlds than our physical cosmos.
2. It is by a metaphysical necessity that God and world coexist and co-determine one another, so that God influences the world and temporal experiences flow into the actual nature of God; all that exists necessarily participates in divine life.

Qualified (Christian) Panentheism, Defined

1. While the world cannot exist without God, God could exist without a world; accordingly, the soul-body is at the most a useful metaphor for the intimacy of the God-world relation once the world is created out of divine love.
2. It is by divine grace that the world is codetermining God, so that temporal events may influence God and creatures share the life of God; all that is redeemed participates in divine life.

Defining panentheism as a distinct position, however, faces the problem of demarcation. What differentiates panentheism from classic tradition? Proponents of panentheism often claim it better articulates the immanence of God than classical theism. I believe, however, that this claim is unwarranted, for classical theism, even in the form of substance theism, entails a very strong doctrine of divine immanence. Hear the answer of Thomas Aquinas to the question "whether God exists in everything": "God exists in everything; not indeed as part of their substance or as an accident, but as an agent is present to that in which its action takes place. . . . Now since it is God's nature to exist, he it must be who properly causes existence in creatures, just as fire itself sets other things on fire. . . . So God must exist intimately in everything" (ST I 8 a 1).[5] Thus the immanence of God in the creatures is indeed asserted by classical theism, since God is identified as the power to exist in and above all that exists. Without the creator becoming a creature ("part of their substance") and without God being an emergent property of the world (an "accident"), God creates the world as if from within. At this juncture Thomas is able to use both the body-soul metaphor and the container metaphor. In fact, Thomas is able to use panentheistic imagery, but he makes clear their metaphorical status: "That in which bodily things exist contains them, but immaterial things contain that in which they exist, as the soul contains the body. So God also contains things by existing in them. However, one does use the bodily metaphor and talk of *everything being in God* inasmuch as he contains them (ST I 8 a 1 ad secundum)."[6] Thus the real demarcation line between panentheism and classic philosophical theism is neither the immanence of God nor the use of the metaphor of the world's being "in" God.

The real difference, according to Thomas, is that the natures and activities of the creatures do not have a real feedback effect on God. There is, in other words, no return from the world into God. As pure activity *(actus purus)*, God is the eternal realization of all positive predicates. Accordingly there is nothing God can "learn" in relation to the creatures, no "challenges" to be met, no free acts to "wait for." The world is utterly dependent on God for its existence, while the world cannot really affect the being or mind of God (*Summa Theologiae* 1.28.a.1). In short, Thomas rejects not the first but only the second tenet of generic panentheism, as defined above.

Soteriological Panentheism in the Context of Trinitarian Thought

What follows is thus an attempt to sort out different ways of developing the intuitive idea of the world's being "in God." I see at least three ways something can be "in" something else. The first way of in-being is like a ball placed in a bowl in a physical sense. Most would agree that this container model does not work when talking about the God-world relationship. However, there is also the case where a finite realization of some possibilities is placed in a wider set of possibilities. In this quasi-mathematical sense the world's being in God can be expressed as follows: something real but finite (the world of creation) is carved out, as it were, and allowed to exist out of infinite divine possibilities. This is a far more suggestive way of understanding the world's being in God, especially if it is made clear that natural events are not simply "parts" of the divine but realizations made possible by divine creation. But third, and most importantly in our context, something can be in another thing in a qualitative sense, such as when the beloved is present to the lover, even when physically absent, or when the playing of a symphony orchestra is so sensitive that each member of the orchestra becomes one of many in the unified experience of the symphony. The experience of attunement is here at the forefront. This third understanding of our "being in God" is the one emphasized in trinitarian thought.

As is well known, Thomas developed his philosophical theology within the confines of an Aristotelian substance metaphysics. According to Aristotle, relations are only "accidents" that cannot and do not change the "essence" of things. Relations are external, not internal, to substances, and so is the relation of the world to God. There is, however, another route to follow within classic Christian thought which starts out from a reflection on the three divine persons rather than from a presupposed model of divine simplicity. This is the preferred way of Eastern Orthodoxy.[7] The "essence" *(ousía)* of the divine life is thus a result of the reciprocal relations between the Father, the Son, and the Holy Spirit, so that, for instance, the Fatherhood of God is coconstituted by the Son, and vice versa; likewise the Holy Spirit is not a free-floating force but has the personal character of wanting to accomplish the will of the divine community. Accordingly, the life of God is a *community* constituted by the interdependencies of divine persons. God exists as God only in the eternal mutual relations of self-donation and interpenetration *(perichoresis)* between the Father, Son, and Holy Spirit. Trinitarian doctrine is thus one way of explicating the biblical message that "God *is* love" (1 John 4:16).

In his influential book *Being as Communion,* John D. Zizioulas has further argued that the trinitarian dogma entails a more general ontology: there is no true being without community, and no individual is conceivable in isolation from others. This ontology, according to Zizioulas, also entails a vision of created personhood: "Communion which does not come from a 'hypostasis,' that is, a concrete and free persons, and which does not lead to 'hypostases,' that is, concrete and free person, is not an 'image' of the being of God."[8] Now the question is whether this trinitarian idea of divine relationality can be extended so as to encompass the world and thus allow for a "return" of the world into the being of God. It should here be noted that seen from a historical perspective, there is no such direct way from a trinitarian view of God to asserting a two-way traffic between God and world. But there might be an indirect route. For what is characteristic of trinitarian thought is a highly developed notion of a human participation in divine life.[9]

Key elements of this idea of a sharing of divine life are thus present in broad strands of the biblical traditions, not least in the context of the Spirit of God who in the last days shall be poured out on all flesh (Joel 3:1-5 [2:28-32]; Acts 2:17). And 2 Peter 1:4 sets forth the promise that "you may be partakers in the divine nature."[10] More than anything else, however, it was the Johannine tradition that gave the impetus for patristic trinitarian reflection and for the idea of a human participation in God. The prologue of Saint John's Gospel reads, "In the beginning was the Word *(Logos).* The Word was with God, and the Word was God. It was with God at the beginning. All things came into being through the Word, and without it not one thing came into being. What has come into being in it was life, and the life was the light of all people" (John 1:1-4). The Logos (which in v. 14 is identified with Christ) is here said to be (1) "one with God" and thus to share the divinity with the Father. But the Logos is also (2) the principle of creation, through which "all things came into being," and finally (3) the principle of revelation, "the light of all people." Thus the divine Logos has both a cosmological and a revelational function.

The difficulty was to convey this message in Latin. The later standard translation of the Vulgate from around 400 translates "Logos" with the Latin *Verbum* (Word), which is still the usual translation. However, the earlier church fathers knew well that "Logos" could be translated both with *ratio* (Reason or Pattern) and *sermo* (Sermon or Dialogue).[11] In fact, the idea of a divine Pattern/Dialogue, putting the two together, expresses the unity of the two functions of the Logos as the principle of creation and revelation. Accordingly we could translate the opening passage of Saint John's Gospel as follows, "In the beginning was the Pattern *(Logos = ratio)*, and the Pattern was with God, and the Pattern was God. . . . All things came into being through this Pattern, and without it nothing came into being." On this account every configuration within the world of creation is a specified pattern elicited by the all-pervasive creative Pattern of the Logos. Being a creature simply means participating in a creaturely network of configurations, which is continuously reshaped by the creative information of the divine Logos. In this perspective the being in God of the creatures is not like a ball in a bowl, but they are specified configurations out of the endless fecundity of the divine Logos. However, God is not only creative, but also communicative. Each and any creature is addressed by the Logos. Here the informational or revelational aspects of the Logos come to the fore, and we could translate the prologue as follows, "In the beginning was the Dialogue *(Logos = sermo)*, and the Dialogue was in God, and the Dialogue was God. . . . All things came into being through this Dialogue, and without it nothing came into being." The world, we might say, is "in God" insofar as nothing can exist apart from the network of relations shaped and sustained by the divine Pattern, which also provides the divine milieu for all communication taking place within the world.

In the farewell discourses of John 14–17 (the main exegetical basis for the doctrine of the Trinity), we find a stronger sense in which the divine *perichoresis* extends to a *perichoresis* with worldly creatures. The basic formula is that Christ is "in the Father," and the disciples are "in Christ." There is, first, the mutual indwelling of the Christ (on earth) and the transcendent Father: "I am in the Father and the Father is in me" (14:10). This mutual indwelling expresses itself in the conformity between the works of Jesus and the will of God.

But there is, second, a similar relation between Christ and his followers. Jesus encourages his disciples by promising them that the Spirit will come to liberate them and fulfill the work of Christ and the Father. At that time, finally, there shall be a mutual coinherence between Christ and the believers, which leads to a union with God: "On that day you will know that I am in my Father, and you in me, and I in you" (14:20). In this trinitarian vision ultimate salvation means participating in the divine community. However, the statement of the disciples being in God is not a proposition about a present state of affairs, but is part of a future-oriented promise: "On that day you will know. . . ."

In this temporal world, however, we are not yet there. Only that which is born out of love is attuned to the love that God eternally is, and only that which is attuned to divine love can dwell in God. While the prologue of John spoke of the world as participating in the life and light of the Logos, elements of the world are here said to be present in God in the qualitative mode of an indwelling. Eastern Orthodox theology does not shrink away from saying that salvation means becoming like God, *theosis,* or even being deified in a process of *theosis.* Even though the being *(ousía)* of God is incommunicable, it is claimed that the uncreated activities *(energeia)* of God do include human beings.[12]

At this juncture, however, the spiritual tradition of Christianity distrusts a general metaphysical doctrine that holds that just anything, regardless of all its qualities, is "in God." It would be asked, Are all things really united with God? Is small-mindedness, miserliness, hatred, torture, terror, war? The biblical tradition denies this by saying that expressions of sin ("flesh and blood") shall not inherit the kingdom of God (1 Cor. 15:50). Only faith, hope, and love can abide in the extended divine network of personal relations (1 Cor. 13:13). "God is love, and those who abide in love abide in God, and God abides in them" (1 John 4:16). To be "in God" is possible only by being attuned to the self-giving, communicative Love that binds all things together. In this sense the "in" of pan-*en*-theism is highly qualified. Panentheism could not be affirmed as a matter of fact, but only as a movement of conversion and attunement to God, a movement not fulfilled until after the resurrection. Soteriological panentheism could thus also be referred to as an "eschatological panentheism," to use the term employed by John Polkinghorne.[13]

Expressivist Panentheism in the Context of German Idealism

We now turn to the expressivist version of panentheism in romanticism and idealism. The very term "panentheism" was coined as late as 1829 by the post-

Kantian philosopher and mystic Karl Christian Friedrich Krause (1781-1832). Notorious for inventing new and often obscure neologisms, he has had a considerable degree of success with the term "panentheism."[14]

Following the subjective idealist Fichte, Krause took his point of departure from the experiencing ego. His point was that anyone who realizes his or her own finitude also reaches a spiritual intuition of the infinity of God as the primordial being. With Schelling, the thinker of objective idealism, Krause referred to God as the one who in himself — as *Orwesen* (another neologism!) — is beyond all dualisms, but who nonetheless — as *Urwesen* in relation to the world — manifests both Contrabeing *(Gegenwesen)* and Unified Being *(Vereinwesen)*. Hereby Krause emphasized that God's internal being contains more than is manifest in the world. Yet at the same time all divine activity is motivated by the divine love, which promotes otherness and brings back the world into the divine life: "Love is the living form of the inner organic unification of all life in God. Love is the eternal will of God to be lovingly present in all beings and to take back the life of all his members into Himself as into their whole life."[15] We immediately recognize the important motif of the world returning into divine life. Human reason and nature are seen as subordinate beings, ontologically distinct from, yet somehow lying within, God. Each in their way, humanity and nature express the richness of divine life. However, since humanity epitomizes the synthesis between nature and reason far beyond that of plants and animals, humanity is seen by Krause as particularly expressive of the divine life. In this way the pious strife for a union with God *(Gottesinnigkeit)* is part of a comprehensive metaphysics of love according to which nature is contained within the human community, and the human community within the life of God. Krause's panentheism shares the goal of romanticism and idealism, viz., to overcome the split between humanity and nature and to move beyond the alternatives of a supernaturalist theism (as epitomized by Leibniz) and the idea of pantheism (as formulated by Spinoza).[16] The remedy was the idea of nested hierarchies: nature in humanity, and humanity in God.

This expressivist view of divine love emerged in a situation when philosophical theologians attempted to find a third way between pantheism and supernaturalism. The challenge of Spinoza's pantheism was his thesis that there is "a oneness of the supreme God with nature itself, or with the universe of all things."[17] In his *Ethics* from 1677, Spinoza distinguished between God as the "one substance" of all things and all things as the "modes" or "affections of God" (bk. I, def. 3).[18] God is not the external creator, but the "immanent cause" of all things (bk. I, prop. 18). In this context also Spinoza can occasionally use the panentheistic formula that "everything is in God" (bk. I, prop. 15).

However, Spinoza's first-cause theology implies quite a few philosophical problems. First, he presupposed a deterministic worldview. Whether one perceives the world from the "vertical" perspective of the creative principle of "God" *(natura naturans)* or from the "horizontal" perspective of natural networks *(natura naturata)*, all is determined by God or nature (bk. I, prop. 29, 33). Secondly, Spinoza had difficulties in accounting for the ontological status of individual beings. The stone on the beach, the horse on the field, and the mathematical argument are all "modes" of the same substance, but not really discrete events. Finally, Spinoza found that the world is perfect, because it derives its existence from a perfect divinity (bk. I, prop. 33; bk. III, preface).[19] The romanticists were for good reasons not willing to subscribe to any of these implications.

Paradoxically Leibniz's perfect-being theism had come into disrespect for similar reasons. Also Leibniz subscribed to a doctrine of determinism, a doctrine which was not seen by the German idealists to give proper room to human freedom. And while Leibniz certainly was able to safeguard the reality of individual beings (the "monads"), he subscribed to the idea that the world must be "the best possible world" since it originates from an omnipotent and benevolent God.

Thus both pantheism and supernaturalism seemed to face unsurmountable problems. Add to this the critique of Fichte that the very notion of divine personhood implies a finitization of divine infinity. Being a person means to stand in a relation to another, but the idea of true infinity seems to exclude the borderlines of a person "here" standing in a relation to another person "there."[20]

Here Hegel came to the rescue by proposing a deeper concept of infinity which also implied a new view of divine perfection. According to Hegel, Fichte was right in insisting that infinity should not be understood in contrast to finitude. Infinity is not that which starts on the other side of finitude. Neither is infinity just the endless process of transcending, in analogy to an endless series of numbers. These examples constitute only the concept of a "bad infinity" *(das schlecht Unendliche)*. The concept of genuine infinity *(das wirklich Unendliche)* is rather that which includes finitude within itself. In this sense the finite world has its being "in" the infinite God. Panentheistic formulations seemed almost unavoidable.

From this infinity-based concept of God Hegel reconceived the idea of divine causality and divine perfection, while also safeguarding the subjectivity of God. Hegel did so by expanding the dogma of the Trinity into a universal vision for the God-world relation. To create a world is not a free option for God, but is an implication of the self-giving nature of God. It belongs to the perfection of God to set free and to include finitude. As absolute being, God (the "Father") is no longer the remote inaccessible deity of a first-cause theology, but the kenotic, self-divesting, and relational Being, who manifests himself in the history of humanity (the "Son"), and does so in the form of a self-consciousness ("Spirit"). The overarching model of God is here one of a self-conscious subjectivity who creates the otherness of creation in order to bring it back into divine life. As expressed in Hegel's *Encyclopedia,* "God is only God to the extent that God knows godself; God's self-knowing is, further, a self-consciousness in humanity and humanity's knowledge *of* God, which proceeds to humanity's self-knowing *in* God."[21] Thus the Spirit both proceeds from God and returns to God, enriched by the experiences in the world of creation. Hegel is here an heir of the Western version of trinitarian theology that gives priority to the unity of God, here in the form of the self-manifesting subjectivity of the Father. However, when Hegel sees the creation and redemption of the world as the self-realization of divine life, the divine life opens up and embraces the world. The internal divine life will thus in the end coincide with the history of divine redemption. Thus the concept of divinity includes three elements in which the Absolute presents itself, "(a) as eternal content abiding with itself in its manifestation [Father]; (b) as differentiation of eternal being [Son] from its manifestation, which through this differentiation becomes the phenomenal world into which the content enters; (c) as infinite return [Spirit] of the alienated world and its reconciliation with eternal being."[22] The characteristics of a generic panentheism (as defined above) are no doubt present in Hegel. But note also the continued presence of the soteriological pattern of Christian trinitarianism. That is, the world is not yet fully in God, but is destined to be reconciled with God. Hegel is not compelled to say, with Leibniz in his *Theodicy* from 1710, that our world, as it is, is "the best possible world." Evil exists, and evil cannot exist — as evil — in God. However, evil is a necessary by-product of the self-alienation which logically follows from finite knowledge. (This is, according to Hegel, why the fall of Adam and Eve is connected to the eating of the fruits of the tree of knowledge in Genesis 3.) Stones, plants, and animals don't sin. But the evils of self-alienation are necessary stages of human emergence. (Here Hegel appropriates the old idea of a *felix culpa* or felicitous fall.) In this manner God's creation of finite awareness coincides with the fall away from God. Only in the long process of returning into the divine will the alienated world be reconciled with God.[23] Evil shall then be "sublated" or absorbed by God. Put in traditional terms: only at the consummation of world history will the "economic Trinity" (God's relation to the world) coincide with the "immanent" Trinity (God's internal life). This whole process is guided by the idea of the self-expressive yet self-divesting divine Spirit.

In this sense the core of the romantic-idealist tradition of philosophical theology has helpfully been termed "natural supernaturalism."[24] For it is *in* the "natural" world that God's love becomes manifest. And yet it is only in the return to God that the world of nature participates in "supernatural" life, liberated from the alienations of finitude.

Dipolar or Whiteheadian Panentheism

We have seen that straightforward panentheistic formulas can occasionally be found in both Thomas and Spinoza. I also argued that the defining feature of the world's return into God can be traced back to some forms of trinitarian theology that were later highlighted in expressivist romanticism. However, it was not until the work of the process philosopher Charles Hartshorne that the idea of panentheism was promoted as a distinct option in philosophical theology. Already in the programmatic article "A Mathematics of Theism" from 1943,[25] Hartshorne argued that among the formally possible forms of theism, panentheism commended itself as the "higher synthesis" of theism and pantheism. Whereas traditional theism claims God to be the universal cause (C) and pantheism understands God as the all-inclusive reality of the world (W), panentheism holds that God, without contradictions, is CW, i.e., both the universal cause and the all-inclusive reality.

This solution is semantically stable only if one distinguishes between two aspects or "poles" of the one and same God. The backbone of Hartshorne's panentheism exactly lies in his dipolar concept of God. In one respect God is essentially unchangeable, but in another respect God is dependent on all that is encompassed by God. According to Hartshorne, no power is conceivable which is not influenced by that over which the power is exercised. Therefore Hartshorne rejects the idea of a divine creation "out of nothing" resp. "out of God." God necessarily stands in relation to a necessarily preexisting world. God is the world's creator insofar as God gives form and shape to everything, but God is also a creature of the world who absorbs and coordinates the events that from time to time enter into divine experience. The world transcends God as well as God transcends the world.[26] Irrespective of the manner in which the universe is actually developing, the absolute self-identity or essence of God is thus preserved: "God as CW 'transcends' the world, not only as every whole transcends each and every one of its parts, but in the uniquely radical way of containing an essence or element of self-identity absolutely independent of whichever among possible contingent things are actual as parts of the Whole."[27] Hartshorne's dipolar concept of

God is thus the key to his revision of first-cause theology. As rightly observed by Hartshorne's collaborator William L. Reese, it is the dipolar concept that specifies Hartshorne's panentheism, and not the other way around.[28]

In the same vein, Hartshorne proposed a highly influential reconception of the idea of divine perfection. In classical philosophical theism, divine perfection is understood as the prior possession of all possible predicates. God is the perfect absolute (A). By contrast, pantheism understands God as the perfect relative (R). But also here panentheism follows the "golden mean" that God is AR, i.e., both the unsurpassable perfect and the self-surpassing perfect that ever grows in perfection.[29]

On the classical understanding as represented by Thomas or Leibniz, God is the *actus purus* who leaves no values unrealized in divine experience. God therefore cannot discover anything, since no knowledge is new to God. Nor can God be affected by the creatures. But according to Hartshorne, the capacity for universal empathy also belongs to the perfection of God. God is the unsurpassable nature, but divine perfection includes a capacity for surpassing Godself by being "sympathetically dependent" on all that happens in the world.[30]

This important idea of divine relativity changes the understanding of divine love. A love which is not sensitive to the particular needs of the beloved is not perfect love. Love is to stretch out and surpass oneself in the direction of the other. It belongs to the greatness of God to be empathically related to all individual events, not only as a passive receptacle for worldly events but also as the one who provides the creative impetus for further developments in the world.

Hartshorne should be given credit for developing a thoroughly social conception of God within philosophical theology. He succeeds in preserving a high degree of divine self-identity, and his panentheism gives full weight to the idea of individuals or "parts" of creation. Hartshorne's worldview, in contrast to Spinoza's, is one of freedom and individuality. It seems to me, however, that the problem of the persistence of evil is not appropriately reflected in Whiteheadian panentheism. For sure, Hartshorne avoids the Spinozistic presupposition that the world is perfect as it is, and process theology provides a theoretical solution of the "theodicy problem" by removing the omnipotence of God. But thereby the practical problem about how to overcome evil is only worsened! There seems no redemption possible for the tragically unfilled aspirations of life, nor for the problem of horrendous evils of wickedness. The closest we come are formulations like these: "What is in the parts is in the whole; so, for example, our misdeeds are in God; but not as his misdeeds, or his deeds at all — rather as his misfortunes. They make his overall satisfaction less than it otherwise would be, but not his goodness of decision."[31] God's moral identity seems here to be bought at the expense of the tragedy of those creatures who — both as perpetrators and as victims — fail. Dipolar panentheism expresses the passive absorption of experiences into God but has difficulty in speaking about the active transformation of creatures. A soteriological deficit is obvious, because Hartshorne's theory of the God-world relation is general in nature. By contrast, trinitarian panentheism is centered on the soteriological vision of transforming the world into the complex community of divine and creaturely lovers.

There are also important differences to the expressivist version of panentheism. Both Hegel and Hartshorne expound universalist models of the God-world relationship, models that entail a two-way flow between God and world. However, the process view of divine action seems to endanger the idea of divine infinity. Since the creativity of the world is an eternal principle alongside God, God cannot be truly infinite but will always be one factor among other factors. For sure, the divine lure is a factor in all events, but the Christian naturalist assumption that God is at work "in, with, and through" natural processes cannot be articulated. For in a relativistic cosmology based on autonomous local prehensions, God may provide the stimulus for creaturely activity *prior* to natural events and God can absorb the worldly events *after* their occurrence, but God cannot be *simultaneously present* with the creature. To the mind of God, actual occasions remain black boxes.[32] This is an unavoidable consequence of Whitehead's presupposition that God is subdued under the general metaphysical principles as their "chief exemplification."[33]

On this point there is hardly a mediation possible between Hartshorne and the understanding of divine causality in the Abrahamic tradition, which was also presupposed by Hegel. The point of demarcation is whether creativity derives from God the creator or belongs to the everlasting world.[34] We here face a genuine metaphysical alternative: either the matrix into which the transient creatures are woven is the energies and actions of the living God, or God and world share a third common platform within which God and world coexist and subsequently coadapt to one another.[35] For Palamas and the Eastern tradition, the matrix for the divine-human communion is the uncreated energy of God; for Hegel the matrix is the twofold movement of the divine Spirit itself; for process thought the matrix is coconstituted by several actors and principles: (1) the world of eternal objects or possibilities (as envisaged by God), (2) the creativity inherent in actual occasions (be they divine or worldly), and (3) the actual occasions themselves. On the latter account, God and world are different sorts of actual societies whose influences go from here to there. But never is the one the creator and the other the creature. On the former accounts, however, the infinity of God does not inhibit the freedom of finite beings, since it is the very divine activity that elicits, upholds, and embraces creaturely freedom. On this crucial issue there seems to be no way of mediating between the solution of an infinity-based theology and that of process theology.[36]

Concluding Perspectives

If my observations so far are essentially correct, panentheism should not be regarded as a perennial philosophy. Panentheism came up in the specific context of German idealism as part of various attempts to escape the alternatives of Leibniz's supernaturalism and Spinoza's pantheism. Only later, in the mid–twentieth century, did Hartshorne turn the vexed term "panentheism" into a clear position guided by the specific premises of dipolar theism.

But even though panentheistic systems are relatively new, we have seen that the basic intuitions and metaphors of panentheism can be traced further back in religious tradition. The metaphor of the world's "being in God" is present in many traditions, albeit with different meanings. In the present context I have confined myself to the Christian tradition, but similar metaphors appear in the sacred writings of Hinduism.[37] As argued by the cognitive scientists George Lakoff and Mark Johnson, a spatial thinking in "containers" and "contained" is virtually universal.[38] We even found the container scheme in Thomas and Spinoza.

I have therefore proposed the supplementary criterion that in order to count as panentheism (in the broad generic sense), the world is not only in some sense internal to God but there must also be some feedback from world to God. On this definition part of trinitarian tradition as well as Hegel's philosophy of religion can also be termed "panentheist" (even if the term itself is not used). Thus, reading backwards, we come to the threefold typology of soteriological, expressivist, and dipolar panentheisms.

The critical lesson to be learned from this essay is that anyone who wants to describe himself or herself as a panentheist should from the outset make clear what kind of panentheism he or she is endorsing. Panentheism should not be seen as a solution to the problem of thinking about God in a contemporary context. But it may serve as a fruitful heuristic concept, which then immediately requires a specification in order to avoid confusions. I have thus argued that while there is a substantial overlap between soteriological and expressivist panentheism, dipolar panentheism is incompatible with both of them. A clear choice of metaphysical principles will have to be made.

However, even if panentheism is not a stable philosophical "doctrine," its metaphors can still be illuminating. Understanding all things to be in God, as it were, means that we can be at home with God anywhere in the universe. The logic of infinity permits us to think of the presence of God in the midst of reality — without replacing the finite with the infinite. Since there exists no matter without God being present in it, we have the interesting formulas: *God + nature = nature* while *nature - God = o*. This is another way of stating an old principle from my own Lutheran theological background: *finitum capax infiniti* (finitude allows for the presence of infinity). The infinite God is in principle graspable within finitude. This is aptly expressed by Wolfgang Goethe in the sentence placed at the beginning of this essay: "If you want to enter the infinite, walk in the finite world, and look to all sides." God speaks both in the starry heaven which attracts our eyes and in the cry of the child, who demands our attention. God is to be discovered in the miniatures of life.

The difficulty lies in grasping it, or in being grasped by it. This is why the concept of revelation becomes so important to religion. God's ambiance can in principle be felt by swimming in the ocean as well as in the intricate pattern of the snowflake. For all that is exists as a specified pattern somehow carved out of the creative pattern of God. But to grasp it or not to be grasped by it, that's the crucial question.

Summary

It is argued that the concept of panentheism, attractive as it is, is far from stable. That God is present everywhere in the world, and that the world is somehow present "in God," was already made explicit by the substance theist Thomas Aquinas and the pantheist Spinoza. Against this background a generic concept of panentheism is developed, according to which panentheism contends that (1) the world is somehow contained by God and (2) the world affects God and returns to God. Against this background a typology between three distinct types of panentheism in Western thought is developed. In classic trinitarian thought, dating back to the fourth century, we find resources for what might be dubbed a *soteriological panentheism*. In the context of nineteenth-century romanticism, especially in Hegel, we find a universalized *expressivist panentheism*. In the twentieth century, finally, Charles Hartshorne developed a *dipolar panentheism* in continuation of Whitehead's process philosophy. It is argued that the dipolar panentheism is not compatible with the two other forms of panentheism, and that a metaphysical choice has to be made between them.

Panentheism: A Postmodern Revelation

DAVID RAY GRIFFIN

My thesis is that panentheism is the content of a divine revelation that has been occurring in the cultural life of the West, primarily through religious, moral, scientific, and philosophical experience, roughly over the past two centuries. It is "postmodern" in that it goes beyond, while incorporating the central truths of, the dominant worldviews of the early and late modern periods in the West.

The term "panentheism" can be used generically or more specifically. The generic meaning has been explained in the introduction to this volume. Other essays spell out various positions that can, insofar as they incorporate this generic meaning, legitimately be called panentheistic. In this essay I discuss the version of process panentheism, based on the process philosophies of Alfred North Whitehead and Charles Hartshorne, that I advocate.[1] My thesis about panentheism as a postmodern revelation applies especially to process panentheism, which in my view most fully embodies the distinctive features of the panentheistic alternative to atheism, pantheism, and traditional theism. In the first and second sections I mention various reasons why the dominant worldviews of the early and late modern periods have proven inadequate. The third section explains process panentheism and how it overcomes these inadequacies.

Early Modernity's Supernaturalism

The "scientific revolution" of the seventeenth century was primarily a change in worldview, in which the atomism of Democritus, revived by Galileo, was

36

joined with the supernaturalistic theism of Augustine, which had been revived in the nominalistic voluntarism of the fourteenth century (called the *via moderna*) and then popularized by the Protestant Reformers. According to this supernaturalistic version of theism, God created our universe *ex nihilo*, with the *nihil* understood to mean absolute nothingness.

This supernaturalism can be called extreme voluntarism, because the fact that a universe of finite beings even exists is said to be due solely to the divine will. This idea implies that all the general principles involved in our universe — not only what scientists call the "laws of nature" but also the more general, underlying principles, such as the principles of causation — are purely contingent, having been freely established by an act of divine will. The implication of this position is that the divine power is absolute, not restricted in the slightest by any power inherent in the creatures or any causal principles inherent in the nature of things. This implication is brought out explicitly by contemporary evangelical theologian Millard Erickson, who says: "God did not work with something which was in existence. He brought into existence the very raw material which he employed. If this were not the case, God would . . . have been limited by having to work with the intrinsic characteristics of the raw material which he employed."[2] Erickson affirms, he says, "a definite supernaturalism — God resides outside the world and intervenes periodically within the natural processes through miracles."[3] In this view the "laws of nature" can be interrupted because they are not really *natural* in the sense of being inherent in the very nature of things. This same understanding was expressed by the nineteenth-century Calvinist Charles Hodge in response to the question of how God is related to the laws of nature. "The answer to that question . . . is, First, that He is their author. . . . Secondly, He is independent of them. He can change, annihilate, or suspend them at pleasure. He can operate with or without them. The 'Reign of Law' must not be made to extend over Him who made the laws."[4]

Although this doctrine of *creatio ex nihilo* was long assumed to be biblical, recent scholarship has revealed otherwise. The Hebrew Bible, shows Harvard's Jon Levenson, affirms a doctrine of creation out of chaos.[5] And Germany's Gerhard May has shown that *creatio ex nihilo* is also absent from the intertestamental literature (including 2 Maccabees) and the New Testament.[6] The Christian thinkers throughout the first and most of the second century simply took for granted the standard view, which was that our world had been created out of chaos, with many of them explicitly affirming Plato's version of this view, according to which although *our* world is a contingent creation, it was created out of matter in a chaotic state.

As May shows, the doctrine of creation out of absolute nothingness —

according to which the creation of our world was the beginning of finite existents as such — was an innovation, adopted by some theologians
(Theophilus, Hippolytus, Tertullian, Irenaeus) near the end of the second
century in response to Marcion's gnostic theology, which said that our world
was created out of evil matter. The best way to fight this idea, they thought,
was to deny that the world was created out of *anything*. Although
Hermogenes, a Platonic Christian theologian, warned that this innovation
would lead people to blame God for the world's evils, these innovators went
boldly — and, as I argue in an essay that takes issue with May's own endorse-
ment of *creatio ex nihilo*,[7] foolishly — forward. The doctrine of creation out
of absolute nothingness soon became the standard Christian doctrine. In
later centuries it was also widely affirmed by Jewish and Islamic theologians,
so that "traditional theism" within all the Abrahamic religions is extreme voluntarism.

In Christian theology in the Middle Ages, certain positions, such as
Thomism, mitigated this voluntarism. But early modernity involved a resurgence of extreme voluntarism over against not only Thomist mitigations
but also Renaissance naturalisms of various types — atheistic, pantheistic,
and panentheistic. A central motivation behind this resurgence was to cur-
tail any adoption of religious pluralism by supporting the supernatural
character of Christianity's miracles as divine testimony to its status as the
one true religion.[8]

Much of the cultural history of the following centuries has involved
multiple reasons to reject this supernaturalistic worldview. One reason is the
problem of evil, which, given the doctrine of *creatio ex nihilo*, is truly severe,
because this doctrine implies that any evil that has occurred — from the rape
of a child to the Nazi Holocaust — could have been unilaterally prevented by
God. This doctrine also implies that all the structural causes of evil in our
world, such as the fact that birth defects, cancer, and nuclear weapons are
possible, were freely created by God — even though God, by hypothesis,
could have created a world with all the positive values of this one but without
the possibility of all these evils. Hermogenes' prediction has come true, as one
of the main reasons behind the widespread atheism in modern times is the
feeling that "God's only excuse," as one wag put it, "is that he doesn't exist."

Throughout the Middle Ages and the early modern period, this conclusion was not widely drawn, even though theologians were not able to provide a
satisfactory answer to the problem of evil,[9] because the idea that religious belief rests on authority, to be accepted by faith, was generally accepted. Central
to the Enlightenment, however, was the adoption of the "modern commitment" to support all beliefs on the basis of common experience and reason.[10]

Given this new commitment, which implies that religious beliefs are not worthy of acceptance unless they can pass reason's tests of self-consistency and adequacy to the facts, the conflict between the world's evils and omnipotent goodness has led to widespread atheism.

The supernaturalist version of theism also came into conflict with the naturalistic attitude induced by the scientific mentality. Although Mersenne, Descartes, Boyle, and Newton were central figures in the resurgence of supernaturalism, so that it was at first integral to the "scientific worldview," science soon became identified with a naturalistic outlook that ruled out any miraculous interruptions of the "laws of nature." Although the term "naturalism" has recently taken on an even more restrictive meaning (to be discussed below), I am here simply referring to naturalism in the generic sense, which I call naturalism$_{ns}$ (with "ns" standing for "nonsupernaturalist"). The supernaturalist idea that there is a divine being who can occasionally interrupt the world's normal causal principles, sometimes called a "God of the gaps," has been increasingly rejected.

The rise of evolutionary theory provided more reasons to reject supernaturalism. It ruled out the Genesis-based view that the universe is only a few thousand years old, thereby raising the question why omnipotence would take so long to create our world. It contradicted the view that our present biological species were created *ex nihilo*. And it undermined the argument for supernatural design. All these so-called conflicts between evolution and theism, it should be noted, are conflicts only with the form of theism created by Hermogenes' opponents, who saddled God with a kind of power that would not need to work slowly, through a step-by-step, evil-filled process, to create a world such as ours.

In any case, just as natural scientists increasingly saw no reason to affirm any gaps in the natural causal sequences, historians increasingly saw no reason to assume that historical events involved any such gaps. In particular, although supernaturalist assumptions had supported the idea that the Bible reflected infallible revelation, historical-critical study of the Bible found no evidence of supernatural causation in its production. The modern study of the Bible, in other words, falsified the hypothesis that divine inspiration overrode the fallibility of the biblical authors.

The early modern reaffirmation of supernaturalism was used, as mentioned earlier, to undergird the idea that Christianity is the one true religion. But this idea, especially after the splintering of Protestantism into warring sects, came to be seen as the cause of violence. This fact motivated many leading thinkers to reject the theism behind this idea.

Still another factor behind the rejection of traditional theism was the rise of the social critique of religion — which portrayed religion as sanctioning the status quo by regarding it as divinely ordained. This critique, by leading to the conviction that belief in God is more harmful than helpful, provided a motive to focus on the reasons against, rather than the reasons for, theistic belief.

Given the rise of the commitment to support all beliefs on the basis of experience and reason rather than authority, "natural theology" became vital to rational belief in God. Philosophers such as Hume and Kant, however, realized that reasoning on the basis of common experience alone could not support the existence of a supreme being that had created the world *ex nihilo*.[11]

Late Modernity's Atheism

Through the combined effect of these factors, the dominant worldview in intellectual circles moved from theism to deism and then to complete atheism (or in some cases to pantheism, which is similar to atheism in denying that there is a divine actuality distinct from the world). This shift was part of the more general transition from early to late modernity. Early modern thinkers, as mentioned earlier, affirmed Democritean atomism and thereby a purely materialistic, mechanistic view of the basic units of nature. But they did not understand the created world as a whole in materialistic terms. They affirmed, instead, that human beings have minds or souls, which are different in kind from the bits of matter making up their bodies. This dualism between mind and matter was affirmed, most famously by Descartes, to protect belief in human freedom and life after death.

Equally crucial to early modernity was the sensationist doctrine of perception, affirmed most famously by Locke and Hume, according to which we can perceive things beyond ourselves only by means of our physical sensory organs. One motive behind the denial of nonsensory perception was to exclude a naturalistic (which we would today call a parapsychological) explanation of Jesus' "mental miracles." Another motive was to rule out "enthusiasm," meaning the direct experience of God, through which some people claimed to have personal revelations that contradicted church doctrine. This denial of a capacity for religious experience was not, however, seen as undermining religion, because the existence of supernatural revelation in the Bible was still presupposed.

As supernaturalism lost its appeal, however, the religious dimensions of early modernity were undermined. Besides the fact that there could be no more talk of supernatural revelation, the decline of supernaturalism also undermined the affirmation of a soul. In response to the question of how the soul, with its consciousness and freedom (final causation), could interact with the brain's matter, said to be wholly insentient and to interact solely by efficient causation, Descartes and his fellow dualists could only say "God does it." That is, God, being omnipotent, had simply ordained that mind and matter would interact — or at least, as Malebranche and other "occasionalists" said, *seem* to interact. "For thinkers of that age," wrote William James, "'God' was the great solvent of all absurdities."[12] But once this kind of answer could no longer be given, dualism collapsed into materialism. All that remained of the early modern worldview was its mechanistic-materialistic view of matter and its sensationist doctrine of perception. Naturalism$_{ns}$ came to be embodied in what I call naturalism$_{sam}$ (with "sam" standing for "sensationist-atheist-materialist").

Although naturalism$_{sam}$ has been the dominant worldview of the late modern period, at least since the middle of the nineteenth century, this period has involved a growing realization that this doctrine is problematic in many ways. Some of the problems result from its materialism, which implies that the mind (or soul) is somehow identical with the brain. Although this "identist" doctrine was adopted to avoid dualism's mind-body problem, it has an equally difficult problem, which is to understand how the brain, understood as consisting of billions of bits of matter devoid of experience, can give rise not only to a *unified* experience but even to any *experience* whatsoever. Although many thinkers believe this can be explained as simply one more example of "emergence," the alleged emergence of experience out of nonexperiencing things is different in kind from any of the nonproblematic kinds of emergence — such as the emergence of wetness out of the combination of hydrogen and oxygen into H_2O.[13] As some materialistic philosophers now admit, such an emergence, apart from the assumption of a supernatural deity, is completely mysterious.[14]

Materialism, with its equation of the mind with the brain, also makes human freedom unintelligible. Some materialists admit this to be a problem, because although their worldview has no room for human freedom, they cannot help presupposing in practice that they are partly free and hence responsible for their actions.[15]

Some of the problems of naturalism$_{sam}$ are rooted primarily in its sensationism. For one thing, as we saw, it denies that we have any capacity for religious experience, and yet such experience seems to be common to the cultures of all times. Naturalism$_{sam}$ has yet to come up with an explanation of the origin, persistence, and variety of religion that remotely approaches adequacy.[16]

Sensationism also denies the capacity for moral experience. Early modern thinkers were able to avoid the moral relativism to which this denial might lead by appealing to divine omnipotence. Locke said the moral law was revealed in the Bible, whereas deists such as Adam Ferguson and Thomas Jefferson said God, in creating us, had implanted moral norms in our minds. Once this supernaturalist answer could not be given, however, sensationism led modern moral philosophers to conclude that moral principles are merely human creations. Although some of these philosophers admit that moral experience *appears* to be objective, they must, given their sensationist and atheistic premises, regard this appearance as illusory.

Naturalism$_{sam}$ also cannot do justice to the apparent objectivity of mathematics and logic. Although virtually all mathematicians and logicians presuppose in practice that they are in touch with objective principles, the atheism and materialism of naturalism$_{sam}$ imply that the universe has no place for such principles, and its sensationism implies that, even if they existed, we could not perceive them.[17]

The atheism of naturalism$_{sam}$ creates still more problems. It has great difficulty explaining the order of the universe, a fact that has become even more obvious with the realization that our universe has been able to develop so as to support life only because of many "cosmic constants" that appear to have been "fine-tuned" at the beginning of our universe. Also, neo-Darwinism, which provides naturalism$_{sam}$'s framework for understanding evolution, is unable to explain the novelty, the directionality, and the apparent saltations in the evolutionary process.[18] Finally, whereas supernaturalism had difficulty explaining the world's evil, naturalism$_{sam}$ has difficulty explaining its goodness.

Thanks to a growing appreciation of these inadequacies, many intellectuals have concluded that naturalism$_{sam}$ must be abandoned. Some of them, perhaps unaware of another alternative, have reaffirmed traditional theism. But a growing number are exploring panentheism, seeing that it has many advantages. In the next section I discuss process theology's version of panentheism, pointing out several of its advantages.

Process Panentheism

According to process panentheism, God is essentially soul of the universe. Although God is distinct from the universe, God's relation to it belongs to the divine essence. This does not mean, however, that our particular universe — with its electrons, inverse square law, and Planck's constant — exists necessarily. This universe was divinely created, evidently about 15 billion years ago. It was even created out of "no-thing" in the sense that, prior to its creation, there were no enduring individuals sustaining a character through time (such as quarks and photons), which is what is usually meant by "things." With Berdyaev, therefore, we can say that it was created out of *relative* nothingness.[19] This relative nothingness was a chaos of events, each of which embodied some modicum of "creativity," which is the twofold power to exert self-determination and then efficient causation on subsequent events. Each event in this chaos, therefore, influenced future events after being influenced by prior events, so that the creation of our universe was not the beginning of temporal relations and hence of time.[20] It was, however, the beginning of the particular, contingent form of order that physicists have been progressively discovering. Our universe began when God got this order instantiated in what had previously been a chaotic situation consisting of extremely brief, trivial, random happenings in which no significant values could be realized.

Although this situation was chaotic in comparison with the order that followed, it was not completely devoid of order. The realm of finite actualities always embodies various necessary (metaphysical) principles, including *causal* principles about how finite actualities are related to each other and to God. To say that God is *essentially* soul of the universe means, accordingly, that it belongs to the essence of God to be related not only to *our* universe (now that it exists) but also to *the* universe, in the sense of a realm of finite actualities instantiating these metaphysical principles.

The most important implication of this point is that it shows process panentheism to be a version of *naturalistic* theism. Besides the fact that the universe — in the sense of *some* realm of finite actualities — exists as necessarily and therefore as naturally as does God, the most fundamental causal principles of the universe exist naturally, being inherent in the nature of things, because they exist in the very nature of God. They cannot be divinely interrupted, because such an interruption would be a violation of the very nature of God. These causal principles — including the twofold principle that every finite individual embodies at least some slight power of self-determination and has causal effects on other individuals — cannot be overridden by divine power. Accordingly, although there is divine influence in every event, there is divine determination of no events.

Another central feature of process panentheism is its affirmation of divine dipolarity. There are, in fact, two senses in which God is dipolar. The dipolarity emphasized by Hartshorne says that, besides having an *abstract essence* that is strictly unchanging, God also has *concrete states* that — contrary to the traditional doctrine of divine immutability — involve change. For God as a concrete individual, time or process is real, so that God constantly has new experiences by virtue of being related to the world, which is constantly changing. To say that God changes in this sense does not imply, however, change in God's character or essence. For example, God's (concrete) knowledge changes because the creatures, with their power of self-determination, constantly do new, unpredictable things. But God always embodies the abstract attribute of omniscience — of knowing what is knowable at any particular time. Likewise, God's love changes in that it now includes billions of human beings who did not exist a century ago, but the fact that God is perfectly loving never changes. According to this first dipolarity, therefore, God has both contingent and necessary aspects,[21] and to affirm change in God is not to deny divine perfection.[22]

The second dipolarity, which is reflected in Whitehead's distinction between God's "primordial" and "consequent" natures, emphasizes the fact that God both *influences the world* and is also — contrary to the traditional doctrine of divine impassibility — *influenced by the world*. This interaction between God and the world is understood by analogy to the relation of soul and body. As with any analogy, there are features of the soul-body relation that do not apply to the God-world relation, such as the fact that the soul emerges out of the body and is thereby dependent on it for its very existence. The point of the analogy, however, is to emphasize the intimacy and directness of the relation. My body is the part of the universe that I directly influence and that directly influences me, being so intimately related to me that I feel its sufferings and enjoyments as my own. To call the world the body of God is to say both that God directly influences all things and that God has the kind of sympathy with all creatures that we have for our bodily members.[23]

The idea that there can be causal interaction between God and the world has, to be sure, been problematic in the modern period. If the world is composed of insentient, unfeeling bits of matter, how could God sympathize with it? And if the only mode of perception that we creatures have is sensory perception, how could we be influenced by God, who is clearly not an object of sensory perception? Process philosophy's answer is based on the fact that it breaks with all three aspects of naturalism$_{sam}$. Besides replacing its atheism with panentheism, it also replaces its materialism with *panexperientialism*, according to which all individuals have at least some slight degree of experience and spontaneity, and its sensationism with a *prehensive* doctrine of perception, which says sensory perception arises out of a deeper, more fundamental, nonsensory mode of perception (prehension), which we humans have in common with all other creatures.

These two doctrines explain how the mind can interact with its brain cells: although the mind is *numerically distinct* from the brain, as dualism said, the mind and the brain cells are *not ontologically different in kind*, so they can interact: the mind feels or "prehends" its brain cells, and they feel or prehend it in turn. Besides overcoming the problems of both dualism and materialism, this doctrine, which can be called *nondualistic interactionism,*[24] also provides an analogy for understanding the interaction of God and the world. Part and parcel of process panentheism, therefore, is a pan-experientialist doctrine of the world and a prehensive doctrine of perception. Process panentheism is, in other words, an integral feature of a worldview that can be called naturalism$_{ppp}$ (with "ppp" standing for "prehensive–panentheist–pan-experientialist").

This version of naturalism, like any other, rules out a God of the gaps. Thanks, however, to its pan-experientialism and its doctrine of prehensive perception, it allows for ongoing divine influence in the world. Furthermore, even though this theism is naturalistic — meaning that God never acts in some events in a way that is formally different from the way God acts in other events — it can affirm *variable* divine causation in the world, so that some events can be "acts of God" in a special sense, being especially revelatory of the divine character and purpose. The analogy is with our mind's influence on our bodies, which is formally always the same and yet varies greatly in content, so that some of our bodily acts express our character and purpose in an especially direct way.[25]

The fact that God acts variably in the world, however, does not mean that the world's evil contradicts the goodness of God. Although God has perfect power — the greatest power that any one being could have — this is not coercive power, because the creatures necessarily have their own power. On this basis process theology recovers Plato's doctrine "that the divine element in the world is to be conceived as a persuasive agency and not as a coercive agency," which Whitehead called "one of the greatest intellectual discoveries in the history of religion."[26] The second major element in the process theodicy, which I have developed at length elsewhere,[27] is the fact that among the metaphysical principles necessarily instantiated in any world that God could create is a set of variables of power and value. These variables rise proportionately with each other, so that to increase one is necessarily to increase all the others. The upshot of this point is that God could not have created beings capable of enjoying life who would not be capable of suffering pain, and God could not have created beings capable of enjoying mathematics, music, and mysticism who would not also have been capable of madness, murder, and mayhem. Even divine power cannot create the good without the risk of the evil.

It is sometimes suggested that the literal meaning of "panentheism," according to which *all* things are in God, is problematic because it would mean that there is evil in God. But the way to solve this apparent problem is not to deny that some things are in God, as if only the good events of the world could enter. Divine omniscience means that God knows *all* things, and for God to know something is for it to enter into the divine experience. The solution to the apparent problem involves asking precisely in what sense the creatures are "in God." The distinction between the essence and concrete states of God is relevant here. It belongs to the essence of God to be related to *a* world — some world or other — but not to our particular world. The good and evil events of this world are only in God's concrete states — in God's *experience* — not in God's essence. The other dipolarity — between God as influencing and as influenced — is also important. It would indeed be offensive to speak of "evil in God" if this meant that God's causal influence in the world were based on evil intentions. But in Whitehead's position God's primordial nature, in terms of which God influences the world, can be called the "creative love" of God, because it is always aiming at the greatest possible good that can be achieved. Insofar as there is evil in God, it is only in God's "consequent nature," which is God responding sympathetically to the world,[28] which means that God rejoices with its joys and suffers with its pains and sorrows. This can be called the "responsive love" of God.[29] From the perspective of Christian faith, with the cross of Christ as its central symbol, this doctrine should, far from being considered a stumbling block, be seen as bringing out part of faith's deepest meaning. In any case, there is evil only in God's experience, not in God's intentions. There is no moral evil in God.[30]

Summary and Conclusion

Naturalism$_{ppp}$, with its panentheism, has all the advantages of supernaturalism and of late modern naturalism without their respective problems. Like naturalism$_{sam}$, it embodies naturalism$_{ns}$, so that it is not in tension with the basic ontological conviction of modern science. But it can, like supernaturalism, explain not only how moral, mathematical, and logical principles exist in the nature of things, but also why the world has an order that supports the existence of creatures capable of enjoying high-level forms of value. Unlike supernaturalism, however, its explanation of these things is not embarrassed by the world's evils and the slowness of the process through which the present state of the world was created, and unlike naturalism$_{sam}$, it is not embarrassed by the directionality of evolution and the evidence from the fossil record that evolution involved many saltations. Process panentheism can, like supernaturalism, explain why human beings always and everywhere have had religious experience. But it is not embarrassed by the fact that there is no infallible revelation to give us *the* truth about religious matters. Unlike naturalism$_{sam}$, panentheism's naturalism$_{ppp}$ can do justice to the reality of human experience and freedom. Unlike dualism, however, naturalism$_{ppp}$ requires no appeal to supernatural causation to explain the relation of the human soul, with its consciousness and freedom, to its body. Finally, because it has all the strengths of traditional theism without its insistence on creation out of *absolute* nothingness and its resulting problem of evil, process panentheism provides a far stronger basis for a natural theology in the sense of arguments for the existence of God.[31]

My title refers to panentheism as a "postmodern revelation." The panentheistic doctrine presented here, being part of the naturalism$_{ppp}$, is a *postmodern* doctrine not only by going beyond the theism of early modernity and the atheism of late modernity, but also by rejecting the two fundamental pillars of distinctively modern thought: the mechanistic-materialistic doctrine of nature and the sensationist doctrine of perception. It can be considered a *revelation* for two reasons. On the one hand, insofar as we have come to see both supernaturalism and naturalism$_{sam}$ to be false, we have done so largely because of our drive to discover truth, which is a divinely instilled drive. On the other hand, many of the features of our experience to which naturalism$_{sam}$ cannot do justice, including our distinctively moral and religious experiences and our experiences of logical and mathematical principles, result from our direct experiences of God — which is to say, God's direct influence on us.

Theistic Naturalism and the Word Made Flesh: Complementary Approaches to the Debate on Panentheism

CHRISTOPHER C. KNIGHT

What Does "In" Mean? — the Need for Dynamic Categories

The main advantage of panentheism, it is often argued,[1] is that it represents a via media that can avoid the pitfalls associated with pantheism, on the one hand, and classical philosophical theism on the other. Among those who wish to avoid speaking of the cosmos as being either "identical with" or "outside of" God, however, the precise meaning of describing it as being "in" God has proved difficult to articulate. There is, as a result, a plethora of uses of the term, not all of which are mutually compatible.

For some, for example, panentheism represents a way of expressing a relationship of the world to God that is analogous to some relationship within the created order — such as that of the body to the mind or of an embryo to its mother's womb. There is no consensus, however, as to which relationship of this sort constitutes the best analogy. For others, by contrast, any understanding of this sort is reckoned misleading, and panentheism implies either a set-theory model or one that expresses some other sort of intrinsic relationship of a formal kind. There is, however, no broad consensus about how this relationship should be understood.

There is, nonetheless, one factor which is common to many of these otherwise disparate accounts, and which may be a major factor in the doubt that some have expressed about panentheism's legitimacy. This is that they assume — or at any rate are susceptible to interpretation in terms of — an essentially static ontology, which contrasts strongly with the essentially dynamic categories used by others. This factor is, however, only rarely recognized adequately. As a result, debate often proceeds as if the terms and models on which it hinges are clearly defined, whereas in practice a variety of ontological assumptions can often be read into them.[2]

John Polkinghorne's opposition to panentheism, for example, seems to be based at least in part on the static overtones that he reads into the term. For while he is adamant that the creation should not be seen as being "in God" (except in an eschatological sense), it is noteworthy that he is quite happy with the concept of it being "within the *life* of God" — a notion which, he notes, has "overtones of the Orthodox concept of the active presence of divine energies."[3] Given that this concept of divine energies[4] is at the heart of the sort of dynamic panentheism that some Orthodox have affirmed,[5] this poses the question of whether Polkinghorne's position might be best interpreted as a rejection not of panentheism itself, but of the static, ontological overtones of the terminology sometimes used to defend it. Might it be, for example, that a panentheism based on a traditional Eastern Logos cosmology — of the sort that we shall note presently — would meet at least some of the objections that he voices?

Considerations of this sort suggest, at any rate, that it might be more fruitful to step back from questions about the validity of panentheism, as they are usually posed, and ask instead what its advocates seek to affirm or deny through it. Here, however, we must recognize that there are — as the other chapters of this book bear witness — many starting points for discussion, and that even those who share the same starting point often follow different trajectories in their subsequent thinking. There is no consensus, for example, even among those who share what is perhaps the most common starting point for discussion: the "noninterventionist" understanding of divine action developed within the current dialogue of science and theology.

"Noninterventionist" Divine Action

The fundamental assumption of this "noninterventionist" understanding — based in part on a rejection of a "God of the gaps" model[6] — is that the laws of nature are fully operative at all times. Divine action, it is therefore asserted, never involves a "supernatural intervention" during which those laws are temporarily set aside. Instead, it is held, God acts *through* the laws of nature.

Some of those who take this view believe, as we shall see, that these laws have been designed in such a way that all divine purposes are brought to fruition naturalistically — that is, without further divine guidance. According to this naturalist viewpoint, all divine providence is of the "general" sort that arises from the way the laws of nature have been designed with a providential end in view.

The majority of advocates of a noninterventionist view do not, however, take this purely naturalist standpoint. They assume, instead, that there do occur, at least occasionally, genuine divine responses to events in the world — to prayer, for example. These responses, it is held, bring about phenomena that would probably not occur if the laws of nature — assumed to remain fully operative — were not in some way divinely guided. In this sense most defenders of a noninterventionist view of divine action have not, in the way that radical naturalists have, rejected the concept of temporal divine interference with the world. Their approach remains noninterventionist only because they believe the laws of nature are sufficiently supple for God, without actually setting aside those laws, to be able to change the probability of some particular event occurring.

The guidance of the laws of nature that is required by this viewpoint is possible, it is argued, because there exists some sort of temporal *causal joint* (or perhaps a whole range of such joints) through which the laws of nature may be manipulated by God for particular, providential ends. This view has been made plausible by the way it has proved possible to speculate about the nature of possible causal joints in a scientifically literate way. Candidates range from Arthur Peacocke's concept of "whole-part constraint"[7] to John Polkinghorne's "cloudy unpredictabilities of physical process, interpreted . . . as the sites of ontological openness."[8]

There has been, however, no straightforward correlation between the causal joint, identified by those taking this sort of position, and the attitude to panentheism they adopt. Thus, for example, Philip Clayton's judgment that Peacocke's account of the causal joint is inadequate[9] seems to be very similar, both in content and motivation, to Polkinghorne's.[10] While Clayton has been one of the chief advocates of panentheism, Polkinghorne, as we have noted, has taken a highly critical view. This disagreement arises neither from a fault of logic by one or the other, nor, entirely, from the sort of broader ontological issues that we have noted. It arises, rather, from the fact that panentheism is neither precluded nor required by the sort of approach to divine action that Clayton and Polkinghorne share. Differences on the panentheism issue can, in fact, legitimately arise from any particular view about the causal joint of divine action. It is only from the way such a view interacts with wider theological presuppositions that conclusions about the concept can be drawn.

The Naturalistic Dimension

One theological issue which may be of importance in this respect arises from the widespread recognition, even among the fiercest critics of a purely naturalistic approach, that not all divine action need be seen as requiring causal joint explanation. At least some of the purposes of God, it is acknowledged, are fulfilled through the coming to fruition — without additional divine guidance — of the intrinsic potentialities of the cosmos.

Where this recognition is not a major aspect of an account of divine action, this issue is perhaps not a significant one. In those accounts which put a particular stress on this naturalistic aspect of divine action, however, only a panentheistic understanding seems able to allow an avoidance of what Polkinghorne has characterized as "an implicit deism . . . whose nakedness is only thinly covered by a garment of personalized metaphor."[11] For unless God is intimately involved in every event as a participant — and not just as a sympathetic observer — naturalistic strands of thinking do stand in danger of failing to satisfy the requirements of any but the most abstract theism, especially in relation to theodicy. A panentheistic framework seems, however, to allow for direct divine participation in purely natural processes in a way that classical philosophical theism does not. Thus, one can argue, the stronger any account's stress on naturalistic strands of divine action, the stronger the need for a panentheistic framework.

Peacocke's account, for example, strongly emphasizes the way "it is chance operating within a lawlike framework that is the basis of the inherent creativity of the natural order, its ability to generate new forms, patterns and organizations of matter and energy."[12] It is now clear to the theist, he says, "that God creates *through* what we call 'chance' operating within the created order, each stage of which constitutes the launching pad for the next."[13] This leads him to see God's creative action as being one of essentially "exploring" the inherent, divinely ordained potentialities of the cosmos, rather than interfering through a temporal causal joint to bring about particular ends. His understanding of God's creative activity is thus an essentially naturalistic one, and only the panentheistic framework, within which it is set, enables this aspect of his thinking to avoid the dangers to which Polkinghorne has pointed.

Considerations of this sort suggest that any classification of accounts of divine action needs to take fully into account their naturalistic component. In particular we must recognize that some accounts, which are often seen as essentially identical in panentheistic implications, may in this respect manifest important differences. Thus, for example, we must surely qualify Clayton's statement that Peacocke's defense of panentheism and his own are essentially complementary,[14] since Peacocke's account, though not a fully naturalistic one, as we shall see, is far closer to being such than is Clayton's. This is evident not only from the latter's objections to the naturalistic overtones of Peacocke's views of revelation and Christology,[15] but also from his belief — essentially antinaturalistic in intent — that Peacocke's view of the causal joint of divine providence needs supplementing.[16] His contention that human mental activity involves "a level of reality that breaks the bond of naturalism"[17] also challenges Peacocke's antidualistic and naturalistic stress on emergent properties.

Theistic Naturalism

If we are to use degree of naturalism as a measure of the intrinsic panentheism of any understanding of divine action, it is essential that we understand the term properly — and especially when we come, as we shall, to discuss in more detail positions that are fully naturalistic. For, as Willem Drees has noted, the term "naturalism" does not refer to a "single, well-defined philosophical position," but rather indicates "family resemblances among a variety of projects."[18] Some of these projects are, like Peacocke's, only partly naturalistic. While holding that some of God's purposes are brought about by naturalistic processes, they assert that there are also more direct divine responses to events in the world which are brought about through some temporal causal joint. As we have noted, however, other accounts exist that are fully naturalistic, in the sense of denying *any* temporal response of this sort.

Of these fully naturalistic accounts, some, like that of Drees, tend toward an essentially instrumentalist understanding of religious language.[19] Others, however, find the arguments for denying reference in theological language unconvincing,[20] and despite denying the occurrence of temporal divine response, affirm the objective reality of God. This latter position — *theistic naturalism,* as it is usually called — asserts not merely that a purely naturalistic understanding of temporal causality *can* be interpreted theistically — something Drees acknowledges[21] — but that it *should* be so interpreted.

A theistic naturalism of this kind has, for some, clear advantages over a more conventional theism. It extends the widespread recognition that God should not be understood as "a thing among things" to embrace the parallel recognition that he is not a cause among causes. It allows the vexed question of precisely how God affects the world — the temporal "causal joint" problem

— to be seen as a false one. It can even be developed — by an expansion of the concept of "regime" used by Polkinghorne[22] — in such a way that it does not necessarily deny the occurrence of "miraculous" events.

A theistic naturalism denies the objective reality neither of God nor, necessarily, of particular types of providential experiences. All it does deny is that a recognition of these objective realities entails a belief that the cosmos is at least occasionally "interfered" with — either in a supernaturalist or in a weakly "noninterventionist" way. Rather, as Drees has noted, it can affirm "an ontological form of transcendence . . . via a scheme of primary and secondary causes, with the transcendent realm giving effectiveness and reality to the laws of nature and the material world governed by them." In such a theistic naturalism, he goes on to recognize, "God would be the ground of all reality and thus intimately involved in every event — though not as one factor among the natural factors."[23]

"Special" Providence

This is not to say that there do not exist objections to theistic naturalism which need to be taken seriously. Clayton's opposition, for example, does not rely simply on what Drees has called his "package of panentheism and an anthropology with dualistic elements."[24] It relies also on a stress on specific acts of "special" divine providence which he, like many others, sees as precluding a fully naturalistic position. Even Peacocke, for example, who has perhaps done more than anyone to foster a naturalistic view of God's action as creator, has for this reason taken up an antinaturalist position as far as "special" divine providence is concerned.[25]

This argument for eschewing a naturalistic position is not, however, as conclusive as often seems to be assumed. In particular, the concepts of objective divine action associated with the classical view of God's eternity — those posited by neo-Thomism[26] and by Maurice Wiles's "single act" account,[27] for example — can be developed in a way that allows for a fully naturalistic account of divine providence. Moreover, quite apart from any technical argument about the relationship of a temporal cosmic process to a God who is assumed to be beyond temporal categories, a simple human analogy suggests a way in which even a temporal God might have arranged all divine providence naturalistically.

This argument is based on the observation that human providence — parents' financial support of their children, for example — can be given in three ways:

1. It can be unmediated. ("Here's your regular allowance, and here's some extra cash for the new bike you need.")
2. It can be mediated. (E.g., through fixed instructions to a bank: "Transfer such and such an amount every week to my children's accounts and, if a new bike becomes necessary, transfer such and such an extra amount to pay for it.")
3. It can be either mediated or unmediated, depending on circumstances. ("The money that comes automatically into your bank account will cover only your normal expenses, so here's some more for the new bike you need.")

Most accounts of divine providence opt for a model that is equivalent to the last of these, making a distinction between the general providence that has been built into the way the world is and the special providence required as a response to particular needs. The "financial support" analogy suggests, however, that this is not the only option. Because human parents are not infinitely wise, they are unable to predict all possible circumstances in which extra money will be needed. Support through "fixed instruction" will at least occasionally, therefore, need to be supplemented by the human equivalent of "special" divine providence. The wisdom of the God Christians call their heavenly Father is, however, not limited in this way. He could in principle, therefore, have arranged the "fixed instructions" of the natural world so that there would be no need to supplement the "general providence" provided by the character of that world.

God need not have done this, as humans must, in the rather clumsy form of a set of "if . . . then" statements. He could, for example, have set up the sort of goal-oriented providence suggested by certain interpretations of human psychology,[28] supplemented perhaps by the sort of "synchronicity" or mind-matter complementarity that has been suggested within both physics and psychology.[29] A naturalistic understanding does not, however, depend on any particular model of this sort. What it does depend on — at least if it takes seriously the history of providential experience — is the validity of the belief that underpins such models: that the creation is far more subtle and complex than our present scientific understanding indicates. (In this sense a theistic naturalism suggests specific scientific research programs aimed at establishing the reality of "new emergents" or "regimes" in the cosmos over and above those already recognized. As indicated by the history of research into the "paranormal," however, such programs are likely to involve major and perhaps insuperable methodological problems.)

The Sacramental View of Matter

Considerations of this sort suggest, at the very least, that it may be possible to affirm the reality of divine providence while at the same time affirming a naturalistic understanding of all causality. And indeed, when we look at the objections to this type of understanding that appear to have been most persuasive within the science and religion debate, they seem to have been not so much philosophical as more broadly theological.[30] These theological objections may, however, seem far less persuasive when viewed in the light of other theological considerations.

One starting point for these is, in fact, identical to one of the main theological roots of Peacocke's own approach. For while that approach clearly arises in part from his scientific perspectives on the intrinsic potential of the created order, it arises also from the theological tradition that he himself both reflects and advocates: one with a strong stress (as he puts it) "on the doctrine of the Incarnation, and on a sacramental understanding of the world with its concomitant emphasis on the sacraments of the church."[31] For there is, in his view, "a real convergence between the implications of the scientific perspective on the capabilities of matter and the sacramental view of matter which Christians have adopted. . . . Briefly, it looks as though Christians, starting, as it were, from one end of their experience of God . . . acting on the stuff of the world, have developed an insight into matter which is consonant with that which is now evoked by the scientific perspective working from matter towards persons, and beyond."[32]

What Peacocke calls the *sacramental view of matter* has, we should note, less to do with the usual Western concept of a sacrament — as a "sign" of grace — than with another, related concept. This is the understanding of a sacrament as an actualization of the potentiality of matter to become fully transparent to the purposes of God. In Peacocke's own Anglican tradition, this understanding is manifested less in formal theology than in spiritual writing — especially that of the seventeenth century.[33] Doctrinally it is more highly developed in strands of Orthodox theology, and especially, in modern times, in the work of Alexander Schmemann.[34]

In this understanding the "outward and visible sign" of a sacrament (or of a quasi-sacramental object, such as an icon) is an aspect of the cosmos that has been returned or redeemed to its essential significance and purpose. It is a foretaste of the redemption of the whole cosmos. A sacrament is, as Schmemann puts it, "understood primarily as a revelation of the genuine *nature* of creation, of the world, which, however much it has fallen as 'this world,' will remain God's world. . . . [It] is primarily a revelation of the *sacra-*

mentality of creation itself, for the world was created and given to man for conversion of creaturely life into participation in divine life."[35]

Pan-sacramental Naturalism

It is, I have argued in my book *Wrestling with the Divine,* a theological understanding, comparable to this Orthodox one, that has allowed Peacocke to use his scientific knowledge to develop an essentially naturalistic understanding of God's creative activity. This understanding — *pan-sacramentalism* as I call it[36] — is also able, I go on to argue, to lead beyond the point at which Peacocke himself stops, and to allow us to incorporate God's providential activity in a naturalistic framework.

An essentially new form of theistic naturalism thus, I suggest, becomes possible — a *pan-sacramental naturalism,* in which both the natural world perceptible to the scientist and our religious experience within that world may be understood naturalistically, "in terms of divine action through the sacramental potential of the cosmos."[37] Just as the world as perceived by the sciences has a God-given natural tendency to develop in fruitful directions — the sort of "teleology without teleology" of which Paul Davies has spoken[38] — so in the realm of spiritual understanding we can, I argue, perceive an equally God-given "natural" tendency toward development through psychological processes.

The use of the term "pan-sacramental" does not, of course, imply that the sacramental potential of all created things can be actualized independently of context. Just as the specific sacraments of the church can be effected only in a particular ecclesial context, so, for example, the emergence of a new species requires, from a purely scientific perspective, the particular context provided by a specific ecological niche. Similarly, I have argued, any particular revelation of God will take place only in what I call an appropriate *psycho-cultural niche.*[39] One aspect of such a niche is a particular sort of openness to God, since (as Karl Rahner has emphasized) there is an essentially contemplative dimension to revelatory experience, from which arise the thoughts or visions that constitute the outer form of that experience.[40]

I develop this idea in terms of what I call a *psychological-referential model of revelatory experience,* which is related to important strands of thinking about revelation in the work not only of Rahner, but also of Yves Congar and Keith Ward.[41] Any authentic revelatory experience of God that occurs through this divinely given "natural" tendency always, I argue, takes a form that is appropriate to a particular cultural and psychological environment.

Because of this it can never be absolute. It has a genuinely referential component, recognizable in principle through the "puzzle-solving" character of the theological language to which it gives rise.[42] It also, however, inevitably has a culturally conditioned instrumental component that makes the link between experience and referential doctrine a complex one. Moreover, I note, not only is there, in this understanding, no a priori reason for believing that genuine revelatory experience can occur only among members of some particular religious grouping. In addition, a number of factors suggest rather strongly a pluralistic (though not necessarily relativistic) understanding of the faiths of the world.[43]

The Word Made Flesh

Despite its origins in strands of traditional Christian theology, this type of theistic naturalism will seem to some to represent an extreme position which is barely compatible with the Christian tradition. Indeed, adherents of that tradition have often eschewed a naturalistic understanding, not so much because of general considerations about divine action, but because they regard naturalism, in a quasi-instinctive way, incompatible with the central, "supernaturalist" tenets of their faith.

In particular — as indicated by attacks on what are seen as the naturalistic overtones of Peacocke's christological thinking[44] — there is a widespread sense that the doctrine of the incarnation can be safeguarded only through a strong antinaturalist stance.[45] It is important, therefore, that we recognize that the type of theistic naturalism that I have described may be more consonant with the doctrine of the incarnation than is usually recognized. This possibility can be acknowledged, however, only when the doctrine is understood in a way that takes into account the breadth of the biblical accounts on which it is based, incorporating in particular both the Pauline concept of the cosmic Christ and the Fourth Gospel's linking of creation and incarnation in terms of God's Logos — his Word.

Arguably it is only in what we might call the Logos cosmology of Greek patristic and later Byzantine thinking that this has been adequately done. In the work of Maximos the Confessor, in particular, this cosmology is expounded in a detailed way. Maximos perceives the Logos of God not only in the person of Jesus, but in the words — logoi — of all prophetic utterance, and in the logoi — in the sense of underlying principles — of all created things from the beginning.[46] Because of this understanding of the economy of the divine Logos, Maximos does not see the incarnation simply as a historical "event." Rather — as Lars Thunberg has put it — Maximos's thinking presupposes "almost a gradual incarnation."[47] The divine aspect of the person of Jesus represents, in this understanding, not something essentially alien to the natural world — a supernatural intrusion — but rather the coming to fullness of something present in it from the beginning.

The wider presuppositions of this sort of understanding are of considerable significance when we ask what its implications are for the development of a contemporary theistic naturalism. In particular, it is important to recognize that this sort of patristic and Byzantine approach involves an understanding of "nature" that is different from that assumed by the Western medieval approach to divine intervention or by the modern, causal-joint approach which attempts a more subtle understanding of divine action. Both types of approaches — albeit in different ways — assume a "natural" or "normal" state, to which something must be added in acts of grace. In the patristic and Byzantine traditions, by contrast, this assumption is not held in anything like the same way.

Convergent Perspectives

Like strands of modern Orthodox theology, these traditions posit a more dynamic, teleologically oriented universe in which, as Vladimir Lossky has put it, there is "no natural or normal state, since grace is implied in the act of creation itself. The world, created in order that it might be deified, is dynamic, tending always towards its final end."[48] Even sin and its effects — which these traditions tend to interpret in a more far-reaching way than most would now find acceptable — are seen as failing to destroy completely the image of God in creation. Rather, if these effects are seen as inhibiting the purposes of God — and thus as subnatural — there is still a strong sense of a teleological movement, in which all things, sin included, are taken up and used for the divine purpose.[49]

This concept of an intrinsically "dynamic" universe immediately has a strong resonance for those who acknowledge the validity of the modern scientific perception of the universe's evolutionary development. It represents, in fact, another facet of the sacramental view of matter that Peacocke has noted, and of the resulting convergence between scientific and theological perspectives that he has recognized. Here, however, the theological perspective has a deeper rooting than in Peacocke's understanding, since it is based not simply on an "incarnationist" instinct about the sacramental nature of matter, but on a fully developed doctrine of the incarnation. This affirms not simply that in the person of Jesus the Logos became flesh, but also — in a way that is underdeveloped in most Western theology — that this same Logos is active throughout creation both as its source and its final purpose.

Convergence between naturalist and incarnationist perspectives does not of course imply identity. These traditional perspectives may not have been "supernaturalist" in the late medieval or modern sense, but neither were they "naturalist" in the way the term is usually now understood. What is implied in a recognition of convergence is not a simplistic reconciliation of science and theology through a theological interpretation of a contemporary naturalism. Rather, what is suggested is the need for a deeper exploration of this sense of the complementarity of a traditionalist Logos cosmology and a philosophical theistic naturalism.

My own attempt to develop a pan-sacramental naturalism already indicates how such lines of exploration are likely to challenge the assumptions about the character of the natural world that are shared by both naturalists and their opponents. It also points to the necessity of a far more subtle theistic naturalism than that usually discussed — one which, instead of being largely a philosophical construct, is rooted fully in the Christian revelation, and as such is far closer to a traditional Logos cosmology than anything the term now connotes.

Panentheism and Beyond

One example of how this complementarity may be explored lies precisely in the way the two approaches illuminate the debate about panentheism. For, as we have seen, any theistic naturalism seems to have strong panentheistic implications, and a pan-sacramental naturalism in particular may be said to point toward what we might call a *pan-sacramental panentheism*. It is noteworthy, therefore, that these implications are reinforced when we interpret this type of naturalism in terms of a traditional Logos cosmology, since the logoi of created things, in the sense in which writers like Maximos use the term, are a manifestation of the divine Logos itself and not something separated from it.[50]

This is related to the fact that, as Philip Sherrard has stressed, when Eastern writers spoke of creation out of nothing — ex nihilo — they often did so in a way that was significantly different from the way that phrase is usually understood. For, he says, the term "nothing," as used by at least some Eastern writers, "does not denote an absolute blank, the privation of every quality or an entirely negative quality. . . . It refers to that in God which is free from all form. . . . In so far as we can envisage it at all, it may be envisaged as the fathomless, incomprehensible ground or depths of God's uncreated energies and possibilities, the pre-ontological 'nihil' from which all things proceed. In this way it refers not to something that is outside or privative of God, or that is void of His presence. It refers to what is within God."[51] Thus, Sherrard goes on to argue, these writers had a strong sense that the creation is not separate from God in the way that is often read into the term "ex nihilo." Rather, he says, their use of the phrase was intimately linked to a "contemplative path, whose goal is not so much to see God in all things as to see all things in God — not so much pantheism as *panentheism*."[52]

Sherrard's perspectives on a Logos cosmology point, moreover, beyond the issue of panentheism. They also have a strong pluralistic dimension which complements in a remarkable way that which, as we have noted, seems to be implied by a pan-sacramental naturalism. For in the early patristic period there was often, as he says, a positive attitude toward pre-Christian religious frameworks. This was based on an understanding of the incarnation in which the Logos was seen as incorporating himself, "not in the body of a single human being alone but in the totality of human nature, in mankind as a whole, in creation as a whole."[53] Only later, he notes, was this view overlaid by the narrower, purely historical understanding of the incarnation which led to the exclusivism that has since been characteristic of conservative Christian theology.

This narrower view must, Sherrard asserts, "be replaced by a theology that affirms the positive attitude implicit in the writings of Justin Martyr, Clement of Alexandria, Origen, the Cappadocians, St. Maximos the Confessor and many others. The economy of the divine Logos cannot be reduced to His manifestation in the figure of the historical Jesus." He then continues, in a way that has remarkable parallels with the approach that arises from my own pan-sacramental naturalism, to declare that

> the Logos in His *kenosis*, His self-emptying, is hidden everywhere, and the types of His reality, whether in the forms of persons or teachings, will not be the same outside the Christian world as they are within it. Yet these types are equally authentic: any deep reading of another religion is a reading of the Logos, the Christ. . . . At different times and in different places, The Supreme . . . has condescended to clothe the naked essence of [the principles underlying all reality] in exterior forms, doctrinal and ritual, in which they can be grasped by us and through which we can be led into a plenary awareness of their preformal reality.[54]

It would seem, then, that it is not only the validity of a pan-sacramental panentheism that is suggested in complementary ways by a radical theistic naturalism and a traditional Logos cosmology. A strategy which uses the two in combination in fact has significant ramifications which go far beyond this issue. Indeed, by suggesting the basis for both a theology of creation and a theology of the world's faiths, it can surely claim to be among the most important research strategies of early-twenty-first-century theology.

The World as the Body of God:
A Panentheistic Metaphor

KEITH WARD

Ramanuja

The doctrine that the world is the body of God is primarily associated with the twelfth-century Indian philosopher and religious thinker Ramanuja.[1] One of the six main classical philosophical systems of the Indian traditions is Vedanta. It is a philosophy which is based on acceptance of the revealed authority of the Veda and the Upanishads, as interpreted in the Vedanta Sutras of an early commentator, Baradayana, who probably lived in the first century C.E.

There are various forms of Vedanta, but they are all committed to accepting, in some sense, the Upanishadic doctrine that the ultimate reality (Brahman), individual selves, and the cosmos as a whole are identical. A crucial phrase from the Upanishads is *Tat Twam Asi*, "That you are" (*Chandogya Upanishad* 6.10.3). Each self, and indeed each thing, is identical with Brahman, the absolute Real. There are many ways of interpreting this view, but Vedantins all accept this as a central doctrine which needs to be interpreted. It looks almost directly opposed to the Semitic (Jewish, Christian, and Muslim) view that God, who is the absolutely real, and the universe are totally different in kind.

One reason for this difference is that most European philosophical systems have assumed that effects are different from causes, so that if God is the cause of the world, then the world is different from God. But Indian philosophy often works with the idea that the effect is the same as the cause, that it is the same sort of thing and made of the same sort of stuff. Thus if God is the cause of the world, then the world is one with God.

European philosophers have often held that the effect must in some way be like the cause (a thing cannot cause something totally unlike itself, according to Aristotle), and the cause must be at least as great in reality as its effects. So Aquinas held that God, the cause of the world, must contain in the divine being the natures of all created things, though in a higher and more perfect manner. Nevertheless, they have held that though God is the efficient cause of the world, God is not the material cause of the world. The stuff of which the world is made, matter itself, is quite different from God, who is wholly immaterial. So although European philosophers have tended to affirm that in some remote sense God and the world are similar, they have insisted that they are made of different stuff (spirit and matter, respectively).

Indian philosophers, on the other hand, have often assumed that matter must, like everything, arise from God, and so it must be contained in the divine being. This view is held in conjunction with a general cosmology for which matter exists without beginning or end, arising from Brahman, and in some way expressing what Brahman is. Ramanuja's distinctive way of putting this is to say that the universe and individual souls are all parts of the body of God, the material expression of the being of Brahman. Brahman necessarily has a body. The universe arises from Brahman by inner necessity. Yet Brahman wills it to be, and it is the "joyful play" of the Supreme Lord. Some universe has always existed. More precisely, this universe is one of an infinite series of universes, which alternate with states when all universes are hidden in Brahman in unmanifest form.

It is important to see what Ramanuja means by "body" in this context. He writes that a body is completely under the control of the self. So if the universe is the body of the Lord, it is completely under the control of the Supreme Self, and the Lord is as close to it as the human self is to the human body, present to every part immediately. The body is that through which the self acts and expresses itself, and the vehicle of sense-knowledge. So the universe is that through which the Lord acts and expresses the divine self, and by means of which the Lord has knowledge of material things in their particularity and diversity.

The universe and the Lord are one, as the body is one with the self. But one must be clear that for Ramanuja this means that the universe is totally under the control of God, and is that by which God expresses a small part of the infinite divine nature. Of all the millions of souls which exist, as parts of God, only some exist in this material universe. For this is a universe in which souls come under the sway of ignorance *(avidya)* or illusion, thinking that they are quite different from the Supreme Self and devoting themselves to the pursuit of sensual pleasures. When they come to knowledge of what their true nature is, they will be released from the round of reincarnations in the material universe, and live in a paradisal world in which they will be fully aware that they are parts of the body of God, and will delight in being servants of the Supreme Lord, members of his body in a fully obedient and conscious way.

Though God necessarily manifests himself in many material forms, having as his body an infinite number of worlds, Ramanuja holds that God is not in any way bound by matter or by the laws of karma. On the contrary, all the laws of the universe are under the complete control of God. So the main import of calling the cosmos the body of God is to affirm that the universe is a necessary self-expression of the divine being. It is freely, or intentionally, produced by God, and does not limit God in any way. And the destiny of embodied souls is to see and enjoy the nature of their lives as finite embodiments of the divine Self.

Hegel

In Europe the philosopher who comes closest to the thought of Ramanuja is Hegel.[2] Hegel sees the universe as an emergent historical process which is the self-realization and unfolding of Absolute Spirit *(Geist)*. Like Ramanuja, Hegel assumes that the ultimate cause of all things is Spirit. He also assumes that the Spirit is complete in itself, eternally self-conscious and perfect, not bound by the material universe in any way. However, he gives to the history of the universe an importance it had not had in classical thought. Time becomes the form of the divine self-unfolding, by which Spirit realizes successively the perfection which actually belongs to it eternally. As Hegel puts it, "Being-in-itself," which is the potential for all possible beings, expresses itself in the universe as "Being-for-itself," and then unites the universe fully in self-conscious experience in the completed phase of divine being, "Being-in-and-for-itself." Although time is real and important for this view, it is actually present as a completed whole in the full reality of Spirit. This involves what is now sometimes called a "block time" view — time is really existent from beginning to end, as perceived in God, but temporal beings progress through it successively. Thus history is essential to God, but Spirit in and for itself, as Hegel puts it, is the completed process of history as a whole, the complete unfolding of the potencies of the divine nature into the actuality of the completed world process, as reintegrated, "eternalized," into the divine being.

Despite the obvious similarities to the philosophy of Ramanuja, of which Hegel was almost certainly unaware, Hegel does not use the idea of the world as the body of God. That is because of a difference in the way the relations of self and body are conceived in the Indian and European classical traditions. In India the self is causally prior. Bodies exist to enable the karma of spirits to be worked out. The body is the instrument of the self, more like clothing than like skin. In Europe, at least where the Jewish-Christian view has been influential, body and self come into existence together, and the self is "enfleshed" in such a way that the nature of the body, including its genetic structure, is at least partly constitutive of the self. Persons are embodied selves, and bodies are not clothing but integral parts of what the self is. Thus the mainstream Jewish, Christian, and Muslim hope is for the resurrection of the body, not for the liberation of the self from all material embodiment.

This makes it impossible for Hegel to see the universe as the body of God. For him the universe has no independent causal role in the constitution of the divine being. It cannot limit God in any way. If selves do not, in general, wholly control bodies, God cannot be thought of as the self of the universe — a view which for Hegel would limit God and subject the divine being to the constraints of time and suffering. Sometimes Hegel's view has nevertheless been called "monistic" or "pantheistic," because it makes the universe part of the self-expression of God, making it part of God in a way. And I think it would be correct to call his view panentheistic, since he explicitly holds that the divine being includes, as part, but only a small part, of itself, the whole temporal process of the history of the universe.

The Hegelian view is different from the classical theistic view of Thomas Aquinas[3] and most other Christian thinkers. The difference can be seen most clearly in their respective uses of the idea of infinity. Both Aquinas and Hegel hold that God is infinite. But for Aquinas this means that God can include nothing finite, and God thus excludes the whole cosmos from the essential, unbounded, divine being. For Hegel, however, to say that God is infinite means that God can exclude nothing (for if there were something else in existence, that would form a boundary to God). So God includes the whole cosmos, and it becomes in some sense part of what God essentially is.

The most extreme form of these views would lead to saying, for the Thomist, that God has no real relation to the world, being essentially perfect and unchanged in any way by what happens in the world or even by creation itself, whereas for the Hegelian, God is incomplete without some world, which is part of the self-expression of the divine nature and part of the divine perfection.

There is an associated difference between the Thomist and Hegelian views in their respective ideals of perfection. For the Thomist the perfect must be changeless (or it would get more or less perfect). For the Hegelian perfection must include change, and the values of creativity, action, and relationship which only change makes possible.

If one tries to compare the views of Ramanuja with these two European traditions of thought about God, it seems that he would fall somewhere between them. Ramanuja thinks the divine perfection is essentially changeless, and it is not changed by what happens in time. Yet the world is a necessary expression of God, as the body of God. Possibly the nearest analogy in Christian tradition is the doctrine of incarnation, for which two quite distinct natures, human (temporal) and divine (eternal), are united in one person. So in Ramanuja the temporal universe and the changeless divine nature are united in one person, the divine nature being the Supreme Self and the temporal nature being the body of that Self.

It might then seem that Ramanuja is saying that the whole universe is an incarnation of God. This would, however, not quite be right, for he affirms that selves in this universe exist in ignorance of their true nature and in attachment to the desires of the world. It is only when they are liberated, to live with Krishna, who is the true incarnation of the Supreme Lord, fully aware of his nature as divine and free from attachment to material desires, that they can become truly conscious and intentional members of the body of the Lord. In the meanwhile, individual souls are still to be regarded as parts of the body of the Lord, but they are enmeshed in desire and largely unaware of their true nature, so that it would be misleading to call them "incarnations." There are incarnations of the Lord in the world for Ramanuja, and Krishna is one of them, indeed the main one. But in this world, "fallen" into desire and attachment, such true incarnations are the exceptions rather than the rule.

This view may seem uncannily like some Christian views, and that is a reminder that it is misleading to speak of sharp oppositions between Indian and Semitic thought, as though the former was "monistic" and the latter "dualistic," so that they are bound to be fundamentally opposed to one another. Indian monism is sharply qualified in Ramanuja — whose system is actually called *visistadvaita,* or qualified nondualism. And Semitic dualism is sharply qualified in Hegel. It is not that all these systems are really the same. On the contrary, every new synthesis of diverse traditions begets a new system of its own, without dissolving the old traditions. Yet it is important to see how many diverse interpretations there are of the basic religious symbols and doctrines which make up religious traditions, and how none of them are free of the influence of others, whether consciously acknowledged or not.

One major problem for both Ramanuja and Hegel is the place of individual causality in the history of the universe. They both want to say that humans are free and morally responsible. Ramanuja is committed to accepting that humans enjoy and suffer what they do because of their freely chosen past deeds in former incarnations. Hegel wants to give individual action an important place in the development of history. But do individuals have a real causal role to play, in the sense that nothing, not even God, determines what they will do, that only their own free choice causes their morally free acts?

The problem is a familiar one, and the most obvious solution is that of compatibilism, to say that divine determinism is compatible with human freedom. If that is true, then God can determine everything, while human freedom can be preserved. Surprising as it may seem, the difference now between Hegel, Luther, and Calvin becomes a very fine one — it is no coincidence that Hegel trained to be a Lutheran pastor. They all see the whole universe as completely determined by God, so that everything that happens expresses the divine will. Since the divine will is identical with the divine essence (a commonly accepted scholastic doctrine), it looks as though the universe is essentially what it is in all its details, and in expressing the divine will it also expresses the divine nature. If freedom and necessity are compatible, then when we say the creation is God's free act, this is quite compatible with saying that it arises by necessity from the divine nature. The differences between Indian, idealist, and Christian views begin to disappear before our very eyes!

Why, then, should Christians react strongly against the idea that the world is God's body, as they usually seem to? I have pointed to one factor — that within the Judeo-Christian tradition to say that *x* is my body leads me to think I am constrained by or partly dependent upon *x*, whose nature is not constituted by me. So to call the universe God's body seems to make God unduly dependent upon some independent material reality.

Another factor is that I think most people are actually, whatever philosophers might tell them, uneasy about compatibilism. People often feel that if God determines everything I do, it is not really fair to punish me for my misdeeds, or even to reward me for my good deeds — though I probably would not worry so much about unmerited rewards as I would about unmerited punishments. So if I am truly free, reality must be indeterministic to some degree — not wholly determined by anything other than my own decisions, not even by God.

Whitehead and the Post-Hegelians

The philosopher who confronts both these factors without shrinking from their implications is A. N. Whitehead, whose system of "organic atomism" turns most European philosophical assumptions on their head.[4] To the objection that God might be dependent upon the independent character of matter, he says: yes, indeed. Matter is independent and eternally existing, and it does limit the sorts of things God can do. To the objection that freedom seems to require that God does not determine everything, he says: yes, indeed. God is not the all-determiner. God's acts are limited to those which do not undermine human freedom. They will be attempts to guide or influence perhaps, but not exercises of a wholly sovereign will.

What is at first surprising is that he also seems to be a panentheist. That view makes clear sense when the whole universe is seen as the self-expression of the divine nature. Then the universe is part of what God is, since without it God would not be God, and it makes a difference to the nature of God. But now if you have an independently existing matter — and indeed, an infinite number of atomic actual events (or "occasions") — that is not subject to divine sovereignty, and lots of individual human beings who are at least partly not under the control of God, how can such a universe be called "part" of God? It will no longer be the self-expression of God, since it expresses the decisions of millions of causal entities.

However, once again Whitehead accepts the unexpected, turns the tradition on its head, and affirms that the universe is not the self-expression of God. Rather, God is the result of the decisions of the millions of atomic entities which constitute the universe. Without the universe God would not exist at all, as a concrete individual, though God would exist in the primordial divine nature. That nature, however, is in a sense incomplete, and requires some form of actual existence to become what it should be. The universe makes such actual existence possible, and thus helps to make God what God is. Now we have a completely different sense of the world as the body of God. The world is not the means of divine self-expression. It is the organic unity of infinite numbers of causal processes which together make up the consequential nature of God. The body constitutes, even creates, the self. I am not forgetting the primordial and superjective aspects of Whitehead's God. But the former is relatively abstract, setting forth possibilities of being, and the latter is influential but not primarily causative. The heart of the doctrine lies in its stress on the consequential nature of God. This God really suffers everything that the universe suffers, because this God is the organic process of the universe as a whole, insofar as it is received into one all-inclusive superconsciousness. This is a strong form of panentheism. It should just be clearly noted that it is at the opposite extreme from Ramanuja's notion of the world as the body of God.

If the classical views face the problem of individual freedom, Whitehead's view faces the problem of divine sovereignty. Is there any room for it at all? God expressing the divine being wholly and without constraint in the universe is very unlike the relation the human self bears to its body. But God being constituted in the consequential divine nature by the universe is also very unlike the human self-body relation. Human bodies neither completely express nor wholly constitute human selves, so the body-self metaphor is not perhaps a totally helpful one in either of these senses. The metaphor of the world as God's body in fact raises a complex of different debates about the nature of God, which are of great intrinsic interest. Four of these debates are of particular importance.

First, for many theists it is important to affirm that the perfection of God is beyond the dualities of good and evil which are so obvious in the universe, and that it cannot be fundamentally impaired by what happens in the universe. In the universe there are struggle, suffering, and a competitive will to power. Those German romantic philosophers who increasingly denied the idea of a separately existing, perfect God, philosophers like Schelling, Schopenhauer, and Nietzsche, came to think of the will to power as the ruling principle of the universe. If there is a God at all, it is an emergent, morally ambiguous God, who comes into being only after a long process of struggle, emerging from blind necessity.

That is the sort of "pantheism" of which many theists are afraid. For most believers in God, God does not develop out of matter (as human minds arguably develop out of matter) and God is not "made up of" matter, as bodies are made up of cells and atoms. If panentheism asserts anything like that, it throws doubt on the original perfection and creative priority of God. The debate here is about the nature of divine perfection, about whether it grows or develops, or whether it is an original and indefectible property of God.

Many panentheists, however, have something rather different in mind. They want to stress that the universe, or some universe, is necessary to God's complete perfection. God's perfection is necessarily expressed by the generation of finite realities. Classical theists have usually denied any such necessity of creation, and there is a second major area of debate here. Whether panentheism is the best label for a view of necessary creation, however, is unclear. For it may be the nature of God as love which necessitates the creation of persons who are genuinely other than God, whose existence makes relational, mutual love possible, and so makes possible the realization of God's nature as love. Insofar as that element of "otherness" is indissoluble, it may seem hard to call finite persons "parts" of God. That would seem to deny their otherness. In addition, if one wishes to stress that the cosmos depends wholly for its existence on God, as its one ultimate cause, that throws doubt on the process claim that matter exists independently of God's willed causality.

69

Process thinkers like David Griffin hold that this is a positive strength of the process view, since it makes the problem of evil easier to solve. That is undeniably true, but some theists may wish to affirm that God does have causal priority, even though there may be necessities of any creatable universe containing free creatures which limit divine power. In other words, it might be possible to have a process-type solution of the problem of evil (that some actual, and much possible, evil is necessary in any universe like this), while also accepting the causal priority — and therefore the assured ultimate triumph — of God and goodness. At any rate, this is another point of theological debate, the degree to which God has total causal priority in creation.

Process thinkers stress that God's knowledge, if it is to be the greatest possible knowledge, must include the actual experiences of all finite beings, so that their experiences are "parts" of a wider divine experience. This is a strong argument, but God cannot experience things exactly as finite persons do. The experience a murderer has in murdering a victim is not an experience God could actually have, as the murderer has it. So one might wish to say that God knows what it is like to have such an experience. God feels its affective tone. But God also reacts negatively to such experiences, and that is an essential part of how God experiences them. God's perfection distances the experiences of sinful and ignorant beings from God, makes them not really "part" of God, but rather causes of affective representations in God of finite experiences. This difficult question marks a third problematic area which panentheism raises, about the nature of divine knowledge, and about whether events in the world change God at all.

A fourth area of debate is whether the universe is the realization or self-expression of the divine will. I have noted that process thought denies this, but both Hegel and Ramanuja affirm it. The qualification one might want to make here is that if creatures possess true autonomy, perhaps they can frustrate the divine will. God's will may triumph in the end, but it may have to be by eliminating evil wills, if there are any wills which remain always unrepentant. Process thought can allow fully for finite freedom, but it raises the difficulty that it is hard to see how God can ever finally triumph, since God lacks finally decisive causality. It does raise the possibility, however, that God's action in the present world might be persuasive rather than irresistible, and many people feel that is deeply consistent with belief in a God whose nature is love.

Panentheism raises at least these four important areas of debate about God. I do not wish to claim that it is obvious which side of the debate is stronger, but it may be useful to separate out the diverse strands of debate which are sometimes bundled together, or even confused, in discussion of panentheism. My own view would be that the thesis of panentheism has brought to the fore considerations of divine passibility, the necessity of creation, the relational nature of love, and the importance of finite freedom, which need to be taken more seriously by believers in God than they often have been. But I have grave reservations about saying that the conflict and suffering and evil in the world are actually parts of the divine being, and to that extent it does not look as if the world is the body of God.

The Body of Christ

However, there is a form of panentheism that might survive these reservations, for Christians in particular. A Christian might say that God creates finite persons who are distinct from God, who are morally free, and to whom God can relate as others, empathizing and cooperating with them but neither being constituted by them nor including them nor dictating all their actions. It could be that the divine perfection realizes itself in personal relationship, in love which is for what is other than oneself. In this way God would exclude all imperfection from the divine being, but change by relation to persons, so that the complete goodness would lie in a communion or social unity of persons.

A major reason for not using the model of the universe as the body of God is to stress the autonomy of finite persons, the importance of a fully interpersonal relationship of love, and the perfection of God, which does not develop or evolve but does realize itself in relations of empathy and synergy with created persons. The model is that of a communion of persons, with God taking the lead as the primary causal agent, but finite persons as related in real creative and responsive ways to God, and so as making possible a community of love, creativity, and empathy as the goal of creation.

Yet within the Christian faith there is quite clearly to be found a key metaphor of the body, which is mostly used with reference to the "body of Christ." This does point to a deeper relationship between God and created persons than that of external relationship. It points to a sort of unity of being in which persons retain their creative freedom but are open to the activity of the divine Spirit which acts in and through them. When the church, consisting of the many communities of believers, is spoken of as the body of Christ, this statement can be taken in an optative sense. That is to say, it is God's wish that created persons should become instruments and vehicles of the divine love, the hands and feet of Christ the eternal Word, as Catherine of Siena put it. The church exhibits this possibility partially and ambiguously. But the Christian hope is that at some stage, in this universe or more probably beyond it, all evil and imperfection will be eliminated, and we can become fully and unambiguously coworkers with God, filled with the divine Spirit, in an integrated and organic communion with the divine Wisdom.

Then and only then we may speak of created being as the body of the Lord, expressing the divine will through the free cooperation of created wills, and affecting the divine being through its fully empathetic knowledge of the creative actions and experiences of created wills. With John Polkinghorne, I would thus feel it helpful to speak of "eschatological panentheism" — the destiny of created persons is to become "sharers in the divine nature" (2 Pet. 1:4), united to God in knowledge and love. But I would not feel it very helpful to describe the relation of God to the present universe, in which there is so much evil and corruption, as panentheistic, or to say that this universe, just as it is, is part of God, or is the body of God. If we took such a view, we could say that we are not parts of God; but we hope that, by grace, we shall one day become such, and that the final purpose of God will be realized, "to bring all things in heaven and on earth together under one head, even Christ" (Eph. 1:10).

Panentheism in Metaphysical and Scientific Perspective

PHILIP CLAYTON

In an array of publications I have defended panentheism as an outcome of developments in modern philosophical theology, as a framework for speaking of divine action in the context of modern science, and as a response to specific conundrums within Christian systematic theology. Reading the chapters in this volume has made me think again, however, about the basic question: How, if at all, could one make an effective case for panentheism with a discussion partner who was skeptical about this theological program? Like several of the other authors, I am interested in the question of why one might espouse panentheism — and why one might decline to do so.

In recent years scholars have advanced a variety of reasons that might lead one to adopt panentheism. Consider this rational reconstruction of some of the central options:

- One might hold that classical philosophical theism (CPT) or "supernaturalistic" theism or traditional theism is no longer viable, without being convinced that atheism is the most compelling answer.
- One might be convinced that panentheism is more compatible than traditional theism with particular results in physics or biology, or with common features shared across the scientific disciplines, such as the structure of emergence.
- One may be convinced of the truth or preferability of a particular metaphysical position (process philosophy, German idealism), and panentheism either lies closer to, or is actually entailed by, that metaphysical position.
- One might hold that panentheism can do a better job at preserving cer-

tain religious beliefs than classical theism can. So, for example, one might argue that viewing the world as within God allows for the development of an adequate theory of divine action, whereas classical theism, if it succeeded in avoiding deism, could support only an "interventionist" theory of divine action.

- In the process of searching for a mediating metaphysic between Western and Eastern religious philosophical systems, one might come to believe that panentheism provides the most convincing available answer.

- One might find panentheism religiously more viable or more attractive than the alternatives. Some have argued, for instance, that traditional Christian theism is burdened by unanswerable objections such as the problem of evil, whereas panentheistic theologies are able to avoid these objections.

- One might be convinced that classical theism has unacceptable ethical or political implications, while panentheism does not have these implications.

The recent debate, however, reveals a rather remarkable breakdown in the actual debates for and against panentheistic theologies. In order to understand what kind of a debate is involved in pro-and-con discussions concerning panentheism, a few methodological observations are in order.

First, a quick survey of the literature reveals that panentheism is advocated much more often by philosophical theologians than by systematic or biblical theologians. The term is found most frequently in authors who are wrestling with connections between theology and other disciplines: science, or metaphysics, or ethics and social-political philosophy, or the contemporary cultural context. The shared argument paradigm among these authors runs something like this: "Theology faces some serious difficulties when it enters into interdisciplinary debates, and traditional doctrinal language has not been effective in responding to these difficulties. By contrast, a panentheistic understanding of the God-world relationship is able to make connections with other academic fields. Until we find a conceptual structure that does a *better* job of addressing these problems, we are justified in turning to panentheism as a framework for making sense of God-language in the face of its detractors. Even if this move involves some revisions vis-à-vis traditional formulations, it is a cost one should be willing to pay."

Second, an overview of the papers in this volume will reveal how difficult it is to express shared criteria for deciding the panentheism question: even the most rigorous argument in one category may fail to interest those whose motivation stems from another field or set of questions. Likewise, thinkers who are moved by one or another criticism *against* panentheism are sometimes unmoved by even the strongest arguments in its favor. For some, the steps panentheism takes away from traditional Christian formulations already constitute sufficient reason to reject it.

Perhaps the best case for panentheism, then, would be a cumulative one: because there are so many difficulties (and dissatisfactions) with classical philosophical theism, and because panentheism offers a potentially attractive response to various (theological, philosophical, ethical, social-political) difficulties, the authors in this volume are drawn to it as a model. Only a multifaceted defense of this sort could make the case that recent work on panentheism constitutes a progressive research program,[1] one that brings new resources to unresolved religious and philosophical debates. If it can be shown to open up new solutions to theology's contemporary difficulties, and if classical philosophical theism is not able to do the same, then one will have reasons for pursuing the panentheist option. It is hoped that a diverse collection of essays like the present one may be the right venue to begin to make the cumulative case.

A single paper, however, can develop only one or two specific arguments in any detail. In what follows I reconstruct two of the central arguments in more detail, one stemming from developments in the modern "metaphysics of the subject" and the other from the theory of emergence as it is being developed today in the philosophy of science and the philosophy of mind. I believe these two arguments, when combined with the other arguments in this book, are sufficient to advance panentheism as a very serious option within philosophical theology today.

On God and Persons

Theologians in the twentieth century were particularly drawn to person language. Rarely do recent defenses of the continuing relevance of theism in today's intellectual climate or "in light of modern science" explain the God-world relationship in terms of interacting substances, for example, as one might have done in the fourth century. And contemporary philosophers, though they have worked in detail on the problems of personhood, have made scant use of the concepts of *hypokeimenon*, *hypostasis*, and *substantia* (though some of the essays in this volume suggest that it would behoove them to do so).

Instead, when theists attempt to explain why theism should still be viewed as a live option, they most often have recourse to language about persons. God's nature, it is argued, is not less than personal, even though it is infinitely more; God is a personal agent who forms intentions and acts in the world; the divine being consists of the "persons" of Father, Son, and Spirit; and in God's relations *ad extra,* God is personally present to the world. Indeed, person-based arguments are sometimes even used against panentheists: panentheism must be false, it's sometimes said, because we really are persons — agents who engage in personal relationships and who initiate personal activity within the world — whereas panentheism would make us merely "parts" of some larger divine whole.

Unfortunately, however, "person" is not a self-explanatory category. It's my contention that although the Latin term *persona* first arose in a context in which the metaphysics of substance was dominant, it has today largely lost contact with that particular context of origin. Indeed, one of the major reasons for panentheism's significance as a theological resource, I suggest, is that the "panentheistic analogy" provides a rigorous way of specifying what we mean when we apply person language to God — a sort of rigor too often lacking in discussions of God and personhood. (Of course, the argument will be convincing in the end only if supported by both metaphysical and scientific considerations.)

In the struggle to reestablish a credible theory of personhood after the demise of substance metaphysics, modern thinkers have turned to the natural sciences; to sociobiology and evolutionary psychology; to social sciences such as psychology, sociology, economics, and cultural anthropology; to history, literature, and the arts; and of course, to metaphysical reflection. Among the lessons that this modern "quest for the person" teaches[2] is that no simple appeal to an alleged "commonsense theory of the person" will suffice for rehabilitating the God-world relation. Contemporary deconstructive treatments of personhood alone, for example, are probably sufficient to undermine "commonsense" language about persons (esp. the personhood of God!); for additional evidence, one need only consider the radically different understandings of personhood across the world's cultures and religious traditions.

Theologians in the Western traditions have typically maintained that the closest analogy for the relationship between God and humans is the person-to-person relationship, rather than the relation of impersonal forces or deterministic causes. "God relates to us as one person relates to other persons," it is often said, even if God remains infinitely more than "just a person."

But it is one thing to use the notion of personhood as an intuitive starting point, quite another to treat the assertion "God is personal" as all the philosophical basis one needs for determining God's relation to the world. When theologians leave unexplained the sense in which God is personal, has intentions, or relates to the world in a personal fashion, their lacuna is not filled simply by turning to biblical theology for data on the God-world relationship or by providing a historical survey of the various things doctrinal theologians have said on the topic through the ages.[3]

If one were satisfied with this mode of proceeding, one might well have no motivation for developing a panentheistic theology. The trouble, however, is that the expression "relating to us as persons," especially when applied to God, expresses a desideratum — it's the placeholder for an answer rather than the answer itself. Gesturing in the direction of personhood is not enough; theology faces serious theoretical objections, and new conceptual work is necessary to answer them.

Central Moments in the Modern Philosophy of the Subject

The dawn of the modern period in the West coincided with a growing sense that inherited notions of the God-world relation were in trouble. Philosophers and theologians began to give new explications of what it is to be a person in the world — and what it would mean for an infinite God as ground and source of all that is to interact with the created world. Indeed, almost as soon as one formulates the question, one recognizes that the history of modern thought has been a continual attempt to find a metaphysics adequate to express what is meant by "personal being."

Descartes fired the opening salvo by sharply distinguishing persons from all other living things (a move that placed him solidly within the Aristotelian and much of the scholastic tradition). Famously, he divided the world into *res extensa* and *res cogitans:* body and mind are essentially different; the human being consists of both; and it is *res cogitans* that we first and fundamentally know ourselves to be.

Unfortunately, this turned out to be an unstable attempt at a solution. The mind-brain interaction proved impossible to specify conceptually in the Cartesian context — surely the pineal gland was not going to suffice! The problem was so intractable that Malebranche was driven to pay the extremely high ransom of occasionalism to avoid it: perhaps at every instance where mind-body interaction should occur, God directly intervenes to cause the appropriate changes. For all of Leibniz's brilliance, his metaphysical solution was no less expensive: windowless monads contain all their properties essentially, such that an infinite intellect who knew your individual concept or *haecceity*[4] could predict all your actions. According to his doctrine of pre-established harmony, God coordinates all the concepts of all monads in advance, producing the fortuitous appearance that you are responding to the words on this page and that I am touched by your criticisms. The British empiricists, quick to abandon a sinking ship, gradually managed to set aside the notion of human substance altogether, settling finally (in David Hume's philosophy) for a view of the human subject as a "bundle of perceptions" without a discernible principle of metaphysical unity.

Kant provided a philosophically viable way of thinking the self *sans* Cartesian dualism (albeit with some new dualisms of his own). As William James comments wryly, "At first, 'spirit and matter,' 'soul and body,' stood for a pair of equipollent substances quite on a par in weight and interest. But one day Kant undermined the soul and brought in the transcendental ego, and ever since then the bipolar relation has been very much off its balance."[5] The cost of Kant's move was to make each of the constitutive elements of the person primitive, rather than giving them a metaphysical grounding. On his view there is input to the human knower from we-know-not-what (Kant called it *das Ding an sich* or just "x"). Two forms of sensibility and twelve categories of the understanding, he held, are necessarily imposed by sentient beings on their perceptual input, though why this should be the case cannot ever be specified, even in principle. And the result is our experience of other persons and things in the world — the whole human world of experience that we inhabit, the only world we will ever know.

Nonetheless, Kant did realize one thing more clearly than anyone before him: basic to a metaphysics of personhood is the active principle of unifying diverse experiences into a single whole which he called the "transcendental unity of apperception." Basic to being a human subject is transforming variegated inputs into the core experience of "thought by me" or "felt by me." Interestingly, Augustine had already recognized this phenomenon, as in that passage in the *Confessions* in which he speaks of an extended "present" of attention that is able to experience a temporally extended progression of musical notes as one single melody.[6] But Augustine, according to Kant, lacked an adequate "transcendental" framework for exploring the conditions of the possibility of agenthood. Certainly the German idealists from Jacobi to Hegel went further in working out such a "phenomenology" than had any other thinkers in the Western tradition. One thinks, for example, of Schleiermacher's lectures on dialectics, in which subjective experiencing and the objective "what is experienced" became the fundamental categories, from which he derived theological conclusions such as the categories of *tranzendenter Grund* (God) and *Welt*.[7]

Clearly something new was afoot here. For the first time, steps were being taken from the "thing"-based ontology of substances toward a living ontology of subjects. It turned out, however, that the entire furniture of metaphysics had to be rearranged: you simply can't get to subjects if you start with substances in the sense of the Aristotelian tradition. As Hegel wrote famously in *The Phenomenology of Spirit,* being first had to be reconceived as subject *(Sein als Subjekt).* Contemporary theories of personhood ignore these developments at their peril.

Whether because of the horrors of German political history or because of the opacity of the German language, English-speaking philosophers and theologians have only partially appropriated the conceptual developments stemming from the explosion of thought between Kant and Hegel. In these years the ontology of personhood was rewritten and new foundations were established for a metaphysics of the subject. Fichte's *Science of Logic (Wissenschaftslehre),* for example, tried to defend a consistent version of "subjective idealism," the view that all things and all change stem from the self-unfolding subject or ego. But this program, it turned out, faces an insuperable dilemma: beginning with the finite ego leads (at best) to agnosticism about God, since God as absolute ego would stand outside of or above the development of the ego as presented in the *Science of Logic* itself. Yet beginning with the creative act of an infinite ego leads to agnosticism about humans, since subjective idealism could then no longer explain the process by which the finite ego — its own core principle — comes to be.[8] By contrast, Schelling's early "objective idealism" followed Spinoza in beginning with the notion of the Absolute. But his early attempt failed because the idealist principle of pure subjective activity — the synthetic activity of conscious awareness — cannot be derived from a starting point in which it is absent.

Already by 1802 Hegel had seen that the only answer must lie in a fusion of subjective and objective idealism. According to his "dialectical idealism," the activity of the emerging human subject produces reality in an iterating, dialectical process whereby the subject is repeatedly confronted with an "other" *(das Andere seiner selbst)* and overcomes the difference in a new synthesis that both transcends and preserves *(hebt auf)* their difference. Thanks to this principle of movement, which is Hegel's core achievement, the old metaphysics of substance was replaced with a new metaphysics of subjectivity. On this new view, *being has come to be understood as subject:* the idealist theory of the structure of subjectivity can now play the role that substance once played, with no less sophistication but with greater success.

From "Being as Subject" to Panentheism

Here is where panentheism enters: the metaphysical framework that was developed during the modern period from Descartes to Hegel necessitates a rethinking of the God-world relationship. One can't merely tack the new meta-physics of subjectivity onto the old metaphysics of substance with its separate notions of God and world.

Interestingly, already Descartes had seen that the substance idea was pointing in a different direction than the scholastics had thought. In the *Principia* he wrote, "By *substance* we can understand nothing other than a thing which exists in such a way as to depend on no other thing for its exis-tence. And there is only one substance which can be understood to depend on no other thing whatsoever, namely God."[9] Spinoza picked up the hint, appropriating it in a far bolder fashion than Descartes ever did. His *Ethics* is an extended argument for the claim that it makes more sense to say that there is only one substance, all things being merely modes or affections of that one substance, that is, manners in which its infinite essence is expressed. Among the infinite attributes of the one whole, which he called *deus sive natura,* are thought and extension. If thought and extension cannot be sepa-rate types of substances, à la Descartes, they must be distinct aspects of the One (hence Spinoza's "dual aspect monism"). To every mode in the world corresponds an idea; and just as the modes proceed upward in an interlock-ing hierarchy to the physical totality we call nature, so also the hierarchy of "ideas of ideas" proceeds upward to the interlocking whole that Spinoza called "God or Nature."

The trouble is, Spinoza was unable to conceptualize the principle of ac-tivity. Of course, he *asserted* that ideas were both active and passive, and he spoke of nature both as fact *(natura naturata)* and as activity *(natura naturans).* But he did not recognize that there must be a center of agency — what Kant called a "transcendental unity of apperception" — to serve as the unifying force behind any center of conscious experience. It is fascinating to observe how the commentaries of Spinoza's three most important interpret-ers prior to Kant (Lessing, Jacobi, and Mendelssohn) gradually pull the Spinozistic system in the direction of an active unifying principle.

Were Spinoza to have added the transcendental unity of apperception, however, he could not have maintained the strict pantheism for which he is so famous, the complete unity of God and nature *(deus sive natura).* One can in-deed speak of the whole of nature as corresponding to the idea of all ideas, but in order to preserve the attributes of both thought and extension, one must then also add, above and beyond the totality of facts or ideas, *the active principle of thinking* that conceives all those ideas. Note, however, that this ac-tive principle cannot be identical to the world (or to any part of the world) if it is to be able to form an idea of the world; it must be an entity that is *more than* the world, that transcends it. Had Spinoza followed out the logic of his own position in this fashion, he would thus perforce have become a panentheist.

The critical literature on Kant, Fichte, Schelling, and Hegel describes how Spinoza served as a formative influence on each of these four thinkers. All four of these core figures in the modern theory of the subject accepted some form of the transcendental unity of apperception; hence all four, tacitly or explicitly, accepted this modification of Spinoza in the direction of panentheism: Kant in the latter part of the first critique and in the *Opus postumum,* albeit in aphoristic form; Fichte in his contributions to the *Atheismusstreit* and especially in his later philosophy; Schelling most clearly in the essay *On Human Freedom;* and Hegel throughout.

One other advance characterizes these four thinkers: the movement away from a medieval "metaphysics of perfection" — God understood primarily in terms of the logic of the *ens perfectissimum* — to a new focus on the implications of divine infinity. Again, if space allowed, we could trace the influence of Spinoza's understanding of infinity on modern thought about God.[10] The net result of these developments, seen perhaps most clearly in the work of Fichte and Hegel, was the insight that the infinite God could not exclude the finite. Two mistakes in particular were identified. Fichte showed in an early essay that God could not be conceived as *an* infinite person.[11] Either God would be absolutely infinite, and in that case not limited by (hence not in relationship with) any other subjects, or God would be a person in relationship with (hence limited by) other persons, and hence not infinite. Hegel later argued that an infinite that stands over against a finite to which it must then be related is not truly infinite *(das schlechte Unendliche).* The truly infinite includes the finite within itself. If God is to be truly infinite, then God must include the world within Godself. As Hegel showed, this can be done without eliminating either the agency and essential finitude of created beings *or* the infinity and agency of God. If you will, this (panentheistic) notion of the finite world logically contained within the infinite God represents the inevitable by-product of the modern theory of subjectivity — that same approach to subjectivity that was first able to express the distinctiveness of personhood as over against objects.

The Panentheistic Analogy

As it turns out, these two major strands in the history of philosophical theology — the concepts of the infinite and the perfect — tend to link with monistic and pluralistic understandings of reality respectively. In *The Problem of*

God in Modern Thought I tried to show that these two separate families of concepts — infinity-based ultimate unity and perfection-based irreducible pluralism — help form the terrain on which modern theology moves. When one emphasizes the complete perfection of God, one has reason to separate all created, less-than-fully-perfect beings and objects from the divine, because the perfection of God would be compromised if God took into Godself other objects before they had been sufficiently cleansed (sanctified) from their imperfection (sin). Much of the history of Calvinism exhibits the outworking of this logic. By contrast, the logic of the notion of infinity ultimately excludes anything that might be "outside" the infinite; all must be included within it.[12] The emergence of panentheism in the nineteenth century reflects this conceptual world.

As neat as this conceptual division may appear, there are theological reasons to suspect that neither of the two approaches can stand on its own. On the one hand, a strong monism leaves inadequate place for individual difference or the integrity of creation — precisely the criticism raised again and again of Spinoza's philosophy. On the other hand, a sharp distinction between God and world has led in the modern period to deism and to the apparent impossibility of divine action.[13]

What to do, then? When two factors are both desirable yet neither can stand alone, one looks to the possibility of combining them. Admittedly, the rules of metaphysical debate tend to push one to choose one option *or* the other in the interest of simplicity and systematicity. But must we consent to this pressure? Sometimes the conjunction supplies the better answer; sometimes the position that's more adequate to the data is the one that is *less* simple. Perhaps, among the options, the best is the one that preserves both the essential, eternal nature of God and the essentially temporal process of God's relations to others. Herein lies the continuing attraction of "dipolar theism" as it has been defended by process theologians over the last decades. Dipolar theism is the view that God consists of two natures: an "antecedent" nature, which is fixed and unchanging, and a "consequent" nature, which is fully responsive to the world and arises only in interaction with it.

What happens when we return with this result to the question of God's relation to the world? Earlier we found ourselves pulled between the monism of Spinoza's "one substance with many modes" and the separation of God and world based on the demands of divine perfection. Dipolar panentheism suggests a more dialectical answer: not unity or difference, but unity-in-difference. The world is neither indistinguishable from God nor (fully) ontologically separate from God. Univocal language breaks down here, as it often does when we try to express dialectical relations. Arguably, one of the great weaknesses of the line of thought from Whitehead to Hartshorne was to advance dipolar theism with insufficient emphasis on the dialectical nature of the relationship. A Hegelian (or Peircean) revision of process thought would retain the "two-ness" of the two poles in God but would attempt to add as a third moment the movement of relation between them. The resulting trinitarian form of process theology represents a fascinating new research program.[14]

The more abstract (metaphysical or logical) presentation of panentheism is not for everyone; some will wish for a paraphrase that uses metaphors or analogies. But what kind of metaphor could express the truth that the infinite must comprehend all finite things? Highly concrete metaphors — e.g., the world exists in the womb of God — are evocative but too specific to be of broad theoretical interest. For a truth of this generality, one would need to make use of the most general metaphors that language offers.

Herein lies the justification for the central metaphor of panentheism — the "in" metaphor — which is built into the very etymology of this position (panentheism = all-in-God). "In" is a metaphor — an expression that defines or explains by identifying nonidenticals — because it ascribes spatiality to God (at least in God's relation to the world) even though God as the creator of space cannot be intrinsically spatial. Indeed, that the "in" is used metaphorically should be obvious from the fact that panentheists use it in two different directions — the world is in God, and God is in the world — whereas in mundane spatial relations this is impossible: the pie can't be in the cupboard and the cupboard in the pie at the same time! Like the tensions that are created by all living metaphors,[15] this tension drives one beyond any literal interpretation of the twofold "in." It is not difficult to paraphrase the fundamental claim being made by the metaphor: the *inter*dependence of God and world. The world depends on God because God is its necessary and eternal source; without God's creative act it would neither have come into existence nor exist at this moment. And God depends on the world because the nature of God's actual experience depends on interactions with finite creatures like ourselves.

Thus the analogical relationship suggests itself: the body is to mind as the body/mind combination — that is, human persons — is to the divine. The world is in some sense analogous to the body of God; God is analogous to the mind which indwells the body, though God is also more than the natural world taken as a whole. Call it the panentheistic analogy (PA). The power of this analogy lies in the fact that mental causation, as every human agent knows it, is more than physical causation and yet still a part of the natural world. Apparently, no natural law is broken when you form the (mental) intention to raise your hand and then you cause that particular physical object in the world, your hand, to rise. The PA therefore offers the possibility of conceiving divine actions that express divine intentions and agency without breaking natural law. On the PA there would be no *qualitative* or ontological difference between the regularity of natural law conceived as expressing the regular or repetitive operation of divine agency and the intentionality of special divine actions.

Emergence, Reduction, and Complexity

If one is to speak of the divine at all, one must speak analogically — even though all finite, human analogies are inadequate to the infinite God. *If* one chooses to speak, one will wish to use the best analogies available, while openly acknowledging their limitations. After all, isn't it appropriate to take the highest level of emergence one can find and to apply it, limitations and all, as a model for the divine nature? The strength of the panentheistic analogy is that it takes the highest level of emergence known to us and uses it as a model for the divine reality. The highest level we know is the level of human personhood: the emergence of mind (or mental properties) from the most complicated biological structure yet discovered, the human body and brain.

Given that the panentheistic analogy makes tacit appeal to the principle of emergence, an appeal to it will therefore require some explanation of that notion. In providing that explanation, we turn from metaphysics to science.

Various pieces of the argument appear elsewhere in this book and will not be repeated here. Thus in his contribution Arthur Peacocke shows how the hierarchical structure of the natural world lays the foundation for panentheism. Robert Herrmann draws an analogy between the role of consciousness in contemporary neuroscience and the relationship of God to world within panentheism. David Griffin draws a compelling conceptual line from the pervasive role of process in the world to panentheistic conclusions. Each of these could be shown to be features of an emergentist account of the God-world relation. And as Paul Davies writes elsewhere, "[The evidence] provides the strong impression that the cosmos is poised, exquisitely, between the twin extremes of simplicity and complexity. . . . The universe is neither a random gas nor a crystal, but a menagerie of coherent, organized, and interacting systems forming a hierarchy of structure."[16] The goal of the following paragraphs is to draw out the connection between emergence and panentheism more explicitly. After a few words on how emergence has become important in the understanding of science, we consider the ways it might be related to panentheism.

The method of reduction was once viewed as so fundamental to science that many equated science with reductionism. The equation was tempting: one of the greatest intellectual achievements of humanity was the modern scientific revolution, in which complex properties and states of affairs were reliably explained in terms of the behaviors of their parts acting in accordance with absolutely general, mathematicizable laws. I assume that readers are familiar enough with the history of physics, chemistry, and astronomy, and with the more recent breakthroughs in microbiology and biochemistry, to be suitably impressed with the powers of this method.

The twentieth century, however, brought to the fore what appear to be inherent limitations to reductive explanation. Relativity theory introduced the speed of light as the absolute limit for velocity, and thus as the temporal limit for communication and causation in the universe; Heisenberg's uncertainty principle placed mathematical limits on the knowability of both the location and momentum of a subatomic particle; the Copenhagen theorists came to the startling conclusion that quantum mechanical indeterminacy was not merely a temporary epistemic problem but reflected an *inherent* indeterminacy of the physical world itself; so-called chaos theory showed that future states of complex systems like weather systems quickly become uncomputable because of their sensitive dependence on initial conditions — a dependence so sensitive that a finite knower could *never* predict the evolution of the system, which is a staggering limitation given the percentage of natural systems that exhibit chaotic behaviors; Kurt Gödel showed in a well-known proof that mathematics cannot be complete . . . and the list goes on and on. To the innocent observer, it certainly appears that the project of omni-reduction within scientific explanation collapsed, perhaps permanently, at what should have been its moment of greatest victory.

The scientific interest in emergence has arisen, at least in part, in response to these inherent limitations in the project of reduction. Often in nature, it turns out, "the whole is greater than the sum of the parts." Or, to put it differently, explaining the behavior of a system often requires understanding both the parts and the way the system as a whole influences the behavior of the parts. Numerous scientific examples can be given: superconductivity is a strongly emergent feature of quantum systems, which cannot be reduced, even in principle, to the behavior of individual particles; thermodynamic properties such as are manifested in the Bénard phenomenon (but for that matter, even entropic processes) are not specifiable without consideration of the entire thermodynamic system (Prigogine, Peacocke); chemical properties (viscosity, acidity) require analyses at the structural level of molecules; the life of cell functioning introduces a genuinely new mode of functioning into natural history; organisms show a striving to feed, fight, flee, and reproduce that could not be predicated of any of their parts; and a number of animals (especially the higher primates) manifest qualities of inner experience that emerge from, but are not reducible to, the complexity of their central nervous systems.

The focus on emergence is related yet not identical to the new science of complexity.[17] Harold Morowitz alludes to the logic of complexity in his contribution to this volume, and Niels Gregersen has published extensively on the subject.[18] It is possible, at least in some cases, to quantify the complexity of systems and to observe changes in behavior as the complexity is increased. As the complexity index of a system increases, computations predicting its future states become more and more difficult; eventually the predictions become uncomputable. At the point of breakdown, if quantitative predictions and testing are still to be possible, simplifying assumptions have to be made (cf. the role of pruning algorithms described by Morowitz in his chapter). One has to switch the index of analysis: where explanations were formerly given in terms of the parts, one now begins to analyze and describe the behavior of the system as a whole — be it the molecule, the cell, the organism, or whatever. In many cases it turns out that the most empirically fruitful strategy is to describe and explain the emergent whole in its own terms. For there are patterns in its behavior; laws or quasi-laws describe these patterns; and other organisms (for example) evidence similar behaviors. At this point a new, emergent science may be developed.

One of the reasons some scientists resist emergence in this sense is that it forms a sort of bridge between the sciences as we know them and the humanities. One can study emergent phenomena like superconductivity within physics, as Robert Laughlin is now doing at Stanford, without breaking the bounds of physics; the same is true of studies of the relation between physics and physical chemistry or physical chemistry and biochemistry. Stuart Kauffman's recent *Investigations* shows how emergent complexity points toward a "general biology";[19] yet this new biology (if successful) will remain a genuine science emerging from physics, even if it is different from physics. But studies of the evolution of species are not as quantitative as studies of the genome, and environmental studies are even less so. By the time emergence leads us to speak of the role of emergent culture in influencing the behavior of individual human organisms, for example, we have clearly moved beyond the quantitative and lawlike framework of the physical sciences.

A word of caution: emergence is not equivalent to holism. It does not involve rejoicing in obscure "feelings of the whole," and it is not antirational in orientation. At least at some points in the ladder of complexity, emergent phenomena can be studied with all the rigor of fundamental physics. Still, emergence does set something in motion — and the outcome is not what the physical reductionists hoped for.

Emergence and Panentheism

Much remains to be said beyond this brief sketch of emergence.[20] But time and space are short, and the links to panentheism must now be drawn. My thesis is simple: emergence provides the best available means, for those who take science seriously, to rethink (i.e., establish a new conceptual basis for) the immanence of God in the world. Where emergence seems to make God *too* immanent and not transcendent enough, there are reasons *internal to the emergence argument itself* to correct it back in the direction of transcendence.

It is widely acknowledged that during the modern period the emphasis on God's transcendence of the world merged with the growing power of naturalist explanations to break the delicate balance between transcendence and immanence that theists had established in previous centuries. Unfortunately it turned out that if God is transcendent and the world is fully explained by natural law, then there *is* no place for any divine involvement in the world. Naturally, theists still wanted (and want) to affirm that God is omnipresent, aware of and responding to the world. But — and this is the point many theologians still need to acknowledge — the *conceptual basis* for these claims, which had undergirded divine-action claims in the patristic and medieval periods, gradually collapsed under the pressure of modern science and modern philosophy. Conservative evangelicals and fundamentalists have responded by encouraging us to ignore or contradict modern science. But that is an answer that neither I nor the other authors in this book are willing to countenance. Instead, we accept the thrust of modern science and look for a new conceptual basis — or a rediscovery and renewing of older conceptual resources — for asserting the immanence of God. Like the other authors, I find panentheism to provide the most adequate means available, and particularly in the combination with emergence that we have called emergentist panentheism.

Arthur Peacocke has already nicely described the way emergent systems represent a sort of nested hierarchy: parts are contained within wholes, which themselves become parts within greater wholes, and so forth. Martinez Hewlett diagrams them as in the illustration on page 88. As the diagram shows, the emergence concept is a viable means for expressing the relation "in" or "is internal to." If the same structure could be applied to God's relation to the world, it would comprehend the world as internal to God — pre-

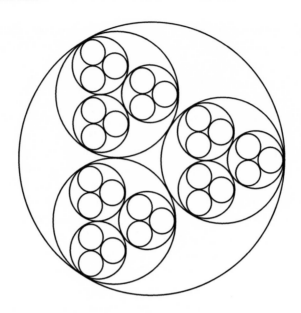

cisely the sort of intimate connection of God to world that the theological doctrine of immanence has traditionally offered. Indeed, the connection is closer than is often recognized. For example, note that the terms "in" or "internal" are used metaphorically by emergence theorists as well. What emergence actually offers, put in more formal but less evocative terms, is the self-inclusion relation "⊂": "belongs to," "is a member of," etc. This is a relation of logical inclusion rather than (primarily) one of location. Conceptually it's much closer to the (Hegelian) case for the finite being included within the infinite, sketched above. Emergence thus represents a powerful answer to misgivings about the preposition "in."

Note that the nature of the "in" or self-inclusion relation changes as one moves up the hierarchy of complexity in nature. As long as one remains with the nested hierarchies that constitute actual objects in the world, the "in" is indeed locative: atoms are in molecules, molecules in cells, cells in organs, organs in organisms, etc. By contrast, organisms are in an ecosystem in a rather different sense. Consider the further differences introduced by "William is in the army," "Vermont is in the Union," "her love is in her heart," "we live in community," and "no man is an island; all persons exist in society."

This diversity of usages is important for understanding those complex emergent properties that we collectively call "the mental." The diversity suggests that one doesn't have to be a dualist to account for the relationship of thought to the brain and central nervous system (CNS). Conceptually this relationship counts as yet another instance of emergence, albeit a unique one. The increasing complexity of neurophysiological structures over the course of evolution has given rise to an emergent level we might call mentality. Thoughts, intentions, and wishes are complex properties emergent from the brain — influenced by but not reducible to their physiological substrate. In a fashion both analogous to and yet different from previous levels of emergence, the brain and CNS give rise to mental qualities that are dependent on the brain as a whole and yet qualitatively different from it.

Cells represent a real explanatory level within science because they possess properties not ascribable to the molecules that compose them and because they exercise causal powers that one cannot ascribe to their parts. Likewise, what we call "the mind" — the sum total of mental properties associated with a given organism or person — possesses properties not ascribable to neurons and ganglia, properties such as *hoping to win this chess game* or *comprehending general relativity*. And mental occurrences such as thoughts and wishes exercise causal influence on each other and on bodies, which makes them irreducible components in any adequate causal explanation of the world. Consider, for example, to what extent the surface of the earth must today be explained in terms of the intentions of agents.

Using and Limiting the Panentheistic Analogy

To understand the mental as an emergent property is not sufficient for comprehending God's relation to the world, but it may be a necessary step in the process. Consider the tension between mind as property and mind as object. To conceive mind as an object invites dualism, since (as Descartes argued) an object that is nonphysical, immaterial, not composed out of parts, and not located in space and time must be a very different kind of thing altogether, which he called *res cogitans*. (Think also of the Aristotelian-Thomistic concept of the soul as the form of the body.) Given the dangers of such a dualism, one is tempted to speak only of mental *properties*: complex, emergent properties predicated of the brain as an object. Certainly there is no problem locating brains among the furniture of the universe and "parsing" them in terms of our knowledge of the physical world. Yet "physicalizing mind" doesn't remove all the tensions either, for mental properties are so radically different in kind from the object that is said to produce them that linking the two (brains and consciousness) remains the "hard problem" of neuroscience.[21]

The same tension arises in applying the notion of emergence to God. If applied directly — that is, in analogy with cases of emergence in the natural world — emergence theory would suggest that "God" or "the divine" is an emergent level or property within (or "of") the natural world. Let's call this view *radically emergent theism*. On this view there is no substance or thing that is God. Rather, "deity" is a quality that *the universe* comes to have increasingly over time. This emerging quality of spirituality is imagined to feed back onto the world the way mental phenomena affect physical states in the world. God does not exist in any literal sense, but there may be an increasing "deification" of the universe over time.

In a classic but underappreciated work entitled *Space, Time, and Deity*,[22] Samuel Alexander defends radically emergent theism in this sense. As he writes, "God is the whole world as possessing the quality of deity. Of such a being the whole world is the 'body' and deity is the 'mind'" (p. 366). Alexander's theology endorses a God who is in the process of coming to be: at one time there was no God, and now — to put it strangely — there is only partly God. God is radically dependent on the world:[23] this "finite God," he writes, "represent[s] or gather[s] up into its divine part its whole body" (pp. 367f.). Alexander accepts, one might say, a verbal notion of God: the deity "deisms," and these "deisings" are things the world does (*nota bene:* the atrocious neologisms are Alexander's). The *world* is the subject of these actions; *it* does them; but what the world *does* is to deify itself. God is verb only — as in the famous book by Rabbi David Cooper, *God Is a Verb: Kabbalah and the Practice of Mystical Judaism.*[24] God does not create the world; the world "deises" itself.

Now, it is possible that Alexander offers all that can reasonably be saved out of traditional theism. But I believe that conclusion would be mistaken. Theists have certainly *meant* to attribute divine properties to an actually existing being or Ground of Being rather than to the physical cosmos; although radically emergent theism is an option, it's not clear that it's the only one. Suppose instead that panentheists comprehend "divinity" not merely as an emergent property of the natural world, but also as a quality of one who is also an agent, whom we call God. The logic of emergence *allows for* this move, but it does not require it. Put differently: God *can be* understood on analogy with properties such as "reproduction," "life," or "thought," which we ascribe to cells, organisms, and minds respectively. But there are good reasons to think that the properties generally associated with divinity — eternality, perfection, love, justice, and the role of Creator and Source of all that is — are different in kind from such intramundane properties. How can God be source of all things and yet at the same time *a* thing or agent that arises in the course of the history of the cosmos?

It is this conundrum that has forced many panentheists to accept a form of ultimate or theological dualism. We remain dissatisfied with Alexander's treatment of divinity (or, as we might say today, spirituality) within the context of the finite universe and the sciences that explain it. Instead we make the move to metaphysics, postulating a broader framework in which the cosmos exists and which helps to sustain and explain it. God is, for us, the source and (we hope) ultimate culmination of this cosmos, the alpha and omega, the force or presence within which all is located.

Emergence is therefore a conceptual structure, born in the crucible of the sciences, that can lead to the category of divinity or spirituality as an emergent property in evolution. But emergence is not in the end adequate to fully explain this property. Emergence propels one to metaphysics, and metaphysical reflection in turn suggests a theological postulate above and beyond the logic of emergence. Emergence helps with models for thinking the relationship of world to God (e.g., the nested hierarchy model given above), and it serves as a constant reminder of the radically different sorts of inclusion relations found in the natural world; panentheism provides a means for incorporating these inner-worldly relations into an explicitly theological model. Emergentist panentheism thus represents a superior means for thinking God's relation to the world in comparison with the older models that are associated with classical philosophical theism.[25]

II Scientific Perspectives
on the God-World Relation

Teleology without Teleology:
Purpose through Emergent Complexity

PAUL DAVIES

In this paper I offer a modified version of the standard uniformitarian view of divine action.[1] According to the standard view, God acts not only by creating the universe "at the beginning" together with its laws (something even Deism asserts), but also uniformly, sustaining the universe moment by moment. That is to say, the existence of the universe is contingent on God's continuous involvement. In addition, the unfolding of the potentialities embedded in these laws through the processes of nature could be considered God's action as well. In seeking to develop and adapt this view, I wish to focus on the form of the observed laws of nature, and argue that these laws are *very specific* with remarkable properties. In particular, they allow not only for chance events in the routine sense, but for the emergence of genuinely novel complexity in nature, an emergence that requires these laws but goes far beyond a mere unfolding of their consequences.

Thus my view of divine action depends on a much more fecund understanding of nature than the one usually given by scientists. As I see it, the development of complexity is not just an outworking of the laws of nature; it also depends on the kind of radical chance permitted by, and yet transcending the determination of, these very laws.[2] This claim has striking scientific implications: it means that the full gamut of natural creativity cannot be explained scientifically if one is limited in biology to neo-Darwinism and in

I am particularly indebted to Robert Russell of the Center for Theology and the Natural Sciences for his detailed critique and assistance with the original draft of this paper. I am also very grateful to Philip Clayton for his careful comments and guidance relating to panentheism.

physics to the fundamental laws of relativity and quantum mechanics. That is not to say that these aspects of science are wrong; rather, they form only part of the story. Indeed, the laws of nature as we currently understand them are *essential* for my worldview, because they give rise to genuine openness in nature. I shall argue that the intrinsic creativity of nature results from the inherently self-organizing potentialities of the laws of nature. Thus the emergence of complexity in no way warrants appeal to special divine action in particular events, especially if this in turn entails an interventionist view of divine agency. (My openness, however, to newly developing "noninterventionist" views of special divine action will be noted below.) In essence, although nature's complexity *appears* to be the product of intentional design and purpose, it is entirely the result of natural processes. In effect it introduces into nature an implicit teleology, without inserting one explicitly in its underlying operation; hence my theme of "teleology without teleology."

I begin with a brief discussion of three models of divine action: interventionist, noninterventionist, and uniformitarian. I then introduce the modified uniformitarian approach, modeled after the game of chess and elaborated through an extended discussion of complexity in nature. Following this I comment on recent attempts to explain the apparently contrived and teleological aspects of nature by appealing to some sort of multiple-universe scenario. I include specific suggestions about how my ideas can be tested scientifically in terms of assessing the complexifying trends in nature and the search for extraterrestrial life in the universe. Finally I consider how the view presented here links to the theological position known as panentheism, which is the focus of this volume. I believe panentheism is the theology that most closely matches my understanding of the relationship between God and the physical universe.

How Can God Act in the World?

According to theological tradition, God not only creates and sustains the world but acts to bring about special events in nature and history. But what does it mean to say that God acts in nature? Can such acts be reconciled with the scientific picture of nature that is subject to lawlike principles? We may distinguish three ways in which God might be said to act in nature.

Interventionist Divine Action

Perhaps God's special actions break the ordinary flow of physical processes and entail a violation of the laws of nature. Conservative Christians typically approach divine action in this "interventionist" way.

a. According to one form of interventionism, God acts as something like a physical force in the world. God moves atoms and other objects about to achieve God's purposes, but to do so God must violate the physical laws revealed by science. To be explicit, if a particle would naturally follow trajectory X, then as a result of God's intervention it contravenes the laws of physics and follows trajectory Y. If God intervenes at the atomic level, we may call this "bottom-up" action, since the effects at the atomic level may percolate up to the macroscopic realm where they result in events such as those recorded as miracles in the Bible. Of course, once the principle of divine intervention is accepted, one may entertain the possibility of God acting directly on a macroscopic scale too, but somehow the degree of violence done to the laws seems worse the larger the system involved.

The problem with the foregoing approach is that the idea of a god as *a force* pushing and pulling matter about alongside the other forces of nature is decidedly unappealing to scientists — and to many theologians, since it reduces God to an aspect of nature in competition with other aspects. But one need not entertain something so crude as a "cosmic magician."

b. One could eschew any attempt to explain physically God's action and simply assert the purely abstract claim that God acts per se. Even then, if such action entails violating or suspending the laws of nature, the claim is still deeply antiscientific. Moreover, it raises its own theological problems, since the laws of nature are themselves attributed to God; in other words, we are appealing to God violating God's own laws, creating the image of a shoddy craftsman who is obliged to intervene from time to time to fix up a flawed product. But these problems notwithstanding (and in spite of its pagan overtones), this version of God's action is still the one favored by many religious people.

Noninterventionist Divine Action

An alternative "hands-off" approach being developed by several scholars enables God to act effectively in nature through specific events — making a real difference in what actually comes to pass — but in ways that do not interrupt these processes or violate the laws of nature. Instead, it is precisely the special

97

form of these laws that permits a "noninterventionist" action.[3] This "having your cake and eating it" approach appeals to the inherent indeterminism of nature.

a. One option is to locate the effects of God's acts at the atomic level where quantum physics pertains. Here the concept of unique, causally closed particle trajectories melts away. Instead, quantum indeterminism permits a range of possible trajectories consistent with the laws of physics. The future evolution of a system is not fully determined by the physical forces at work; instead, nature is ontologically indeterministic.[4] This indeterminism provides a loophole through which God might act in the world without violating (at least the letter of) the laws of physics.

At face value this proposal seems to be merely a more subtle variant of the traditional God of the gaps. But this objection can be easily met, since in this case the gaps are not *explanatory* gaps due to human ignorance, but are *physical* gaps inherent in the structure of nature itself. A second, stronger objection is that if God were to act repeatedly in this way on a specific physical system (e.g., on a particular atom), then the spirit, though not necessarily the letter, of the statistical laws of quantum physics would be violated, thus running into some of the objections associated with the crude interventionist approach. Nevertheless, it is easy to imagine that God may achieve God's purposes with ease by simply "loading the quantum dice" only exceedingly slightly by involving large numbers of particles or even the entire universe. Such a stratagem would almost certainly go unnoticed; we would never spot a "conspiracy" among widely separated atoms destined to merge in some specific end goal at one location in space.

But even this is not necessary. God could act entirely within a "fair dice" universe by introducing a degree of determinism within the range of indeterminism allowed by quantum physics. That is, within the range of quantum alternatives offered to a set of physical systems, God could "pick the choices" in each case in such a way as to respect the statistical laws but nevertheless to determine the outcome (perhaps only to some level of probability). There is obviously a spectrum of intervention ranging from occasional and minor acts of "selection" to the extreme case of God's will totally "soaking up" the residual indeterminism left by the quantum laws.

b. Quantum indeterminism is not the only possibility for grounding the apparent behavioral openness of physical systems. Although closed dynamical systems are described in textbooks, no real (finite) physical system is in fact physically closed, if for no other reason than that external gravitational disturbances cannot be screened out. Furthermore, many physical systems fall into the category of being chaotic, which means that their behavior is exceedingly sensitive to minute external influences, including gravity.[5] Now I concede that, as Wildman and Russell have carefully argued,[6] epistemic unpredictability does not necessarily entail ontological indeterminism. Moreover, we still use *deterministic* equations to describe chaotic systems in many domains, in spite of the fact that they are in practice unpredictable. Still, unless one assumes that the universe *as a whole* is closed and deterministic,[7] it may in fact turn out that at least some chaotic systems are ontologically open. Thus in my opinion it is rash to discuss physical systems as if they were closed and deterministic, even when neglecting quantum effects.[8]

The fact that physical systems may well be "open to the future" implies that there is room for such systems to be affected by God. Indeed, a common analogy for such divine action is the kind of "top-down" causality presupposed in many discussions of human agency. The mind-body interaction may include both bottom-up "nudging" of specific key quantum events as well as various forms of top-down causation.[9] The precise mechanism whereby downward causation might operate remains mysterious — we do not yet understand how minds and brains relate to one another. But in considering the problematic nature of God's action in the world, the fact is often overlooked that *our* minds can act in the world (perhaps through downward causation), so there would seem to be no logical impediment to God also acting in a somewhat similar manner.[10] Indeed, panentheists frequently appeal to the analogy between our minds acting on our bodies and God acting on the universe as a whole.

Uniform Divine Action

I should now like to discuss a type of divine action that is in a sense weaker than interventionist or noninterventionist yet in some ways more impressive. This is the traditional liberal Protestant and Anglo-Catholic view of God's action "in, through, and under" the laws of nature, to use Arthur Peacocke's helpful phrase.[11] It too comes in various forms.

a. In its more deistic mode, this approach views God as playing the role of designer or grand architect by selecting a suitable set of laws from among the infinity of possibilities. These laws are chosen because of the inherent self-organizing and self-complexifying properties they confer to matter when it is subject to them.[12] This is the model of the universe I sought to develop in my book *The Cosmic Blueprint*.[13]

b. In its more uniformitarian view of divine agency, this approach adds to God's initial choice an emphasis on God's continuing role of creating the universe afresh at each moment, though without in any way bringing about particular events which nature "on its own" would not have produced.

It is the latter view that I wish to explore in more depth in the following sections of this chapter, though in a new and sharply modified form. When I use the term "panentheism," I mean it to express the relationship between God and the universe that fits most naturally this type of divine agency.

Modified Uniformitarianism: God as Chess Player

T. H. Huxley likened nature to the game of chess, with the pieces representing physical systems, the rules of chess the laws of nature, and the game itself the evolution of the universe.[14] It is a useful analogy. Suppose you were given a checkerboard and pieces and asked to invent a game. If you didn't give a lot of thought to the problem, the chances are the game you invented would be either boringly repetitive or a chaotic shambles.[15] In contrast, the rules of chess have been carefully selected to ensure a rich and interesting variety of play. More importantly, the end of any given game of chess is not determined by these rules alone, *but also by the specific sequence of moves* taken by each player, and is thus open to human whim or ingenuity. The rules serve to constrain, canalize, and encourage certain patterns of behavior, but they do not fix the goal in advance. The game thus becomes an exquisite mix of order and unpredictability, which is why it is so fascinating to play.

We may exploit the chess analogy and suggest that God, on the one hand, acts by selecting from the set of all possible laws of nature those laws that encourage or facilitate rich and interesting patterns of behavior (e.g., by making some laws nonlinear, inherently statistical, etc.). On the other hand, the details of the actual evolution of the universe are left open to the "whims" of the players (including chance operating at the quantum or chaos level, the actions of human minds, etc.). I will call this proposed mode of divine action "modified uniformitarianism." I believe it has a number of appealing features.

First, God need never suspend, manipulate, bend, or violate God's own laws since their statistical character allows for the action of divine — and perhaps human — agency. There are no miracles, save for the miracle of existence itself. Second, God does not exercise an overbearing influence on the evolution of the universe, thus reducing it to a pointless charade. There is room for human freedom, and room for even inanimate systems to explore unforeseen pathways into the future. A third advantage of this approach is that it enables one to discuss a concept of design in nature that is impervious to a Darwinian-style rebuttal. So long as it is agreed that the universe as it exists is not necessary — that it could have been otherwise — then clearly the actual universe has selected (or had selected for it) a particular set of laws from the (probably infinite) list of all possible laws. In my experience almost all scientists, including hard-nosed atheists, concede this point. Thus the contingent nature of the world inevitably begs the questions: Why those laws? and, Is there anything special or peculiar about the actual set of laws selected?

The answer to the latter question seems to be a definitive yes. Much has been written about various "anthropic" coincidences, the astonishing intelligibility of nature, its beauty and harmony and so on.[16] Here I wish to dwell on the fact that the laws encourage the universe to behave creatively. This property of the laws makes them look to me as though they are the product of an ingenious — even loving — designer. Before such a conclusion can be drawn, however, we must consider the alternative possibility: whether the remarkable nature of the laws of the universe might only *appear* to be designed but is in fact the product of pure chance in the "blind watchmaker" sense, to use Dawkins's apt phrase.[17] After all, Darwinism in the biological realm mimics design where there is none. So might a kind of cosmic Darwinism account in a similar way for the distinctive nature of the laws of physics? Might the suggestion of an element of intentional input in the laws be an illusion masking the fact that there is none?

I believe the answer is no, because unless multiple universes are allowed, the concept of Darwinian selection is meaningless. Of course, some people have tried to argue that there *is* an ensemble of universes, and the fact that our universe is so ingeniously contrived is simply because most of the less contrived universes are incompatible with life, and so go unobserved.[18] In some versions of inflationary big bang cosmology, the visible universe occupies only one domain in a vast, possibly infinite, set of domains of the whole universe. Proponents of quantum gravity depict our universe as part of a mega-universe characterized by "eternal chaotic inflation," to use the phrase of Andrei Linde.[19] In all these examples the laws and constants of nature may vary considerably among these different domains.[20] Lee Smolin has even gone so far as to suggest a sort of cosmic Darwinism whereby baby universes, and cosmic natural selection, operate in a way analogous to biological natural selection.[21]

There are, however, several objections to these ideas. (1) Invoking an infinity of unseen (and perhaps unseeable) universes just to explain the one we do see is the antithesis of Occam's razor. (2) In many variants of the many universes theory, the existence of the "other universes" can be neither verified nor falsified — they are merely implied by the theory — so the status of the conjecture as a scientific theory is questionable. (3) It is hard to see how the appearance of law and rationality can emerge from total randomness. Anthropic selection cannot explain regularities in nature the failure of which would not be life-threatening. Yet we know of many such regularities. For example, the law of conservation of electric charge is known to great precision. Slight and rapid violations of this law in atoms would have only trivial consequences for chemistry and life. Why don't such violations occur? (4) An ensemble of universes, each lawlike in differing ways, would still require an explanation for the origin of "law" as such, even if one could explain how, given such lawfulness, the actual laws of this universe can be explained. (5) In any case, it is likely that the "multiverse" explanation does not improve on naive theism (i.e., the prior existence of a selector Deity) in terms of explanatory economy: indeed, I suspect it *is* simply naive theism dressed up in scientific language. The application of algorithmic information theory[22] to these competing explanations would show them to be of equivalent (high) complexity (both require us to discard an infinite amount of information). Although I have not carried out the formal steps to determine their equivalence, I offer here a heuristic argument. If the multiverse hypothesis is taken to its logical extreme, there must be at least one universe in which a technological civilization reaches the point of being able to simulate consciousness using fast computers or some other technological system. This civilization would then be able to create virtual worlds in the manner of the science fiction movie *The Matrix*. For any given "real" world, there would be a vast, possibly infinite, number of possible virtual worlds. A randomly selected observer would be overwhelmingly more likely to experience a virtual simulation than the real thing; there is no reason to suppose that "this" world is other than a simulated one. But the denizens of a simulated virtual world stand in the same ontological relationship to the intelligent system that designed and created their world as human beings stand in relation to the traditional designer/creator Deity. Therefore the multiverse is ontologically equivalent to naive theism. Of course, many people would regard my argument as a reductio ad absurdum of the multiverse concept, rather than as a justification of naive theism with God in the guise, not of a grand architect, but of a grand software engineer.

A key concept in the model of the divine selection of laws is that the laws themselves are in a certain sense timeless and eternal. To appropriate the wisdom of Augustine,[23] God does not act *within* a preexisting and endless time, picking a suitable set of laws at some moment in the past and then making a universe to try them out on. Instead God acts to create all that is, including space, time, and the laws of nature, and thus these laws are in this sense eternal, too. Indeed, one of the purposes in choosing these laws is that they permit the universe — including space and time — to originate spontaneously "from nothing" in a lawlike manner, without the need for a further, special divine act.[24] Thus the eternal selector God is, in this function at least, outside of time altogether. However, it is important to stress that "creation" is not a once and for all act at the big bang, but ongoing and inherent in nature itself. Nature is highly creative *through* time in ways that go beyond the mere genetic evolution of complexity. If God sustains the continually creative universe through time, then in this sense God possesses a temporal as well as an atemporal aspect. These insights have led me to the modified view of uniformitarian divine action, which I will present next.

Modified Uniformitarianism and the Creative Cosmos

Among the infinite variety of possible laws will be a subset — some assert a very small subset — that permits what we would now call self-organizing complexity to emerge in the universe. One example that has been much discussed is the complexity associated with life and consciousness. The existence of these phenomena imposes rather stringent restrictions on the values of the fundamental constants of nature and on the cosmological initial conditions. If the laws of physics and the structure of the universe were not rather similar to the actual state of affairs, then it is unlikely that life and consciousness, at least as we at present understand them, could exist.

It is likely that many complex systems (snowflakes, turbulent eddies, sandpiles) are highly sensitive in their specific details to the form of the laws of physics. The source of most natural complexity can be traced to the existence of nonlinearity in the controlling forces. Such nonlinearity depends in turn upon the form of the underlying laws of physics (e.g., the specific Lagrangian), and on such quantitative details as the values of coupling constants, relative particle masses, etc. Of course, the very complexity of the subject of complexity precludes any general conclusions at the present state of our knowledge. All one can really say is that if one were able to "twiddle the knobs" and alter some of these fundamental quantities, then the nature of most complex systems would vary greatly; indeed, the very existence of these systems may well be compromised. This is a subject area ripe for scientific investigation, and the results would have an important bearing on the whole question of divine selection and purpose. The narrower the range of lawlike possibilities that permit rich complexity, the more contrived, ingenious, and purposeful the universe will appear. Some scientists expect that there are quasi-universal principles of organization and complexity that will describe similar features in systems as disparate as embryos and spin glasses. These "organizing principles" would not usurp the fundamental laws of physics, but complement them. They would not be reducible to, or derivable from, the laws of physics, but neither would they be some sort of mystical or vitalistic addition to them. Instead, the organizing principles I have in mind would arise from the logical and mathematical structure inherent in all forms of complexity. At least that is the hope.

Central to this entire philosophy is that the emergence of organized complexity is lawlike, spontaneous, and natural, and not the result of divine tinkering or vitalistic supervision. In other words, life and consciousness *emerge* as part of the natural outworking of the laws of physics. Thus from the uniformitarian perspective taken in this paper, I am proposing that God "initially"[25] selects the laws and the laws then take care of the universe, both its coming into being at the big bang and its subsequent creative evolution, without the need for direct supernatural intervention. By selecting judiciously, God is able to bestow a rich creativity on the cosmos, because the actual laws of the universe have a remarkable ability to canalize, encourage, and facilitate the evolution of matter and energy along pathways leading to greater organizational complexity. Indeed, I have suggested that there may be a strict mathematical sense in which the laws optimize organizational complexity — what Freeman Dyson has termed "the principle of maximum diversity." Again, this is a subject ripe for scientific investigation: one may be able to prove that the familiar laws of physics form an optimal set.[26] If such ideas are correct, then in a certain scientific sense we may well live in the best of all possible worlds.

Still, it is important to realize that the particular form of the uniformitarian argument being proposed here goes far beyond its usual "garden-variety" form of theism that often tends toward Deism. My point in appealing to panentheism is to propose that in choosing these particular laws God also chose not to determine the universe in detail but instead to give a vital, cocreative role to nature itself. Remember, the selection of the laws, and even the cosmological initial conditions, does not serve to determine the fate of the universe in detail, seeing as the laws that have in fact been selected contain an element of indeterminism. Instead, the role of chance is a two-edged sword. In most uniformitarian approaches to divine action, chance could be viewed as neglect or abandonment by God — the world left vulnerable to the vagaries of happenstance. In my modified approach, however, God's choice of chance bestows an openness — a freedom — upon nature, crucial for its impressive creativity, for without chance the genuinely new could not come into existence and the world would be reduced to a preprogrammed machine.

The exquisite and crucial feature of the actual arrangement of the statistical laws of physics — the specific amalgam of chance and necessity that pertains to the actual universe — is that chance is not mere anarchy, as it could so easily be if the laws were simply chosen entirely at random. Instead, chance and lawlike necessity conspire *at the basic physical level* felicitously to produce (incredibly!) emergent lawlike behavior at the higher levels of complexity.

This point cannot be overstressed. Many scientists have the misconception that complex order (e.g., mental activity associated with brains, universality in chaos, the ubiquity of fractal structures) is really no surprise because nature is ordered at the fundamental level of the basic laws of physics, and that this underlying order somehow reappears in complex systems. This argument has even been used to "explain" how human beings are able to create the mathematics needed to describe the lawfulness of nature. In my view this is a totally erroneous connection.[27] The regularities observed in complex systems, which are often quasi-universal (e.g., Feigenbaum's numbers in chaos theory), are *emergent* phenomena, not pale manifestations of the "underlying" laws of physics. To be sure, if the laws were different, these regularities would be different (probably, I have argued, nonexistent), but the regularities are not derivable from, or reducible to, those underlying laws, for they depend in a crucial way on the openness and indeterminism of the complex systems involved. Thus the laws of physics produce order — the order of simplicity — at the micro, reductionist level, while the felicitous interplay of chance and necessity leads to the emergence of *a different sort of order* — the order of complexity — at the macro, holistic level. It is this *specific* view of chance, which acts as a prerequisite for emergence and thus bequeaths the universe the conditions for the possibility of creativity, which underlies my modified uniformitarian view of divine action.

The fact that there has emerged an entirely new form of order — the order of complexity — in the organization of matter and energy on the macro level, is part of the striking ingenuity of the laws of physics. How much easier it would be for an omnipotent deity to "cobble together" the complex systems "along the way" by crude manipulative intervention (as in the first approach, above), but how much less impressive! To select a set of laws that through their subtle interplay bring about a *natural* creativity of an orderly and organizational form, a spontaneous self-organizing potency that is not anarchic but hierarchical and constructive, which is both ordered yet open, determinate in its general trend yet undecided in the specifics, is altogether more wonderful and a cause for celebration!

In the earlier divine teleological schemes of pre-Darwinian Christianity, God directly selected a final outcome (e.g., the existence of "Man") and simply engineered the end product by supernatural manipulation. By contrast, the concept I am discussing is "teleology without teleology." God selects very special laws that guarantee a trend toward greater richness, diversity, and complexity through spontaneous self-organization, but the final outcome in all its details is open and left to chance. The creativity of nature mimics pre-Darwinian teleology, but does not require the violation or suspension of physical laws. Nature behaves *as if* it has specific preordained goals — it exhibits purposelike qualities — while in fact it is, at least to a limited extent, open to the future.

How can we test these ideas? The clearest example I can think of for where to begin is the emergence of life, consciousness, and culture, and — the crowning achievement — intellectual schemes such as mathematics and science that capture the very laws upon which this magnificent edifice is constructed, completing the loop of existence that links the highest organizational level (mind) back to the lowest level (particles and fields of matter).

How many of these features are due to chance and how many to necessity? I contend that the general trend of matter → mind → culture is written into the laws of nature at a fundamental level; i.e., it is part of the natural outworking of ingeniously selected laws. But I also contend that the specific details (the human form, our mental makeup, the character of our culture) depend on the myriad accidents of evolution. If this argument is correct, we would expect the same universal laws to work themselves out along a similar trend elsewhere in the universe, to bring forth life, consciousness, and culture in other planetary systems too.

The acid test of my thesis is therefore whether or not we are alone in the vastness of the universe. If we are, then contrary to my hypothesis, it suggests that life on earth is either the product of a supernatural interventionist act in a universe of mind-numbing overprovision (given the 10^{20} or so stars within the observable universe) or a hugely improbable but purely accidental series of events of staggering irrelevance. My hope and expectation is that we are not alone, and that life on earth, including the emergence of mind, will be seen as a natural consequence of the outworking of universal laws. That is why I attach such importance to the search for extraterrestrial life.[28]

Finally I should say that even the modification to uniform divine action that I am proposing here will be regarded by many as too impoverished and remote a concept of God. There is, however, the option to combine noninterventionist divine action with uniform divine action, and consider that God may be more immediately involved in the process of evolutionary change when the laws of nature themselves are an expression of noninterventionist divine agency.

How Does This Fit with Darwinism?

I will be very interested in the reaction of biologists to the concept of "teleology without teleology." I expect the reaction might be very favorable for at least two reasons. First, biologists have already incorporated the general themes of self-organization and emergent complexity as part of the neo-Darwinian account of biological evolution. For example, although genes carry information only about the linear sequence ("primary structure") of amino acids in a protein or enzyme, the secondary, tertiary, and quaternary structures (all having to do with three-dimensional organization and functionality) are examples of self-organization. The developing embryo provides another remarkable example of self-organization.[29] My question to my biologist colleagues, then, is how much biology can be accounted for in terms of spontaneous self-organization (i.e., random factors operating together with general laws as in the previous example of the Bénard instability)? Cell development provides an example for my question. It seems clear that the formation of cell structure results from a threefold combination: (i) random factors such as chemical diffusion and spontaneous symmetry breaking; (ii) deterministic factors such as the information contained in the DNA; and (iii) the laws of nature provided by physics and chemistry. Does the role of genetics in helping to determine the development of the structure of a cell, along with the laws of physics and the random variables, provide a case in which a term like "supervised self-organization" is appropriate?

Secondly, there seems to be some evidence of complexifying trends in biological phenomena. For example, the rate of mammalian encephalization is often cited in this regard.[30] Some biologists find the suggestion of trends unacceptable since they seem to imply "progress." Any such talk of "trends" or "progress," they argue, is the misguided result of anthropocentrism, of our chauvinistically placing value on our own species and regarding humans to be at the top of an evolutionary ladder.[31] Instead, they claim, evolution is blind; it is a random walk through the space of possibilities. Because life necessarily began (relatively) simple, and diffused into the boundless space of possibilities as a result of random variation, there is the illusion of progress, of the trendlike advance of complexity. Stephen Jay Gould has forcefully argued that no such trend exists.[32] Others, however, take a more moderate view of the notion of progress. Francisco J. Ayala, for example, has written a number of papers on "progress in evolution."[33]

Moving into the context of theology, I intend that my term "teleology without teleology" will allow theologians to speak in a more subtle and scientifically congenial way about divine purposes being achieved in evolution —

that is, in a way entirely consistent with science. To summarize my position, we may explain the appearance of goal-oriented design in nature without miracles or supernatural tinkering. Instead, I appeal to the outworking of peculiarly creative and felicitous laws *selected for these very purposes.* Although the general trend of this process is basic to the laws, the actual details of evolution are left to the vagaries of chance.

On the view that I have presented, the theological interpretation of nature's creativity and complexity is by no means obligatory. A scientist could still shrug it aside with the remark: "That is just the way the world is. It's amazing, but I'll simply accept it as a brute fact." However, for those who wish to mesh the worldview I have presented with a formal theological position, then panentheism best expresses the concept of "teleology without teleology." Classically, panentheism entails that the world is located within the divine, although God is more than the physical universe. The three central contentions of this article are, first, that God can be thought of as logically prior to the universe and responsible for the set of laws that allow self-organizing complexity to emerge in the universe. That is, the rational order of the physical universe is grounded in God. Second, the process of emerging complexity rests uneasily with "interventionist" divine action, but it need not exclude panentheist agency. The laws of nature can themselves be regarded as expressions of God as long as nature's novelty and creativity are identified with, not separated from, divine agency. As I noted in the opening, the unfolding of the potentialities contained in nature's laws in the course of natural history can now be considered God's action as well. Finally, panentheism allows one to think together these two dimensions of divine agency. The activity of complex processes eventually produces agents who are able to "glimpse the mind of God," comprehending (at least in part) the underlying laws of the universe. Creation "in the beginning" and creation through self-organizing complexity may therefore be regarded as merely two aspects of a single divine creativity.

God in and beyond Space and Time

RUSSELL STANNARD

In this paper I wish to share with nonphysicists our current views on the nature of time. These I believe to have a strong bearing on how we are to see God in relation to time. Indeed, by the end of the paper you might well have formed the conclusion that modern-day physicists probably experience less difficulty accepting traditional doctrines — such as that concerning God's foreknowledge — than certain theologians!

Let us begin with our "commonsense" ideas of time.

It is divided into past, present, and future. The past consists of those things that have happened — events that once existed. These happenings might well have left memories and other lasting effects, but the past events themselves no longer exist. As for the future, by that we mean all those events that might one day happen but as yet do not exist. The present is that instant in time we label "now." It divides the past from the future. We live in the present. All that exists belongs to the present — what is happening right *now.*

Time moves on. We are being swept toward the future. Future events fleetingly become actuality, before passing once more out of existence in the past. We call this the "flow of time." The future is open, uncertain. Through what we do now we can affect the future. The past on the other hand is fixed; we have no power to change it now.

We exist in time; we also exist in space. Space and time are very different from each other. We measure distances in space using rulers, and intervals of time by clocks. There is just the one three-dimensional space, and the one one-dimensional time.

These, then, are some of our commonly shared ideas about space and time. As for how God is thought to relate to time, we note that when we pray we are interacting with God at a particular point in space and at a particular instant in time. In this context God is immanent — within space and time. But we also think of God as transcendent — beyond space and time. This belief manifests itself, for instance, in the way one traditionally regards God as having foreknowledge. Although for us creatures the future is undecided — it does not exist — God has a different perspective — one that is all-embracing and somehow takes in the full sweep of time — past, present, *and* future.

Such a belief has always been hard to accept. After all, is it not a physical, indeed a logical, impossibility to know something if that something does not yet exist? If even I do not know what I shall be doing tomorrow, how can anyone else — including God — know what those actions will be? If our future behavior could be predicted with certainty, would that not imply that we were nothing more than automatons? What then of our supposed free will?

To understand how a *physicist* views time, we must draw upon Einstein's theory of relativity. Not that it is my intention to put you through a crash course on relativity theory! It is sufficient for our purposes merely to highlight some of the theory's more startling consequences — consequences which I hasten to assure you have been fully vindicated by experiment.

I want you to imagine an astronaut in a high-speed spacecraft and a mission controller at Houston. The astronaut leaves the earth bound for another planet. Relativity theory is able to show that, with the astronaut and mission controller in relative motion, they do not agree on the distance the craft has to travel to reach its destination. For example, at a speed nine-tenths the speed of light, the astronaut would calculate the journey distance to be about half that estimated by the mission controller.

The two also disagree over the time taken by the journey. According to the controller, time for the astronaut is passing at about half the rate it does for himself. Thus everything happening in the spacecraft — the ticking of the clocks, the astronaut's breathing rate, her heartbeats, her aging processes — has slowed down by a factor of a half. Not that the astronaut will be aware of this; a slow clock looked at by a brain in which the thinking processes have been slowed down by the same factor, appears perfectly normal.

Which of the two observers has the right assessment of distance and time? It is impossible to say. But why? Won't the astronaut realize that something must be wrong with her observations when, because of her sloweddown clock, she arrives at her destination in half the time it should have taken? No. Remember, she thinks the journey distance is only half that which the controller claims it to be. Both the astronaut and the mission controller have sets of measurements that are entirely self-consistent.

Confusing? It certainly appears that way when one comes across the ideas of relativity theory for the first time. We are so accustomed to thinking in terms of us all sharing the one space and the one time, that it requires a severe mental wrench to conceive of something radically different: namely, that we each inhabit our own space and our own time, and these will differ from each other if we are in relative motion. The reason most people go through life unaware of this is that for the speeds we normally encounter in everyday life, the differences between our various estimates of distance and of time are so small as to make no practical difference. Nevertheless, the effects are there all the time.

So, how are we to understand these differing spatial and temporal measurements? Let me give you an analogy. I hold up a pencil. What do you see? It depends on where you are sitting relative to the pencil. If you are viewing it from the side, you see a long pencil; view it from an end, and it appears foreshortened. Are these differing perceptions a source of concern? No. We think nothing of them. We realize that what we actually see is merely a two-dimensional projection of what in reality extends in three dimensions. The two-dimensional projection is at right angles to the line of sight, and this line of sight will vary depending on where you are placed relative to the pencil. We are unperturbed by the different observations because we know that when we make due allowance for how the pencil extends along whatever line of sight we have adopted, we come up with identical results for the true length of the pencil in three dimensions.

Now we can use this as an analogy for the case of the astronaut and the mission controller and their differing perceptions of the distance and the time of the journey. Einstein's solution to the problem is that we are *not* dealing with a three-dimensional space and a separate one-dimensional time. We are dealing with a *four-dimensional reality:* the three dimensions of space plus a fourth dimension closely related to time. We call this combination *space-time.*

What kinds of "objects" are we dealing with in four-dimensional space-time? They must depend on the four quantities: the three spatial directions and the time. This means we are dealing with *events.* An event takes place at a particular location, or position in 3-D space; it also takes place at a particular point in time. One event might be the launch of the spacecraft from earth at a specific time. Another would be its arrival at the distant planet at some later time. Having specified these pointlike events in the four-dimensional space-time, we can now ask what the four-dimensional "distance" is between the events marking the beginning and end of the journey. We have already seen that the astronaut and the mission controller do not agree on either the spatial separation of these events or the temporal separation. But this need worry us no longer. Why? Because once you start thinking of reality as four-dimensional, then the spatial separation between events is merely a three-dimensional *projection* of that reality. Likewise, the temporal separation is a one-dimensional projection. From our analogy with the pencil, we know that projections are liable to change as one changes one's viewpoint. It turns out that where four-dimensional space-time is concerned, "changing one's viewpoint" means more than simply being at a different spatial position. Because of the way space-time mixes up space and time, changing one's viewpoint means having a different speed. Two observers in relative motion (like our astronaut and mission controller) have differing perspectives on space-time by virtue of that relative motion.

So, differing spatial and temporal projections are nothing to worry about; they are merely appearances. What counts is what these observers get when they calculate the true separation of the events in four dimensions. When they each plug in their own versions as to what the spatial and the temporal separations are, they obtain identically the *same* value for the four-dimensional space-time separation. You recall that the astronaut thought the distance covered by the journey was shorter, but she also thought the time of the journey was shorter; the two cancel out and she gets the same overall result as the controller. The four-dimensional separation is the one thing they can agree upon. It is for this reason that one is led to the conclusion that what really counts is not the individual estimates of spatial distance or temporal interval but the four-dimensional space-time separation. Einstein himself once declared that henceforth we must deal with "a 4-dimensional existence instead of, hitherto, the evolution of a 3-dimensional existence."

It is an extraordinary conception. There is little point in trying to visualize four dimensions — you just get a headache. The best I can do is to stretch out three of my fingers (representing the three spatial dimensions) and my thumb (representing the time dimension). But of course, this is seriously inadequate. I'm cheating. Strictly speaking, all four digits ought to be mutually at right angles, and that is a physical impossibility to demonstrate. But it is the best I can do by way of visualizing the situation.

Actually, the preferred course of action among professional physicists is to ignore such visual aids and just allow oneself to be guided by the mathematics. Mathematically speaking, one can handle any number of dimensions — one just adds on further terms in the relevant equation.

I have already said how one must stop thinking of a separate time outside three-dimensional space; space and time are welded together like the fingers and thumb of my hand. One must also not get lured into thinking of a separate time outside four-dimensional space-time. Time is not outside those four digits of my hand; time is already there represented by my thumb. What that means is that four-dimensional space-time does not change. Something can only change *in time.* But space-time is not "in time." *All* of time is there in the thumb. One point along the thumb represents the instant you began to read this chapter; next comes the knuckle, which stands for this present instant; and the next point along the thumb is the instant you finish (or give up) reading this chapter. It's all there: *past, present, and future.* It's static. We call it a *block universe.* Just as each point in space exists on an equal footing with any other, so does each point in time. We are accustomed to think that all of space exists at each point of time. So, for example, at this instant in time not only does your present location exist, but also New York, London, planet Jupiter, distant galaxies, etc. What we are now saying is that likewise at each point in space, all of time exists. At the point of space where you are sitting, everything that has ever happened at that location, or will ever happen there — it all exists, in some sense. Don't press me to be more precise than that! I don't know "in what sense."

This is such a counterintuitive notion, it is perhaps not altogether surprising that while the majority of physicists subscribe to the block universe idea as the most reasonable interpretation of the differing spatial and temporal measurements, not all do. A sizable number of scientists and philosophers (John Polkinghorne, Arthur Peacocke, Richard Swinburne, John Lucas, David Pailin, to name but a few) disagree with the conclusion. While one may appreciate their reservations, it is not easy to see what might be put in place of the block universe. One can hardly stick with the familiar notion that existence is confined to whatever is happening at the present instant. Why? A further, and indisputable, finding of relativity theory is that observers in relative motion cannot agree on the simultaneity of events occurring at a distance. For instance, the mission controller at Houston and the astronaut flying at high speed above Houston cannot agree on what event located in London is to be regarded as happening at the same instant as one in Houston. That being so, they would not be able to agree on what exists in London at the present instant. This loss of agreement on the question of simultaneity poses no problem for the block universe idea; the relative motion merely causes the two observers to make different time assignments to the events — *all* the events being considered to exist.

One of the consequences of the block universe interpretation is that there is nothing special about the particular instant we label "now"; as I have said, all points in time are on an *equal* footing. Also the future, in itself, is *not* uncertain. We do not *know* what the future holds because all we are directly experiencing is what exists at this particular instant, now. At this particular instant we might possess data regarding past events, but not the information that would allow us to predict with certainty what lies in the future. Nevertheless, our modern understanding of time would seem to indicate that whatever the future holds, in some sense it is already there, fixed, waiting for us to come across it.

That being the case, it would appear to me to add plausibility to the idea that God might have knowledge of it. According to the block universe idea, it is all out there, it is fixed. All God has to do is find a way of looking at it — which should not be too difficult for a god!

To my way of thinking, these considerations lend credence to the panentheistic view of God's relationship to the world. As we have already noted, God is present within space and time (as evidenced by our interactions with God through prayer). But now we discover that even we creatures, confined to live out our lives within space and time, can nevertheless discern intimations that there might be another way of regarding space and time — a somewhat detached, distant viewpoint from which all that exists, past, present, and future, is laid out in its entirety. Space-time does not, of course, manifest itself to us in this fashion; for us it has to be a conclusion inferred from data that *are* available to us: the spatial and temporal measurements. But perhaps it presents itself to God directly in that fashion. If so, God not only permeates the very fabric of space and time, he can also, in a sense, be all-encompassing.

But, you might be wondering, if physics does not pick out any special instant in time to be called "now," where does the concept of now come from? And if nothing is changing (the block universe idea), what about the flow of time — where does that come in?

Here we touch on one of the truly great mysteries: the fact that we have two entirely different approaches to the concept of time. So far I have spoken of time exclusively in the way the concept is addressed in physics. Let us now see how this same word "time" is used in a different context — the description of what it is to be a conscious human being.

On examining the contents of the conscious mind, we find mental experiences — feelings, decisions, sensory experiences, etc. These occur in sequence. What separates one experience from the next? We call it "time." The experiences occur in time. We are able to estimate and compare these separations or intervals of time. This might be done through noting the extent to which the memory of a past experience has faded — the greater the separation in time, the greater the degree of fading. In addition, there might be an indication of the time interval based on the number of other notable experiences we have had subsequent to the one in question. The precise mechanism by which we subjectively assess time intervals is not at all well understood, but we do know that we do have our own internal, mental way of doing it — semiquantitatively at least.

For each experience there are other experiences on either side of it along the sequence, with one exception — the experience that marks the end of the sequence. This end point of the sequence we designate "now." It is only in consciousness that the "now" acquires its special status.

Although we use the word "time" to describe the separation between our mental experiences, it does not follow that this is the same "time" as is used in the description of what exists in the physical world. For one thing, mental states occur in time but not in space. (It would be absurd to ask how much space a big decision like getting married takes up, compared to a small decision such as which tie to wear today.) And yet we know how indissoluble is the link between physical time and physical space.

Only through the recognition that we use the word "time" in two distinct ways can it make sense to say that all of time, including the future, exists now. What this means is that all of *physical* time exists at the instant of *mental* time called "now" — and indeed at every other instant of mental time.

It is perhaps unfortunate that the same word "time" is used in two such dissimilar contexts. The reason it is, of course, has to do with the fact that despite the distinctiveness of physical and mental time, there is a close correspondence between them. A sensory experience which is part of the mental sequence (e.g., the hearing of a bang now) is correlated to a feature of space-time (the firing of a gun at a particular point in space-time). The "now" of mental time is correlated to a particular instant of physical time. Although, as I have said, *all* of physical time exists now, consciousness (not physics) singles out one particular instant as having special significance for the "now" of mental time.

That focus of consciousness does not remain static. It moves steadily along the physical time axis. The mental "now" correlates with one particular instant of physical time. But a short while later (judged according to mental time) the "now" correlates to a different physical time. The difference between the two physical times, judged on a clock, when compared with the perceived lapse in mental time, gives rise to a "flow" of time. Note that without there being two types of time, there could be no flow. A flow is a change of something in a given time. The flow of water from a hosepipe, for instance, is the amount of water emitted in a given time. But what possible meaning could be given to the phrase "a flow of time"? The amount of time passing in a given time? It cannot mean anything — unless we are talking about *two* different times.

I began by mentioning prayer. But you might be wondering: How can my asking God for anything *in* time affect the outcome when the future, in *physical* terms, is fixed?

As I see it, there is no difficulty. The future outcome can already have built into it the effects of one's prayer to God now. Indeed, I and some other Christians think nothing of praying for events that have already happened, but about which we do not as yet know the outcome. It might be some oversight that we did not pray about it earlier. We are confident that an all-knowing God will be aware that we will be offering up such a prayer later, and he will take that into account in determining the outcome. Thoughts of a block universe can really transform one's thinking about what can and cannot be done.

There remains one final worry: Do not the foregoing considerations compromise our sense of free will? How can we be free if in some sense the future is known — not known to us, but known to God? Another analogy: You have taken a video recording of some family event. You have viewed it on numerous occasions and are familiar with its contents. On sampling any excerpt, you know exactly what will happen next. Does such predictability mean that you are now viewing the actions of automatons? Of course not. The videotape remains a record of the free will actions of the participants. Their freedom of action is not in any way altered by the fact that you, the viewer of the tape, are now in the privileged position of having random access to the whole sequence of events.

In our analogy, that videotape is somewhat like the record of our lives as they are etched into the four-dimensional fabric of the world. God is the viewer of the tape. From his privileged standpoint he encompasses the whole of space-time; he has access to it all (much as I am able to survey in one sweeping glance the whole of the three fingers and thumb I hold up stretched before me). But such random access is denied to us; we still have to make the free will choices that are the determinant of the future — a future unknown to us.

Indeed, the analogy can be made even closer. Imagine that in making your video recording you from time to time set up the camera on a tripod so that you yourself can participate in the events. The tape is thereby not just a dispassionate record of the activities of the rest of your family, it includes you. Not only are you the viewer of the completed videotape, you are also an active participant on the tape; you are watching yourself interacting with the rest of your family. So it is with God. As God transcendently surveys the four-dimensional world with its record of our lives, he sees in it not only us but also himself immanently relating to and interacting with us — helping to determine the nature of the sequence of events. The world is not a cassette he has rented from the video store; it is a panentheistic God's own home video.

Let me now move on to one more important development in our modern understanding of the nature of time. It arises out of the recognition that time might have had a beginning.

Twelve thousand million years ago all the contents of the universe were together at a point. There was a big bang. Distant galaxies of stars are even today receding from us in the aftermath of that violent explosion. The big bang was such a cataclysmic event, it is natural to suppose that it marked the origin of the universe. That being the case, it seems only reasonable to ask what *caused* the big bang.

The religious response is to say that God created the world. But there is a problem. Cosmologists claim that the big bang marked not only the coming into existence of the contents of the universe but also the start of time. There was no time before the big bang. There could, therefore, have been no cause of the big bang (a cause having to precede the effect). "What place then for a creator?" as Stephen Hawking asks in his best-seller *A Brief History of Time*.

To answer this, let us first examine why scientists hold the view that time had a beginning.

The big bang was not like other explosions. It did not take place at a particular location in space. Not only was all of matter concentrated initially at a point, but also all of space. There was no space outside the big bang. An analogy might help: Imagine a rubber balloon. Onto its surface are glued some small coins. The coins represent the galaxies. Now we blow air into the balloon. It expands. Suppose a fly were to alight on one of the coins; what would it see? All the other coins moving away from it. But that, of course, is the observed behavior of the galaxies.

Physicists attribute the motion of the galaxies not to them moving *through* space, but rather to the space between them *expanding*. The galaxies are being carried along on a tide of expanding space, just as the small coins are moving apart because the rubber between them is expanding. And just as there is no empty stretch of rubber surface "outside" the region where the coins are to be found (a region into which the coins progressively spread out), so there is no empty three-dimensional space outside where we and the other galaxies are to be found.

It is this interpretation of the recession of the galaxies that leads scientists to conclude that at the instant of the big bang, all the space we observe today was squashed down to an infinitesimal point. The big bang not only marked the origins of the contents of the universe, it also saw *the coming into existence of space*. Space began as nothing, and has continued to grow ever since.

That in itself is a remarkable thought. But an even more extraordinary conclusion is in store for us. Recall how we earlier spoke of space and time being indissolubly welded together as a four-dimensional space-time. One cannot have space without time, nor time without space.

This being so, we can immediately conclude that if the big bang marked the coming into existence of space, it must also have seen the coming into existence of time. This in turn means there was no time before the big bang — and hence there could have been no preexistent cause of the big bang.

This certainly gets rid of the kind of creator God that most people probably have in mind: a God who at first exists alone, then at some point in time (note: *in* time) decides to create a world. The blue touch paper is lit, there is a big bang, and we are on our way.

But does this entirely dispense with a creator God? Before jumping to that conclusion, let us consider this famous passage from Augustine's *Confessions:*

> It is idle to look for time before creation, as if time can be found before time. If there were no motion of either a spiritual or corporeal creature by which the future, moving through the present, would succeed the past, there would be no time at all. . . . We should therefore say that time began with creation, rather than that creation began with time.

If the archaic expression "either a spiritual or corporeal creature" had been replaced by a more up-to-date one — such as "a physical object" — one might well have thought the quote came from Hawking or some other modern cosmologist. In fact, those are the words of Saint Augustine. (Modern cosmologists find it hard to come to terms with the fact that where the beginning of time is concerned, it was a theologian who got there before them — and by fifteen hundred years!)

How did he do it — bearing in mind he obviously knew nothing of the big bang and 4-D space-time? He argued somewhat along the following lines: How do we know that there is such a thing as time? It is because things change. Physical objects (for instance, the hands of a clock) occupy certain positions at one point in time, and move to other positions at another. If nothing moved, we would not be able to distinguish one point in time from another. There would be no way of working out what the word "time" referred to. A fortiori, if there were no objects at all, moving or stationary (because they had not been created), time would clearly be a meaningless concept.

In this way Augustine cleverly deduced that time was as much a property of the created world as anything else. As such, it needed to be created along with everything else. Thus it makes no sense to think of a God capable of predating the world. Despite this, Augustine remained one of the greatest Christian teachers of all time. His realization of the lack of time before creation clearly had no adverse effect on his religious beliefs.

To understand why this should be so, we have to draw a distinction between the words "origins" and "creation." Whereas in normal everyday conversation we might use these terms interchangeably, in theology they acquire their own distinctive meanings.

So, for example, if one has in mind a question along the lines of: How did the world get started? that is a question of origins. As such, it is a matter for scientists to decide, their current ideas pointing to the big bang description.

The creation question, on the other hand, is different. It is not particularly concerned with what happened at the beginning. Rather it is to do with, Why is there something rather than nothing? It is as much concerned with the present instant of time as any other. Why are *we* here? To whom or to what do we owe our existence? What is keeping us in existence? It is a question concerning *the underlying ground of all being.*

For this reason one finds that whenever theologians talk about God the creator, they usually couple it with the idea of God the sustainer. His creativity is not especially invested in that first instant of time; it is to be found distributed throughout *all* time. We exist not because of some instantaneous action of God that happened long ago — an action that set in train all the events that have happened subsequently — an inexorable sequence requiring no further attention by God. We do not deal with a God who lights the blue touch — and *retires.* He is involved at first hand in *everything* that goes on.

An atheistic response to this discussion would be to dismiss the "creation question" as meaningless. Why not simply accept the existence of the world as a brute fact? What is to be gained by saying that God created the world — that only raises in its turn the question of who created God?

This is to misunderstand how we are using the word "God." God is not an existent object. One cannot say that God exists in the same way as we say an apple exists. If that were the case, then postulating one more existent thing — God — would not be any real advance in understanding. No, the point is that God is the *source* of all existence. "God" is the name we give to whatever is responsible for the existence of things — including you and me.

It can be argued that such considerations give added credence to the panentheistic view of God's relationship to the world. As the source of existence, God's presence can be discerned in the world, but God is not to be identified with that world. Still less is God to be viewed as merely functioning as a temporal "cause" of the big bang.

A reason why many believers resist the idea of there being no God before the big bang, is the thought that this seems to imply that God too must have come into being at that instant. How could God have made himself? The trouble here is that not only are we once more mixing up existent things with the source of existence, we are compounding the mistake by regarding God as an object confined within the limits of space and time; it assumes that God can exist only *in* time. The panentheistic idea serves as a useful antidote to the tendency to fall into that trap.

Emergence of Humans and the Neurobiology of Consciousness

ROBERT L. HERRMANN

As a trustee of the John Templeton Foundation for a number of years, I have viewed with considerable interest the series of symposia sponsored by the foundation to explore Sir John Templeton's humble approach to the knowledge of God. In these endeavors we are asked to put ego aside and enter into a searching experience, realizing that we know so very little about the Creator and the vast universe of which we are such an infinitesimal part. Yet, despite the enormity of the project, we are asked to be eager to study, understanding that exploration into God is the highest form of learning. In the present symposium, on panentheism, we are asked if this early theological construct may represent an example of the humble approach to theology, a searching among the biblical and scientific texts to seek a more comprehensive model for God's action in the world.

Panentheism

The picture of the creation which science now gives us appears to be very much a seamless whole. The remarkable process begins in a cataclysmic explosion, evolves through galaxies, supernovae, recondensation, and planet formation, to set the stage for the biogenesis of life. There would seem to be little room for God to interfere after the process was begun, hence a difficulty in arriving at an understanding of the traditional God of action, one who works miracles in nature and answers the prayers of his people.

Because of this outlook, I have found panentheism's emphasis intriguing. The idea of God working in and through the cosmic evolutionary process, intimately involved in what are nevertheless free and natural processes which twist and turn yet climb inexorably upward to yield self-conscious creatures, is arresting. Then joining this self-consciousness with a uniquely human awareness of God, so evident in anthropological evidence from our very recent evolutionary past, makes God's immanence a salient feature of the creation. It would seem reasonable that God not only gives continuous being to the creation, but as panentheism suggests, God also includes and penetrates the whole yet is infinitely more than the whole, as a high view of God's transcendence would dictate. But God's intimate involvement in the whole sweep of creation to finally create self-conscious free agents who can know their Creator suggests an incredible closeness and intimacy and a form of trust which gives new meaning to the concept of immanence.

Emergence

The origin of human beings can be seen to be an example of an emergent phenomenon. Arthur Peacocke, in his chapter, describes the way the enormous diversity of species in the biological world can be understood in terms of the formation and unique behavior of complex systems. Among the systems so described, human beings, which are best understood as psychosomatic unities — with physical, mental, and spiritual capacities — are among the most complex.

In viewing the emergence of our own species, the scientific data for human evolution point back to hominid ancestors who diverged from our closest primate relative, the chimpanzee, some 5 to 7 million years ago. From that point hominid evolution appears to have proceeded exclusively on the African continent until the emergence of the toolmaking bipedal *Homo erectus* about 1.8 million years ago. Shortly thereafter, *Homo erectus* spread to other continents; fossil remains have been found in Java, China, the Middle East, and Europe. According to evolutionary biologist Francisco Ayala, the transition from *Homo erectus* to modern humans began around 400,000 years ago.

Homo erectus persisted for some time in Asia, until 250,000 years ago in China, and perhaps until 100,000 years ago in Java. We now know that modern humans *(Homo sapiens)* appeared more than 100,000 years ago, with the weight of evidence favoring an African or Middle Eastern origin, followed by migration to the rest of the world. A near relative of *Homo sapiens*, *Homo neanderthalensis*, appeared in Europe around 200,000 years ago and persisted until 30,000 or 40,000 years ago. Modern humans appeared in Europe at least 100,000 years ago, and coexisted with Neanderthals, whom they gradually re-

Paleolithic Age

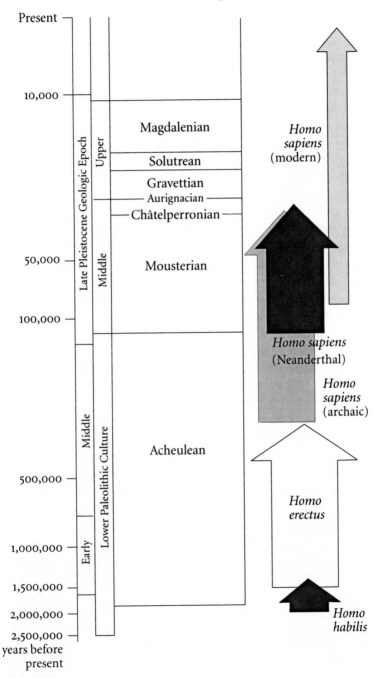

placed. These latter two species are especially interesting to us because they evidence what we might call spiritual characteristics: compassion for the sick, burial of the dead with flowers and preparations for future life, many evidences of ritual and symbol. With the early moderns there was also a virtual explosion of artistic expression, with vivid drawings found in over two hundred caves in Europe dating to some 20,000 to 30,000 years ago.

When one considers that the transition from *Homo erectus* the toolmaker and hunter to *Homo sapiens* the compassionate artist and worshiper took perhaps 100,000 to 150,000 years, a mere tick on the evolutionary clock, it is clear that we are viewing a special emergence. As can be seen in figure 1, the advent of *Homo sapiens* is remarkable even in comparison with its competitor, *Homo neanderthalensis,* for once modern humans became established there was a veritable explosion of innovation. Painting, engraving, and tool manufacture changed so quickly that archaeologists divide the period from 35,000 years ago to 10,000 years ago into six separate cultural periods, each with its own style of technology and innovations. David Wilcox points out that by contrast the Neanderthal populations displayed cultural stasis like *Homo erectus.*[1] The Mousterian tool culture they developed appeared around 100,000 years ago and remained basically uniform across Europe for 65,000 years. The modern humans who replaced the Neanderthals were, in less than half their tenure, walking on the moon. Of course, based upon the principle of humility toward God, it would be appropriate to anticipate still further emergences, the next perhaps to humans with a profound understanding of their spiritual nature.

Neurobiology of Consciousness

In neurobiological terms the most interesting features of the emergence of artistry, technology, and compassion are traceable to a greatly enlarged and complexified brain. The loci which seem most probably involved include the evolutionarily ancient limbic system and portions of the temporal lobe. The latter has been implicated in intense feelings of religiosity during seizures in patients with temporal lobe epilepsy. Other recent research points to a role for the parietal lobe, which helps regulate the sense of self and physical orientation, and the frontal lobe, which is evidenced to be involved in heightened concentration during meditation.

The advent of brain imaging by functional magnetic resonance (fMRI) and positron-emission tomography (PET), which measure cerebral blood flow, has added powerful new methodologies for the monitoring of brain activities when specified tasks are performed by human subjects. For example, when a research subject is asked to look at faces, an fMRI scan shows increased blood flow in the part of the visual cortex that recognizes faces. For many neurobiologists, all of this seems to point to an eventual understanding of events of the mind as simply events of the brain. Yet there are many who see an irreducibility in mental events such as consciousness. Philip Clayton has pointed out the importance of the latter view, especially because of its theological significance in providing a powerful mechanism for explaining divine action. That mechanism, which he calls the panentheistic analogy, portrays God's action in the world as in some ways similar to our mind's relationship to our body. As Clayton says of this relation:

> If humans have a purely spiritual soul associated with their body, one that can influence events in the physical world, then there is in principle no difficulty with a spiritual being such as God influencing events in the physical world. It is only necessary that God's relation to the world be understood as sufficiently analogous to our relation to our bodies for similar principles to apply. By contrast, what if human mental functioning can be fully explained in terms of neuro-physiological states and laws, and in this sense be reduced to them? In that case, it would appear, everything that "folk psychology" calls mental or consciousness would be better accounted for in physical terms. It would seem to follow that there could be no real mental or spiritual causation within the world — or at least none that could be intersubjectively known.[2]

In light of this critical question of the nature of human consciousness, it would be useful to examine the state of progress in neurobiology toward the understanding of the mind-brain relationship. In this connection we recently conducted a program for the John Templeton Foundation in which we invited neuroscientists and also theologians and philosophers with some scientific background to submit ideas for neurobiological research into deeper realities. Among suggested topics for study were love, purpose, moral sense, worship, mystical experience, creativity, genius, imagination, curiosity, and the search for meaning. Respondents were asked to submit a two-page précis describing their creative research idea and the deeper reality it would address. One hundred one précis were submitted, and forty-eight of these were deemed of sufficient merit to invite their writers to submit an essay of four thousand words detailing their approach. Forty-three essays were submitted, and the list of essayists includes representatives from a number of well-known neurobiology laboratories in the United States, Canada, Europe, and Asia, as well as theologians in the United States, Germany, and Switzerland.

The topic of consciousness was addressed by approximately half the essayists. Among the ten winners, whose essays are published on the John Templeton Foundation web page, are three who give insight into the direction of contemporary neurobiological research into consciousness.[3]

Mary Colvin, from the Department of Physiological and Brain Sciences at Dartmouth, proposes that consciousness is an emergent behavioral state, one that follows a convergence of perceptions, memories, and emotions. She asks the question, "If consciousness is an emergent state, how long does it take to become aware of the stimulus?"[4] Colvin prefaces her essay with a description of the work of Benjamin Libet, who wrote a widely read and controversial article on conscious awareness in which he measured brain activity with the EEG.[5] He concluded from his observations that voluntary acts begin unconsciously, with a 300-500 millisecond separation between intention and subjective awareness. This proposal, that "mind and body are not temporally aligned," Colvin says, caused some neurophilosophers to "imply that our current conscious thoughts, feelings and acts play very little role in determining future behavior." Colvin disagrees with the Libet conclusions, pointing out that more recent studies favor an erasure theory in which information which is rapidly acquired (within 500 milliseconds or less) during a series of stimuli will "not remain activated long enough to stabilize reportable conscious awareness." With the erasure theory, then, the goal is to discover how long a stimulus must be attended to, to achieve a constant state of awareness. Colvin's experimental approach consists in testing the performance of a simple response to a visually presented stimulus as an automatic response, and comparing the timing of that response to the same situation when the subject is asked to lengthen his or her response time by the smallest possible amount. She hypothesizes that there will be a unique neural activation in the delayed situation which represents the process of becoming consciously aware of the stimulus prior to the execution of the motor response. Concurrent measurement with fMRI would localize the neural systems involved. Colvin assures us that this activation may not represent a single "locus of consciousness" but may reflect activation of one or more of a myriad of higher-level cortical systems mediating awareness and attention.

It is interesting to note that she believes that consciousness will eventually be fully explained. She concluded, "It is my belief that consciousness can be explained in the philosophical traditions of reductionism and causality.... While a biological explanation of the neural processes involved in producing the mental state that many would uphold as the hallmark of the human species may reduce the associated mystique and romance, it will unify the study of the separate brain systems giving rise to human behavior."

Todd C. Handy, another winner in the Creative Ideas in Neurobiology program,[6] is at the Center for Cognitive Neuroscience at Dartmouth. He proposes to explore an important aspect of the phenomenon of selective attention. Cognitive psychologists refer to our ability to selectively attend to stimuli in our environment as a way that our brain assigns meaning and importance to specific kinds of information. Trivial information is not immediately processed, whereas other kinds of information — particularly those that serve as a warning — are processed quickly, even at the expense of less valuable data.

Handy begins with the assumption that this "moment to moment" search for meaning can be operationally defined in relation to selective attention. At the level of information processing in the brain, selective attention can be measured in terms of what information should be attended to as well as the specific kinds of operations that are performed on that information. Competition arises within this system as to which information is going to be vigorously processed since we all possess a brain that has a limited capacity.[7] This limitation is not in reference to how much information can be learned and later recalled. Rather, it refers to the fact that our perceptual system is capable of overwhelming the processing mechanisms, with too much information being collected in a very brief period of time. The deciding factor as to what information is given priority is based upon that information's meaning.

Dr. Handy builds upon this knowledge of meaning-based selective attention to make the creative proposal that this phenomenon may have application to our search for meaning over longer time periods. In his words, "can one's belief about the deeper meaning of life influence how they pay attention to the world?" He concludes: "at issue are the most profound questions we as humans can ask. What is the purpose of life? What is the reason for corporeal existence? What happens to our being when the transition is made from life to death?" Dr. Handy hypothesizes that a search for meaning over very long timescales, as in a religious belief system, can be explored by examining the influence of one's belief system on selective attention as measured at short timescales. The very interesting question to be answered is whether a person's beliefs about the meaning of life can have consequences for information processing in the cortex. He asks, "For example, do people of Islamic faith attend to their world in the same way people of Christian or Jewish faith do? If not, how do they differ and how is this manifest in cortical processing?"

These are questions Dr. Handy believes can be approached by present neurobiological methods, studying event-related potentials with EEG and brain-imaging technologies such as fMRI which measure blood flow and oxygen consumption by the neurons of the brain.

The third winning essay in the Creative Ideas program which relates to consciousness research is authored by Curt Paulson of the Strategic Learning Institute and Michael Persinger of the Neuropsychology Department at Laurentian University.[8] These authors are trying to understand that part of consciousness that involves the sense of self and, beyond that, the religious experience of the "sensed presence." The latter, they say, has been documented for centuries in scriptural writings of Western religion "that stem from revelations and communications received by individuals from sources that have been reported throughout human history and within all cultures."

To explore the nature of these experiences, Paulson and Persinger have developed a new technology that enables them to artificially produce the "sensed presence" in normal individuals. The key is to apply weak yet complex magnetic fields around the brain. The magnetic field is generated by small solenoids that are clustered into a montage across the surface of the skull. These solenoids are activated by subtle changes in positive and negative voltages that are delivered and controlled by proprietary software and hardware components. They add that "the software of the computer also allows for different pairs of solenoids to be activated at a given time so that there occurs a spacial rotation of the field through brain space as well."

The typical experiment involves having the subject sit in a quiet room while blindfolded. The magnetic field is applied to the right hemisphere for twenty minutes to "affect the proportion of alpha and particularly theta activity over the temporal lobes." Then a "burst-firing" magnetic field is applied to both cerebral hemispheres for another twenty minutes. When this is applied, they report that many people feel "marked peacefulness" as if they have accessed the "allness or wholeness" of the universe. The "critical factor," the researchers say, "is that the applied fields must simulate the temporal and spacial complexity of those generated during specific states of consciousness."

Other essayists in the competition who considered consciousness provide further evidence of its complexity. Several essayists, using specialized computer techniques, suggest approaches to consciousness which treat the brain as a chaotic, self-organizing system. In some cases rat brain preparations and isolated individual rat neurons were proposed for study, based upon data for spontaneous organization of neural tissue.[9]

What seems to be suggested by these essays is that even the simplest and best-defined approaches for studying human consciousness still leave us with only the very beginning of an understanding of consciousness.

For example, Colvin's explanation for the "slow condition" in her experiments — where the subject is asked to delay the response to the visual stimulus by the smallest possible amount — is to postulate a unique neural activation representing the process of becoming consciously aware of the stimulus prior to the execution of the motor response. This activation, she says, "may reflect activation of one or more of a myriad of higher-level cortical systems mediating awareness and attention." Taking this together with her statement that "consciousness is an emergent behavioral state, one that follows a convergence of perceptions, memories and emotions," we are impressed with the daunting complexity of conscious awareness.

The essay by Todd Handy adds "fuel to the fire" as he elaborates on work with the study of selective attention. Most impressive is his proposal that meaning-based attention, which already implies a highly integrated process involving memory, emotion, and perception, may be a major factor in the long-term search for meaning as in a religious belief system.

Relating these neurobiological studies of consciousness to what we have learned about human evolution, with its evidence of a veritable explosion of artistry, toolmaking, ritual, and symbol at the advent of *Homo sapiens*, it seems very likely that in our very rapid evolution we are viewing the effects of a highly integrated and complex brain with consciousness as its primary driving force.

Consciousness would seem to be a primary example of emergence, a phenomenon in which a complex network gives rise to new and unique properties, whether seen in the evolution of hominids or in the integration of a myriad of neural elements in awareness and attention. I am tempted to agree with Philip Clayton that consciousness is of a different order than the physical aspects of the brain. David Chalmers has divided consciousness into two segments — problems which are easy, and may be defined neurobiologically, and hard problems which deal with how physical processes in the brain give rise to subjective experience.[10] The easy problems concern what he calls objective mechanisms of the cognitive system. The hard questions, which he believes are irreducible, include the inner aspect of thought and perception: the way things feel for the subject.

The phenomenon of consciousness would appear to us to pose a very large number of hard problems. Accordingly, its complexity suggests that it may remain a puzzle indefinitely, and so be part of that "purely spiritual soul" which Clayton believes will remain unexplained. In that case the analogy of the human soul in relation to our body and God's spiritual activity in relation to the world seems very apt and appropriate to a panentheistic model for God's action in the world.

In another more speculative view, the possibility that brain systems are organized in a nonlinear fashion and subject to spontaneous, creative activity might provide added support for the value of the brain-body analogy as a picture of God's creative activity in the universe.

Finally, I reiterate my wonder and amazement at the whole picture. As Keith Ward has said, "what is wrong with materialism is that it takes too low a view of matter."[11]

The "Trinitarian" World of Neo-Pantheism: On Panentheism and Epistemology

HAROLD J. MOROWITZ

Pantheism is the search for God and the understanding of the divine in the laws of nature and the stuff out of which the universe is made. In its Kantian form it identifies God with the *Ding an Sich,* the thing-in-itself, which Immanuel Kant regards as unknowable. The epistemology of science, which was influentially formalized by Kant in the *Critique of Pure Reason*[1] and later refined by Henry Margenau in *The Nature of Physical Reality,*[2] begins with the mind, both as the site of the a priori rules and as the processor of the a posteriori sensations. From the sensory and the cognitive are constructed the things of science (such as material objects, cells, atoms, electrons); it is the mind that is involved in the search for the *Ding an Sich.* When I first studied physics, the most fundamental objects were thought to be nuclei and electrons; now they are at the level of quarks and superstrings. The ongoing changes support Kant's assertion that we will never get to the *Ding an Sich.* Karl Popper's rules regarding verification and falsification are used to arrive at the currently accepted science,[3] which is always subject to revision by new experiments or changes in the operative paradigm.

Knowledge is thus constructed and organized in a hierarchical series from the sensory cognitive mind down to the "most fundamental" entities. To move down toward the most fundamental entities is the task of reductionism, which is not an ideology, as some maintain, but a methodology for explaining happenings at one hierarchical level in terms of happenings at lower hierarchical levels. In addition to reductionism, we have recently come to understand that science can also operate in the other direction: up through the hierarchies. This is known as emergence,[4] which occurs when the properties, rules, and agents at one level are generated from those at lower levels. A classical but very constrained example of emergence is statistical mechanics, where thermodynamics is generated from the rules of molecular mechanics. The constraint comes from the equilibrium point as the universal attractor.

In most cases the number of agents at any hierarchical level is large and the interaction rules are complicated and nonlinear, so that the number of possible computational solutions becomes unmanageable because of a combinatoric explosion of states. It requires pruning rules or selection rules if we are to arrive at humanly manageable emergent solutions.

When we focus on these problems of emergence, which we are just beginning to understand, it is clear that selection introduces something new into the loop — sensory data to theory to predicted data — which characterized the epistemology of the past and was formalized by Karl Popper. Emergence thus calls for a radical rethinking of epistemology.

The new speculative question is, Where do the pruning rules come from, and how are they validated? Given multiple sets of pruning rules which predict observations, how do we choose among them? The problem of the nature and status of pruning rules is a serious one for contemporary science. It is clear that they have a different status from the underlying laws of nature — laws that Spinoza associated with the immanence of the pantheistic God. Pruning rules may be laws of nature, but they are laws of a different kind.

I would like to introduce a metaphor here that may be theologically instructive. I propose that emergence is how scientists climb the hierarchical ladder from *Ding an Sich* (by which I mean the Unknown Source or Ground of order) to atomicity to life to mind. From atomicity to biota, we might say, is how the "word" becomes flesh. Emergence goes beyond immanence in the sense of Spinoza, for whom immanence was the "word" (or logos or all-determining law). Instead, rules of emergence associate more closely with what theologians call the Holy Spirit. I think both scientists and theologians have a great deal of work to do in understanding emergence and the epistemic nature of selection rules.

The concept of emergence, while rapidly changing, has been a part of biology for almost a century. The various biological selection principles have been lumped in the concept of "fitness," which prunes by death and extinction. The current-day discussion of emergence has come from computer modeling, where pruning algorithms are introduced to tame combinatoric explosion. Many of the biologists' concepts go back to C. Lloyd Morgan, whose 1923 book *Emergent Evolution* discussed various competing theories.[5] Emergence in almost every application implies a universe of levels or a hierarchy. It also recognizes novelty as a key feature of evolution. The mechanism of emergence was unspecified by Morgan and remains so. Some of the discussions about the locus of novelty in the biological world are still relevant. Possible causes of novelty are:

1. Frozen accidents
2. Rules of emergence
3. Biogenic laws
4. Design

Frozen accident and design lie outside of science, since we are unable to subject them to experiment. Biogenic laws, as proposed by Walter Elsasser,[6] and rules of emergence are subject to scientific study and should be vigorously pursued. An example of a rule of emergence at the level of physics is that all functions representing states of two electrons must be of the antisymmetric variety. This form of the Pauli exclusion principle prunes the possible behavior of systems of nuclei and electrons to generate the laws of chemistry. Thus chemistry emerges from physics. An example of a biogenic law is probably the universality of cellularity, which lies deep within coacervate chemistry and organic chemistry.

Pruning by design is a possible theological explanation. It implies a God who is not exhausted by the rules of immanence and who interacts from outside the system to form each new domain. Such an explanation is a form of the "God of the gaps." If this pruning by design has a volitional character, it lies outside the scope of science. It can be regarded as a form of panentheism.

The hierarchical climb from the *Ding an Sich* (the Unknown Source) to atoms to flesh then comes to the emergence of mind. The emergence of mind happens in many ways in animalia and may be studied using the tools of evolutionary psychology. Eventually it leads to the human mind, both individual and social. The study of the emergence of mind is clearly in its infancy.

At the point of the emergence of the mental, we encounter an epistemic loop: we start from mind; we construct part of the path (using reductionistic methods) from the mind back toward the *Ding an Sich;* and then we proceed in the reverse direction, step-by-step upward to the human mind, which we try to understand in terms of our own constructs. The move from the mind to the constructs is epistemic; the move from the *Ding an Sich* to the human mind, using the same constructs, is evolutionary psychology. The epistemic loop of science is therefore circular, moving from mind to mind. This may come as a surprise, but it has provided the philosophical background of science since Kant's *Critique of Pure Reason.*

The mind is the beginning and the end of scientific epistemology. It is the locus of verification and falsification, which permits us to formulate and revise our paradigmatic science. Since science is a social activity, it is the collective mind of the practitioners in each domain that establishes the paradigm. Contingent truth is established by vote — except everyone's vote is not equal, as anyone might suspect who knows the social system of the practitioners.

Mind is a real emergent novelty in the evolution of biota. Hints of it occur in the prokaryotes, for example in the directional migration of motile cells. Stronger hints occur in the predation, feeding, and protective activities of a variety of protists. In a series of books Donald Griffin explores the animal mind, its roots, and its evolutionary contributions to fitness.[7]

Mind is not a unique construct, but it takes different forms in different taxa. The evolution of the primates and the primate mind shows a number of unique features, which led at some point to the evolution of a mind that combines a priori concepts with a posteriori sensations in the manner described by Kant. With the emergence of human mind, the universe, at least locally, underwent a profound change in three senses. First, the epistemological loop was completed, and a portion of the universe was able to think about itself. Second, the volitional aspect of human thought meant an escape from the rigid determinism and the rules of emergence, thereby introducing a novel aspect into the world: transcendence arising from immanence. Third, I suggest, mind is a feature of the immanent, emergent God. This thought has resonated in the Western religions, which have spoken of humans as being in God's image, of prophets as the voice of the divine, of Jesus as the Son of God, and of Muhammad as the messenger of God.

Given this framework, we may now speculate that humanity is the transcendence of the immanent, emergent God. This postulation does not violate the purest pantheism, but nevertheless it is trinitarian in form. For according to this theory there are three origins: the origin of the universe, the origin of life, and the origin of mind. This consequence of emergence is genuinely novel (and genuinely heretical within the Abrahamic religions): humanity viewed as the transcendence of the emergent, immanent God.

Note that at each stage of emergence the features become more local. The origin of the universe presumably gave rise to laws that obtain everywhere and for all time. The origin of life encompasses all domains where life actually in fact emerges. Finally, the origin of mind — what we might call transcendence or the God within our minds — extends only to the domain of the noosphere; it may in fact encompass only our planet.

Ethics, morality, and religion have their home in the noosphere. Since the mind has volitional properties, some aspects of the local universe are under our influence. Prayer may be directed inward to our volitional selves, or public prayer may be directed to the public noosphere. We may stand in awe of the God of immanence; we may struggle to understand the mind of the God of emergence; and we may put our bodies on the line to fulfill the potential of the God of transcendence for the world of humans.

Science deals with public knowledge. By contrast, there is no epistemology to deal with individual experiences that are not available to all. Religion deals with such experiences when they are told to others, who then incorporate the stories and beliefs into the public domain. Recent science, which includes complexity and emergence, supports the reformulation of pantheism in the direction of panentheism. The God of immanence, transcendence, and emergence is vastly different from the traditional Father, Son, and Holy Spirit; yet there is enough connection between them, metaphorically at least, to let the dialogue go on.

A theology centered on epistemology like this one is of necessity anthropic. It has to be. The only world we know, we participate in constructing. It may seem brazen to some to identify the noosphere with divine transcendence, but I find that it induces humility. It is our unending task to create a better local universe, and we have a long, long way to go.

In viewing the ideas outlined above in relation to the other contributions in this volume, I perceive a major difference. My coauthors start with a series of diverse scriptural views and proceed to examine a number of philosophical, theological, and scientific arguments. They operate under the constraint of returning to the scriptural "truth," which is different for each tradition. In the world of the three Abrahamic religions, the scriptures are the Hebrew Scriptures, the New Testament, and the Qur'an. For adherents, each scripture has a truth outside of epistemological and standard historical investigation. Each religion posits a God who is beyond understanding and who interacts with human beings and societies in ways revealed in the scriptures. The requirement of returning to scripture demands a panentheism rather than pantheism, for the God of philosophy must be supplemented by the personal anthropomorphic God of scripture.

The philosophical view that I have defended can be described as trinitarian, since it consists of the three moments of immanence, emergence, and transcendence. This "trinity" maps onto the trinity of the origin of the universe, the origin of life, and the origin of mind. If one requires a scriptural deity in addition, the panentheistic view becomes quarternarian. The God of scripture must be accepted on the basis of faith and uncertain reports of historical events. This is, as noted, a philosophical constraint on the Abrahamic religions.

Can we have a religion outside of the historical traditions? If one is to be developed, I believe we must interpret the Creator as being that feature of existence that is needed if human existence is to have meaning. This *"Gott an Sich"* which I postulate is unknowable in the same sense as the *Ding an Sich* is unknowable. We can certainly stand in awe of the immanent God who made the anthropic principle possible. Likewise, we can adore the God of emergence who provided the route from the laws of immanence ("the Word") to flesh (living matter in the most general sense). We have not yet reduced emergence to science, although modern science is in the process of attempting to do so. The evolution of the mind is the least understood part of the theology I have discussed. This evolution does, however, embody transcendence: the ability to manipulate the world for the benefit or detriment of humankind. But transcendence shows no evidence of going beyond the human mind, as would be demanded by most forms of panentheism. Transcendence is the divine in us. To choose good, not evil, is our responsibility.

The religion I have explored promises us nothing beyond our days. It generates an ethics that demands much of us: to do good, to love mercy, and to walk humbly with our fellow humans, who are also expressions of the divine transcendence. It resonates with the ethics of the Abrahamic religions, and yet it does not demand belief beyond what we can ascertain by our investigations.

Articulating God's Presence in and to the World Unveiled by the Sciences

ARTHUR PEACOCKE

> The WORLD is unknown, till the Value and Glory of it is seen;
> till the Beauty and the Serviceableness of its parts is considered.[1]

Thomas Traherne's deeply sacramental — and, eventually we shall have to say, "panentheistic" — vision of the world, especially as expressed in the golden prose of his *Centuries*, from which the above epigraph was taken, was historically coincident in England with the quite differently motivated insights of his great contemporary Isaac Newton. Traherne died in 1674, some thirteen years before the publication of the *Principia* gave a defining impetus to the scientific revolution in its modern form, bringing with it the widespread recognition of the universe as lawfully embedding rational principles discoverable by experiment. The implications of Newton's scheme led his contemporaries, notably Robert Boyle, to envisage the universe in terms of a mechanistic clockwork, and his successors in the eighteenth century to an excessively transcendent perception of God as creating the world, as it were, "outside" of the divine life — in spite of an ancient immanentist strand in Christian theology. Inevitably "creation" came to be seen by many as an event in which God brought into existence (in time) an autonomous world, which was then free to run according to its divinely endowed laws, so that God tended to become the redundant clockmaker, or absentee landlord, of Deism.

Many developments in science itself have led to a radical transformation of that mechanical picture of the natural world; these in turn have led to a profound reconsideration by Christian theists (and others) of how, in the light of the sciences, to conceive of God's relation to the world as it is now perceived to be and to be becoming.

137

To discern the direction that must be taken in this new exploration of God's relation to the world, it is necessary briefly to recount the relevant features of the scientific perspectives.

The World of Science

A Synchronic Scientific Perspective

First, the world as it is, in a kind of "still shot." The underlying unity of the natural world is evidenced in its universal embedded rationality, which the sciences assume and continue to verify. In the realm of the very small and of the very large — the subatomic and the cosmic — the extraordinary applicability of mathematics in elucidating the entities, structures, and processes of the world continues to reinforce that it is indeed one world. On the one hand, the early-twentieth-century unification of space-time-matter-energy within one mathematical framework by Einstein anticipated current attempts to unify also the four fundamental forces operating in the world. On the other hand, the diversity of this world is apparent not only in the purely physical — molecules, the earth's surface, the immensely variegated systems of the astronomical heavens — but even more strikingly in the biological world. New species continue to be discovered in spite of the destruction caused by human action.

This diversity has been rendered more intelligible in recent years by an increased awareness of the principles involved in the formation and constitution of complex systems. There is even a corresponding "science of complexity" concerned with theories about them. The natural (and human) sciences more and more give us a picture of the world as consisting of complex hierarchies — a series of levels of organization of matter in which each successive member is a whole constituted of parts preceding it in the series. The wholes are organized systems of parts that are dynamically and spatially interrelated. This feature of the world is now widely recognized to be significant in relating our knowledge of its various levels of complexity — that is, the sciences that correspond to the different levels.

The concepts needed to describe and understand — and also the methods needed to investigate — each level in the hierarchy of complexity are specific to what is distinctive about it. Sociological, psychological, and biological concepts are characteristic of their own levels and quite different from those of physics and chemistry. It is very often the case (but not always) that the properties, concepts, and explanations used to describe the higher-level wholes are not logically reducible to those used to describe their constituent parts. Thus sociological concepts are often not logically reducible to, that is, translatable into, those of individual psychology (e.g., the difference between communities of more than three, three, and two); psychological concepts are not reducible to those of the neurosciences; biological concepts to those of biochemistry; etc. Such nonreductionist assertions are about the status of a particular kind of knowledge (they are "epistemological"), and are usually strongly defended by the practitioners of the science concerning the higher level of complexity. When the nonreducibility of properties, concepts, and explanations applicable to higher levels of complexity is well established, their employment in scientific discourse can often, but not in all cases, lead to a putative, and then to an increasingly confident, attribution of a distinctive causal efficacy to the complex wholes that does not apply to the separated, constituent parts. It has often been argued that for something to be real, new, and irreducible it must have new, irreducible causal powers. If this continues to be the case for a complex under a variety of independent procedures and in a variety of contexts, then new and distinctive kinds of realities at the higher levels of complexity may properly be said to have "emerged." This can occur with respect either to moving up the ladder of complexity or, as we shall see, through cosmic and biological evolutionary history. This understanding accords with the pragmatic attribution, in both ordinary life and scientific investigation, of the term "reality" to that which we cannot avoid taking account of in our diagnosis of the course of events, in experience or experiments. Real entities have effects and play irreducible roles in adequate explanations of the world.

All entities, all concrete particulars in the world, including human beings, are constituted of fundamental physical entities — quarks or whatever current physics postulates as the basic building constituents of the world (which, of course, includes energy as well as matter). This is a "monistic" view that everything can be broken down into fundamental physical entities and that no *extra* entities are thought to be inserted at higher levels of complexity to account for their properties. I prefer to call this view "emergentist monism" rather than "nonreductive physicalism." In addition to the incoherence in the latter view (notably pointed out by J. Kim),[2] those who adopt it, particularly in speaking of the "physical realization" of the mental in the physical, often seem to me to hold a much less realistic view of the higher-level properties than I wish to affirm here — and also not to attribute causal powers to that to which the higher-level concepts refer.

If we do make such a commitment about the reality of the emergent whole of a given total system, the question then arises of how one is to explicate the relation between the state of the whole and the behavior of parts of that system at the micro level. The simple concept of chains of causally related events (A → B → C . . .) in constant conjunction is inadequate for this purpose. Extending and enriching the notion of causality now becomes necessary because of new insights into the way complex systems in general, and biological ones in particular, behave.

It has become increasingly clear that one can preserve the reality, distinctiveness, and causal powers of higher levels relative to lower ones while continuing to recognize that the higher complexes are complex assemblies of the fundamental building blocks currently being discovered by physicists. No new entities are being *added* to the constituent parts for such parts to acquire the new distinctive properties characteristic of the wholes. For example, in the early twentieth century it was proposed that something had to be added to matter to explain the difference between living organisms and the inorganic. Such "vitalism" is now universally rejected by biologists. Even more significantly with respect to human beings, one can affirm the distinctiveness of the language of the "mental" as not, in principle, reducible to that of neurophysiological without asserting the existence of an entity, the "mind," in a realm other than the physical world.

The new challenge then becomes how what we have regarded as physical entities can in the human-brain-in-the-human-body-in-society be so organized to become a thinking self-conscious person. Persons are better regarded, it transpires, as psychosomatic unities with physical, mental, and spiritual capacities — rather than physical entities to which a "mind" and/or a "soul/spirit" has been added. This is in fact the biblical understanding, as H. Wheeler Robinson expressed in a famous epigram: "The Hebrew idea of personality is an animated body and not an incarnated soul."[3] Talk about the "soul" or "spirit" of human beings as entities, and especially as naturally immortal ones, no longer represents the best explanation of the emergence of spiritual capacities in the light of what we now know about the kind of complexity that constitutes a human being. Dualism of that kind seems to be incommensurate with any picture of the world consistent with scientific observations. This does not, of course, undermine the reality and validity of mental and spiritual activities and capacities. Those Christians who have affirmed not the natural immortality of the "soul/spirit" but the biblical doctrine of resurrection of the whole person can welcome this development.

A Diachronic Scientific Perspective: The "Epic of Evolution"

The foregoing describes only one way of perceiving the natural world through the sciences. For since the time of Newton and his eighteenth-century Deist successors, our whole perspective on the world has been transformed through studies in geology, biology, and cosmology — indeed, in all those sciences which may be dubbed "historical" insofar as they are inevitably concerned with the processes that have been occurring in the past throughout the universe, on the surface of the earth, and in its living organisms. By inferring to the best explanation of the succession of states of these systems from the relevant data, we are now possessed with a remarkably coherent picture of the origin and development to the present state of the universe, of planet earth, and of life on the earth. This account is a naturalistic, intelligible, and well-evidenced story of the development over the last 12 billion years or so of the observable universe from a primal concentration of mass-energy expanding with space in time to the present observable universe, including earth. This story joins up with the contemporary epic of evolution which describes how inorganic matter on the earth has acquired the property of self-copying particular patterns in complex structures — and so to be living — and through the processes of natural selection, perhaps supported by some other natural factors facilitating complexification, has generated the multiple diverse forms of past and present living creatures on the earth, including *Homo sapiens.* The general sweep of the story is too well known to need repeating here. But certain features must be stressed, for these were quite unknown until a century and a half ago — or were at the most but dimly intuited — by those who developed classical Christian (and indeed, Muslim and Jewish) theism in relation to the world as it was then understood.

The nexus of causality is unbroken and now requires no *deus ex machina,* no "God of the gaps," to explain inter alia the cosmic development, the formation of planet earth, the transition from inorganic to living matter, the origin of species, and the development of complex brains that have the capacity to be aware. Much remains unknown and obscure, but the sequences are supported increasingly by hard science and new observations that become available as technology enhances the subtlety and power of scientific instrumentation. The picture is one of all-pervasive, incessant change. Although the second law of thermodynamics entails an inexorable overall increase in entropy (and so of randomness and disorder) in the universe as a whole, it is now understood, in terms of both irreversible thermodynamics and stochastic kinetics, how new complex structures can arise even within homogeneous physicochemical systems, especially when they involve a flux of matter and/or energy. In fact, studies of complex systems of many kinds (e.g., sets of lightbulbs, cell formation in liquids, snow crystal growth, gene complexes, immune systems, neural nets, conglomerations of economic centers) show that when certain rules apply to the relationships prevailing between their constituent units, and when there are fluxes of matter/energy, they can self-organize into surprisingly few and recurring patterns.[4] Indeed, it is proposed that such factors are involved in the appearance of more complex living organisms.[5] Through the operation of natural selection favoring those developments which increase descendants' chances of survival, biological evolution evidences a propensity[6] toward an increase in complexity, information processing and storage, consciousness, sensitivity to pain, and perhaps even self-consciousness, which is a prerequisite for human social development and the cultural transmission of knowledge down the generations. Moreover, the operation of random factors (e.g., mutations in DNA) within the constraints of some wider lawlike system (e.g., the environment exerting a selection effect) is not at all inconsistent with the whole process manifesting purposes, such as those of a creator God.[7] Yet it is significant for how we understand God as creator to note that this process of "things making themselves" is a purely naturalistic one, built into the very nature of the systems and of their constituents. As T. W. Deacon recently expressed it, "in an evolutionary emergent account of natural 'design,' the creative dynamic is understood to be *immanent* in the world rather than external to it, and this can be extended to subjective issues as well."[8]

The processes of the world by their inherent properties manifest a spontaneous creativity in which new properties emerge. One can even agree with Deacon when he also asserts that

> The subjective experience of being a locus of incessant novel self-organised mental activities is consistent with evolution-like emergence of spontaneously ordered neural activity. . . . Emergent phenomena, including subjective states and relationships, are not contingent in form because they are highly constrained by this self-organising holistic dynamic that gives rise to emergence. So, although emergent subjective states and relationships may in some sense be contingent products of the material world, this does not entail that their realised forms are either arbitrary or merely relative.[9]

It is this situation that any understanding of the creativity of God, the giver of existence to all-that-is and all-that-is-becoming, must now take into account — not reluctantly but as a new illumination of the divine activity. It is but a further elaboration and development of the "emergentist monism" which was required in our "synchronic" consideration of the relations within the hierarchies of complexity in the world as it now *is* — and, we now have to add, as it is *becoming*.

These new scientifically originating perspectives on the world, including humanity, and on its processes in time urgently press upon us the need for theological reconstruction.

Theological Reconstruction

Clearly the deistic conception of a God external to nature — dwelling in an entirely different kind of space and being of a "substance" sufficiently different that it could not be involved continuously in the created order — does not cohere with these new insights into the world and its processes. As an Anglican theologian expressed it, as long ago as the 1880s, "Darwinism appeared and, under the disguise of a foe, did the work of a friend. . . . Either God is everywhere present in nature, or He is nowhere."[10] Both a later archbishop of Canterbury, Frederick Temple, and Charles Kingsley in *The Water Babies* (1863) could express the idea that "God makes things make themselves."[11] Recent concepts of self-organization would indeed have been welcomed by these authors, but unfortunately their insights, although appropriated by many theologians (in Britain, at least) in the earlier part of the twentieth century, were overshadowed by the influence of Barthian neoorthodoxy, with its repudiation of "natural theology" in the midcentury. Today the impact of the perspectives of the sciences impels us to develop further those earlier insights prompted by theological reflection on "Darwinism." The following gives an account of those themes which are becoming prominent and pressing for reconsideration.

Immanence: A Theistic Naturalism

God must now be seen as creating in the world, often through what science calls "chance" operating within the created order, each stage of which constitutes the launching pad for the next. The Creator is unfolding the created potentialities of the universe through a process in which its possibilities and propensities become actualized. God may be said to have "gifted" the universe, and goes on doing so, with a "formational economy" that "is sufficiently robust to make possible the actualization of all inanimate structures and all life forms that have ever appeared in the course of time."[12]

We have to emphasize anew the immanence of God as creator "in, with, and under" the natural processes of the world unveiled by the sciences in accord with all that the sciences have revealed since those debates in the nineteenth century. At no point do modern natural scientists have to invoke any nonnatural causes to explain their observations and inferences about the past. The processes constitute a seamless web of interconnectedness and display emergence, for new forms of matter and a hierarchy of organization of these forms appear in the course of time. New kinds of realities emerge successively, each with its own specific environment, with its specific boundary conditions, and with specific adjacent possibilities open to it in its specific situation.

Hence there is inexorably impressed upon us a dynamic picture of the world of entities, structures, and processes involved in continuous and incessant change and in process without ceasing. This picture impels us to reintroduce a dynamic element into our understanding of God's creative relation to the world — an element which was always implicit in the Hebrew conception of a "living God," dynamic in action, but often obscured by the tendency to think of "creation" as an event in the past. God has again to be imagined as continuously creating, continuously giving existence to what is new. God is creating at every moment of the world's existence through perpetually giving creativity to the very stuff of the world.

All of this reinforces the need to reaffirm more urgently than at any other time in Christian (and Jewish and Islamic) history that, in a very strong sense, God is the immanent creator creating through the processes of the natural order. The processes are not themselves God, but the *action*[13] of God as creator. God gives existence in divinely created time to a process that itself brings forth the new — thereby God is creat*ing*. This means we do not have to look for any alleged extra gaps in which, or mechanisms whereby, God might be supposed to be acting as creator in the living world.

A musical analogy may help: when we are listening to a musical work, say, a Beethoven piano sonata, there are times when we are so deeply absorbed in it that for the moment we are thinking Beethoven's musical thoughts with him. Yet if anyone were to ask at that moment (unseemly interrupting our concentration!), "Where is Beethoven now?" we could only reply that Beethoven-as-composer is to be found only in the music itself. Beethoven-as-composer was or is — for this could have been said even when he was alive — other than the music (he "transcends" it), but his communication with us is entirely subsumed in and represented by the music itself: he is immanent in it and we need not look elsewhere to meet him in that creating role. The processes revealed by the sciences are in themselves God acting as creator, and God is not to be found as some kind of *additional* influence or factor added on to the processes of the world God is creating. This perspective can properly be called "theistic naturalism" and is not Deism redivivus, for it conceives of God as *actively* and (in the light of an analogy developed below) *personally* creating through the processes of the world.

Panentheism

The scientific picture of the world has pointed to a perspective on God's relation to all natural events, entities, structures, and processes in which they are continuously being given existence by God, who thereby expresses in and through them God's own inherent rationality. In principle this should raise no new problems for classical Western theism, which has maintained the ontological distinction between God and the created world. However, classical theism also conceived of God as a necessary "substance" with attributes and posited a space "outside" God in which the realm of the created was located — for one entity cannot exist in another and retain its own (ontological) identity when they are regarded as substances. Hence, if God is also so regarded, God can only exert influence "from outside" on events in the world. Such intervention, for that is what it would be, raises acute problems in the light of our contemporary scientific perception of the causal nexus of the world being a closed one. Because of such considerations, this substantival way of speaking has become inadequate in the view of many thinkers. It has become increasingly difficult to express the way in which God is present to the world in terms of "substances," which by definition cannot be internally present to each other. This inadequacy of Western classical theism is aggravated by the evolutionary perspective which, as we have just seen, requires that natural processes in the world be regarded *as such* as God's creative action.

We therefore need a new model for expressing the closeness of God's presence to finite, natural events, entities, structures, and processes; and we need the divine to be as close to them as it is possible to imagine, without dissolving the distinction between Creator and what is created. It is therefore not surprising that many contemporary theologians,[14] especially those with a scientific background, have resorted to the idea of "pan*en*theism": "The belief that the Being of God includes and penetrates the whole universe, so that every part of it exists in Him, but (as against Pantheism) that His Being is more than, and is not exhausted by, the universe."[15] One recalls the description of God in the speech at Athens attributed to Saint Paul, who is depicted as quoting a Greek poet to the effect that it may be said of God: "in him we live, and move, and have our being."[16] Since God cannot in principle have any spatial attributes, the "in" (Gk. *en*) expresses an intimacy of relation and is clearly not meant in any locative sense, with the world being conceived as a "part of God." It refers, rather, to an ontological relation so that the world is conceived as within the Being of God but, nevertheless, with its own distinct ontology. It is as if the world has a mode of being created by, but distinct from, God. Jürgen Moltmann, drawing on the kabbalistic notion of *zimsum* (meaning a "withdrawing into oneself"), has argued that this creative act of God involves a self-limitation by Godself.[17] In order to create a world other than Godself and in that sense "outside,"

> God must have made room beforehand for a finitude *in himself*. It is only a withdrawal by God into himself that can free space into which God can act creatively. (p. 86, italics added)

> God does not create merely by calling something into existence, or by setting something afoot. In a more profound sense he [God] "creates" by letting-be, by making room, and by withdrawing himself. (p. 88)

> But if creation *ad extra* takes place in the space freed by God himself, then in this case the reality outside God still remains *in* the God who has yielded up that "outwards" in himself. Without the difference between creator and creation, creation cannot be conceived of at all; but this difference is embraced and comprehended by the greater truth . . . : the truth that God is all in all. (pp. 88-89)

In these quotations in defense of panentheism, Moltmann is clearly using "space" in an ontological sense — as in that vision of Saint Augustine of "the whole creation" as if it were "some sponge, huge but bounded . . . filled with that unmeasurable sea" of God, "environing and penetrating it through every way infinite . . . everywhere and on every side."[18]

The language of Moltmann and the striking image of Saint Augustine both use the "in" (the *en* of "pan*en*theism") to express the idea of the world, including humanity, as enveloped by God without it losing its true distinctiveness and as a way of intensifying the traditional belief in God's immanence in the world. It is this kind of panentheism, emphasizing the coinherent presence of God and the world, which I wish to espouse here — rather than one that allows any kind of identity of the world with God, even in the form of the "world as a part of God." The latter too easily merges into pantheism and weakens the necessary emphasis on God's ultimate transcendence of all-that-is (the "more than" in that definition of panentheism quoted earlier). The "in" metaphor has advantages in this context over the "separate but present to" terminology of divine immanence in Western classical theism. For God is best conceived of as the circumambient reality enclosing all existing entities, structures, and processes, and as operating in and through all, while being "more" than all. Hence, all that is not God has its existence within God's operation and Being. The infinity of God includes all other finite entities, structures, and processes; God's infinity comprehends and incorporates all.

The pan*en*theistic model as propounded here is intended to be consistent with the monist concept that all concrete particulars in the world system are composed only of basic physical entities, and with the conviction that the world system is causally closed. There are no dualistic, no vitalistic, no supernatural levels through which God might be supposed to be exercising *special* divine activity. In this model the proposed kinds of interactions of God with the world system would not be from "outside" but from "inside" it. That's why the world system is regarded as being "in God."

These panentheistic interrelations of God with the world system, including humanity, I have attempted to represent in the figure on page 148. This is a kind of Venn diagram representing ontological (including logical) relationships; the infinity sign represents not infinite space or time but the infinitely "more" of God's Being in comparison with everything else. The diagram has the limitation of being in two planes so that the "God" label appears dualistically to be (ontologically) outside the world; although this conveys the truth that God is "more and other" than the world, it cannot represent God's omnipresence in and to the world. Arrows have been placed within this circle to signal God's immanent influence and activity *within* the world. It may also be noted that "God" is denoted by the (imagined) infinite planar surface of the page *on* which the circle representing the world is printed. For, it is assumed, God is "more than" the world, which is nevertheless "in" God. The page underlies and supports the circle and its contents, just as God sustains everything in existence and is present to all. So the larger dashed circle, representing the ontological location of God's interaction with all-that-is, really needs a many-dimensional convoluted surface not available on a two-dimensional surface — something like Saint Augustine's sponge? — though we continue to recognize the limitation of this inevitably locative model, as of all others.

In this model there is no "place outside" the infinite God in which what is created could exist. God creates all-that-is *within* Godself. This can be developed into a more fruitful biological model based on mammalian, and so human, procreation. The classical Western concept of God as creator has placed too much stress on the externality of the process — God is regarded as creating in the way the male fertilizes the female from outside. But mammalian females nurture new life within themselves, and this provides a much-needed corrective to the purely masculine image of divine creation. God, according to panentheism, creates a world other than Godself and "within herself" (we find ourselves offering this as the most appropriate image — yet another reminder of the need to escape from the limitations of male-dominated language about God).

A further pointer to the cogency of a panentheistic interpretation of

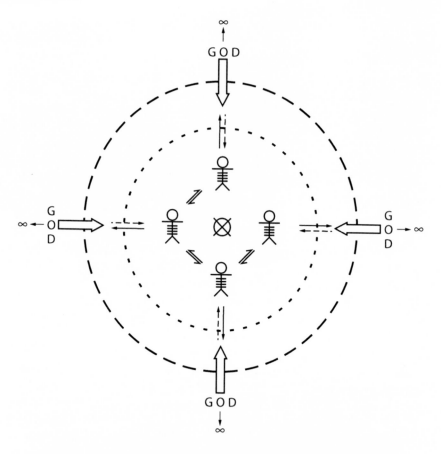

Diagram representing spatially the ontological relation of, and the interactions between, God and the world (including humanity).
— *Paths from Science towards God: The End of All Our Exploring*
Arthur Peacocke

God's relation to the world is the way the different sciences relate to each other and to the world they study — the hierarchy of sciences from particle physics to ecology and sociology. The more complex is constituted of the less complex, and all interact and interrelate in systems of systems. It is to this world discovered by the sciences that we have to think of God as relating. The "external" God of classical Western theism can be modeled only as acting upon such a world by intervening separately at the various discrete levels. But if God incorporates both the individual systems and the total system of systems within Godself, as in the panentheistic model, then it is more conceiv-

Key

GOD   God, represented by the whole surface of the page, imagined to extend to infinity (∞) in all directions

the world, all-that-is: created and other than God, and including both humanity and systems of nonhuman entities, structures, and processes

the human world: excluding systems of nonhuman entities, structures, and processes

God's interaction with and influence on the world and its events

a similar arrow to the preceding one but perpendicular to the page: God's influence and activity within the world

effects of the nonhuman world on humanity

human agency in the nonhuman world

personal interactions, both individual and social, between human beings, including cultural and historical influences

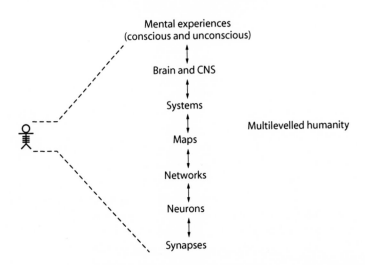

Mental experiences
(conscious and unconscious)
↑
Brain and CNS
↑
Systems
↑
Maps   Multilevelled humanity
↑
Networks
↑
Neurons
↑
Synapses

Apart from the top one, these are the levels of organization of the human nervous system depicted in Patricia S. Churchland and T. J. Sejnowski, "Perspectives on Cognitive Neuroscience," *Science* 242 (1988): 741-45.

able that God could interact with all the complex systems at their own holistic levels. God is present to the wholes as well as to the parts.

At the terminus of one of the branching lines of natural hierarchies of complexity stands the human person — the complex of the human-brain-in-the-human-body-in-society. Persons can have intentions and purposes that can be implemented by particular bodily actions. Indeed, the action of the body as a whole in its multiple levels just *is* the intended action of the person. The physical action is describable, at the bodily level, in terms of the appropriate physiology, anatomy, etc., but it also expresses the intentions and purposes of the person's thinking. The physical and the mental are two levels of the same holistic psychosomatic event.

Personal agency has been used both traditionally in the biblical literature and in contemporary theology as a model for God's action in the world. "We" as thinking, conscious persons appear to transcend our bodies while nevertheless remaining immanent in their actions. This psychosomatic, unified understanding of human personhood partly illuminates the use of a panentheistic model for God's relation to the world. For, according to the model, God is *internally* present to all the world's entities, structures, and processes in a way analogous to the way we as persons are present and act in our bodies. This model, in the light of current concepts of the person as a psychosomatic unity, is then an apt way of modeling God's personal agency in the world as in some sense "personal."

As with all analogies, models, and metaphors, qualifications are needed before we too hastily draw a parallel between God's relation to the world and our relation as persons to our bodies. The *first* is that God who, it is being suggested, relates to the world like a personal agent, is also the one who creates it, gives it existence, and infinitely transcends it. Indeed, the panentheistic model emphasizes this in its "more than the world" concept. However, our capacity for intentional (and other) thinking is a natural emergent within the world of brains-in-bodies, and *we* do not create our own bodies.

The *second* qualification of the model is that, as human persons, we are not conscious of most of what goes on in our bodies' autonomous functions such as breathing, digestion, and heart beating. Yet other events in our bodies are conscious and deliberate. So we distinguish between these functions, but this can scarcely apply to an omniscient God's relation to the world — God knows all that it is logically possible to know, hence God's knowledge of the world would include all patterns of events in it, namely: (1) those, relevant to the panentheistic analogy developed here, which are analogous to autonomic functions in human bodies and which constitute God's general providence in continually and actively giving existence to the world's entities, structures, and processes; and (2) those patterns of events in human bodies that implement particular intentions and may therefore be held to be analogous to any implementation of any particular divine intentions. The separate discussion of how (2) could occur continues intensively,[19] and without any general consensus, but note that both kinds of patterns of events would be observed as natural, meaning here consistent with the scientific accounts. The *third* qualification of the model is that in using human personal agency as analogous to the way God interacts with the world, we are not implying the "world is God's body" nor that God is "a person" — rather that God is more coherently thought of as "at least personal," indeed as "more than personal" (again the "more than" of panentheism). Perhaps we could even say that God is "suprapersonal" or "transpersonal," for there are many essential aspects of God's nature which cannot be subsumed under the categories applicable to human persons.

In my view the panentheistic model allows one to combine a strengthened emphasis on the immanence of God in the world with God's ultimate transcendence over it. It does so in a way that makes the analogy of personal agency both more pertinent and less vulnerable than the Western externalist model to the above distortions of any model of the world as God's body.

The fact of natural (as distinct from human, moral) evil continues to challenge belief in a benevolent God. In the classical perception of God as transcendent and as existing in a space distinct from that of the world, there is an implied detachment from the world in its suffering. This renders the problem of evil particularly acute. For God can do anything about evil only by an intervention from outside, which provokes the classical dilemma of either God can and will not, or he would but cannot: God is either not good or not omnipotent. The God of classical theism witnesses, but is not involved in, the sufferings of the world — even when closely "present to" and "alongside" them.

Hence, when faced with this ubiquity of pain, suffering, and death in the evolution of the living world, one is impelled to infer that God, to be anything like the God who is love in Christian belief, must be understood to be suffering in the creative processes of the world. Creation is costly *to God.* Now, when the natural world, with all its suffering, is panentheistically conceived of as "in God," it follows that the evils of pain, suffering, and death in the world are internal to God's own self: God must have experience of the natural. This intimate and actual experience of God must also include all those events that constitute the evil intentions of human beings and their implementation — that is, the moral evil of human society.

The panentheistic model of God's relation to the world is therefore much more capable of recognizing this fundamental aspect of God's experience of the world. Moreover, the panentheistic feminine image of the world, as being given existence by God in the very "womb of God," is a particularly apt one for evoking an insight into the suffering of God in the very processes of creation. God is creating the world from within, and the world being "in" God, God experiences its sufferings directly as God's own and not from the outside.

In a more specifically Christian perception, God in taking the suffering into God's own self can thereby transform it into what is whole and healthy — that is, be the means of "salvation" when this is given its root etymological meaning. God heals and transforms from within, as a healthy body might be regarded as doing. The redemption and transformation of human beings by God through suffering is, in this perspective, a general manifestation of what is, for Christians, explicitly manifest in the life, death, and resurrection of Jesus the Christ. In brief, this redemptive and transforming action of God is more congruent with the panentheistic model than with the Western classical externalist interpretation of God's relation to the world.

Theological Resources for Imaging a Theistic Naturalism and Panentheism

In the foregoing I have been referring to this classical kind of theism as "Western" because it has been dominant in Western Christianity (Roman Catholic, Anglican, Protestant), with some notable exceptions, such as Hildegard of Bingen. But it is the Eastern Christian tradition that is most explicitly panentheistic in holding together God's transcendence and immanence.[20] For example, Gregory Palamas (ca. 1296-1359) made a distinction-in-unity between God's essence and God's uncreated energies in the world, and Maximus the Confessor (ca. 580-662) regarded the Creator-Logos as characteristically present in each created thing as God's intention for it — its inner essence *(logoi)* which makes it distinctively itself and draws it toward God.

I confine myself to mentioning some other threads in the Christian inheritance (East and West) pertinent to articulating God's presence in the world as expressed in the more abstract concepts of theistic naturalism and panentheism.

The Wisdom (Sophia) and the Word (Logos) of God

Biblical scholars have in recent decades come to emphasize the significance of the central themes of the so-called Wisdom literature (Job, Proverbs, Ecclesiastes, Ecclesiasticus, and Wisdom). In this broad corpus of writings, the feminine figure of Wisdom *(Sophia),* according to J. G. Dunn, is a "convenient way of speaking about God acting in creation, revelation, and salvation: Wisdom never becomes more than a personification of God's activity."[21] This Wisdom endows some human beings, at least, with a personal wisdom that is rooted in their concrete experiences and in their systematic and ordinary observations of the natural world — what we would call science. But it is not confined to this and represents the distillation of wider human, ethical, and social experiences and even cosmological ones, since knowledge of the heavens figured in the capabilities of the sage. The natural order is valued as a gift and source of wonder, something to be celebrated. All such wisdom, imprinted as a pattern on the natural world and in the mind of the sage, is but a pale image of the divine Wisdom — that activity distinctive of God's relation to the world.

That wisdom is an attribute of God, personified as female, has been of especial significance to feminist theologians, amongst whom Celia Deane-Drummond has argued, on the basis of a wider range of biblical sources, that the feminine in God refers to all persons of the Christian triune God and Wisdom *(Sophia)* becomes "the feminine face of God."[22] In the present context, it is pertinent that this important concept of Wisdom *(Sophia)* unites intimately the divine activity of creation, human experience, and the processes of the natural world. It therefore constitutes a biblical resource for imaging the panentheism we have been urging.

So also does the closely related concept of the Word *(Logos)* of God, which is regarded as existing eternally as a mode of God's own being, as active in creation, and as a self-expression of God's own being and becoming imprinted in the very warp and woof of the created order.[23] It seems to be a conflation of the largely Hebraic concept of the "Word of the Lord," as the will of God in creative activity, with the divine logos of Stoic thought. This latter is the principle of rationality as manifest both in the cosmos and in human reason (also named by the Stoics as logos). Again we have a panentheistic notion that unites, intimately, as three facets of one integrated and interlocked activity, the divine, the human, and the (nonhuman) natural. Needless to say, it is significant that for Christians this Logos was regarded as "made flesh"[24] in the person of Jesus the Christ.

A Sacramental Universe

The evolutionary perspective recounts in its sweep and continuity over aeons of time how the mental and spiritual potentialities of matter have been actualized above all in the evolved complex of the human-brain-in-the-human-body. The original fluctuating quantum field, quark soup or whatever, has in twelve or so billion years become a Mozart, a Shakespeare, a Buddha, a Jesus of Nazareth — and you and me!

Every advance of the biological, cognitive, and psychological sciences shows human beings as naturally evolved psychosomatic unities — emergent as persons. Matter has naturally manifest personal qualities — that unique combination of physical, mental, and spiritual capacities. (I use "spiritual" as meaning "relating to God in a personal way.") For the panentheist, who sees God working in, with, and under natural processes, this unique result (to date) of the evolutionary process corroborates that God is using that process as an instrument of God's purposes and as a symbol of the divine nature, that is, as the means of conveying insight into these purposes.

But in the Christian tradition, this is precisely what its sacraments do. They are valued for what God is effecting instrumentally and for what God is conveying symbolically through them. Thus William Temple came to speak of the "sacramental universe,"[25] and we can come to see nature as sacrament, or at least as sacramental. Hence my continued need to apply the phrase "in, with, and under," with which Luther referred to the mode of the Real Presence in the Eucharist, to the presence of God in the processes of the world.

Conclusion

With such reflections we begin to touch the hem of the finely spun robe of the Christian claim that the self-expressive, creative Word *(Logos)* that was and is God-in-the-world was incarnate in a historical person, Jesus of Nazareth. The panentheistic framework, upon which I have concentrated as encapsulating my other themes and resources, is very congruent with the affirmation that God-as-Word could be expressed in a human being evolved within the world. For panentheism implies a much tighter coupling between the transcendent God and the created order than in classical theism. The incarnation can thus be more explicitly and overtly understood as the God *in whom the world already exists* becoming manifest in the trajectory of a human being who is naturally in and of that world. In that person the world now becomes transparent, as it were, to the God in whom it exists: the Word which was before incognito, implicit, and hidden now becomes known, explicit, and revealed. The epic of evolution has reached its apogee and consummation in God-in-a-human-person. Indeed, the preceding could be regarded as a footnote to and paraphrase of the Johannine prologue — "In the beginning was the Word, and the Word was with God, and the Word was God. . . . All things came into being through him. . . . What has come into being *in him* was life . . . and Word was made flesh."

III Theological Perspectives on the God-World Relation

EASTERN ORTHODOX

God Immanent yet Transcendent:
The Divine Energies according
to Saint Gregory Palamas

KALLISTOS WARE
BISHOP OF DIOKLEIA

> Thee, God, I come from, to thee go,
> All day long I like fountain flow
> From thy hand out, swayed about
> Mote-like in thy mighty glow.
>
> *Gerard Manley Hopkins*

Nearness yet Otherness

In her classic work *Worship,* the Anglican writer Evelyn Underhill uses the memorable phrase "the nearness yet otherness of the Eternal."[1] She alludes here to a paradox, an antinomy, constantly affirmed in the three great "Abrahamic" religions, Judaism, Christianity, and Islam. The living God is both transcendent and immanent. Above and beyond all things, he is yet at the heart of everything; mystery surpassing all understanding, he is yet more intimate to us than we are to our own selves. Looking at the creation, we may affirm a phrase used by the poet and theologian Charles Williams, "This also is Thou, neither is this Thou."[2]

In the Hebrew Scriptures the radical transcendence of the Divine is eloquently proclaimed in the answer — or rather the question — that God gives to Job out of the whirlwind: "Where were you when I laid the foundation of the earth?" (Job 38:4). For the Hebrew prophets God is a mystery beyond our comprehension: "Truly, you are a God who hides himself" (Isa. 45:15). Human beings cannot fathom the divine mind: "My thoughts are not your thoughts, / nor are your ways my ways, says the LORD" (Isa. 55:8). But at the same time the Lord is "a God near by . . . and not a God afar off"; "Do I not fill heaven and earth? says the LORD" (Jer. 23:23-24). In the words of the psalmist:

> Where can I go from your spirit?
>   Or where can I flee from your presence?
> If I ascend to heaven, you are there;
>   if I make my bed in Sheol, you are there. (Ps. 139:7-8)

The New Testament likewise affirms the otherness yet nearness of God. As transcendent Creator, God preexists his creation: the Logos, so it is said, subsists prior to all things, "in the beginning" (John 1:1). But at the same time, this transcendent God is "not far from each one of us. For 'In him we live and move and have our being'" (Acts 17:27-28). He is immanent as well as transcendent: all things have been created "in him . . . through him and for him . . . and in him all things hold together" (Col. 1:15-17). God is *pantokrator*, a term which means not only "almighty," "all-powerful," but "he who holds all things in unity."

This double emphasis upon God transcendent yet immanent has been continued in the Christian tradition whenever it has remained faithful to its own true self. So the eucharistic anaphora in the Divine Liturgy of Saint Basil the Great, used by the Orthodox Church today particularly during Lent, commences with the acclamation, "O He Who Is! . . . without beginning, invisible, incomprehensible, indescribable, changeless. . . ." At the same time, in other prayers used in the Christian East it is stated of Christ and the Holy Spirit that they are "everywhere present and filling everything." The divine omnipresence is beautifully expressed in words attributed to Christ by the second-century *Gospel of Thomas:* "Cut the wood in two, and I am there; lift up the stone, and there you will find me" (logion 77).

As for Islam, it is often assumed that this is a religion of transcendence rather than immanence, but such a view is one-sided and misleading. It is true that in the words of the Sufi master Abdul Aziz, writing to Thomas Merton in 1966, "Islam is iconoclastic par excellence";[3] as the Qur'an states concerning Allah, "Nothing is like unto him" (42:11). But at the same time, in the Qur'an God says, "We are nearer to him than the jugular vein" (50:16), and elsewhere it is affirmed, "He is with you wherever you are" (57:4). Within the mystical tradition of Sufism the contrasting demands of divine transcendence and divine immanence are in fact balanced with deep subtlety and sensitivity.

There are thus good grounds for asserting that Judaism, Christianity, and Islam are all fundamentally "panentheist," if by "panentheism" is meant the belief that God, while *above* the world, is at the same time *within* the world, everywhere present as the heart of its heart, the core of its core. Regrettably, from the seventeenth century onward, among all too many Christian thinkers — chiefly Western but sometimes also Eastern Orthodox — the delicate equilibrium between transcendence and immanence has been impaired and God's otherness has been overemphasized at the expense of his immanence. There has been, that is to say, a widespread tendency to speak as if God the creator were somehow external to the creation. The universe has been envisaged as an artifact, produced by its divine Maker from the outside. God has been likened to an architect, a builder or engineer, a potter — even, on the eighteenth-century Deist model, a clockmaker who sets the cosmic process in motion, winding up the clock but then in effect leaving it to continue ticking away on its own.

This will not do. All such imagery is sadly defective. If the doctrine of creation is to mean anything at all, it must signify that God is on the inside of everything, not on the outside. Creation is not something upon which God acts from the exterior, but something through which he expresses himself from within. Our primary image should be that of *indwelling*. Above and beyond creation, God is also its true inwardness, its "within."

Moreover, the work of creation is surely not to be understood as a once-for-all event occurring in the remote past, an initial act that constitutes a chronological starting point. It is not a past event but a present relationship. We are to think and speak not in the aorist but in the present tense. We are not to say, "God made the world, once upon a time, long ago," but "God is *making* the world, and you and me in it, here and now, at this moment and always." In this sense it is legitimate to talk of "continual creation." When it is said, "In the beginning . . . God created the heavens and the earth" (Gen. 1:1), the word "beginning" (in the Greek Septuagint, *archē*) is not to be interpreted exclusively or even primarily in a temporal sense. It does not merely mean "God started it all off, many millions of years ago." Much more profoundly it means that at each and every instant God is the constant and unceasing *archē*, the source, principle, and sustainer of all that exists. It means that without the active and uninterrupted presence of God in every part of the cosmos, nothing would remain in existence for a single moment. If the divine Maker did not exert his creative will at every split second of time, the universe would immediately collapse into the void of nonbeing. As Saint Philaret, metropolitan of Moscow (1782-1867), expresses it: "All creatures are balanced upon the creative word of God, as if upon a bridge of diamond; above them is the abyss of divine infinitude, below them that of their own nothingness."[4]

Word and Energy

During the early Christian and the Byzantine periods, Greek patristic authors employed two ways in particular to articulate this double truth of God as transcendent yet immanent, as beyond and above, yet "everywhere present and filling everything." First, some of them — above all, Saint Maximus the Confessor (ca. 580-662) — think in terms of Logos and logoi.[5] According to Maximus, Christ the creator Logos has implanted in every created thing a characteristic logos, a "thought" or "word," which is God's intention for that thing, its inner essence, that which makes it distinctively itself and at the same time draws it toward the divine realm. By virtue of these indwelling logoi, each created thing is not just an object but a personal word addressed to us by the Creator. The logoi are described by Maximus in two different ways, sometimes as created and sometimes as uncreated, depending upon the perspective in which they are viewed. They are created inasmuch as they inhere in the created world. But when regarded as God's presence in each thing — as the divine "predetermination" or "preconception" concerning that thing — they are not created but uncreated.[6] The divine Logos, the second person of the Trinity, the wisdom and the providence of God, constitutes at once the source and the end of the particular logoi, and in this manner acts as an all-embracing and unifying cosmic presence.

Alongside this Logos-logoi model, other Greek Fathers use a second approach, not contrary to the first but complementary: they speak in terms of God's transcendent essence *(ousia)* and of his immanent energies or operations *(energeiai)*. In his essence God is infinitely transcendent, utterly beyond all created being, beyond all understanding and all participation from the human side. But in his energies — which are nothing else than God himself in action — God is inexhaustibly immanent, maintaining all things in being, animating them, making each of them a sacrament of his dynamic presence. So we may interpret in terms of essence and energies the saying invoked by Charles Williams and quoted earlier: "This also is Thou [= the energies]; neither is this Thou [= the essence]." While present in created things, these energies are not themselves created but uncreated and eternal.

The essence-energies distinction goes back at least as far as the first-century Jewish author Philo of Alexandria, who asserts that while God is unknowable in his nature *(physis)*, he is revealed to us in his "acts of power" *(dynameis)*.[7] The distinction is taken over from Philo by the Christian author Clement of Alexandria (ca. 150–ca. 215): God is "far off in his essence *(ousia)* but very near in his power *(dynamei)*, which embraces all things."[8] "God is in essence *(ousia)* outside the universe," states Saint Athanasius of Alexandria (ca. 295-373), "but he is present in everything through his acts of power *(dynameis).*"[9] The distinction is developed more fully in the letters of Saint Basil of Caesarea (ca. 330-379), who writes: "We claim to know our God from his energies *(energeiai),* but we do not profess that we can draw near to his essence *(ousia).* For his energies come down to us, but his essence remains inaccessible."[10] The thinker, however, who provides the most systematic exposition of this essence-energies distinction is Saint Gregory Palamas, archbishop of Thessalonica (ca. 1296-1359), the greatest Byzantine theologian of the Palaeologan period. Sometimes Palamas has been accused of misinterpreting the standpoint of the various earlier authors, such as the Cappadocians, in whom the essence-energies distinction is to be found in a less clear-cut form. Certainly Palamas gives to their teaching a greater precision, but I see here a legitimate development rather than a distortion.[11]

Maximus and Palamas are both concerned with God's relationship to his creation, but their perspective is somewhat different. Maximus, when speaking of the logoi and the Logos, is predominantly christological in his approach. Palamas, on the other hand, following the teaching of the Cappadocians, emphasizes that the divine energies are always trinitarian; it is an error to say that any one person in the Godhead has an "energy" in which the other two persons do not share.[12] (Maximus would not in fact have disagreed over this point.) Maximus is chiefly concerned with the vocation of the human person as priest of the creation, as microcosm and mediator. Palamas for his part is preoccupied with the vision of Divine Light seen by the saints during prayer, and with the relationship of this Light to the glory revealed at Christ's transfiguration upon Mount Tabor. But fundamentally the two concur in their understanding of God as both immanent and transcendent and in their appreciation of "the nearness yet otherness of the Eternal." Indeed, there is even a passage where Maximus speaks specifically of the logoi as "energies."[13]

"He Is Everywhere and Nowhere"

Let us explore in greater detail what Palamas means by the distinction — more exactly, we should style it the "distinction in unity" — between the divine essence and the divine energies. It enables him to insist without compromise on both the transcendence and immanence of God. On the one hand, he is firmly committed to the standpoint of apophatic theology and insists without compromise upon the ontological gap between Creator and creation, but on the other hand he wishes also to underline the divine omnipresence:

Every created nature is far removed from and completely foreign to the divine nature. For if God is nature, all else is not nature; but if every other thing is nature, he is not a nature, just as he is not a being if all other things are beings, and if he is a being, then all other things are not beings. . . . God both is and is said to be the nature of all things, in so far as all things partake of him and subsist by means of this participation. . . . In this sense he is the Being of all beings, the Form that is in all forms as the Author of form, the Wisdom of the wise and, simply, the All of all things. Yet he is not nature, because he transcends every nature; he is not a being, because he transcends every being; and he is not nor does he possess a form, because he transcends every form. . . . Not a single created being has or can have any communication with or proximity to the sublime nature.[14]

God, that is to say, is not a "nature" or "being," in the sense that he is not to be regarded as one existent object among a plurality of such existent objects. If we say "God exists," then the word "exists" bears in his case a connotation fundamentally different from what it has when applied to created things. For this reason Palamas employs the *hyper* language, prominent in the writings ascribed to Dionysius the Areopagite (ca. 500): God, he says, is *hyperousios*, "beyond being"; he is "the beyond-essence, nameless and surpassing all names."[15] Yet, if God is "no-thing," in the sense that he is not one among many existent objects, yet he is also "All," in the sense that without his continual indwelling and the uninterrupted exercise of his creative power, no created person or object could exist in any way whatsoever. Thus Palamas would have seen no reason to disagree with the dictum, "Either God is everywhere present in nature, or he is nowhere."

Palamas, as so many other mystical writers have done, resorts here to the language of antinomy and paradox: "He is both existent and nonexistent; he is everywhere and nowhere; he has many names and he cannot be named; he is ever-moving and he is unmoved and, in short, he is everything and nothing."[16] Here, as elsewhere, it is helpful to spell out "nothing" as "no-thing."

God, Palamas continues, remains totally within himself, and yet he totally indwells all created beings: "Those who are counted worthy enjoy union with God the cause of all. . . . He remains wholly within himself and yet he dwells wholly within us, causing us to participate not in his nature but in his glory and radiance."[17] As Palamas's older contemporary Meister Eckhart (ca. 1260–ca. 1328) puts it, God is *totus intra, totus extra*:[18] "The more he is in things, the more he is out of things; the more in, the more out, and the more out, the more in."[19]

The distinction made by Palamas, in the passage just quoted, between God's "nature" and his "glory and radiance," is more frequently expressed in the Palamite corpus in terms of *essence* and *energy*. It is important to note, however, that Palamas does not simply employ a dyadic contrast between essence and energy within God, nor yet a dyadic contrast between essence and hypostases, but he deliberately insists upon a three-pointed contrast between essence, energy, and hypostasis. Dyadic distinctions fail properly to convey the divine mystery; we need to think always in terms of a threefold differentiation. As Palamas himself puts it:

> Three realities pertain to God: essence, energy, and the triad of divine hypostases. As we have seen, those privileged to be united to God so as to become one spirit with him — as St Paul has said, "He who cleaves to the Lord is one spirit with him" (1 Cor. 6:17) — are not united to God with respect to his essence, since all the theologians testify that with respect to his essence God undergoes no participation. Moreover, the hypostatic union is fulfilled only in the case of the Logos, the God-man. Thus those privileged to attain union with God are united to him with respect to his energy.[20]

The fact that Palamas, in discussing the threefold distinction between essence, energy, and hypostasis, chooses to speak here in terms of *union* with God shows us where the main focus of his concern is to be located. He is not a philosophical theologian, seeking to apply in the realm of Christian doctrine certain notions borrowed from Plato, Aristotle, or Proclus, but he is a monastic or mystical theologian, seeking to interpret the vision of God attained in prayer by the saints of his own day. If, then, he affirms the essence-energy distinction — or more precisely, the essence-energy-hypostasis distinction — he does so not for philosophical but for experiential reasons. He does not advance the essence-energy differentiation as a metaphysical theory. He is par excellence a theologian of living experience.

Palamas envisages, then, three levels of union. First, there is union "according to essence," such as exists between the three persons of the Holy Trinity, Father, Son, and Holy Spirit. But the mystical union between God and human beings cannot be on this level. On Palamas's presuppositions, if we were to participate in God's essence, then we should become God in a literal sense, in the same way the three divine persons are God. But *theosis* (deification) is not to be understood in such a crude and unqualified way: for, although united to God, the saints do not become additional members of the Trinity.

Second, there is union "according to hypostasis," such as occurred at the incarnation, when Godhead and manhood were united in the single person of Jesus Christ the *Theanthropos*. Once more, the mystical union cannot be of this kind, since the hypostatic union brought about at the incarnation is altogether unique. It is indeed our vocation to become "sons in the Son," to use a phrase of Eckhart. But this does not mean that we and God constitute a single person, as in Christ's hypostatic union; for in the mystical vision, face-to-face, the saints still preserve each their own individual identity.

There remains, then, the third possibility: the mystical union is a union "according to energy." The human person in such a union is made one with God, yet is not absorbed or annihilated. Each of the saints, although "deified" or "divinized" — filled, that is to say, with the life, glory, and power of God — nonetheless continues to be a distinct personal subject. God is "all in all" (1 Cor. 15:28); yet, in the words of the Macarian homilies (fourth century), "Peter is Peter, Paul is Paul, Philip is Philip. Each one retains his own nature and personal identity, but they are all filled with the Holy Spirit."[21] In the "I and Thou" relationship between God and the saints, the "I" still remains an "I" and the "Thou" still remains a "Thou," however close the two approach in mutual love. The distinction-in-unity between God's essence and his uncreated energies thus enables Palamas to avoid monistic pantheism, and yet to affirm the possibility of an unmediated union in love between creature and Creator.

The teaching of Saint Gregory Palamas concerning the divine energies has been severely criticized, not only in his own time but also up to the present day. It has been argued that there is no need to speak of energies in the way he does; all he wishes to affirm about the immanent presence of God in the world can be spelled out — so it is argued — in terms of the Holy Spirit, without invoking the concept of *energeia*. To this Palamas answers that it is necessary to differentiate between the hypostasis of the Spirit and the charismata or gifts of grace that he bestows; that is, between his personal existence, which is distinctive to himself, and the activity or energy he shares with the other two divine persons. More fundamentally, it is argued that the essence-energies distinction undermines the divine simplicity, turning God into a composite being. This charge was brought against Palamas during 1338-41 by his chief opponent, Barlaam the Calabrian, who accused him of "ditheism." The charge was repeated, after Palamas's death, by the brothers Demetrios and Prochoros Kydones, who approached the issue from a Thomist viewpoint (Palamas's own presuppositions were very different).[22]

In Palamas's defense it may be argued that Christianity envisages God not just as an undifferentiated monad, but as a Trinity of three hypostases, dwelling in each other through an unceasing movement of mutual love. Divine unity is an organic or organized unity, an interpersonal unity. The distinction between the divine essence and the three divine persons does not overthrow the simplicity of God; equally this simplicity is not destroyed by the essence-energies distinction.

It has to be remembered, moreover, that the divine energies are not an intermediary between God and humankind, not a "thing" that exists apart from God. They are, on the contrary, *God himself*, God in action, God in his self-revelation, God indwelling his creation through his direct and unmediated presence. Furthermore, the energies are not a part or division of God, but they are severally and individually the whole deity, *God in his entirety*. Just as the whole God is present without diminution or subdivision in each of the three persons of the Trinity, so he is present entire and undivided in each and all of the divine energies. On this point Palamas could not be more explicit and categorical. "Each power and energy is God himself," he affirms;[23] "God is wholly present in each of his divine energies."[24]

There is, then, no synthesis or compositeness in the Godhead, but the one, single, living, and active God is present wholly and entirely:

1. on the level of *ousia*, in the total simplicity of his divine being;
2. on the level of hypostasis, in the threefold diversity of the divine persons;
3. on the level of *energeia*, in the indivisible multiplicity of his creative and redemptive work.

In the words of the Council of Constantinople, which in 1351 confirmed the teaching of Palamas as the true faith of the church: "When speaking of God, we distinguish while uniting and we unite while distinguishing."[25]

Palamite Panentheism

In his teaching concerning the immanent energies of God, omnipresent throughout the creation, Saint Gregory Palamas sets before us a doctrine of God that is intensely dynamic. The emphasis is clearly upon "becoming" rather than "being." Permeating the world, the divine energies are precisely the life and power of God, directly and immediately active throughout the natural order. The God of Palamas is not a remote God, not a detached and distant architect, but a living and personal God, an involved God, unceasingly present and at work in all that he has made: "My Father is still working, and I also am working" (John 5:17). For the Palamite theologian the act of creation is nothing else than the continuing reality of God's indwelling. Yet while permeating the created universe through his energies, God also transcends the universe in his ineffable essence, which remains forever unknowable alike to angels and to humankind, both in this present age and in the age to come. Palamas is in this way a maximalist: the whole God is radically transcendent in his essence, and the whole God is radically immanent in his omnipresent energies.

Does this mean that Palamas upholds "panentheism"? This is of course not a word that Palamas himself uses; it was coined long after his day. In general the Greek Fathers — and equally their Latin counterparts — show little partiality for the abstractions that we today habitually employ. They prefer to speak in concrete terms. They talk about councils, not about conciliarity; about the Holy Spirit, not about pneumatology; about the last things, not about eschatology; about mystical prayer, not about mysticism.

If, however, we wish to use the term "panentheism," then this is a label that may legitimately be applied to Palamism. Whereas the pantheist states that God is the world and the world is God, the panentheist states that God is *in* the world and the world is *in* God; and it is obvious that Palamas is affirming the second of these two positions, not the first. But, as we are all aware, there are many varieties of panentheism; it all depends what is meant by the word "in." Applying the distinction used by Arthur Peacocke,[26] the panentheism of Palamas is "weak" rather than "strong." For while he believes that the being of God embraces and penetrates the universe, he also believes that the divine being is in no way exhausted by the universe, for God remains utterly transcendent in his imparticipable essence. While within, he is also above.

How, more specifically, does Palamite theology relate to the three types of panentheisms posited by Niels Gregersen?[27]

1. Palamas can certainly be regarded as an adherent of *soteriological panentheism*, provided we make a distinction between the ontological and the eschatological levels. Ontologically, from the very beginning God is fully and completely present in the creation through his divine energies. All things necessarily participate in the divine energies; otherwise they would not exist at all. But eschatologically it cannot be said that, at this present juncture, all things subsist in God with total fullness; for the created world around us, and we human beings within that world, exist at present in a fallen state.[28] There is, that is to say, more to come in the future: "at present we see only puzzling reflections in a mirror" (1 Cor. 13:12); "what we shall be has not yet been disclosed" (1 John 3:2). Even now God is certainly omnipresent within the world, but that omnipresence will be revealed in a far more glorious way when at the

final consummation God will be "all in all" (1 Cor. 15:28) in a manner not as yet evident. In that sense it can indeed be said on Palamite principles that the existence of the world "in God" is not merely a static datum but a dynamic gift of grace, a gift that is to be revealed to an ever increasing extent through the voluntary cooperation of humankind.

2. What of Gregersen's second type, *expressionist panentheism*, whereby the divine Spirit expresses itself in the world by going out from God and then returning back to God, enriched by its experiences in the world? Palamas sometimes uses the triad found in Dionysius the Areopagite (and before him in Proclus): stability, procession, and return *(monē, proodos, epistrophē)*. But Palamas is no Hegelian, and he would not have spoken of the Holy Spirit, or of God in his divine energies, as being "enriched" through experiences in the world. God is complete in himself, and the world does not add anything to the perfection of his being. But if we think as before in eschatological rather than ontological terms, perhaps we can effect a certain rapprochement between Palamas and the expressivist panentheists. The theology of the divine energies, as we have already emphasized, is to be interpreted in vividly dynamic terms. The uncreated energies, through their presence in creation, transform and divinize the world, continually bringing all things to ever new levels of reality, constantly transfiguring them "from glory to glory" (2 Cor. 3:18). So the penetration of the world by the uncreated energies does not enrich God, as he is in himself, but it certainly enriches the creation in its relation to the Creator.

3. Between Palamas and Gregersen's third type, *dipolar panentheism*, there seems to be a far sharper discrepancy. Palamas certainly did not wish to ascribe to evil any kind of "ontological" status. In common with traditional theism, both Eastern and Western, he believed that evil has no substantive existence. Evil is no more than a parasite, a twisting and distortion of things that, in their essential nature as created by God, are fundamentally good; it is an adjective, not a noun. Moreover, the Palamite doctrine of the divine energies in no way signifies that there is a "necessary interdependence" between God and the world, such that the world contributes to God as much as God contributes to the world.

On the contrary, Saint Gregory Palamas would have agreed wholeheartedly with the words of his predecessor Saint Maximus the Confessor: "God, full beyond all fullness, brought creatures into being, *not because he has need of anything*, but so that they might participate in him in proportion to their capacity and that he himself might rejoice in his works, through seeing them joyful."[29]

In creating the universe, that is to say, God acted in entire freedom. Any form of panentheism that restricts God's total liberty vis-à-vis the created world would have been altogether unacceptable to Palamas. Nothing compelled God to create, but he chose to do so. God is as free *not* to create as he is to create. God is necessary to the world, but the world is not necessary to God.

Yet, having said all this, it is important for us to add something more. Even if dipolar panentheism, as expounded by process theologians such as Alfred North Whitehead, is unacceptable to Palamas — and to traditional theism in general — yet hidden within the "dipolar" viewpoint there is a vital spark of truth which no Palamite would wish to deny. While the creation of the world is totally an act of divine freedom, at the same time this act is in no way arbitrary, casual, or accidental. God did not have to create, but in creating he was in fact expressing his own true self. For God is a God of love, and love is by its very nature self-diffusive. It implies sharing, exchange, self-giving, and response. This is true on the eternal level of God as Trinity, and it is true equally of God's self-expression as creator. "Divine love is ecstatic," affirm the Areopagitic writings.[30] As a God of "ecstatic," outgoing love, God the Holy Trinity desires to share that love with a world that he has freely created, thereby making possible — as Saint Maximus affirms — mutual participation and mutual joy. Creation, therefore, while an act of unqualified freedom, is at the same time a congruent and convincing disclosure of God's true nature as ecstatic love. Here, then, is a certain point of contact — not, indeed, a complete agreement, yet nonetheless a genuine convergence — between dipolar panentheism and Palamite orthodoxy. The world is not necessary to God; yet at the same time it is in no way peripheral to his being or incidental, for it expresses the self-diffusive love that is precisely at the very heart of the living God.

It is here, in the idea of self-diffusive love, that we find the true point of reconciliation between divine transcendence and divine immanence. Equally, the idea of self-diffusive love sums up the basic meaning of the Palamite teaching concerning God's energies. When Saint Gregory Palamas refers to the divine energies, what he means is nothing else than love in action. And when he speaks of the created world as sustained and interpenetrated by these omnipresent energies, his meaning is exactly that of Julian of Norwich when she marveled at the contrast between the "littleness" and fragility of the world on the one hand and its stability and persistence on the other: "It lasteth, and ever shall, for God loveth it. And so hath all thing being by the love of God."[31]

The Universe as Hypostatic Inherence in the Logos of God: Panentheism in the Eastern Orthodox Perspective

This paper is written with the purpose of elucidating the meaning of the notion of panentheism in the context of the Orthodox Christian tradition. Panentheism, generally speaking, advocates the presence of God in the world by asserting that God is bigger than the world and hence the world is in God. Panentheism does not identify God with the world, following thus the logic of classical theism, which asserts that God in his *essence* is beyond the world but is present in the world through his *economy*. This philosophical position distances it from pantheism, where the difference between God and the world disappears.

The fundamental issue of panentheism, then, is to articulate in what sense the transcendent God is present in the world and to find the means of expressing the presence of God in the world; this implies that all traditional rationalistic philosophical schemes based on the idea of substantial causation cannot be of great help in elucidating the meaning of panentheism. We advocate in this paper a view referred to in the title as "hypostatic inherence" of the world in the Logos of God, and which asserts the union of nature with its principle, the Logos, the union in which not a slightest trace of time, generation, and emergence can be found. It is only in this sense that panentheism can be conceived in the Orthodox context. We provide three different insights in favor of our claim, using some patristic theological ideas employed in modern context.

I am grateful to George Horton for comments and discussion, as well as for help with polishing the language of the paper.

Panentheism in Patristic Perspective

Hypostasis and Nature

The meaning of the term "hypostatic" comes from the Greek word *hypostasis*, which was used in patristic theology to underline the "personal," active as well as intransitive, dimension of existence as different from impersonal substance *(ousia)* or nature *(physis)*. This difference can be found, for example, in the Christian doctrine of *creatio ex nihilo*, which asserts that the world was created out of nothing as an ecstatic act of interpenetrating love among the persons of the Holy Trinity. In patristic theological language there were different expressions of this belief. It was affirmed that the world was created by the will of God, and this implied that the ontology of the world was rooted in God's will but not in his essence *(ousia)* (Saint Athanasius of Alexandria).[1]

This entails that there is an ontological transcendent gulf between God and the world (in Greek *diastēma*), in spite of the fact that God is present in the world, not ontologically (i.e., on the level of the world's substance), but rather relationally and personally, on the level of his loving kindness to the world, expressed through his will and realized by his Word. It has been affirmed since the times of the Gospel of John that it is the Word-Logos of God, the second person of the Holy Trinity, who entered the world by creating it and preparing his incarnation in Jesus as the meeting of the uncreated Divine with created humanity. It is at this point that the cosmological mystery of the presence of the ontologically transcendent God in the world acquires christological (and anthropological) dimension. For the presence of God in the world (usually asserted in patristics either in terms of the divine *uncreated energies* or the *logoi* of created things)[2] cannot be understood without the personal mystery of Christ as a locus of the divine and human.

The distinction between substance *(ousia)* (or nature [*physis*]) and hypostasis was articulated in patristic thought in the context of the trinitarian and christological discussions throughout the fourth through seventh centuries. *Ousia* (as related to universals, families, or species) tends to be used with regard to internal characteristics and relations, or metaphysical reality (in this it is almost identical with *physis*), whereas "hypostasis" regularly emphasizes the externally concrete character of the substance, its empirical objectivity, and the existential aspect of being, expressed through the realization of freedom, movement, and will. It is important to stress that though every individual substance moves and is moved, the personal element in the realization of the potentiality of the substance, i.e., its hypostasis, is not immanent to what is included in the substance.[3]

Nature or substance (in its self-realization, which is accounted for by God's will as creator) can be divided and shared while the hypostasis of a particular being is indivisible. The reality of substance (i.e., its transcendence) is made available to human beings because of God's economy, which relates independent creation to the Creator through communion. In other words, substance becomes evident and real only in hypostases, i.e., in what is indivisible. In a theological context hypostasis is similar to *prosōpon*, i.e., "person" in modern parlance. This implies that the nature of things becomes evident if it is personified, i.e., made articulated and distinguishable. The hypostasis, then, is seen as the foundation of being, for it is that in which nature exists.[4]

The distinction between nature and hypostasis allows one to articulate the unity of all creation in two different senses. On the one hand all varieties of sensible objects share the same nature (the same elementary particles, e.g.). On the other hand, if one considers the world in relationship to its Creator, then natural existence acquires the features of existence for someone, i.e., the Creator, who is not only an impersonal substance or essence of the higher order (in which other individual substances participate), but who is the personal God. Thus when Christianity affirms that the world was created by the Word-Logos of God and that through the Logos everything was made, it effectively affirms that the natural existence of the world is existence in the personhood of God, i.e., in his hypostasis; this means that the whole creation is brought to unity in the hypostasis of the Logos and that the link between God and the world is nonnatural (i.e., nonontological, nonphysical, nonbiological, etc.), but *hypostatic*, which can be expressed as the relationship between the Divine and the world in the personhood of God. The creation of the world and its existence have sense then only in relation to the person who is acting as the creator of and the provider for meaning of existence: there cannot be impersonal creation as well as existence.

The nonpersonal part of the universe, however, being created by God, is not capable of knowing that it has its Creator, for impersonal physical objects are not hypostatic creatures: they have no ability to contemplate their own existence and relate it to their ultimate source. Thus the intelligibility of the universe and its meaning are accessible only to hypostatic human beings, who, according to the biblical tradition, are created in the divine image, and whose hypostasis (being also created by God) is capable of personifying other objects in the universe, i.e., making the universe self-conscious of its own existence and origin. Maximus the Confessor strongly argued that man as a person cannot be isolated from the fact that human nature has its hypostasis in the Logos, and it is in this sense that it can be said that human nature is itself *enhypostasized*; this means that a personal relationship with

God cannot be excluded from human nature and is identical with fully realized human existence.

Hypostatic Inherence

The combination of the two words "hypostatic inherence" is however much
more difficult, for it refers theologically to the Greek words *enhypostatic* or
enhypostasis, which were introduced into theology by Leontius of Byzantium
in the context of christological discussions of the sixth to seventh centuries,
and whose meaning (appropriate for the purposes of our research) according
to *A Patristic Greek Lexicon* can be described as: "being, existing in an
hypostasis or Person," "subsistent in, inherent."[5]

One can refer to a theological view of *participation* in the Divine in order to illustrate the idea of hypostatic inherence of the universe in the Logos
of God. When it is said that created beings know about God, it means that
they participate in God through a mode which is distinct from his essence
(uncreated energies, for example). However, the very ability to participate in
God is willed by God himself, for it is God who brought into existence participating beings; the knowledge of why this participation is possible at all is
concealed by God from participating beings and known only to himself.[6]

It was natural then for Maximus the Confessor to argue that "everything that derives its existence from participation in some other reality presupposes the ontological priority of that other reality" (*Philokalia,* text 6,
p. 165); he meant the priority of the Logos of God with respect to all other
created things which do participate in him (text 3, p. 164). The hypostatic inherence of the universe in the Logos of God can then be interpreted in
Maximus's words as the Logos's eternal manifestations in different modes of
participation by created beings in him. This participation takes place in spite
of the fact that the Logos is eternally invisible to all (i.e., ontologically distinct
from creation) by the surpassing nature of his hidden activity (text 8, p. 166).
But this participation does not assume any ontological causation; for to participate in the Logos means to be made by the Logos a participating being,
i.e., a being in the hypostasis of the Logos himself. This implies that existence
through participation in the Logos is subsistence in his personhood, i.e., the
inherence in his hypostasis. In short, one can say that hypostatic inherence in
the Logos is the same as participation in his person.

Another example, which illustrates what the existence in a hypostasis or
person means, can be brought from the sphere of theological anthropology
which asserts that "man is hypostasis [personality] of the cosmos, its con-

scious and personal self-expression; it is he who gives meaning to things and who has to transfigure them. For the universe, man is its hope to receive grace and to be united with God."[7] The universe as *an expressed and articulated existence* is possible only in human hypostasis; i.e., it acquires some crucial qualities of existence only when it is reflected in the personality of humanity. Using the words of Maximus the Confessor, every thought about the universe inheres as a quality in an apprehending being.[8] The universe thus acquires a new form of existence in the being who apprehends it.[9] The link between the universe as articulated existence and the apprehending being is not ontological, but rather hypostatic or personal. A patristic theologian would say that existence of the universe as an articulated existence is hypostatic existence, i.e., the universe is *enhypostatic.*

Can human beings, given their apprehension of the universe as inherent in the Logos, then interact with the Logos and change him? Maximus the Confessor has already prepared a response to this question by saying that the Logos, who is beyond comprehension (intellection), unites himself to human comprehension, which is purified from any manifold and temporality, and makes it his own, giving it rest from those things which by nature change and diversify it with many conceptual forms they impose upon it (text 5, p. 138). This means that human intellection of the universe does not affect the Logos, which is beyond intellection. The link between the Logos and the world is not subject to temporal change or to the instability of nature, to which the human intellect is bound. The world is in the hypostasis of the Logos of God from ages to ages, so that the Logos experiences the world as being in rest from his works just as God did from his (Gen. 2:2; Heb. 4:10) (*Philokalia*, text 5, p. 138).

One should not think the ideas about "hypostasis" are some outdated relics of the old tradition which have no links with modern philosophical development and its fusion with theology; for example, the term "hypostasis" was used by a contemporary French phenomenological philosopher, Emmanuel Levinas, in a very special way.[10] Levinas puts a stress on the difference between the *transitive* existence of beings, through relationships for example, and the absolutely *intransitive* element of one's own existing as freed from intentionality and relationship. The *existent* and its *existing* do not coincide together in every creature. For if, according to Levinas, the existent "contracts" its existing,[11] it forms an event he calls hypostasis. One can say the hypostatic existence of human beings, as existents (and of all of humankind), is the event of their engaging with their existing. What will happen then if we consider the situation when the existent cannot engage with its own existing, but can be existent in the existing of the other? Are we still obliged to talk about the "event" of hypostatic existence? For example, some physical object has no inclination to perceive its own existence. This means there is an existent without its own existing. But at the same time, the same object can be articulated in the existing of a human being, so that it receives its existing in the other, i.e., in human being. A human being, being itself a hypostatic event, makes the engagement of an existent physical object with its existing in the apprehension of human being an event, so that the "hypostatic inherence" of a physical object in the knowing subject has some features of temporality and emergence, which follow from the event of human hypostasis. The situation drastically changes if the existent receives its existing from the Logos of God whose eternal being is not involved in any chain of worldly relations and events. In this case the "hypostatic inherence," as the receiving by the universe of its existing in the hypostasis (person) of the Logos of God, has no features of emergence and temporality. This is the reason why we do not want to express the existence of the universe in the personality of the Logos of God, in order to deliver the reader from the temptation to think about the universe as "personalized" by the Logos. Personalization is an emergent notion usually applied to something which has already been in existence. This is why the Greek term *enhypostasization* would be more appropriate for us in order to affirm that "the universe is *enhypostasized* by the Logos of God." We express this thought by using the language of "hypostatic inherence" in order to make it easier for a modern reader to comprehend the term; by so doing we avoid the danger of affirming the link between God and the world in emergent terms.

The creation and existence of the universe thus can be seen as enhypostatic in two senses: (1) the universe as mere nature exists in the person of the Logos; (2) but the knowledge of this, i.e., the transcendence beyond substance from within the universe, can be achieved only if nature is contemplated in the human hypostases (which in turn exist in the hypostasis of the Logos). The universe thus acquires the features of its hypostatic inherence in a twofold sense: in the Logos of God, who brings matter into existence through his effected words, and in hypostatic human beings, who through analysis and differentiation of this matter lead the universe to self-awareness of its purpose and end, i.e., bring it toward realized existence in God and for God. It is in this sense that one can argue that human beings are, in a way, co-creators of the universe: the universe is brought into being as a meaningful and self-conscious existence in the personhood of humanity, which is, in turn, inherent in the Logos of God. The human phenomenon, or, as we prefer to say, the humankind event in the universe, is hypostatic in the sense that it is contingent upon the personhood of the Logos. The universe, as articulated existence in the human hypostasis, can be treated in turn as the happening, contingent upon the humankind event, which constitutes an element of God's economy for salvation.

Ultimately one can conclude that the link between the Logos of God and the universe is hypostatic; i.e., the universe is seen as inherent in the person of the Logos of God. But this signifies that once the universe is apprehended by us in its connection and unity with the primordial ground of the Logos, it becomes for us something greater and other than "only the universe," because the specific "worldly" character of the universe is overcome without the universe itself being "removed" or "eliminated." The meaninglessness of the universe, its pure factuality and impersonality, its indifference to the divine truth, are overcome; this also signifies that the presence of God in the world can be detected only through manifestations of the enhypostatic mode of the world's existence. It is clear then that a panentheistic claim about the presence of God in the world can be developed in a sophisticated way, avoiding any danger of articulating the link between God and the world on the level of their substances (natures). In what follows we intend to provide some "pointers" as to how to detect this enhypostatic mode.

Panentheism and Coinherence

But before turning to the "pointers" of the personal presence of the Logos in the universe, we must discuss one particular claim of "generic" panentheism, namely, its affirmation that God is not only present in the world, but also that God is influenced by the world, and that the relations between God and the world are bilateral. Our reaction to this claim is already present in the title of this paper. We stress the patristic belief that God is hypostatic being (the person) but the world is not. Since the link between God and the world is hypostatic (as we have argued above), any bilateral relationship between God and the world would be possible only if the world as such exhibited its own hypostatic features. Then the bilateral relationship between God and the world might be understood as the relationship between two persons: God and the world. But it is exactly at this point that our position states clearly that the created world as such is not a person at all. It has a mode of existence which is inherent in the person of the Logos of God; that is why the relationship between the Logos and the world is established through the one-way *diastēma*, i.e., as the permeation from God to the world, but not vice versa.

The claim of generic panentheism about the bilateral relationship between God and the world, as seen through patristic eyes, runs the risk of affirming something similar to the old patristic idea of *perichoresis* (coinherence) of God to the world. Certainly this similarity must be analyzed with caution, for it must not be understood as analogous to the trinitarian formula of coinherence as interpenetration and mutual indwelling of the persons of the Trinity (it would be theological nonsense to affirm that created nature is capable of interpenetrating the Divine).[12] It can rather be paralleled with *perichoresis* in the christological context as the interchange and reciprocity of the human nature with the divine nature in Christ. Then by analogy one might affirm panentheistically the *perichoresis* of the Divine and the created in a sense of "interchange" and "reciprocity" (bilateral relationship) between God and the world. But even in this "weak" form of the *perichoresis,* panentheism must not forget the origin of this *perichoresis,* i.e., that it proceeds from the personhood of the divinity, not from the matter of the world. The Divine, having once permeated through the world, bestows on its matter an ineffable *perichoresis* with itself. The interchange or reciprocity of the Divine and the created is ultimately initiated and held by the person of the Logos of God. One can see again that the process of the divine permeation of the world is one-sided and entirely determined by the Logos himself. This has been demonstrated by God through the incarnation of the Logos in Jesus Christ.

Once again we assert that any interchange and reciprocity between the Divine and the created originates from the permeation of the world by God, and is sustained by the Logos through his intentional immanence to the world. The world as such has no hypostasis of its own and cannot initiate and sustain the *perichoresis* to the Divine. It is possible, however, to speak about hypostatic agencies in the world, i.e., human beings, through whom the world acquires some personal qualities, in the sense we have explained above. Human beings, not being entirely from this world, thanks to the gift bestowed upon them by God to know him, can initiate the interchange between the world and God through the apprehension of the created universe, so that the world, being articulated by human beings, is related to God as its uncreated source. Thus any panentheistic claim about the world which is brought to Godself must be understood in the context of human deification and involvement of the world in the transfiguration, which brings it back to the union with God. But all this is initiated by the Logos of God, who created human beings with such logoi as to allow them to relate to God through personal interaction as well as through apprehension of his created universe. This is why the universe, being personified by human beings, still exhibits its inherence in the Logos of God. Human beings thus become the focal points of creation through whom the evidence of the hypostatic inherence of the universe in the Logos can be seen.

Man and the World: Microcosmic Panentheism

Let us articulate first what we mean by the hypostatic dimension of the human phenomenon in cosmological terms. We start by elucidating the role of human persons in the process of knowing the universe. It can sound tautologous to say that the very fact that physics can speculate about the universe and the place of man in it is based on the ability of humans to contemplate the universe as a coherent world. It is this ability which makes human being fundamentally different from other forms of biological life. In modern terms this simple fact is not regarded as constitutive for knowledge. Human beings in the universe are downgraded to the level of passive observers, so that the problem of human consciousness is excluded from the subject matter of physics. B. Carr described this situation in physics, which models the world, by saying that "yet one feature which is noticeably absent from this model is the Creator, man himself."[13] An obvious incompleteness in this view of man's place in the universe can be easily elucidated by a simple example.

Let us recall a typical and popular scientific argument (usually presented by a diagram) which depicts different objects in the universe in terms of their spatial sizes or masses.[14] The position of human beings in the universe is seen as unnotable: their typical size is 10^{12} times larger than an atom, and the place they occupy in space is 10^{-19} times smaller than the size of the visible universe. In spite of the fact that the existence of human beings depends on atoms and the size (or age) of the universe (this is anthropic-style reasoning), the position of human beings in the universe is seen as insignificant. The internal inconsistency of a purely physical view is hidden in the fact that human reason, which is not present in the diagram explicitly, is encoded in it implicitly, for all objects, starting from atoms and finishing with the universe as a whole, are integrated in a single logical chain, which is possible only because the human insight is present everywhere. Thus all objects in the chain of physical being are united by human reason in a single consciousness of the whole. This unity is sustained from the "vertical" dimension of human intellect, which is linked to the *natural* conditions of man's existence but at the same time transcends them, revealing itself as dependent not only on physico-cosmological factors but also on nonnatural factors (we call them *hypostatic* factors).[15]

One could object to our usage of the term "hypostatic" in this context by pointing out that what we mean by it is human intelligence, which assumes the ability to contemplate objects in nature, form their meaning, and communicate this meaning to all of humankind. Some would say that all these functions of the human intellect have naturally emerged, so that they constitute a part of nature, although quite different from what one means by physical nature.[16] In this case one could say that instead of naming the vertical dimension "hypostatic," it would be easy to call it intellectual (or psychological), and not to make a sharp difference between "horizontal" and "vertical" dimensions. Our response to this would be that the presence of intellect and consciousness, even if treated as epiphenomena of physical and biological functioning, does not explain the *personhood* of human existence. The personhood of human beings implies not only that they have self-consciousness, i.e., the perception of one's own *ego*, but also that there is a fundamental distinction from and *relation* to other existences.[17] Despite the fact that the human hypostasis cannot be communicated, the formation of the personhood goes on only through its *relation* to other hypostases (which does not necessarily imply interaction on the level of substance), and to the common source of their origination in the Logos.[18] This means that when we speak of human being as hypostatic, it stands for the whole of humankind (in contrast to natural man) as the community of beings with a common logos of human nature related to God and realized in different persons.

On the basis of the idea that human beings, in a way, imitate in their composition the whole universe, in an empirical (i.e., explicitly visible) and intelligible fashion (which is invisible), Maximus the Confessor developed an allegorical interpretation of the "universe as man," and conversely of "man as microcosm and mediator" between the parts of the universe, and between the universe and God. A passage from Maximus's *Mystagogy*, chapter 7, elucidates the meaning of this similarity:

> Intelligible things display the meaning of the soul as the soul does that of intelligible things, and . . . sensible things display the place of body as the body does that of sensible things. And . . . intelligible things are the soul of sensible things, and sensible things are the body of intelligible things; . . . as the soul is in the body so is the intelligible in the world of sense, that the sensible is sustained by the intelligible as the body is sustained by the soul; . . . both make up *one world* as body and soul make up *one man*, neither of these elements joined to the other in unity denies or displaces the other according to the law of the one [the Creator] who has bound them together. In conformity with this law there is engendered the principle [*logos*] of the unifying force which does not permit that the [hypostatic] identity unifying these things be ignored because of their difference in nature.[19]

In a scientifico-cosmological context this text can be interpreted as an insight which can lead a cosmologist beyond the sphere of the visible universe (which is accessible to the senses) to that which is invisible and described in terms of mathematical objects (which human reason operates with), because the reason is indwelling in the body, so that through the visible universe the reason reaches the intelligible universe, which also indwells in the visible, in spite of being different from it. It is because of the hypostatic unity of the body and soul in a cosmologist that he can reveal the hypostatic unity of the visible and intelligible universe. A cosmologist relates opposite phenomena: small (atoms) and large (galaxies), visible present cosmos and its invisible past, cosmos as multiplicity of different visible facts (stars, galaxies, distribution of clusters of galaxies, e.g.), and the mathematical cosmos (as uniform and isotropic space), etc.

The human ability to recapitulate in its knowledge all constituents of the universe, and to realize that human being is deeply dependent on the structural and nomistic aspects of the microworld as well as the megacosmos, makes the position of humans in the universe exceptional and unique. The recapitulation of the universe in man takes place not only on the natural level (which is affirmed in the anthropic arguments), but also, and this is much more nontrivial, on the hypostatic level; this implies indirectly that human beings are participating in outward affirmation and articulation (hypostasization) of their own existence by revealing the meaning of various levels of the universe. The latter is possible because human beings can use their own hypostatic mode of existence in order to bring the undifferentiated existents in the universe to their proper, personal existing, through apprehension by persons.

In different words, human persons, or humankind in general, in spite of being physically located at one particular point of the universe, share, through the fusion of knowledge, its existence with all other places and ages of the universe. One can affirm at last that the humankind event, being in its essence the participation in the person of the Logos, is itself the source of further expansion of the inherence of the universe in the Logos of God, which has the form of a revelation of the universe's intelligibility, purpose, and end through human personhood.[20]

The place of man in the universe can be expressed by using the old idea of *microcosm*, as the world in the small. It is however clear, from what we have discussed above, that the major feature which puts man in the "central" position in the universe is the fact that the reality of this universe is articulated by man, i.e., the universe is revealed to itself through the personhood of human beings. This adds to man as *microcosm* the title of *mediator*; for it is man who establishes the link between the universe and God, not naturally, or physically, but hypostatically; i.e., the universe as part of creation is offered to God by man through his "cosmic liturgy" of knowledge.

The fundamental problem, however, in asserting the idea that the universe is made hypostatically inherent in human apprehension, and that the universe appears to us as intelligible reality, is rooted in the origin of the intelligence of human beings and its relation to the intelligibility of the universe. For this to be possible at all, one should assume that the human intelligence is somehow tuned with the intelligibility of the universe through a common root, which is beyond creation and is hidden in the Logos of God. This is the meaning of the analogy between man and the universe made by Maximus.

The central position of man in the universe can now be described in a different formula by saying that man is positioned between God and the universe in the following sense: human beings are created as participants in the person of the Logos of God with the accomplished hypostases, whereas the other objects in the universe are made inherent in the Logos without having their own hypostases, so that their existence is not personal and as such is devoid of the realization of purpose and end. It is only through human apprehension that these objects are brought to a realization of their function in the divine plan, when the objects themselves receive their meaning in terms of purposes and ends.

World as Church: Ecclesial Panentheism

The nontrivial connection between the problem of space in the universe and the concept of the incarnation of the Logos of God in flesh has already been articulated by T. Torrance.[21] The belief in the incarnation of the Logos of God in flesh plays here a central role; for on the one hand Jesus Christ, being in his nature fully a man, lived in the space and time of the empirical world, being located in a body in a particular place and time of earthly history; on the other hand he was fully God, who did not leave his "place" in the Holy Trinity, and who, being God, was present not only in Palestine two thousand years ago but in all places and times of the universe created by him. We have here a nontrivial historico-topological relation between the finite track of Jesus in empirical space and time and the whole history of the visible universe. (A similar relation is established in the humankind event, which, being finite in space and time, is related through human apprehension to the whole universe.) The human nature in Christ was operating within the reality of empirical space and historical time, whereas his divine nature was always beyond the empirical and intelligible aeons, in the uncreated realm of the kingdom of God, which can be expressed symbolically in terms of the boundaries of the created if these boundaries are seen from the vertical (divine) dimension. It is from this "outside" that Christ the Logos of God coordinated the empirical space where he indwelled in the body with the rest of the created universe. This helps us understand space-time in the universe as a manifestation of the hypostatic mode of the relationship between God and the world.

One can rephrase the above by using a different analogy. Clearly space and time are perceived by human beings from within creation. One can then speculate that this space-time is an internal form of the relation of the universe with the transcendent Divine. This internal form of space and time, being contingent and dependent upon the interactions between the parts of the universe and being essential for the existence of human beings, cannot be conceived, however, without its "external" counterpart, i.e., its "boundary," which can be articulated only from "outside," i.e., from the perspective of the uncreated. This argument links the empirical space and time with its moving transcendent "borderline," so that in no way are space and time of the physical universe accomplished and fixed forever in those shapes which we can comprehend at present.

The question is then: What is the principle of the borderline between the universe as the internal space given to us empirically and its nonworldly ground associated by us with the "external" side of the space of the universe? Here the analogy with the union of two natures in the person of Christ can be employed. Indeed, it is because of the hypostatic union of the divine and natural in Christ that one can argue by analogy that the interplay between space and time of the universe and its uncreated ground in God is upheld hypostatically by God in the course of his economy of creation. The fulfillment of this economy took place in the incarnation of the Logos of God in flesh, when the link between the human nature of Christ (in space) and his divinity as the Logos (who is beyond space-time and yet holds all space-time together) was established. The incarnation manifested that space and time are linked to the Divine. It is from this perspective that the assertions of Torrance on the relational nature of space, as the form of rationality created by the Logos of God in order to communicate his presence to us, receive further interpretation. On this view the space and time of the universe represent a physical (natural) manifestation of the relation between the visible universe and its "external" uncreated and divine "form," which constitutes the ground for the natural one. This implies that a particular appearance of space and time in the physical universe is not complete in itself and is open to the unfolding rationality of God, whose presence in space and time of the universe has not an essential but rather a hypostatic character. Indeed, the very relation between the space and time of the universe and its uncreated ground is hypostatic, i.e., it exists only in the person of the Logos of God.

What is important in Torrance's arguments about the links between the incarnation and space and time is that space should be considered in the context of the divine hypostasis, i.e., as the expression of the *personal* rationality of God in the world, accessible to us. One should not, however, understand that space and time and their possible theories represent the embodiment of the Logos of God as was conjectured by Pannenberg.[22] Space and time can be rather treated as a natural counterpart in the constitution of the world in its relation to the Divine which was confirmed through the union between the divine and human in the incarnation of the Logos of God, his Son Jesus Christ; and it is because of this fact — that is, that space and time is linked to the ground in the uncreated via the hypostatic (i.e., nonontological) union — that any particular perception of space and time and its theory is fundamentally open-ended and nonfixed in terms of a natural incarnation of the Logos in flesh in Jesus Christ. It can mean that the space and time of the universe as we know them were important for the Logos to be incarnate in this particular spatiotemporal form, but as we mentioned before, this fact does not preclude space and time deviating in the created future, for the logic of this change follows the logic of the person of the Logos who is balancing his uncreated nature with the world created by him, rather than by any intrinsic processes in the universe.

It is only through this vision of the universe as held in the person of the Logos that it is possible to reaffirm that human hypostatic beings occupy a special position in the universe by being *microcosm* in a very nontrivial sense. In the same way as Jesus Christ, being in his human incarnation in a particular place in space and time of the universe, did not cease to be the Logos who holds all creation in his person, human beings (whom Christ recapitulated in the incarnation), being present in a particular place of the universe, control it in various locations and times not by power but by their knowledge, recapitulating the universe in a single consciousness.

The incarnation of the Logos of God in flesh, which entails the annunciation of the kingdom of God, brings the whole of humanity to the realization not only of their *microcosmic* function, but also of their *ecclesial* function to build the universal church as the body of Christ, and to be a "priest of creation." The whole universe, then, having participated through its creation and through the incarnation in the person of the Logos, is mirrored for human beings in the holy church, which, according to Maximus, being divided in its outward appearance into sanctuary and nave, is held together hypostatically ("through their relationship to the unity").[23] It is from this analogy that one sees again the meaning of the incarnation: the whole church represents the world, and it is Christ who is the head and the foundation of the church; the universe, being mirrored in the church, is held hypostatically by the Logos of God, who is the head of the universe understood as church.

The incarnation thus reveals for Christians, and affirms for modern science, the ecclesial nature of the universe as well as human beings. This is the reason why the knowledge and exploration of the universe, in the context of the science-religion dialogue, can be treated as an activity of uncovering the features of the universe, which manifest the personhood of the Logos and mean the praising of the Creator of the universe. This activity replaces the existing split between the church and the universe with their unity in the communion with God, revealing thus the work of scientists as a *para-eucharistic* work.[24]

The Cosmic Vision of Saint Maximos the Confessor

ANDREW LOUTH

The purpose of this paper is to introduce some aspects of the cosmic vision of Orthodox theology, in the hope that they might serve as a resource for theological reflection on the relationship between God and the universe. This cosmic vision may well be described in some respects as "panentheistic," since it envisages a relationship between the universe and God that stresses God's immanence in the universe and sees the universe as finding its purpose or goal (the Greek term is *skopos*) in union with God, or more boldly in deification. It differs, however, from some modern forms of panentheism in that there is no sense in which God may be said to be affected by the cosmos itself. The aspects of this cosmic vision that express this sense of panentheism are the doctrine of the logoi, "words" or principles, by means of which all creatures exist and participate in God and his perfections, and the doctrine of the energies of God, by means of which God is present to that which is "after him," that is, to the manifold of creation.[1] I write as a historical theologian, and see my task in the collaborative theological enterprise of the church as providing access to the riches of theological reflection of past ages. For the passage of time is a process not only of learning, but also of forgetting; the role of the historical theologian is to keep the memory of the church alive. This is, in fact, quite a humble role, for the memory of the church is preserved principally by its liturgical life, which, in the Byzantine tradition, is especially rich theologically; it is, however, a valuable role, and is a vocation that is especially rewarding.

The two doctrines — of the divine logoi and the divine energies — seem to present very accessible ways of expressing the intimate involvement of God and the created order. It is perfectly natural, and proper, for later theologians to be selective in what they incorporate from earlier theologians. Part of the purpose of this paper, however, is to draw attention to the *context* of the doctrine of the divine logoi in the theological vision of Saint Maximos the Confessor. The point of this is not to suggest that modern thinkers must take the doctrine of the logoi together with its context, in a take-it-or-leave-it manner; rather it is to point to other elements of the Byzantine cosmic vision that, on the one hand, give some sense of the deeper meaning the doctrine of the logoi had for the Byzantine thinkers, and on the other hand, and perhaps more importantly, offer further theological tools that might be of value for current attempts to articulate a fuller theological vision of the universe. To anticipate: the doctrines of the divine logoi and of the divine energies, on their own, offer themselves as ways of articulating a sense of God's immanence; taken in its context, we shall see that the doctrine of the divine logoi, at least, also evokes something like what is nowadays called the anthropic principle. This suggests a particular coinherence — of God, the universe, and the human — that is also to be found in current ideas of the relationship between religion and science.

The historical part of this paper (the bulk of it) focuses on Saint Maximos the Confessor, a seventh-century monk, widely regarded as the greatest of all Byzantine theologians.[2] It is because of the profundity and richness of his vision that I have chosen to concentrate on him. It will perhaps be useful to begin by briefly sketching his life. Born in 580, probably in Constantinople, Maximos seems to have served in the imperial court after the accession of the emperor Heraklios the Great in 610. Within a few years he abandoned this secular career and became a monk, initially in monasteries near Constantinople and then, after the Persian invasion of Asia Minor and the siege of Constantinople in 626, in exile, mostly, it seems, in North Africa. He defended the Orthodox teaching of Christ as one divine person existing in two natures, human and divine, against imperial attempts at ecumenical compromise, and so angered the imperial court that he was eventually arrested, tried, deprived of his tongue and right hand (the instruments of his "heresy"), and exiled to Georgia, where he soon died in 662. His cosmic theological vision is expressed in writings addressed mainly to fellow monks mostly before his struggle against the imperial court, though the same principles underlie both his cosmic vision and his understanding of the incarnation.

We shall consider Maximos's vision of the cosmos under three headings: first, his idea of the analogy between the cosmos and the human person, the idea of macrocosm and microcosm; secondly, his notion of what he called the logoi of creation; and thirdly, his idea of the "divisions of nature," to use the term made famous by the ninth-century Irish monk and scholar, John Scotus Eriugena, who translated into Latin several of Saint Maximos's works and who called his own great synthesis of ideas, largely drawn from Maximos, *On the Division of Nature (De divisione naturae).*

Macrocosm/Microcosm

Let me begin by quoting some words from one of Saint Maximos's most profound commentators from the century just concluded, the Romanian theologian Fr. Dumitru Staniloae, who died in 1993. At the very beginning of his *Orthodox Dogmatic Theology*, the first volume of which has been translated into English as *The Experience of God*, he has this to say:

> Some of the Fathers of the Church have said that man is a microcosm, a world which sums up in itself the larger world. Saint Maximos the Confessor remarked that the more correct way would be to consider man as a macrocosm, because he is called to comprehend the whole world within himself as one capable of comprehending it without losing himself, for he is distinct from the world. Therefore, man effects a unity greater than the world exterior to himself, whereas, on the contrary, the world, as cosmos, as nature, cannot contain man fully within itself without losing him, that is, without losing in this way the most important reality, that part which, more than all others, gives reality its meaning.
>
> The idea that man is called to become the world writ large has a more precise expression, however, in the term "macro-anthropos." The term conveys the fact that, in the strictest sense, the world is called to be humanized entirely, that is, to bear the entire stamp of the human, to become pan-human, making real through that stamp a need which is implicit in the world's own meaning: to become, in its entirety, a humanized cosmos, in a way that the human being is not called to become, nor can ever fully become, even at the farthest limit of his attachment to the world where he is completely identified with it, a "cosmicized" man. The destiny of the cosmos is found in man, not man's destiny in the cosmos. This is shown not only by the fact that the cosmos is the object of human consciousness and knowledge (not the reverse), but also by the fact that the entire cosmos serves human existence in a practical way.[3]

This sums up, more clearly than Saint Maximos himself ever does, the core of his understanding of the analogy between the universe and the human person. The idea of the human as microcosm is of course an old one, and in drawing on it Maximos would not have been thought to be saying anything exceptional. Let us note that the ideas Maximos draws on — philosophical, anthropological, cosmological, medical — would not have seemed strange to his contemporaries; his use of them, however, would have seemed striking, if not actually strange. If we are going to learn from Maximos, we shall have to think through his ideas again, using concepts that are contemporary to us, just as he used concepts that were contemporary to him. If we simply attempt to revive ancient cosmology, we shall probably lose Maximos in the process. And the way Fr. Staniloae restates the insight of Saint Maximos seems to me a step in the right direction. Because of the position of the human in the cosmos — ultimately, because the human is created in the image of God — the human person is a bond of the cosmos, or looked at another way, the human person is priest of the cosmos. It is through the human that the cosmos relates to God, it is in the human that the cosmos finds its meaning. But conversely, if the human fails to fulfill such a priestly, interpretative, relating role, then that failure is not just a personal, individual failing, it is a failing with cosmic consequences. We are becoming dimly aware of this, as we realize how human behavior that fails to recognize the integrity of God's creation, its inherent value, its inherent beauty, and treats it as simply so much material to be consumed — how such behavior is more than simply self-destructive, or destructive of human society, but threatens the ordered beauty of the cosmos itself. Saint Maximos goes further: fallen human activity threatens the very *meaning* of the cosmos, insofar as that meaning is perceived by, and articulated through, the human person. The cosmos ceases to be an ordered, beautiful structure — an idea implicit in the very word *cosmos,* which in Greek suggests something ordered and beautiful — and becomes obscure, dark, dangerous, at least to humans, a forest of symbols, no longer clearly disclosing the divine, but difficult to interpret, and easily misunderstood. The perfect fit, as it were, between unfallen humanity and the cosmos becomes awkward, ill fitting, painful, and mutually harmful.

This is one way Maximos understands the coherence of the universe — a sort of coinherence between the human and the cosmos, more than simply a sympathy between all the different parts of the cosmos — though that is implied, too — but a sympathetic togetherness that is focused on the human person, for good or ill.

Logoi of Creation

The next theme is the logoi of creation.[4] The very word "logos" causes problems: it is a very special word in Greek. Theodor Haecker, the Austrian Catholic lay theologian who died at the end of the Second World War, once suggested that in every language there are one or two untranslatable words — he called them *Herzwörter*, heart words — in which is concentrated something of the genius of the language. In Latin it is *res*, usually translated "thing"; in German *Wesen*, "essence"; in French *raison*, "reason"; in English "sense." In Greek it is, he suggested, *logos*.[5] It can be translated, according to context, "word," "reason," "principle," "meaning"; but this fragments the connotation of the Greek word, which holds all these meanings together.

A lot could be said about the history of the word "logos" in Greek thought, but I shall simply dwell on its use in Greek Christian thought. The universe was created by God, through his Logos, which is identical with the second person of the Trinity, the Son of the Father. To say that the universe is created by the Logos entails that the universe has a meaning, both as a whole and in each of its parts. That "meaning" is logos: everything that exists has its own logos, and that logos is derived from God the Logos. To have meaning, logos, is to participate in the Logos of God. Behind this lurks a Platonic idea, that everything that exists, exists by participating in its form, or idea, which is characterized by its definition; the Greek for definition (in this sense) is, again, *logos*. These Platonic forms, or logoi, to call them by what defines them, are eternal. Between Plato and Saint Maximos much water had flowed down the history of ideas, and for Maximos, because the world has been created by God through his Logos, it can no longer be regarded as a pale reflection of eternal reality, as with Plato's world. The created world has value, meaning, beauty, in itself: because God is the supreme craftsman, his creation is supremely lovely. The beauty and meaning are found in the logoi, so the logoi, in one sense at least, are created: they belong to the created order. In another sense they are uncreated, because they are, as it were, God's thoughts, or intentions, or to use the words Maximos borrows from the early-sixth-century Dionysius the Areopagite, "divine predeterminations and wills."[6] So the logos of a created being means what it is, what defines its nature — Maximos speaks of the *logos tēs physeōs*, meaning or definition or principle of nature — but this means what God intends it to be, what he wills, what he predetermines. This final point needs to be underlined: the divine logoi are expressions of the divine will. Here we find perhaps the most important point at which Maximos, building on his Christian predecessors, advances beyond Plato. For Plato beings participate in the forms; for Maximos created beings participate in God through the logoi, but these logoi must also be seen as expressing God's will and intention, for each created being, and for the cosmos as a whole. There is a dynamism about Maximos's understanding of God's relationship to the cosmos through the logoi that is lacking in Plato; the cosmos itself is moving toward fulfillment, and that fulfillment is ultimately found in union with God, by whom it had received being. This opens out into an aspect of Maximos's thought of which we can catch only glimpses: on the one hand these logoi are inviolable, they may be obscured by the fall, but they cannot be distorted — "nothing that is natural is opposed to God."[7] But on the other hand they are not static, certainly not if we take into account that they represent God's will for each creature. Maximos assumes that natures are fixed — all his contemporaries did — but his thought is open to the idea of evolution, say, as a way of expressing God's providence; and certainly for human beings, who possess rational freedom, the meaning of each human logos is expressed through what he calls logoi of providence and judgment, by which God's providential intention is expressed through a working together with free human actions *(synergeia)*.

But to understand Maximos properly, we have to add something else that we have already begun to adumbrate. For if human beings are created in the image of God, and it is the Logos of God that communicates the divine nature, that displays God's image, this means human beings are fashioned after the Logos of God, something manifest in the fact that human beings are *logikoi*, the adjective from *logos*, usually translated "rational" but really connoting something much broader and deeper. One could say that human beings, as *logikoi*, are capable of discerning meaning, maybe even conferring meaning (is that the implication of the story of Adam naming the animals?): it certainly includes free will, which Maximos designates by the Greek word *autexousia*, which means fundamentally "authority over oneself." Because human beings participate in the divine Logos, they are *logikoi*, and are therefore capable of discerning meaning, that is, logos: they are capable of discerning the logoi of creation, the whole depth of meaning that can be found in creation in all its manifold splendor; this understanding of the cosmos Maximos calls *physikē theōria*, natural contemplation. But alas, because of the fall human beings can no longer fulfill this their role as priest and interpreter of creation: they fail to achieve understanding, and the limpid meaning of the cosmos becomes dark obscurity. What is needed is for the Logos himself, the Son of God, to assume rational humanity and to renew the human function as bond of the cosmos from within, so to speak. That is the purpose of the incarnation: through being born of Mary, the mother of God, the Logos of God lives through human existence from within, renewing it in the course of his life, finally confronting the ultimate meaninglessness of death, and giving it meaning in the resurrection. But that is only part, though the biggest part, of the story, for this renewal worked by the incarnate Word of God has to be appropriated by all who are baptized into the death and resurrection of Christ, and this appropriation takes place through participation in the sacramental life of the church and through the ascetic struggle of the Christian life, the overcoming of vices and growing in virtue. This has the implication that the personal life of struggle against temptation, and growing in virtue, is not simply a personal matter, what Michel Foucault has called *souci de soi*, care for the self; it is a matter of cosmic significance, for such ascetic struggle restores the human capacity of being priest of nature, interpreter of the cosmos. This is true for Maximos in various ways, but one that is immediately relevant here is that through ascetic struggle the Christian attains a state of serenity, and one of the fruits of that serenity is being able to discern the logoi of creation: to see the cosmos as God intended it, to have restored our capacity for spiritual sight.

Maximos, in fact, relates this idea of the Logos and the logoi of creation to two other ways Logos and logoi are related: to the idea of the historical incarnation of the Logos, who, as human, spoke to his fellow human beings in words, logoi, and to the revelation of the Logos in the words, logoi, of Scripture. This is sometimes called by interpreters Maximos's doctrine of the three incarnations, for he speaks of each of these relationships of Logos and logoi in terms of incarnation, or embodiment. All three are examples of the Word making himself understood through words: through the creative principles of the cosmos; through the words of the incarnate One, especially his parables, in which he expressed deep mysteries in simple terms; through the words of Scripture, which again clothe divine mysteries in words that can be understood.

In all these cases there is a double movement: the movement of the Word of God toward us, and our movement toward him of understanding. This answering movement of understanding involves more than an expansion of our knowledge (though it does not exclude that); the understanding gained here involves an inner transformation — requiring personal effort, personal asceticism — that opens us up to that which we know (or the One we know), so that it is through *participation* that our understanding is deepened. How far such participation can go — Maximos certainly speaks of it in terms of union with God and even deification or *theosis*, "becoming God" — is a natural question to raise here. For Maximos this participation in God through the logoi (and through them, through the Logos himself) remains creaturely participation, and takes place only through grace; however deeply one comes to participate in God, one remains a creature, and that movement of participation, or deification, is possible only in response to God's prior movement toward us in incarnation (in any of its forms).

But the point of mentioning participation in this context is less to raise such questions than to draw attention to the kind of understanding attained through participation in God through the logoi. Just as we can understand Scripture only if we let it call in question the smallness of our ideas and the narrowness of our desires, so we can understand the logoi of the cosmos only if we renounce any attempt on our part to understand the world as material for human exploitation, and seek to see it as expressive of the Logos of God. Maximos's doctrine of the logoi of creation is not simply a way of expressing the immanence of the divine will, but is also a way of finding a place for human understanding of that will as expressed in creation — a way of human understanding that has its own ascetic demands of patience and objectivity.

Division of Nature

The notion of the division of nature is again a traditional theme. One can find some of its roots in Plato, with his division between the world of the intellect and the world of the senses. But Maximos's most significant predecessor is Saint Gregory of Nyssa, one of the so-called Cappadocian Fathers, who lived in the latter part of the fourth century. For Gregory the most fundamental division in reality is that between uncreated and created reality — between God the Blessed Trinity, who is alone uncreated, and the whole created order, which is created out of nothing. The recognition of this profound gulf between God and creation has a paradoxical effect: on the one hand it stresses the utter transcendence of God, but on the other hand it means that *within the created order* nothing is nearer or further away from God by virtue of the constitution of its being. As the other Cappadocian Gregory said, the most exalted archangel is, in metaphysical terms, no closer to God than a stone: God transcends all creatures infinitely.[8] More immediately, this means that the human person, composed of soul and body, does not consist of one part close to God — the soul — and one part remote from God — the body; both in body and soul the human person is equally close to and remote from God. That is at the level of being, but for human beings there is another level, and that is the level of what we make of our being, the level of what Maximos sometimes calls "mode of existence," the way we are, which is the result of the life we have led, the decisions we have made — ultimately it is the level of the depth or shallowness of our love. Through love we can become close to God, through love — or rather, failure in loving — we confirm the distance from God that exists as a result of the fall. But Maximos, like many thinkers, sees love as fundamentally a unitive force: it draws beings together, sometimes in a violent, possessive way, sometimes in a healing and reconciling way. It is in this context that Maximos develops the idea of divisions of nature. In one place (in *Ambigua* 41) it is developed like this:

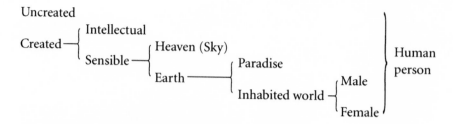

All these divisions are contained within the human person — even, in some sense, the division between uncreated and created, given that the destiny of the human person is deification. As Maximos puts it: "For humanity clearly has the power of naturally uniting at the mean point of each division since it is related to the extremities of each division in its own parts. . . . For this reason the human person was introduced last among beings, as a kind of natural bond mediating between the universal extremes through their proper parts, and leading into unity in itself those things that are naturally set apart from one another by a great interval."[9]

Maximos goes on to show how the human person can embrace all these divisions in his own nature; what emerges is a picture of the spiritual life, in which each stage consists of transcending these divisions, one by one. However, this work of human mediation has been frustrated by the fall, and Maximos shows how through the life, death, and resurrection of the incarnate Word the human task of mediation has been recapitulated, making possible again the cosmic function of the life of ascetic struggle and contemplation. It is interesting to note that these divisions are not resolved by the work of mediation, but embraced or transcended; the divisions remain, but as evidence of the manifold nature of the created order, they do not divide so much as relate. However, in the fallen cosmos — which is the world we know, since the reconciliation achieved by Christ has not been appropriated — these divisions are gulfs of separation and incomprehension. The first we encounter is the divide between the sexes, all too often experienced as a massive fault line in human relationships, and the last of these divisions — that between uncreated and created — is called by Maximos ignorance: ultimately an "unknowing" in which God is known in a way that transcends the operation of the intellect, but all too often simply an experience of the universe as godless and abandoned.[10] When, however, humanity fulfills its mediatorial role, then humanity itself leads the whole created order into union with the uncreated life of the Godhead — to deification.

Deification, or *theosis,* which we have already mentioned a couple times, is a key term in Maximos's theology.[11] Briefly it means the way in which the uncreated God is to share with the cosmos, through humankind, all his divine qualities, save the inalienable quality of being uncreated. As with the notion of deity itself, deification is best approached *apophatically*, that is, by denying what it does not mean. It expresses the *unlimited* parameters of human, and cosmic, participation in the divine — the goal is a diaphanous openness by humankind and the whole of creation to God's will and presence — and in particular includes the insistence that the ultimate purpose of the cosmos is something inherent in God's act of creation itself, with the consequence that a theological understanding of creaturely reality is not limited to considering the restoration of God's purpose to a fallen and fragmented cosmos, but looks beyond that to the ultimate transfiguration of the cosmos, intended from the beginning, a transfiguration in which, in Saint Paul's words, God "will be all in all" (1 Cor. 15:28; cf. Eph. 1:23).[12] It is this point that is most important here: namely, that the goal of deification is not limited to the human, but is the destiny of the whole cosmos.[13] Saint Maximos's divisions of nature may seem to us quaint, but his idea that within the manifold which is the created order there are divisions that can either, when transcended, express the richness and beauty of the created order or alternatively cause gulfs of incomprehension, darkness, and pain seems to me an insight of continuing relevance.

Conclusions

What I have tried to show in my exposition of Maximos's cosmic vision is the way his doctrine of the logoi speaks not only of God's intimate involvement in the cosmos, but also of the central role played by humankind, as microcosm, in both reflecting the cosmos in itself and fulfilling this role by being able to interpret the cosmos. How much of this can we still, in the twenty-first century, *think?* I say "think" because it seems to me it is not so much a matter of accepting certain ideas, but of thinking in a certain way. We must recall what we noticed at the beginning, that Maximos expresses his cosmic vision using ideas that he shared with his contemporaries, both Christian and non-Christian, even if he interprets these ideas in ways that go beyond what many of his contemporaries would have thought. For Maximos and his contemporaries the cosmos was conceived of with the earth at the center (most thought of it as a sphere; the "flat earth" idea, though espoused by some Byzantine Christians, notably Cosmos Indicopleustes [the traveler to the Indies], was not generally accepted in intellectual circles), surrounded by the planets that moved round the earth in cycles that could be represented by spheres, the whole surrounded by the sphere of the fixed stars. It was not very old either:

estimates varied, but Maximos probably thought the cosmos had been created something like six thousand years before his time. And it had all been there — from humans to earthworms, stars to stones — for virtually all of that time.

To see the human as being at the center of such a cosmos, and even to regard the human as mediating between the extremities of the cosmos, would have seemed quite natural. If we are to retain something of Maximos's vision in the context of what we now know about the universe, then we have a good deal of rethinking to do. The universe, as we conceive it, is immensely large: both in time and space. The human presence in the cosmos seems correspondingly minute, and peripheral. We live on the planet of a not very distinguished star, in one galaxy among many, and have been on the scene for only what seems an unimaginably tiny moment, set against the timescale of the universe.

One of the first in Western history to grasp something of the significance of this was the mathematician Blaise Pascal. I find in his reaction to this realization the beginnings of a way in which one might rethink something of Maximos's vision. "Le silence éternel de ces espaces infinis m'effraie" (the eternal silence of these infinite spaces fills me with fear).[14] What kind of fear? Philippe Sellier, in his note to this passage, points to parallels in Augustine (on Ps. 145: "You look to the heavens, and are greatly afraid, you think of the whole earth and tremble") and to the longer treatment of this theme a little earlier in this section, and draws what seems to me the only conclusion: that it is the fear or awe at the magnitude of the cosmos, not an inward intimation of failing faith. The infinity of the universe opened up by science (though it is not a literal infinity, as Pascal thought, only something unimaginably vast) surely only deepens our sense of wonder, compared with what our forefathers felt when they surveyed their rather cozy universe. It only reinforces that characteristic of the thought of the Greek Fathers that has been so attractive over the last century: its emphasis on apophaticism, on the silence of denial of our concepts before the ineffable greatness of God.

Pascal's further steps seem to me even more significant. We tremble before the vastness of the universe; in contrast our humanity seems something puny. "Man is only a reed, more frail than nature, but he is a thinking reed. It does not need the whole universe to wipe him out; a breath, a drop of water, is enough to kill him. But when the universe wipes him out, man will still be nobler that what kills him, since he knows that he dies and knows the advantage the universe has over him. The universe knows nothing."[15] This is what Fr. Staniloae meant in the quotation with which we began: that rather than thinking of the human as a microcosm, it would be more illuminating to think of the universe as a "macro-anthropos," for man can comprehend something of the cosmos, whereas the cosmos comprehends nothing of the human. In an earlier reflection on the *roseau pensant*, Pascal had reflected: "It is not at all in space that I must seek my dignity, but in the ordering of my thought. I would have no advantage at all in possessing the earth. By space the universe embraces me and swallows me up like a point, but by thought I understand it."[16]

Thought — logos: this it is that secures humankind its position in the universe, not a central physical position. It seems to me that Pascal's reflection here converges on modern ideas about the anthropic principle. And it seems to me that we can take these reflections further. Maximos sees the universe given meaning by the logoi through which creatures participate in God. Science sees the universe as governed by laws, to which we humans can give mathematical expression. But for all the impersonal objectivity of mathematics, it is only humans that can know it and understand it. The same seems to be true at the other end of the scale: the discovery that all living beings are structured by DNA. Again it is only to reason that these complex codes can yield any meaning, despite the tendency of some to anthropomorphize and speak, for example, of the "selfish gene."

All this suggests that much of the vision of Saint Maximos can be rethought in terms of current science. Why bother? Why attempt to rethink such ancient modes of thought? Briefly, I would respond thus. Over the last few centuries science has vastly expanded our understanding of the development of the cosmos, the history of life on this planet, and the details of the structures of living beings. But in doing this there has been lost a sense of the whole, of interrelationship between the vast and the tiny, the technical and the meaningful. A monument to this lost coherence might be found in a work like Robert Burton's *Anatomy of Melancholy*, which still preserved the ancient sense of the coherence of all things, from the stars to the humors, in his terms. It is this loss that, many suspect, lies behind the attraction of a host of modern fashions, from New Age religion, revival of paganism, alternative medicine, even ecological concerns: all these witness to the loss of a sense of relationship and coherence. Maximos's vision holds together both a confidence in reason and a sense of the coherence of the whole, and it does this, at one level at least, by having a rich sense of what is meant by reason or logos: not a mere calculating cleverness, a facility for getting results, but a way of making sense that is ultimately participation in the wisdom of the Creator. More than that, Maximos's vision is more than an intellectual theory. One work that brings together many of the ideas outlined above is his brief exposition of the Christian eucharistic liturgy, the *Mystagogia*. In that work the healing power flowing from the incarnation and made effective in personal asceticism is given a cosmic dimension, not through ideas, but through the celebration of the Divine Liturgy, in a symbolism that Maximos shows illuminates everything from the mysteries of the trinitarian Godhead itself, through the glories of the cosmos, to the hidden depths of the human soul. It is this sense of coinherence that the vision of Saint Maximos may help us recover.

WESTERN CHRISTIAN

A Relational and Evolving Universe Unfolding within the Dynamism of the Divine Communion

DENIS EDWARDS

How are we to think about the relationship between a universe of creatures and God? It will be my argument that contemporary science puts before us a universe that can be described as an interrelational world, in which individual entities have their own integrity, and which is evolving at all levels. And in theology the retrieval of a trinitarian understanding of God offers a view of God as a communion characterized by relational unity and diversity. I will propose that when these insights from science and theology are brought into correlation with one another, what emerges is a view of reality in which entities within the universe can be thought of as relational, integral, and evolving. This points toward a relational and evolutionary metaphysics: a relational and evolving universe of entities unfolds within the relational life of the divine communion. This is clearly a view of all-things-in-God, a form of panentheism. In the following section I will attempt a brief clarification of my own approach to panentheism. This will have the advantage of bringing the position taken here into dialogue with other positions represented in this volume.

An Approach to the God-World Relationship

As this volume makes clear, there is a rich diversity of views in philosophy and theology on the God-world relationship. The specific form of panentheism that I embrace can be summarized in the following six points.

1. It is a panentheism that is understood in trinitarian terms.

In this form of panentheism the universe is understood as being created from within the shared life of the Trinity. Creation is understood as the free expression of the fecundity of this dynamic divine life. Creation exists and unfolds from within the communion of the Source of All, the Eternal Wisdom and the Holy Spirit. In the ancient image of Irenaeus, the one who is Source of All acts in creation through the "two hands" of divine Wisdom and the Spirit. All things are created in the Wisdom of God, the same Wisdom who has become incarnate in Jesus of Nazareth. As all things are created *in* Wisdom, so they are created *through* the Spirit of God. The Spirit is the interior divine presence empowering the evolution of the universe from within, enabling a universe of creatures to exist and to become.

2. It understands God as wholly other to creatures and, precisely as such, as radically interior to them.

Along with the great theologians of the past, this form of trinitarian panentheism understands divine transcendence and immanence not as polar opposites but as presupposing each other. Some critics of classical theism misrepresent the past when they suggest that the emphasis on transcendence in theologians like Aquinas makes God remote from creation. Nothing could be further from the truth. It is precisely because God is understood as transcendent that God can be thought of as immanent in creatures in a way that is not possible for a created being. It is because God is wholly other that God can be *interior intimo meo* — closer to me than I am to myself.[1] In this kind of panentheism, then, the infinite ontological distinction between God and creatures is maintained. It is precisely this distinction that enables God to be understood in such radical intimacy with creation.

3. It understands the spatial image of all-things-in-God as an appropriate but limited analogy.

Human beings find it impossible to think of the God-world relationship without some image or analogy. The image of all-in-God is useful in that it appears to fit better with both science and theology than competing mental pictures, such as those of a God in the heavens or of God as a being outside creation who intervenes in it from time to time. Because Christian theology understands God as involved with the whole space-time universe in creation and redemption, but also as beyond space and time, it seems appropriate to think of the universe as evolving within the life of God. While the image and language of all-in-God is useful, I believe it is important that it is not taken in a literal sense. God is not literally any kind of container. In the position taken here, the language of all-in-God is taken as a limited analogy based upon God's creative and redemptive relationship with space and time, which seeks to respect the idea of God's radical transcendence of all finite notions of space and place.

4. It involves the idea of God as a creator who enables creatures to have their own proper autonomy and integrity.

Aquinas saw creation as fundamentally an ongoing relationship between the Creator and the creature — "a certain relation of the creature to the Creator as to the principle of its very being."[2] But he insisted that this creative relationship does not overpower or eliminate a creature's own proper action, but rather enables the creature to be and act with its own proper autonomy. There is an infinite difference between God's *creatio continua* (primary causality) and all the interacting connections and causal relationships between creatures (secondary causality).[3] In this view, which I believe is a foundational insight for all discussion between science and theology, God is understood as creating a world of interacting creatures that have their own integrity. God creates through natural processes that enable a life-bearing universe to evolve. In the light of this insight, it seems appropriate today to think of God as committed to the integrity of natural processes. As God has been understood to respect the integrity of human freedom, so God can be thought of as respecting the creaturely autonomy of nonhuman creation.

5. It sees creation as a free act of divine self-limitation.

Faced with what science tells us about the pain and struggle of the long history of life on earth, theologians have begun to rethink the issue of divine power. Along with a number of others, I would argue that God is freely self-limiting in love. Love involves free self-limitation in making space for another, and God can be thought of as supremely loving in this way. In Jesus, God is revealed not as dominating or tyrannical power, but as defenseless and vulnerable love. This love is certainly also powerful. It involves the promise of life and liberation for all. But the God revealed in the Jesus event is a God present in human history as self-limiting and loving, as a God who accompanies those who suffer, promising freedom and life. This pattern of vulnerable and self-limiting love can be understood to govern not only the story of Jesus but also God's ongoing creation of all creatures. Creation can be seen as a form of divine self-limiting love that enables creatures and creaturely processes to unfold according to their own potentialities and limits. A God committed to the processes of the evolving universe may not be free to override them, but may well be thought of as being present with each creature in faithful, compassionate, and saving love.

6. It understands creation as a relationship that impacts on God as well as creatures.

Along with advocates of process theology, such as Griffin and Bracken in this volume, and with theologians like Moltmann, I believe, against Aquinas and the ancient tradition, that the relationship with creation is real on the side of God as well as on the side of creatures. I would argue that we need to think of the biblical God as capable of suffering — in a divine way — with suffering creation. In this view God can be thought of as supremely and transcendently capable of feeling with finite creatures. The trinitarian God is understood as capable of love that transcends all human loving, as being able to make space for creatures, as being able to suffer with them, to delight in them, to be moved by them, and as being able to bring them to their completion.

Although God radically transcends all notions of space and place, I believe it is appropriate to imagine the divine Trinity as the "place" of the unfolding of the universe. In this kind of theology the Spirit can be thought of as "making space" within the dynamism of the divine trinitarian relations for a world of creatures. In what follows I presume this kind of panentheistic understanding and go further to suggest that insights from both science and theology point to a worldview in which the entities that make up our universe can be understood as *interrelational, integral,* and *evolving* within the dynamism of the divine communion.

All the Entities of the Universe Are Constituted by Relationships

When science looks at any thing at all — whether it be a proton, a galaxy, a cell, or the most complex thing we know, the human brain — it finds systems of relationships. Every entity seems to be constituted by at least two fundamental sets of relationships. First, there are the interrelationships between *the components* that make up an entity. Thus a carbon atom is constituted from subatomic particles (protons, neutrons, and electrons). Second, there is the relationship between the entity and *its wider environment.* So a carbon atom in my body is constituted as part of a molecule, which forms part of a cell, which belongs to an organ of my body. I am part of a family, a human society, and a community of interrelated living creatures on earth. The earth community depends upon and is interrelated with the sun, the Milky Way galaxy, and the whole universe.

Arthur Peacocke tells us that the natural sciences give us a picture of the world as a complex hierarchy, in which there is a series of levels of organization of matter in which each member in the series is a *whole* constituted of *parts* that precede it in the series. He provides an example, expressed (incompletely) in the sequence: "atom — molecule — macromolecule — subcellular organelle — cell — multicellular functioning organ — whole living organism — populations of living organisms — ecosystems — the biosphere."[4] The cosmologist William Stoeger describes the patterns that the natural sciences discover as "constitutive relationships." He asks: "What makes a thing what it is, endowing it with a definite unity of structure and behavior, persistence, and consistency of action?" He says an entity's constitutive relationships make it what it is. He sees constitutive relationships as "those interactions among components and with the larger context which jointly effect the composition of a given system and establish its functional characteristic within the larger whole of which it is a part, and thereby enable it to manifest the particular properties and behavior it does."[5]

When we think about the relationship between a complex entity such as a cell and what makes it up, we find that it is structured in what Peacocke and Stoeger call a "hierarchical" fashion. I will call this the "articulated" structure of nature. It refers to the pattern where one level of a system is nested upon another. At every level from fundamental particles to atoms, molecules, cells, and the brain itself, one level of reality is articulated upon another. Stoeger argues that this kind of articulated structuring is a universal feature of the world that is revealed by the natural and social sciences. At every level this nested organization is realized through the interrelationships between the components, together with the whole-part relationships that determine the distribution and collective function of components.[6]

Constitutive relationships involve all those connections and interactions that incorporate components into a more complex whole, and relate that complex whole into another level of unity. These constitutive relationships may be physical, biological, or social in character. When we move beyond science into philosophy and theology, we can add that the most important constitutive relationship of all, one that operates on a radically different level to all the others, is metaphysical. It is the relationship of creation, the relation of the creator Spirit to each creature that enables it to be and to become.

While science suggests a world of constitutive relationships, theology points to a trinitarian God of mutual relations. Theology understands God's being as communion. God exists only as a communion of persons. In recent writings a number of trinitarian theologians argue that if God's being is communion, then this has implications for the understanding of reality as such. If God's being is radically relational, then this suggests that reality is *ontologically* relational. The very *being* of things is relational being. It is this shared insight of recent theology that I am attempting to bring into a fruitful dialogue with the natural sciences and to develop in the direction of a metaphysical view of reality.

John Zizioulas states that "it is communion that makes things be: nothing exists without it, not even God."[7] He holds that nothing is conceivable as existing only by itself. There is no true being without communion.[8] Walter Kasper argues that understanding the unity of the divine nature as a "unity in love" suggests "breaking out of an understanding of reality that is characterized by the primacy of subject and nature, and into an understanding of reality in which person and relation have priority."[9] Catherine LaCugna writes that "God's To-Be is To-Be-in-relationship, and God's being-in-relationship-to-us *is* what God is."[10] Her trinitarian theology becomes a sustained argument for what she calls an ontology of relation. Hence she writes that an ontology which is proper to the God of the economy of salvation "understands being as being-in-relation not being-in-itself."[11] Colin Gunton writes that "of both God and the world it must be said that they have their being in relation."[12] Elizabeth Johnson holds that "the Trinity provides a symbolic picture of totally shared life at the heart of the universe." She says the Trinity as pure relationality "epitomizes the connectedness of all that exists in the universe."[13]

The theological insight that God is persons-in-relation, that God is communion, can provide a basis for a vision of the fundamental reality of the universe as relational. If the essence of God is relational, if the very foundation of all being is relational, if everything that is springs from persons-in-relation, then this points toward an understanding of created reality that might be called a metaphysics of "being in relation." In such an understanding of reality, not only is God persons-in-relation, but each creature can be understood as a being-in-relation. Science tells us that each creature exists in a nested pattern of constitutive relations. Theology grounds this in the trinitarian relationships of mutual love. There is, of course, an infinite difference between created being-in-relation and the divine communion. But what continuous creation means is that created being-in-relation always springs from the divine persons-in-relation.

Not only human persons, but also all the creatures that make up the universe, in their highly differentiated ways, are radically interrelational and at the same time possess their own individual integrity. In a trinitarian theology of creation, *all* creatures participate in the life of trinitarian communion, and their differentiated relationships with each other are already a limited creaturely reflection of this divine communion. In their different ways every creature, whether it be an insect, a tree, or a star, exists only in a network of relationships. We live in a radically interrelated universe.

Individual Entities Have Their Own Integrity

Individual entities are not only radically interconnected with others, but they also have their own identity and unique autonomy. Individual entities have a degree of self-directedness — whether we think of human beings with their experience of being free agents, of birds with their glorious freedom in flight, or of particles like photons whose individual motion cannot be predetermined. Not everything we come across in nature has an identity of its own. Some things, such as the pile of papers on my desk, are simply collections of other things and do not form a new whole. Stoeger makes the important distinction between things that are simply aggregates or collections of components, such as a pile of logs or a mountain, and those entities that form a new whole and have characteristics that are essentially different from their components. An example of such a new reality would be water, which has characteristics that are distinctive over and above its components of hydrogen and oxygen. Its functions and attributes cannot be reduced to the functions and attributes of its components. Its distinctive characteristics spring not only from its components but also from all its other constitutive relationships. It functions as a whole in a way that cannot be attributed simply to the way its component parts function.[14]

An individual thing like a water molecule exists only in patterns of constitutive relations, yet it has its own identity, characteristics, and functions. It has a level of autonomous existence. It is both relational and substantive. It is precisely its constitutive relationships that allow it to be particular and substantive. It seems clear that in nature, individuality and distinctiveness are not opposed to interrelationality, but can exist only in patterns of interrelationship. Relationships can be of many kinds. A human body has a relationship with the cells that make it up. A predator has a relationship with its prey. The fact that relationships characterize and constitute reality does not necessarily mean that reality is always characterized by what human beings might think of as healthy and good relationships. Feminist thinkers have shown how in human affairs patriarchal relationships damage and limit human life.[15]

What kinds of relationships characterize creation as a whole? In nature we find amazing and beautiful patterns of mutual dependency, cooperation, and shared life. But we also find competition for survival, predation, and death. Our experience of the relationships that characterize the natural world is deeply ambiguous. I would argue that this ambiguity ought not be resolved by any kind of simple synthesis. It is important to celebrate the beauty and wonder of the evolving universe and its creatures. It is important, too, to face the pain, the violence, and the death. If we had only nature as the source for our thinking about relationships, then we would already know that we are part of an interrelational universe, interconnected with all other things. There would already be much to wonder about in this. But we would also find that some of the patterns of interrelationship in nature are highly competitive and exploitative, and we would have to admit that the most exploitative species on earth is our own. Any attempt at understanding human ethical life simply in terms of natural selection and the survival of the fittest can only end in absolute disaster. Clearly a theology of relationships cannot find its source and criteria simply in the relationships that are found in the natural world.

A Christian understanding of relationships springs in part from nature, but has its criterion in the compassionate love of God revealed in Jesus Christ and in the outpouring of the Spirit. Its model of relationships is the trinitarian model of mutual and equal love. In spite of the ambiguity we find in nature, a theology of God dares to suggest that diversity in communion may be the ultimate eschatological nature of all reality, uncreated and created. The theology of God does not resolve the ambiguity we find in created relations. It leaves us like Job before the mystery. But it also functions as a promise. It tells us that the ultimate relationships that undergird the expanding universe and the evolution of life on earth are very specific kinds of relationships. They are relationships of absolutely equal and mutual love, of dynamic shared life. In these kinds of relationships individuals flourish in all their irreducible individuality and otherness. The divine communion is the source of all the constitutive relationships that make up the entities that exist in our universe.

If communion in God is the ultimate destiny of all creatures, then every creature has its own integrity because it is loved by God. From the perspective of science, the individual integrity of things is given in all the constitutive relationships that make the entity what it is. From the perspective of theology, each individual creature has its own independent value within an interrelated universe springing from its relationship with the indwelling Spirit.

The Universe, with All the Entities
That Make It Up, Evolves in Time

The sciences make it abundantly clear that time is a fundamental dimension of the way things are in our universe. The universe evolves over extraordinary lengths of time, and without the patient unfolding of things in time nothing at all could ever happen. It is impossible to conceive of a universe anything like our own that does not emerge in time. Individual entities exist not only in communities of interrelationship in the present, but also in relationship with all the creatures that preceded them, and with all the unknown creatures that will follow. This understanding of ourselves and all other living creatures, as beings who evolve over enormous lengths of time within an evolving universe, demands a different view of reality from anything that was available to Plato or Aristotle, Aquinas or Bonaventure, Galileo or Newton. As individual human beings, we exist only for a brief moment, fragile, contingent, and in the perspective of the universe, as transitory as a butterfly.

Human beings are significant parts of the tapestry that unfolds in time, interconnected with all that comes to be in time. Cosmology offers a prime example of the way humans along with everything else in the universe are time-dependent in what is called "anthropic" reasoning. Cosmologists tell us that the universe has to be roughly as old as it is and as big as it is if it is to be a place in which human beings could evolve. We are made up of atoms of carbon, nitrogen, phosphorus, and oxygen. These elements are cooked in stars, as hydrogen and helium are transformed into heavier elements over billions of years. John Barrow tells us that it takes at least 10 billion years of stellar burning to produce elements like the carbon from which we are made.[16] We exist only because the stars convert hydrogen into the heavier elements that are needed for living creatures. The universe has to be as old as it is for galaxies to form, stars to ignite, elements like carbon to be synthesized, a solar system incorporating these elements to form around the sun, and life to evolve on earth.

A second, obvious example of the way all things within the universe are radically time-dependent comes from our understanding of the evolution of life by random mutation and natural selection. It seems that life first emerged on earth in bacterial form about 3.8 billion years ago, developed into more complex and then multicellular forms over billions of years, expanded rapidly in the Cambrian period half a billion years ago, and then evolved into all the extraordinary forms we find today, including human beings with their complex brains. One way of reflecting on the way this whole process depends on time is to ponder the place of death in the evolution of life. Evolutionary change in complex organisms depends upon death. Without death there could not be a series of generations. Without a series of generations there could be no evolution. It is precisely because of sexual recombination and death that we have the variety of complex creatures we find on earth today. Without death there would be no wings, hands, or brains. Ursula Goodenough writes: "Death is the price paid to have trees and clams and birds and grasshoppers, and death is the price paid to have human consciousness."[17]

All of this suggests that existence depends upon all that has gone before and can contribute to the new that is yet to emerge. We exist only in evolutionary process. There is a necessary incompleteness in the way things are. We are not yet what we shall be. When we turn to the Christian theology of God, we find that it always has an inescapable orientation toward the future. Divine communion has an eschatological character. We live from it yet we do not possess it. It comes toward us from the future. Biblical revelation has the character of promise and hope. For Israel this took the shape of the divine promises, prophetic hope, and messianic expectation. In Jesus it found expression in his preaching and praxis in the light of the coming reign of God. For those who follow the way of Jesus, and live in the light of the promise of resurrection and new creation, it means living in constant expectation of God as the eschatological future.

Karl Rahner sees the biblical God as the *Absolute Future* — the future not only of human beings but also of all creation. He insists that the discovery that we are part of an evolving world demands a new understanding of reality, a new metaphysics. God, now, must be understood not simply as the dynamic cause of the *existence* of creatures, but as the dynamic ground of their *becoming.* In evolutionary history we can find instances when what *is* clearly *becomes something altogether new,* as in the emergence of self-conscious human beings. Rahner argues that we need to think of the divine act of ongoing creation, then, not simply as the divine "conservation" and *"concursus" of* all things, but *as the enabling of creation to become what is radically new.*[18] Rahner calls this process "active self-transcendence." He sees this capacity to become something new as a capacity that nature itself has. He insists that evolutionary emergence has its own autonomy and its own explanation at the level of science. It is to be explained by the laws of nature. But at the deepest metaphysical level, it is God who enables this becoming. God is the inner power of evolutionary emergence.[19]

I see the Spirit of God as the power of the future, immanent in all the processes of the evolving universe, enabling it to become what is new.[20] The Spirit of God is at work in evolutionary emergence whenever something radically new occurs, whenever nature reaches ecstatically beyond itself in the unfolding of the universe and in the dynamic story of life. The divine communion is our eschatological future. It is the eschatological future for all of creation. In all events the Spirit acts to bring creation into a new future. The Spirit enables the new to occur in time. The creator Spirit is immanent in a time-bound universe, deeply involved with its becoming. But the Spirit is also the eschatological Spirit, the Spirit of the divine eternal communion.

Conclusion

The starting point for my own understanding of the God-world relationship is a key insight of the theology of creation of Thomas Aquinas, in which all things exist and unfold with their own integrity only because God holds them in being at every moment. In this view there is an infinite difference between God's ongoing creation of all that exists (primary causality), which is beyond empirical observation, and all the interactions between creatures that can be discovered through the methods of the natural sciences (secondary causality). While I embrace this insight as foundational, I believe it needs to be transformed and developed in four important ways. Two of these I have assumed in this context: first, the ancient tradition needs to be developed in such a way that God is not thought of as immune from the suffering of creatures but is divinely capable of feeling with the pain of creatures; second, God's "almighty power" is not to be conceived as the absolute power of an earthly tyrant, but as the divine capacity for love, which involves a divine capacity for self-limitation that makes room for creaturely integrity and human freedom.

My proposal here has been that two further transformations of the tradition are called for. First, contemporary science points to the fact that created entities are constituted by relationships, while contemporary trinitarian theology points out that God exists only as communion. Taken together, these insights suggest an ontology of relationship in which to be is to be in relationship. This involves a transformation of the classical approach to the theology of creation toward a relational metaphysics in which it is understood that it is *communion that makes things be* (Zizioulas). Second, the discovery that the universe has been evolving over the last 15 billion years and that life has evolved on earth over the last 3.8 billion years means that God's creative action cannot be thought of simply as enabling things to exist. It must be seen as enabling things to evolve and to become what is new. This represents a further radical transformation of metaphysics, so that God is now understood as *enabling and empowering the evolutionary unfolding of creation in a process of self-transcendence from within* (Karl Rahner).

I have sought to describe a relational and evolving universe that is the expression of a relational God who makes space for and embraces the whole and all its parts. This universe can be understood as a radically interrelational world, a world in which individual creatures have their own integrity, and a world which is evolving in time at every level. God as eschatological communion enables an interrelational and evolving universe to be and to become, in and through the creator Spirit's interior presence to each creature.

Panentheism: A Field-Oriented Approach

JOSEPH A. BRACKEN, S.J.

Panentheism is frequently presented as an agreeable compromise between monism and dualism, i.e., between pantheism, in which God is identified with the material universe, and classical theism, in which God is represented as separate from the world as its transcendent creator.[1] At the same time, one must be careful not to caricature thereby either pantheism or classical theism. Many scientists, for example, including Albert Einstein, prefer not to think of God in personalistic terms but rather conceive God as a cosmic force or principle of order within the universe.[2] Likewise, Thomas Aquinas, the premier representative of classical theism, makes clear that God as the subsistent act of being is present to creatures in causing them to be: "God exists in everything, not indeed as part of their substance or as an accident, but as an agent is present to that in which its action takes place."[3] Yet, since God's being according to Aquinas is infinitely other than and superior to the act of being proper to creatures, God is more properly transcendent of creation than immanent within it.

Furthermore, even given the initial attractiveness of the notion of panentheism, that is, creation somehow existing within God, it is not at all clear how this is to be understood. Certainly within classical metaphysics grounded in the Aristotelian category of substance, such a "nondual" relationship between God and the world would seem to be impossible. One substance cannot exist within another substance without being absorbed into the substantial reality of the first substance, as in human ingestion of food.[4] Perhaps the most common explanation of panentheism is the soul-body analogy in which soul and body, though distinct from one another, nevertheless constitute one integral reality. In this way God is represented as the "soul" of the universe, and the universe is seen as the "body" of God. There are, of course, limitations to this analogy. A literal understanding of the metaphor would restrict the ontological freedom of God vis-à-vis the world in that, in order to exist, God must have a body: not necessarily this world, but certainly some world.[5] Likewise, the ontological independence of creatures, above all human beings, would seem to be restricted insofar as they would seem to be reduced to body parts with God as the sole effective agent within the world.[6]

A New Foundational Metaphor

In this essay, accordingly, I will present still another scheme for a panentheistic understanding of the God-world relationship. It will be based on a rethinking of the process-relational metaphysics of Alfred North Whitehead in which the basic category of "society" will be presented as a structured field of activity for its constituent "actual occasions" or momentary subjects of experience. In brief, I will be arguing that the three divine persons of the Christian doctrine of the Trinity co-constitute an all-inclusive divine field of activity which simultaneously serves as the "matrix" or womb of creation. Within this all-inclusive matrix creation has gradually taken shape as an extremely complex, hierarchically emergent set of fields for Whiteheadian actual occasions with varying degrees of interrelatedness. For while it is inappropriate, as noted above, to think of substances within substances, there seems to be no ontological problem with lower-level fields existing within higher-order fields. The lower-level fields presumably operate according to their own laws even as they contribute to the existence and activity of the higher-order fields. Similarly, the higher-order fields regulate in some measure but never completely control the mode of operation of entities within the lower-level fields. In this way the ontological independence of God from the world and the world from God would seem to be better protected than in the organismic model of the God-world relationship as indicated above. Furthermore, as I will indicate below, using this field-oriented model for the God-world relationship, one can philosophically justify two classical Christian beliefs which are effectively called into question by the organismic model, namely, belief in God as triune rather than simply unipersonal, and belief in creation out of nothing (apart from God). For creation, in terms of this scheme, is at every moment emergent out of the divine matrix, existing in its own right here and now, and yet continually being incorporated into the communitarian life of the three divine persons as its ultimate salvation or self-fulfillment.[7]

In advance of my explanation of this hypothesis, however, I wish to make clear that in thus using a field metaphor I am consciously working with a theoretical model or symbolic representation of the God-world relationship. As Ian Barbour wisely commented some years ago, models in both natural science and theology "are to be taken seriously but not literally; they are neither literal pictures nor useful fictions but limited and inadequate ways of imagining what is not observable."[8] Thus I am not suggesting, for example, that the laws of physics governing electromagnetism can be applied without qualification to the divine field of activity constituted by the dynamic interrelationship of the three divine persons. Presumably there are different kinds of fields even within the world of creation, with each operating according to its own internal dynamic. What I am proposing is a new foundational metaphor that seeks systematically to explain reality, something to replace the now outdated Aristotelian notion of substance as the underlying principle of continuity within a world marked by constant change and development. For patterns clearly emerge out of the interplay of ongoing interrelated events, and these patterns must somehow be sustained so as to preserve the order and continuity of nature. My argument is simply that the patterns are indeed sustained in terms of circumambient structured fields of activity or environments which, on the one hand, condition the events taking place within them but, on the other hand, over time are themselves reconfigured by new events and new patterns emergent within them.

"Society" in Whitehead's Metaphysical Scheme

Why then did Whitehead himself not make more use of this notion of field or environment in his metaphysical scheme? He himself evidently prized his key category of actual entity or actual occasion since in his mind actual entities were "the final real things of which the world is made up."[9] Perhaps for the same reason he did not spend enough time reflecting on the correlative notion of "society" even though he recognized that societies remain while actual entities by definition come and go.[10] My hunch is that he was implicitly faced with a conceptual dilemma. If societies are nothing more than aggregates of actual entities, then it is questionable whether societies really endure over time since a new aggregate is generated at every instant with only the pattern or "common element of form" for the next generation of actual entities surviving the passage of time.[11] Yet if he insisted too strongly that societies are more than aggregates of actual entities, then the classical notion of substance as that which underlies accidental changes over time would seem to be indirectly repristinated. Presumably his solution to the dilemma was to say very little about societies as such and to focus on the interplay of the constituent actual entities. In his masterwork *Process and Reality,* to be sure, he briefly talks about societies as hierarchically ordered "environments" or "layers of social order" for any given set of actual entities. Thus "every society requires a social background, of which it is itself a part," with "the defining characteristics" of the supportive societies "becoming wider and more general as we widen the background."[12] By implication, then, societies are not themselves formless but antecedently structured by the interplay of previous generations of actual entities. Thus the pattern or common element of form transmitted from one generation of actual entities to another is, so to speak, imprinted in the structure of the society (societies) to which they all belong.[13]

My own contribution to Whiteheadian scholarship for many years now has been to suggest that this notion of an environment or, as I would phrase it, a field could well serve as the process-relational equivalent of substance in classical metaphysics, that which endures over time and undergoes accidental modifications. And yet it would be sufficiently different from the classical understanding of substance to fit into a process-oriented vision of reality. For example, unlike the substantial form within classical metaphysics which is the active organizing principle for the "material elements," the form or pattern of organization within a structured field of activity for successive generations of actual entities is passive rather than active; at any given moment it is the result of the ongoing interplay of successive generations of actual occasions. Agency is still present within the field, of course, but it is the collective agency of all the constituent actual occasions working in unison rather than the agency of a single organizing principle.[14] Finally, given the ever present possibility of a change in the ongoing pattern of organization for the constituent actual occasions, the overall form or structure of the field of activity is far more contingent and subject to change than would be the case with the substantial form within Aristotelian metaphysics. Priority is thus given within this scheme to becoming over being rather than to being over becoming, as in classical metaphysics.

Application to the God-World Relationship

In any event, given this field-oriented approach to Whiteheadian societies, it is relatively easy to justify, first of all, a trinitarian understanding of God within process-relational metaphysics. Each of the three divine persons can be understood as a personally ordered society of divine actual occasions, therefore, as presiding over an infinite field of activity proper to itself as this divine person.[15] But since each of these fields of activity is indeed infinite, the three divine persons end up sharing a common all-inclusive field of activity which constitutes their objective reality as one God rather than three gods in relatively close interaction. Their ontological unity is grounded in a common field of activity. Just as in classical trinitarian theology the divine persons have everything in common except their relations of opposition to one another,[16] in my theory they have everything in common except their differing roles within one and the same objective field of activity. To be more specific, within their common field of activity the Father and Son share an ongoing I-Thou relation with the Spirit as the personal mediator between them so as to constitute a divine community. Thus the divine field of activity is not empty or formless, but structured according to a definite pattern of interpersonal relations.

Furthermore, if one likewise accepts this field-oriented interpretation of Whiteheadian societies for the world of creation, then creation as a whole can be seen as a progressively more complex, hierarchically ordered set of fields for actual occasions of varying degrees of complexity. Whitehead himself in *Process and Reality* distinguished four grades of actual occasions: "First and lowest, there are the actual occasions in so-called 'empty space'; secondly, there are the actual occasions which are moments in the life-histories of enduring non-living objects; thirdly, there are the actual occasions which are moments in the life-histories of enduring living objects; fourthly, there are the actual occasions which are moments in the life-histories of enduring objects with conscious knowledge."[17] Whitehead proposes that these differing grades of actual occasions exist conjointly here and now. But one can readily imagine how they came into existence successively over the enormous periods of time within the universe since the so-called big bang. Initially, within the field proper to creation there were nothing but "virtual particles," actual occasions basically disconnected from one another which did not endure long enough to form patterns of interrelated activity so as to constitute Whiteheadian societies of any kind. Then after the "primordial soup" resulting from the big bang cooled sufficiently, there appeared first subatomic particles and then by degrees societies of atomic and molecular actual occasions with a minimal pattern of order passed on from one generation to the next. Billions of years later (at least on this planet), societies of actual occasions which constituted first plant life and then animal life came into existence. Finally, with the development of the brain and nervous system within higher-order animals, there emerged that unique structured society of actual occasions which we know as our own species. Yet, as Whitehead maintains, all these grades of actual occasions still exist in dynamic interrelation so as to constitute the overall structured society of actual occasions which is the universe as a whole.

As noted above, with his focus on the key concept of an actual occasion as a momentary self-constituting subject of experience, Whitehead did not attend carefully enough to the correlative notion of society as that which endures as actual occasions come and go. This is especially true of his approach to supraorganic societies or societies in the more conventional sense of the word (i.e., communities, environments for both living and nonliving entities, etc.). Hence, as I have argued elsewhere,[18] it is useful to compare and contrast Whitehead's notion of society with the notion of "system" to be found within the philosophy of Ervin Laszlo and other systems-oriented thinkers. For, like a Whiteheadian society when understood as a structured field of activity for its constituent actual occasions, a system is an ontological totality which is in principle greater than and to some extent other than the sum of its interrelated parts or members. That is, a system is a "relational entity" with characteristics proper to itself which are indeed derived from but not simply reducible to the "mechanical" pattern of interaction among its parts or members.[19] Human communities, for example, are systems in Laszlo's sense since they are clearly more than just an aggregate of human beings living together at the same time and in the same place. As Josiah Royce pointed out years ago in *The Problem of Christianity*, a human community "has a past and will have a future," even though that past and future are largely determined by individual human beings engaged in acts of "interpretation" to one another about their life together.[20] The members of the community, in other words, are inevitably conditioned by the past history of the community in which they live, and at the same time they contribute to its future shape through their own individual decisions or "acts of interpretation." In similar fashion nonhuman social groupings like natural environments are configured by the interrelated activities of the various entities living within them. Over time they acquire a natural history, that is, a distinctive past and future which allow them to be distinguished from other such environments. Furthermore, systems like societies of Whiteheadian actual occasions can be layered within one another and thus be hierarchically ordered from the simpler to the more complex, or (from another perspective) from the more loosely organized to the more tightly organized. The entire known universe, according to Laszlo, can be thus organized into a comprehensive set of interrelated systems or hierarchically ordered fields of activity.[21]

Only a combination of insights from Laszlo and Whitehead, however, allows one to set forth a consistent panentheistic understanding of the God-world relationship. That is, where Laszlo saw better than Whitehead how specifically social realities like systems or Whiteheadian societies must be greater than and in some measure different from their individual parts or members, Whitehead recognized that the ultimate components of such systems must be individual entities capable of dynamic interrelation so as to constitute the systems in the first place. That is, Whitehead realized that "the final real things of which the world is made up" must be actual entities, momentary subjects of experience capable of internalizing their relations to one another through mutual "prehension" and thereby effecting a union with one another deeper than that of a simple aggregate of things spatially juxtaposed to one another.[22] A judicious combination of insights from Whitehead and Laszlo, accordingly, should allow for a trinitarian interpretation of the God-world relationship even as one consistently defends something like an "emergent monism" for one's understanding of creation. In the remaining pages of this essay, I will briefly set forth this scheme.

Emergent Monism within a Trinitarian Worldview

First of all, if, as stipulated above, the three divine persons can be regarded as personally ordered societies of actual occasions which co-create a common structured field of activity for their dynamic interrelation, then all created so-cieties will fit into an intersubjective world that is already constituted by the dynamic interrelation of the divine persons. That is, just as the three divine persons continually "prehend" one another and thereby co-generate their di-vine life together, so all created actual occasions prehend one another so as to form societies of varying degrees of complexity and comprehensiveness. But they also implicitly prehend the divine persons and the pattern of relatedness between the divine persons. Hence, at least when they are properly responsive to what Whitehead calls the divine "initial aim" at the inception of their pro-cess of self-constitution,[23] they find themselves somehow aligned with the Son in the Son's response to the Father in the power of the Spirit. In effect, a trinitarian rhythm governs the universe even though it is at best marginally experienced even by human beings.

Harold Morowitz, in another essay for this volume, likewise takes note of a trinitarian structure to the cosmic process. In his mind evolution in-volves "immanence, emergence, and transcendence," which for the scientist translate into "the origin of the universe, the origin of life, and the origin of mind."[24] His trinity, accordingly, is purely naturalistic since it makes no con-scious reference to the activity of the divine persons within the cosmic pro-cess. Yet in my judgment one can rethink what is meant by transcendence, immanence, and emergence within evolution and come up with a much more traditional understanding of the God-world relationship. The principle of transcendence within the cosmic process, for example, could be readily identified with the person of the Father within the classical doctrine of the Trinity, especially if one accepts the dialogical model of the divine life. That is, if the Father is the "I" within the divine I-Thou relationship, then the Father could well be considered the transcendent principle both within the divine being and within creation. On this view the Father is the initiator both of the divine life within the Trinity and of the world of creation, in that the Father supplies divine initial aims to all created actual occasions to guide them in their individual acts of self-constitution and to group them into "societies" according to a pregiven pattern or common element of form.[25] The Son, on the other hand, as the respondent to the Father within the divine life, can be readily seen as immanent within creation in its collective response to the Father's initial aims. That is, only in and through union with the Son, above all for Christians with the Son as incarnate in the person of the risen Jesus or the cosmic Christ, can creation be said to exist in an ongoing I-Thou relationship with the Father.

Finally, given the classical role of the Holy Spirit within the divine life as mediator between Father and Son, the one who effects the unity of the divine community, one sees how the factor of emergence within the cosmic process can be properly attributed to the activity of the Holy Spirit in the world. Emergence within the world process, in other words, is characterized by the creation of new and higher unities among lower-level systems or societies of individual entities (in the Whiteheadian scheme, interrelated actual occasions). Since the Spirit sustains the unity of the divine life, the Spirit quite properly can be said to be the divine force at work within creation to create and sustain ever higher unities of created entities en route to full union with the Son as incarnate in the cosmic Christ. Thus all three divine persons are at work in creation, although not in a way that human beings would unquestionably recognize as the presence of God in the world. Thus, as Morowitz comments, one can see the cosmic process as inherently possessing the characteristics of transcendence, immanence, and emergence. But to the eyes of faith these same characteristics can be properly attributed to the work of the divine persons in the world.[26]

This raises a further question about the God-world relationship within this scheme, namely, whether or not one can conceive the cosmic process in naturalistic terms as "emergent monism" even as one makes the claim that the world somehow exists in God and is sustained by the power of God. Consider, for example, the essay of Arthur Peacocke in this volume. Therein he argues that "everything can be broken down into fundamental physical entities and that no *extra* entities are thought to be inserted at higher levels of complexity to account for their properties."[27] Within the framework of the neo-Whiteheadian scheme outlined above, there exist only actual occasions as "the final real things of which the world is made up." There are then no "extra entities" inserted at higher levels of complexity to account for new higher-level properties of existence and activity within the created order. There are, to be sure, increasingly complex fields of activity; but their basic constituents are always the same: momentary subjects of experience in dynamic interrelation. Likewise, there are different grades of actual occasions because of the varying complexity of the environment or field in which they arise. But Whitehead's scheme is basically "atomistic"[28] in that at all levels of existence and activity within the world, actual occasions are "the final real things of which the world is made up."

The basic difference between Peacocke's scheme and mine, of course, is that for Peacocke these foundational entities are bits of matter; for me (and Whitehead) they are spiritual entities, momentary subjects of experience, but still physically real. Spirit for me, then, is constitutive of physical reality at all levels of existence and activity; matter is a by-product of spiritual entities in dynamic interrelation. This may seem outrageous until one reflects upon the basic claim of panentheism, namely, that all things exist in God and through the power of God. If God is likewise a transcendent subject of experience or, in trinitarian terms, three dynamically interrelated subjects of experience within an infinite field of activity, what is more natural than for those same three divine persons to bring into existence creaturely subjects of experience capable of responsiveness to themselves in varying degrees? Likewise, what would be more natural as the underlying goal and purpose of creation than to incorporate these created subjects of experience into the divine communitarian life once they have achieved full actuality, that is, taken on specific form and determination within the environment or field to which they belong? Perhaps it is the very nature of spirit to objectify itself in what we loosely term matter. That is, just as the three divine persons continually objectify their relationship to one another so as to constitute the infinite field of activity proper to their divine nature, and just as those same divine persons have objectified themselves in creating the world as an ongoing cosmic process, so must it be necessary for creaturely subjects of experience to objectify themselves, to achieve full actuality within the conditions of space and time before they can be incorporated into the divine communitarian life. Otherwise they would indeed be part of God but not existent in their own right, as the notion of panentheism requires.

The Problem of Evil

One final question remains before bringing this essay to a close, namely, how this scheme deals with the problem of evil and the correlative notions of God's goodness and justice. For if all creatures without exception are incorporated into the divine communitarian life upon cessation of their existence in this world, then how can one defend the idea that God is all good and that no evil exists in God? Furthermore, how is God's justice served if all creatures eventually share in the divine communitarian life, quite irrespective of their malicious or in any case irresponsible activity in this life? An answer to these questions will always remain somewhat speculative, given the inevitable finitude of our human understanding of the God-world relationship. But in terms of the neo-Whiteheadian scheme laid out above, one should initially take note of the fact that both good and evil in this world are the result of "decisions" made by actual occasions or momentary subjects of experience in their process of self-constitution. These decisions in many, if not most, cases are not conscious, still less self-conscious, if one agrees with Whitehead that actual occasions are operative on all levels of creaturely existence and activity (including the subatomic). But objective patterns arise in any case as a result of those decisions, and these patterns are recorded in the structured field(s) of activity or environment(s) to which these actual occasions belong. Hence a decision, good or bad, is never eradicated. But its significance or value can be altered when one looks at the decision diachronically and synchronically. Diachronically the decision of an actual occasion here and now is heavily conditioned by the antecedent structure of the field or environment out of which it arises. Hence it either contributes to a structure or pattern of behavior already present in the field or in some modest way participates in the gradual reconfiguration of that structure. In either case, however, the individual decision, while unquestionably a fact in its own right, nevertheless gains or loses in significance only when one assesses it in the light of the ongoing historical process.

In similar fashion the decision of an individual actual occasion, when viewed synchronically, has to be evaluated not only in terms of the field or fields to which it immediately belongs, but likewise in terms of the entire cosmic process as it is unfolding within the divine matrix or divine communitarian life. Once again, without undercutting the factual reality of a malicious decision and its impact upon an immediate environment, one must be prepared to view it within the broader context of what is likewise going on at the same time. Certainly the divine persons are in a much better position to assess the enduring value and significance of any creaturely decision. Likewise, they and they alone, through the communication of divine initial aims, are in a position to confirm fruitful and productive decisions and to reorient disruptive and irresponsible decisions within the limits of their power to persuade (rather than coerce) subsequent generations of creaturely actual occasions.

The net effect of this line of thought, of course, is not to discount the pain and suffering that can come into this world as a result of such counterproductive creaturely decisions but only to counsel patience and fortitude in dealing with the immediate consequences of those decisions, either made by oneself or by others in one's environment or field of activity. It may well be that in a cosmic process characterized by trial and error at every level of existence and activity, there may be no other way to move forward in the direction of ultimate union with the cosmic Christ. Within this scheme, to be sure, human beings represent a special case since at the moment of death they must presumably say yes consciously and freely to the above-mentioned transformation of the meaning and value of their individual lives within the context of the entire cosmic process. They must, in other words, accept the full truth about themselves, their relations to fellow creatures, and their enduring relationship to the triune God as a precondition of salvation or full acceptance into the divine communitarian life. Hence a period of purgatorial self-reflection might well be necessary before they freely embrace the antecedent divine offer of forgiveness and reconciliation despite the inevitably flawed character of their personal lives. Hell, then, would exist only for those individuals who for whatever reason would not make that decision. They would continue to live within the divine communitarian life but in a state of permanent psychic estrangement from God and their fellow creatures. As Whitehead comments in his "eschatology" in the final chapter of *Process and Reality*, God "loses nothing that can be saved."[29] But not even God can violate the power of choice inherent within human subjectivity in forcing an individual to accept an objectively greater good.[30]

Panentheism and Pansyntheism:
God in Relation

RUTH PAGE

Process philosophy and process theology have made a valuable contribution to theological thought, particularly in their description of the immanence of God as one pole of the divine being, thus emphasizing the proximity of God without surrendering ineffable transcendence. Further, in their view the whole sweep of creation is envisaged in the divine process, not simply the human chapter. The metaphysic of divine presence is expressed in panentheism, well defined in the *Oxford Dictionary of the Christian Church* as "The belief that the being of God includes and penetrates the whole universe, so that every part exists in Him [*sic*], but (as against pantheism) that His Being is more than, and is not exhausted by, the universe."[1]

Some Problems in Panentheism

Given that metaphysical background, however, there are various ways it may be applied to God's action in, and relation to, creation. Creation itself is a multiple conception and has to be considered as a whole project, as an evolving process, and as it affects every creature. Further, a description of what relationship involves will affect accounts of the Divine-creation relationship. Therefore, while accepting totally the definition of panentheism given above, I believe some more particular expositions of God in relation to creation have serious difficulties, which this chapter will discuss. These difficulties may be overcome by a different model of relationship which I shall then proceed to describe in terms of *pansyntheism:* God with everything.

The first problem with some writing on panentheism is that it takes a wide overview of evolution, seeking to give it all a pattern. Thus, what are celebrated are emergent levels of *complexity* ("hierarchies of levels of complexity")[2] and the arrival of *self-consciousness*. This level of abstraction is, first, inadequate in itself as a description of evolution, the history of which is more ambiguous than that would suggest, and second, it leaves God with no more than a guiding hand through the process, an action which falls far short of any sense of relationship.

Certainly there has been an increase in complexity among life-forms. Humans are far more complex than an amoeba, more even than an orangutan, our near relative. But will complexity bear the weight attributed to it as one of the highest values in creation? The achievement is not a simple good. Increasing complexity in one direction decreases flexibility in another. Humans are small, slow creatures in comparison with other forms (which, if they could speak for themselves, might favor speed or size as the preferred value). Further, gains like complexity regularly have negative effects as well, as the cheetah's specialization in speed has sapped it of its fighting strength. A negative effect in the case of the human brain, which has enabled so much civilization and culture (though also so much devastation), is evident in the process of giving birth. The large head of a complex human baby has to descend a birth canal evolved for something smaller. The pains and dangers of childbirth are part of the price paid for complexity which cesarean operations do not adequately overcome.

Consciousness has been equally valued. "The contingency of human being is consistent with the working out of divine purpose in creation, that of eliciting the emergence of self-conscious persons."[3] Yet although consciousness has enabled humans to transcend their immediate situation and needs, it is not without its own ambiguity. To take one small example: it enables regret at the past and apprehension over the future in ways which do not contribute to present well-being. Apprehension is a state readily recognized after the destruction of the World Trade Center in New York. But unself-conscious creatures have no such foreboding. The Scottish poet Robert Burns wrote an apology to a mouse when he broke its nest with his plow. In that poem he expresses poignantly the human condition:

> Still thou art blest compared wi' me!
> The present only touches thee.
> But Och! I backward cast my e'e
> On prospects drear,
> An' forward, though I canna see,
> I guess and fear.[4]

Thus, in the first place, those features of evolution singled out as instances of God's guiding are themselves two-edged, ambiguous like everything in creation — a matter to which I shall return later.[5] Moreover, the celebration of advance ignores or belittles the cost incurred en route. Many panentheistic writers advert to the losses of creatures down the ages, allowing that the cost is prodigious, but not allowing themselves to be deflected from the pattern they are following. Philip Clayton, for instance, writes that "there are significant cases of *disorder* in the biological world, including the pointless death of thousands of species. Should not the case of disorder count against the hypothesis of a cosmic designer?" Nevertheless, he subsumes such unease under the process of *fides quaerens intellectum* (faith seeking understanding), for "*to the eyes of faith* it is impossible not to find signs of God's purpose and designs in the world."[6] I would not disagree with the belief that signs of God's purpose in the world are perceptible to faith, but whether the divine *design* is visible through "the pointless death of thousands of species" is a much more dubious proposition.

Extinction and disorder in the evolutionary process tell against any optimistic perception of divine purpose. When Moltmann gave his Gifford Lectures in Edinburgh, published as *God in Creation,* he expatiated on God's goodness in creating an open system, such that creation was not fixed from the beginning but was free to move and change.[7] Yet an open system is possible only when deaths and extinctions occur and vacant ecological niches are opened up. Thus, before *Homo sapiens sapiens* had even evolved, over 90 percent of species had become extinct. At the Moltmann lectures the dean of the veterinary school commented: "What God creates, God deletes," a view I find contrary to what I believe about God.

God may not be interpreted as directly creating (and hence deleting) living creatures. But if God is in any sense directing evolution toward complexity and consciousness, the losses are part of the process and the cost appears disproportionate. I came to my interest in faith and science issues through my work on ecotheology. In that connection Christians are being encouraged to help save endangered species, and the reason often given is that they are in some sense God's creatures. But it is a real question what Christian faith has to offer to the cause of preservation if before we had even evolved to add our own devastation, God was exercising an influence/effect which resulted in the extinction of over 90 percent of creation.

Finally on this point of emerging complexity and consciousness as the direction of God's movement through evolution, it is clear that the desire to invoke God's effects in this area is as fraught with difficulty as is the desire to see the divine hand in human history. Some time ago I argued that latter case:

"By ignoring the total reticulation of events (C. H.) Dodd is making room for the action of God."[8] Indeed, historians have objected to all patterning of history as doing no justice to actual variety. Thus Pieter Geyl upbraids Toynbee for his *Study of History:* "To see a self-styled historian reducing the whole of the wonderful and mysterious movement of history to one single *motif,* rejecting whole centuries as uninteresting, forcing it all into a scheme of presumptuous construction, strikes [the historian] as going against all that history stands for."[9]

Mutatis mutandis, Geyl's remarks may be directed toward every oversimplification of evolutionary history. The study of evolution is not the same as the study of history. It does not, for instance, have the mind-set of other times to discern. But the strictures against making patterns in history, as blinding their proponents to counterevidence, playing up some aspects while leaving others as irrelevant, are the same as those against the selection of what is to count as important and what is to be dismissed as unimportant ("rejecting whole centuries [in this case aeons] as uninteresting [to God?]") in some versions of evolution within the panentheistic fold.

I am not arguing against the existence of emergence, or complexity, or the dawn of self-consciousness. These have clearly happened and have had many good results, as well as the less happy. I am arguing that the selection of these traits together with the ignoring of "unsuccessful" creatures which became extinct for any reason is to pattern evolution unjustifiably in the direction of human arrival. This is the fault of anthropocentrism, acknowledged now as an oppressive part of the Christian heritage in ecotheology, for it implicitly downgrades the nonhuman and decreases the importance of both human and divine care for the rest of creation. We believe God cares for each individual human, so why not each individual nonhuman? Jesus portrayed God as caring for each individual sparrow (Matt. 10:29), although there was a wider range to care about in humans. Such care, proper to each creature, should also appear in Christian accounts of evolution.

The downgrading of the nonhuman in the valuing of complexity sometimes becomes explicit, as in Charles Birch. "But why rate all life of equal value? If intrinsic value is 'measured' by richness of experience, it follows that creatures such as primates and whales have more intrinsic value than worms or mosquitoes."[10] (This raises another question for me. The post–World War II Britain of my childhood was a drab place compared to the richness of experience I have now. Did my intrinsic value increase, or has it been always the same by pure ontology without reference to context?) Daly and Cobb point out that Birch's hierarchy of richness of experience is different from the one of importance to the planet's survival, in which bacteria would have a much higher standing.[11] But that reinforces my point. Why choose a standard of value which is entirely ontological (a matter to which I shall return) as opposed to one of ecological fitness in interrelationship, which would suit the planet better, while believers must suppose God cares about the state of the planet? In that ecological scenario humans with their casual overuse of creation viewed only as a collection of resources would not rate highly. Gradings require a standard against which they take place. In many panentheistic accounts the acme is clearly an ontological account of chosen aspects of human being — anthropocentrism again — so that all other creatures are assigned a greater or lesser value in relation to human qualities.

This hierarchical view of evolution creates theological problems concerning partiality in God, if God also appears to value creatures more or less according to their richness of experience and proximity to the desired human traits. God surely values creatures for what they are and what they are doing in their own circumstances. (It is worth noting for comparison that I found no deficit in richness of experience during my childhood. It was what it was: whole in itself. It is presumably the same for nonhuman creatures.) Rather than working with hierarchies, theology could rejoice in the *diversity* of creatures and their interrelationship without prior gradings, and understand God to rejoice (or suffer) with creation as well. Considering how recently humans appeared in evolutionary time, God would have spent ages without real pleasure in creation if all that was happening was influence toward future qualities.

As my proposal that God rejoices in the diversity of creation implies, I am not arguing that the perception of ambiguity in evolution overturns all stances of faith. The philosopher Stephen Clark mounted a rigorous logical attack on the rationality of denying validity to any but "neutral" scientific facts.

> Scientists, they say, are only concerned with "facts" and moral (or metaphysical) preferences can never be grounded upon facts or rationally discovered. This does not seem to stop them from counting their own preferences more rational than those of zoophiles, while denying that any such preferences are rational at all. . . . The claim that only the laws of logic and empirical generalisations have any rational status has no rational status: for it is neither a law of logic nor an empirical discovery. . . . The objectivist identifies a *right* approach in the act of denying that there is a right approach.[12]

The matter of metaphysical or theological approaches to such matters as evolution is therefore right to be defended, but it should embrace the widest possible spectrum of information in order to avoid the criticism of partiality.

The sweeping, triumphalist overview of evolution would not be possible if attention were given to God with each creature and each species. Yet insofar as this happens within process thought, the nature of the relationship remains deficient. It is often held within process theology that God gives creatures an "initial aim" or "lure" to achieve the best they can in their circumstances.[13] The lure, as David Pailin describes it, is "to take just this, rather than any other concrete form — although (of course) it is open for the creature to use its creative freedom to actualise one of the other possibilities open to it."[14] This account raises a number of questions. Did God lure to "just this form" the innumerable instances of predator and prey, eat or be eaten, or is that a willful decline from the initial aim? Are all the extinct to be dismissed as not having responded adequately to the lure? What of external factors such as climate change (ice ages) and meteor strikes? On closer inspection, notions of "lure" in connection with evolutionary process have many practical problems. Issues of natural evil remain largely unaddressed and undermine Cobb and Griffin's account of the lure as creative love.[15]

Pailin certainly takes some notice of evil: "Natural evil may be the product of the non-compossibility of several values . . . or the outcome of random chance conjunctions or the result of unsuitable conditions."[16] That indeed seems to be a fair summary of the case. The issue then becomes whether these conditions are numerous enough and compelling enough to make beliefs about a divinely given initial aim impossible. For me there is particularly the colossal extent of extinction, both sudden extinctions like the one in which the dinosaurs perished and the steady background extinctions which go on all the time. Numbers are not everything, but the size of these numbers must give pause if God is said to be exerting a lure. (In all this discussion I take individual death to be a part of life, but the extinction of a life-form, a corner of creation, especially when caused by something as external as climate change, is a more serious theological matter.)

One Solution: Pansyntheism

There are four parts to this proposed solution to the foregoing problems. First I shall discuss what God may be said to have created, and then what the freedom of creation implies. After that come a description of the relationship which exists between God and every last creature, and finally an account of how God makes a difference to what goes on in the world.[17]

First, then, what did God create? I have learned much from process thought on God's creation of possibilities. Yet I find that the next step curtails the application of that notion. "But the sphere of possibility is purely abstract, lacking all agency to provide selectively for the need of new events. There must be an agency that mediates between these abstract forms or pure possibilities and the actual world."[18] But possibility is not a "sphere" in which actualities may be envisaged. Rather it is the condition within which things may or may not happen. Such an understanding moves toward action and relationship, away from the ontological slant within process construction, evident in the initial aim to a form of being, and the hierarchy of creatures with intrinsic value according to their being. Current theology is much more (and rightly) concerned with relationship, and although that may imply an ontology, it does not presuppose one. Thus the role of possibility may be seen as making beings-with-relationships possible rather than setting an ontological goal. Therefore I believe God to have created possibility as the possibility of possibilities without designing any particular forms, including the human, to be aimed at. That anything at all is now, has been, or will be possible is the gift of God in creation making possibility possible. It is a steadfast, loving gift as possibilities continue.

The obverse side of this account of divine creating is the freedom of the subsequent creation to evolve and act as it could within its possibilities. That freedom has produced the world's ambiguity, for it has resulted in, for instance, the earth's tectonic plates which later cause earthquakes, and the welcome production of a breathable atmosphere. Through that freedom of possibility life-forms have come about — often in competition with one another. But they have enjoyed their day and generation and (frequently) perished. This brief account of creaturely freedom extends freedom from the "free will defense" of Augustine concerning human moral evil to a defense of natural evil through the effects of multiple finite freedoms down through all time. In that case neither moral nor natural evil is to be attributed to any kind of scheme by, or influence from, God.

Yet that account on its own would distance God from the world and is little better than a modern form of Deism. For God could have created possibility but then abandoned creation to its own success and failure. But that is exactly where the value of panentheism lies, with its insistence that the world is in God. God cannot be distant from the world. Here also the current emphasis on relationship becomes important again, for God, who gave the freedom of possibility in the first place, is in relationship with every diverse creature which uses possibility to come into being — thereby responding to the Creator's gift. Yet this freedom is at the same time constrained by current circumstances, circumstances which have come about by the results of earlier use of possibilities.

If God may be said to be characterized by freedom and love in relation to creation, the very gift of freedom is loving. But that love also accompanies creation in its use of finite freedoms.[19] The whole of creation is companioned by God, not on the basis of hierarchy, but according to what is proper and necessary to the creature in its circumstances. As Jesus indicated, much is necessary for humans, but that "much" has to do with its widest range of possibilities. Humans form a species to which much has been given, and from which much is expected. As that suggests, the range of possible response from creation will differ according to each creature's possibilities.

Just as process theology has argued that God works by persuasion, so I believe relationship works by attraction. That emphasis on how relationship works does not make God passive as either a cosmic sponge or a pained on-looker. What God does is to establish and maintain relationships with all creation, and that is action as surely as anything more interventionist and directive. One need only think of the problems of relationship which occur in marriages to see that the connection requires attention and work so that lines of communication and support remain open, and that gives some glimpse of what it means to say God acts by making and maintaining relationships. At the same time, the divine must not be thought of as a glorified human establishing "personal" relationships. God relates to all according to their kind, being unlike humans in knowing what it is to be a tree frog or a jaguar, knowing indeed the particular situation of any jaguar better than the animal knows itself. I have used the word "relationship" for this connection, although it is a human term and may not be right for nonhuman creatures. But it is the only word we have for the kind of valuable connection I wish to indicate.

Humans are further limited in not being able to transcend the species barrier to discern what it is for a dung beetle, for instance, to respond to God. It will not respond in any way comparable to humans, but humans themselves need not think that theirs is the only manner of response. Yet one kind of response may be visible in the way nonhuman creatures resist death by fight or flight until their old age. Only humans commit suicide. Such tenacity is a form of response to the divine gift which made life possible. In a way, all divine-creaturely relationships will be one-sided, given that God understands the being, the relationships, the context of each creature perfectly — the actual as actual and the possible as possible — while creatures may respond only out of their own finite, more or less limited capacities. But that too God understands.

On the other hand, a relationship may not be equal, but it comes to fruition and has consequences when it is a known reality and is responded to and acted upon. The nature of the response, moreover, will naturally vary with each individual creature, but its primary component, apart from appreciation of life, may be described in human terms and then attributed with appropriate variation to other creatures. Since God is present but does not intervene, that primary component is creaturely attention, and no one has described what is involved in such attention better than Simone Weil. She illustrates it well through the story of the Good Samaritan. There the sufferer is "only a little piece of flesh, inert and bleeding beside a ditch; he is nameless, no one knows anything about him." In other words, there is no prior connection and nothing attractive to draw the attention. She continues: "Those who pass by this thing scarcely notice it, and a few minutes afterwards *do not even know that they have seen it*"; that is to say, something which is there is just not there for those with no attention. Further: "Only one stops and turns his attention towards it. The actions that follow are just the automatic effect of this moment of attention. The attention is creative. But at the moment it is engaged it is renunciation."[20]

One may go through life entirely taken up with one's own concerns, with the "estranged faces" Francis Thomson said missed "the many-splendoured thing."[21] In Weil's words, such people "do not even know that they have seen it." But to take one's eyes off oneself, to pay attention, is to catch the many-splendored thing, even if it is perceived through some inert and bleeding flesh. Weil may be optimistic in thinking that actions automatically follow from such perception: there may have to be more internal wrestling than that, and less clarity over what exactly to do. But she is right to say that attention is creative — it brings about a new perception of the situation leading to consequent action. It is in this joint way of presence and response that God the companion of all that is acts in the world with free creatures (pansyntheism), a powerful presence when attended to.

But Weil is also right to say that such attention is at the same time renunciation — the renunciation of the creature's self-absorption. Indeed, she interprets the act of creation as renunciation by God who freely allows finitude to come into being within infinity. For Weil the human participation of attention and response "is something sacred. It is what man grants to God. It is what God comes searching for as a beggar among men."[22] In a sense God is a beggar, for God will not remove creaturely freedom to have divine effects. But response opens up the possibilities of powerful divine relationship.

Thus the God who grants freedom to creation is not going to shape evolution toward complexity and self-consciousness, for the powerful presence has always been there, always seeking a response in the attention of all creatures and thus having effects in the world as the response is worked out. Yet again we do not know what counts as response and relationship in other creatures. But with the belief that God's love can never be a matter of more or less, nor given to some and withheld from others, comes the belief that response is always one of the possibilities for all creatures according to their kind.

There is one last important argument concerning relationship. Its proper preposition is "with" (hence pansyntheism) rather than "in" (extended panentheism) — or indeed "over." Thus any extension of panentheism to the proposition that God is "in" creatures, human or nonhuman, is questionable. A relationship is close, but not so close that one is overwhelmed by the other. Thus relationship is not fusion; rather it preserves some space between participants, a to-and-fro even in the coming together. It is the freedom, the attention, the sense of responsibility of each participant which make possible mutuality and joint action. God remains God while men and women (and indeed all creatures) remain themselves, capable of attention and response, but independent enough also to ignore God and wreak the havoc which selfishness can bring about.

A further argument against the notion of God "in" creatures is the ambiguity or the downright evil pervading creation. In a historic debate Reformed theologians argued against Lutherans that *finitum non capax infiniti* (the finite cannot contain/bear the infinite). Their concern was not so much how to fit the infinite into the finite, but rather with the sin of humans and the fallenness of all creation, such that it was held to be unfit to bear this good and holy God. The phrase, however, still has relevance, for even today, when there is no appeal to the fall, and much less absorption with sin, this remains a world of various competing or cooperating finite freedoms. It will be full of unforeseeable change, and always open to varieties of interpretation, and hence ambiguous. General patterns may have the result that what is good for some may simultaneously be bad for others, or that something which is good at one time may later become harmful. Particular instances of this principle could be multiplied. If God is "in" something, it should surely be good without qualification, and there is little that remains, or even appears, that way to everyone involved.

Another question would be what happens if a person or situation "in" which God is seen becomes worse. Has God left? Does God come and go? Or remain "in" even as matters deteriorate? "If God is 'in me,' internally directing my thought and action, what has happened to my freedom and responsibility? Or does God have to be held partly responsible for the ambiguities within my own best but humanly limited actions?"[23] It still seems possible to use "in" of someone or something so transparent to the relationship with God that the small distance of "with" is irrelevant. But in general use the notion of

God with, God alongside, *always* present but not internal, obviates the difficulties of "in" and gives positive gain in the benefits of relationship.

It could be argued against this whole account of possibility and relationship that God, being God, would have foreseen that multiple finite freedoms, however they evolved, would jostle, constrain, and hurt one another. In that case, was the freedom worth it? I can only suggest that God, being freedom and love, desired the possibility of finite freedom and love, and took the attendant risk of constraint and evil, without which freedom and love are not possible in this world.

The Logos as Wisdom:
A Starting Point for a Sophianic
Theology of Creation

CELIA E. DEANE-DRUMMOND

In this paper I argue that if a panentheistic model of the relationship between God and the world is to be *Christian,* rather than simply *theist,* it requires proper reflection on the radical particularity of Christ as the revelation of God expressed in the mystery of the incarnation. I suggest that the Christology that makes most sense in the context of creation themes is a Wisdom Christology.[1] What is the relationship between Logos and Wisdom? Can anything be separate from God? I suggest that Sophia cannot be confined to Christology alone; rather the trinitarian nature of Sophia lends itself to thinking about the relationship between God and the world in dynamic categories. This dynamic God/world relationship is open to the insights of science, but points beyond this to the revelation of God in Christ. Such a Sophianic theology of creation has practical implications for ethics in the way that is more suggestive compared with other models of the doctrine of creation.

Introduction

In a perceptive article Janet Martin Soskice questions the value of much theoretical discussion in science and religion debates about the meaning of creation. She suggests that such theories become more and more remote from anything the Christian tradition ever wanted to say. To put it starkly, she asks: "Why do our collections of essays always have that swirling galaxy on the cover, or a piece of electron-microscopal photography, and never a baby's foot, or a woman drawing water at a well, or — to use a biblical image of creation — a rainbow?"[2] Nonetheless, rather oddly, she draws back from following through such a doubt by suggesting that such obscurity is "neither here nor there." At the same time, she contrasts the "happy meetings of minds" at science and religion conferences with difficult decision making in medical ethics committees, which have become "a conceptual wasteland, one where theological contribution was both peripheral and impoverished."[3] It seems to me that such a challenge to a detached theology of creation *does* need to be addressed at the theoretical level, as well as through the practical concerns of ethics. In some respects this resembles concerns of other feminist writers who have argued consistently against classical theism on the basis that it is too remote from earthly, everyday concerns.[4] However, I am not arguing against classical forms of theism as such; rather I am suggesting something much more subtle, namely, that the way we tend to frame theoretical science and religion debates necessarily leads to detachment from practical ethics. In other words, I am challenging the background assumptions leading to the way certain questions are set up in such meetings, framed in such a way that practical ethical questions are simply not considered to be of any relevance. As I hope to show below, I am more in favor of adhering to a modified version of classical theism inasmuch as it reminds us of otherness between God and the world and it is from this otherness that a developed understanding of relationship can emerge.

I also suggest that where panentheism is understood simply in terms of God/world, equivalent in a metaphorical sense to mind/body, such a detachment from practical problems is almost inevitable, for it is concerned with working out the details of what it means for the world to be in some sense "in" God. Asking questions about how science might be applied in practical ways simply does not enter into the realm of questioning. This is not to deny that panentheism successfully overcomes many of the problems associated with either an acute dualist understanding of the God/world relation, which has Deist leanings, or mergence of God with the world in pantheism.[5] Yet it seems to me that understanding panentheism as a mind/body metaphor simply opens up another set of problems, namely, *how* to relate mind and body and *in what sense* this can be comparable to the relation between God and the world.[6] Arthur Peacocke is correct in his anxiety that understanding the world as God's body in an ontological sense, in the way Grace Jantzen suggests, weakens the idea of God as creator and moves away from panentheism to pantheism.[7] He has also pointed to the dominance of process philosophy in panentheistic thinking, where the total receptivity of God to all events in the world seems to be implied.[8] Process philosophy virtually becomes the measure of the "orthodoxy" of panentheism. I suggest that process philosophy can certainly give us important insights about how to conceive of ways of thinking about God in far less rigid ways than has been the case in much of the Christian tradition. But does process thought have to be the sole measure and criterion through which to understand panentheism? This is where Soskice, it seems to me, is correct in insisting, following the classical theist tradition, that creation is mysteriously *other* than God, and furthermore, that only in declaring creation as *other* can we begin to think in terms of *relation*.[9] The choice is not simply between a fixed form of classical theism or process thought, but something more akin to a modified version of classical thinking that takes into account insights of science and allows a richer understanding of how this might relate to practical ethics.

The Naturalist Dilemma

A further difficulty of panentheistic models, as commonly understood, is that they seem to be too monochrome, they seem to identify the relation of God and the world in such a way that leaves little room for any diversity of understanding, while claiming to offer a liberal interpretation of the Christian tradition. How can such models really convince in a pluralistic religious culture if distinctions are simply ignored? The dilemma for Christian theology is the age-old question of "naturalism," how far is God discernible in science/nature/other faiths, and how far in revealed theology expressed as the revelation of God in Christ? Panentheistic models of God and the world, especially where they equate the world with God's body, seem to leave no room for such a tension between natural and revealed theology, since the radical nature of the incarnation is not adequately taken into account. Hans Urs von Balthasar characterizes the dilemma between natural and revealed theology thus: "the creation's passive character as reflection is necessarily linked to an active splendour . . . on the part of God, a will to reveal himself which is, therefore, already a factual manifestness. We will never be able to determine exactly the extent to which this splendour, given with creation itself, coincides objectively with what Christian theology calls 'supernatural revelation,' which, at least from Adam, was not yet a specifically distinct revelation given in the form of words."[10] For von Balthasar human existence placed "nakedly before the cipher-codes of existence" cannot perceive the call of God's Word. Yet he suggests that we must not pass too quickly over the "creaturely phase," for "It is as creature that man first comes to know the ever-greater and, thus, ever-more-hidden God as his Lord" (p. 449). Moreover, the revelation of grace is "not the establishment of a new form within the created world; it is but a new manner of God's presence in the form of the world, a new intimacy in our union with him, an intimacy to which the child of God has access and in which he participates." Grace does not, in other words, have to be something totally separate or detached from creaturely existence. It is not a "supernatural" intrusion into the world in the way many of those who reject classical theism would like to suggest. Hence "the natural inspiration coming from the Being of the world is the locus and vessel of God's inspiration by grace" (p. 452).

Yet von Balthasar, correctly in my view, argues that because of human sinfulness the internal word of God *within* creation had to become a Word spoken as it were from the *outside,* in the Old Testament as the law and prophets and in the New Testament as the incarnate Word. Hence the revelation of grace through the Word of God is a reminder of the *penitential* nature of human existence. In other words, the understanding of Christ as the Word of God takes into account the broken nature of human lives, the suffering in the lives of other creatures on the planet, and the fact that is obvious all around us, that the world we live in is far from perfect. The sense of brokenness and sin does not have the last word. Human life is challenged and purified by the "fire of the indwelling Word" (p. 455). Yet the Word of God expressed in the events of the incarnation and passion of Jesus Christ shows that God's revelation is both extreme manifestness but also *concealment.* It is manifest as God is explained by the being and life of Christ, but it is also concealed, so that the "translation of God's absolutely unique, absolute and infinite Being into the ever more dissimilar, almost arbitrary and hopelessly relativised reality of one individual man in the crowd from the outset seems to be an undertaking condemned to failure" (p. 457). The revelation of the Word made flesh is *within* creation, not alongside it, and it is in this that the Son becomes the expression of the absolute Being of God. The radical, if shocking, understanding of God made flesh uniquely in the person of Christ shows the importance of an understanding of the incarnation not just for salvation history, but for the whole of creation as well. There is a sense that the Word is *both* from the outside, spoken as a form of address, *and yet* made flesh within creation.

The Logos as Sophia

The prologue to John's Gospel speaks about this mystery in terms of the Word or Logos. Yet his use of the term "Logos" shows remarkable parallels to that of Sophia in the Old Testament, as I have mentioned elsewhere.[11] In general, in the Old Testament the Word and Wisdom of God are often used in an interchangeable way. Gerald O'Collins comments: "Like wisdom, the word expresses God's active power and self-revelation towards and in the created world. Solomon's prayer for wisdom takes word and wisdom as synonymous agents of divine creation; 'God of my fathers and Lord of mercy, you made all things by your Word and by your wisdom fashioned man' (Wis. 9.1-2)."[12] Similarly, John 1:1a echoes Genesis 1:1, so that Logos is identified as preexistent and active with God in creation. In Proverbs 8:22-23 wisdom is presented as the first of God's creatures, in cooperating with God in the creative process. In Proverbs we find Wisdom as agent of creation, but in John Logos fulfills this role (John 1:3). The search for light and life, given by Logos in John 1:4, echoes the thought of Proverbs 8:35, where the search for life is the search for wisdom.

Nonetheless, the portrayal of Christ as the embodiment of Wisdom is not confined to the prologue in John, but extends to the main body of the text as well. For example, Jesus is described as preexistent in terms that echo the characterization of Wisdom. Wisdom is sent from above, as a gift of God, as in Wisdom 8:21; just as Jesus is sent by the Father in passages such as John 3:16-17 and 3:34. The purpose in both cases is that humanity might find communion with God, as in Wisdom 9:10 and John 3:17.

But why did John choose to use Logos rather than Wisdom in the prologue to his Gospel? Was it because, as O'Collins suggests, the female term "Sophia" was "awkward" to use in relation to the incarnation of the *man* Jesus?[13] He also suggests that personified Wisdom as identified with the Torah in Hellenistic Judaism, if John had used it, might have suggested equivalence between the Torah and God, even though later Christians did identify Logos with the law. O'Collins believes Logos offered a more effective bridge with the contemporary culture of the time compared with Sophia. For feminist theologians such as Elizabeth Schüssler Fiorenza, the replacement of Sophia by the Logos reinforced the *patriarchal* culture of the time along with a patriarchal understanding of God.[14] Nonetheless, I suggest that there is another possibility, namely, that it was John's *intention* to highlight the idea of Christ as Sophia incarnate by using the Logos term, since both were largely interchangeable.[15] The Logos became a convenient shorthand for Sophia. Writing to a community imbibed with the wisdom tradition, John could be sure that there would be no misunderstanding in this respect.

O'Collins comments on the *particular* advantages of the idea of Logos to describe the incarnation, rather than the Sophia term.[16] Words are both distinct from, but in some sense identical to, the speaker. The Word "was," which might imply a preexistence in a manner that is not true of Wisdom, which is understood as created by God. The Word of God denotes the revelation of

God and divine will; wherever Logos is, some true light and knowledge of God are to be found. Yet as I showed above, there are also biblical passages that suggest that Wisdom is also in some sense preexistent, even while paradoxically it is spoken of as the "first of God's creatures." The context of Jewish literature sheds some light on the dilemma as to how far either Word or Wisdom can be thought of as preexistent to creation. James Dunn argues that in Jewish literature, words such as "Name," "Glory," "Wisdom," and "Word" are not to be understood as intermediary beings between God and creation, which the idea of preexistence implies. Rather, "these so-called 'intermediary beings' are better understood as ways of asserting the transcendent God's *nearness* to his creation, his involvement with his people. They are ways of speaking about *God* in his relation to the world; they serve to express his immanence without compromising his transcendence."[17] More explicitly: "The Wisdom and Word imagery is all of a piece with this — no more distinct beings than the Lord's 'arm,' no more intermediary beings than God's righteousness and God's glory, but simply vivid personifications, ways of speaking about God in his active involvement with his world and his people."[18]

Dunn's analysis serves to challenge those ways of speaking about Sophia/Word as independent hypostases in the Godhead. The Sophiology of writers such as the Russian philosopher Vladimir Solovyov pointed rather too much in this direction.[19] Yet the purpose of the Hebrew writers was the opposite, namely, to challenge polytheism by domesticating its myths, such as Isis. Both Sophia and Logos are ways of expressing the *presence* of God to God's creation, also expressed as the Hebrew term, the *Shekinah*. Such language enabled the early Christians to relate Christ to creation: he is both Lord of creation, and all things derive their origin in him.[20] The crucial difference between the Christian interpretation of Christ as Sophia/Logos and the earlier identification with the Torah is that while Torah is a book of words, it is in the *man* Jesus that God's revelation can be found. This offered a profound challenge to monotheism, since it is to "attribute to a *man* Wisdom's role in creation."[21] The strength of the Logos/Wisdom Christology was that it allowed *Christ as redeemer* to be identified with the creative agency of God. The Son of Man Christologies, by comparison, could separate the creative and redemptive work of Christ and so allow the emergence of a Gnostic redeemer myth. Dunn does approve of the Son of God Christology that Nicea affirms, as he believes that whereas Logos implies continuity and sameness of partners, the *relationships* in the Godhead would best be thought of through Son of God terminology. To put it more simply, it allowed a trinitarian understanding of the Godhead to develop.

While Dunn is no doubt correct to suggest that impersonal rational being suggested by the idea of the Logos stifles the idea of relationship, is this necessarily true of Sophia? I suggest that it is important to distinguish Logos and Sophia if we are not to lose sight of the ability of Sophia language to express relationality. Furthermore, the evacuation of Sophia Christology by Logos Christology and then Son of God in subsequent Christian interpretation bespeaks the failure of the Logos term to present an adequate portrait of God in relationships. While, as I have shown above, there are parallels between Sophia and Logos, and John would have intended such an identification to be implicit in his writing, subsequent use of Logos Christology has weakened the richness found in Sophia language. For while Sophia includes rational being, she is a more fluid, elusive term, more prone to resist clear definition and bespeak not just the rational energy in the universe, but something more subtle, more akin to God relating to the universe in love.

God as Sophia

Yet it is important to ask if there are any further distinctions we can draw between Logos and Sophia: Are the two so equivalent that *Logos as Sophia* is all we need to say about Sophia? Can, in other words, Sophia simply be restricted to Christology? Irenaeus's theology is powerful, as it allows something of the distinction between Sophia and the Logos to emerge. He speaks not just of Christ as Word, but as the Spirit of Wisdom, thus: "And because God is rational, he therefore created what is made by his Word, and as God is Spirit, so he disposed everything by his Spirit, just as the prophet says: 'By the word of the Lord the heavens were established, and all their power by his Spirit' (Psalm 33.6). Therefore, since the Word establishes, that is gives body and substance, but the Spirit disposes and shapes the variety of powers, the Son is rightly called Word, while the Spirit is called the Wisdom of God."[22]

Subsequent writers, by identifying Sophia exclusively with the Logos, failed to perceive Sophia in a trinitarian way, such that Sophia can be identified with the Spirit as well as the Father. I have argued elsewhere the reasons for preferring to think of Sophia in trinitarian terms rather than exclusively in terms of Christology.[23] The purpose of this paper is not to repeat such arguments, but to demonstrate the radical importance of stressing the mystery of the incarnation in Sophianic language as a way of relating God to the world. Perhaps it would be more correct to say that Logos *and* Sophia are the starting points for such a theology, rather than the Logos *as* Sophia. For the latter opens up once again the temptation to evacuate the significance of Sophia for understanding God's relationship with the world. Moreover, the rootedness of Sophia in the Hebrew Bible in the common practice of living demonstrates that such a relationship cannot be thought of just in terms of detached rational entities, but rather in terms of real-life decision making and ethics. Hence the dilemma of how to relate those "swirling galaxies" that I mentioned at the start of this paper to common problems in medical ethics no longer becomes an issue. One cannot be considered without the other. It is in the man Jesus, precisely in his earthly nature, that we come to realize the true nature of who God is. For, as von Balthasar has suggested, "if man is to truly become the language of God, this cannot occur by straining man's nature towards the superhuman, or by wishing to stand out by becoming greater, more splendid, more renowned and stupendous than all others. He will have to be a man like everyone because he will be man for everyone, and he will exhibit his uniqueness precisely through his ordinariness."[24]

Sophia and Panentheism

Is the idea of a Sophianic theology of God and the world panentheistic in any sense? Of course, this depends on prior presuppositions as to what panentheism might mean. I have argued earlier in this paper that versions of panentheism that equate the world with God's body tend to bypass practical ethical considerations. It might indeed be possible to find the same tendency in a Sophianic model of God if it were confined simply to the relationship between God and the world in the mode of creation. However, Sophia is not simply a way of thinking about God and creation, but necessarily forces us to think in categories of redemption as well. It does this by reminding us of the radical particularity of Christ, the Logos as Sophia, and thence of his cross and resurrection. Creation and redemption are distinguishable, but related. Sophia is not an intermediary or a quaternary in the Godhead, but, as Sergii Bulgakov insisted, Sophia becomes a way of thinking about who God is in Godself.

While more traditional Orthodox theologians prefer to think of Wisdom in terms of the energies of God, bracketing the idea of God's ontology within the realm of mystery and unknowability, it seems to me that as long as we qualify the language used and say that a Sophianic understanding is only a partial insight into who God is, then an adequate apophatic sense can be retained together with an ontological interpretation. The world is in some sense sustained by the *energia* of God, expressed through the notion of Wisdom. It is, as I have suggested elsewhere, like a whisper to the world in its becoming, perhaps on a different plane of reality than that yet discovered by science.[25] In this sense God is fully immanent and involved in the world, without becoming the world. However, the transcendent nature of God as Sophia comes through clearly in that God is more than that which we discover in created existence. It is through a reinterpretation of transcendence that otherness and relationship become possible. Transcendence need not imply immutability or failure to feel any pain or passion. Of course, Wisdom on its own is not all-sufficient in describing such a relationship between God and the world, for the Trinity has been traditionally understood in the language of love rather than Wisdom. However, I suggest that love needs Wisdom if it is to express the true beauty toward which creation groans. Hence the aim and goal of creation in the mode of redemption is not just flourishing, but also beauty — beauty not understood according to human categories of knowing, but beauty in the face of the wounded Christ who, even at his resurrection, shows humanity the scars of his passion and points to the wounds, now healed, in his hands and his feet.[26]

In what sense might this trinitarian understanding of Sophia be open to the insights of science? The early experimental scientists of the seventeenth century, such as the botanist John Ray, believed the Wisdom of God was manifested in the works of creation.[27] Hence experimental science was a means by which such wisdom could be fully appreciated or even experienced. Sharing in the delights of creation was a sharing in the mind of God. Yet for Ray the wisdom in creation remained a partial mirror of God, pointing back to the author rather than saying anything more profound about the meaning of who God is in Godself. The role of Sophia I am suggesting here goes further than this, in that while the discoveries of science can, in some instances, certainly act like a mirror to the mind of God, there may be occasions where science does not demonstrate such wisdom. Wisdom itself acts as a critique on human wisdom, for it is self-referential not just to the mind of God in some Platonic sense, but to the wisdom expressed in the cross of Christ.

It is wisdom learned, then, not just in the joys and glories of creation, and the wonder of scientific discovery, though it is certainly this, but also in the fragility of existence and the pain of creation emerging through evolution. Science can just as easily remind us of this pain as can theology; as Stephen Jay Gould has humorously pointed out, it is a "nonmoral nature."[28] This was the mistake of the early natural theologians, who failed to take into account the radical nature of evil in the universe. For them all of nature was forced into a way of proving the design of the Creator; even those things considered abhorrent in the natural world, such as locusts and other "noxious" creatures, were held to be simply functioning in accordance with divine purposes.[29] A more helpful interpretation is to accept that the brokenness of creation extends to creatures other than simply the human species, so that the suffering of any creature does not have the last word. It is a mystery in the face of which in some sense the human capacity for knowing necessarily falls silent, for to explain away evil in the universe as simply part of God's good purpose renders God either callous or powerless. In the place of silence we can speak simply of God entering fully into that created world and sharing in its suffering and death. Such an entering into the world in the fullest sense is expressed most effectively in the concept of the incarnation. Yet the incarnation looks to a future re-created world. The world is in some sense not finished, so it is in an eschatological key that creation becomes meaningful once more.

Jesus the Sage

Yet we might ask what kind of wisdom did Jesus himself pursue if we are to understand him as in some sense expressing the Wisdom of God. There is a shift from Old Testament to New Testament ideas on wisdom. While later wisdom teaching bases some of its instruction on the law, it also subsequently becomes more eschatological in orientation. As Richard Bauckham points out, it is a mistake to oppose wisdom and apocalyptic worldviews as if they are wholly incompatible. Rather, there is a spectrum between the understanding of wisdom as immanent in the world, subject to observation, and the transcendence of wisdom, revealed by God to God's faithful people.[30] The teaching of Jesus, like James, is radical in that it contains much that is countercultural, negating conventional wisdom. Jesus makes the radical ethical demand to be perfect, to love one's enemies and to show solidarity with the poor. Those who are friends of God have true wisdom, while those who are friends with the world have false wisdom. Such a contrast culminates in the Pauline notion of the cross as the Wisdom of God.[31]

Jesus as the Wisdom of God points toward understanding the relationship between God and the world in terms of friendship. This has some resonance with the understanding of the relationship between God and the world as pansyntheism, the model suggested by Ruth Page.[32] The difference between God as friend of the world according to a Sophianic understanding and that according to pansyntheism is that the idea of God with nature in the latter view implies a sense of God being alongside the world, while deliberately excluding any sense of radical entering *into* the world of nature in and of itself. Of course, such distancing cleverly avoids the problem of how God could possibly be radically involved in a world full of suffering and evil. However, Jesus as friend to the world through Sophia implies not just simply coming alongside, though it certainly *includes* this idea, but also a radical *participation in* its misery, suffering, and even horrible death, as well as, of course, a *participation in* its joys and creativity. While humanity, as made in the image of God, shares in this friendship in a special way, the implication of Sophia as the expression of the creative activity of God suggests a wider understanding of friendship, one that is ecological in a profound sense. Hence it is a friendship that extends to a close participation in the suffering and pain evident in creaturely existence. Of course, it is necessary to qualify such participation by emphasizing the freedom of God and creatures, yet it seems to me that as long as the understanding of God entering into creation is qualified by the idea of participation and friendship, the close intimacy of the relationship is given due emphasis, along with maintaining the distinction between God and creation. Hence true friendship is able to express a deep empathy with the suffering of the other, without necessarily *becoming* that other in the way some panentheistic models of God and creation imply. Such close participation implies, further, that God is pathetic, capable of being influenced by the suffering and joys of the world.

As Denis Edwards has pointed out, contemporary scientific understanding points to a deeper sense of the relationship between ourselves as human persons, other creatures, and the planet.[33] While a Sophianic understanding of the relationships between God and the world is consistent with this view, it seems to me that the radical ethical demand of Jesus moves into the background once we focus too much simply on the cosmological Christ. The cosmic Christ becomes once more a theoretical norm, a distant figure set away from the messy and earthly nature of the incarnation, life, death, and resurrection of Jesus of Nazareth. Instead, I suggest that while affirming the goodness of creation, the challenge of Sophia can be formulated so that it relates as much to ethical practice in the sciences as to more theoretical considerations of God and the world. Edwards has hinted at ways such an ethic might come to be expressed in environmental concern. I suggest further that an ethic of virtue, in particular that of wisdom, comes into consideration. The church, as the expression of Christ's body on earth, then becomes the means through which a virtue ethic is fostered and developed. It is, moreover, an ethic of a particular community rather than isolated individualism.[34]

Sophia, Science, and Ethics

Detailed exposition of how such an ethic might engage with practical issues in science and medicine is the subject of another paper. All I will do here is indicate something of the way such a development could take place. In the first place, an ethic of virtue takes some cues from prudence or practical wisdom. Rather along the lines of Aristotelian thought, we can say that prudence is the "mean" of a particular virtue; it is the way a virtue can be measured in accordance with the particular end of goodness.[35] Prudence as a quality involves, for example, memory, insight into being taught, circumspection, foresight, and caution. Science on its own is good at circumspection, that is, at presenting us with its own understanding of what really is the case from observation. Yet, once we engage the memory, we know that insights from science may themselves be subject to forms of distortion arising not just from the social context in which the science takes place, but also from the motivation of those engaging in the science itself. For example, an understanding of ecology used to be one that promoted an understanding of reality as a stable network of relationships. It drew on the "common knowledge" that there is a "balance of nature," namely, that all creatures exist in networks of stable ecosystems. It seemed also to chime in with the desirable motivation to think of humanity as not isolated from other creatures, but as part of a holistic network of close interrelationships. As such it promoted a conservation ethic. Yet such a precondition of nature as "balance" has now become the subject of considerable challenge amongst ecologists. Ecology today is much more inclined to talk about disturbance, with patchworks of relationships existing only temporarily.[36] Hence it was the social context in which ecology was situated that promoted a particular form of ecology that survived far longer than one might have expected.

Consideration of ethical issues in genetics also requires not just knowledge about what might be possible or feasible, but also a well-developed sense of foresight and caution. It is more than the precautionary principle adopted by scientific ethical committees, in that it tries to consider not just the risks and benefits, but the reasons behind the research and why this particular area needs to take priority. From consideration of the virtue of wisdom, as well as the more secular understanding of prudence, the sense of the ordering of nature through divine Wisdom comes into view. Are humans becoming cocreators with God in manipulating the genetics of different life-forms? Discernment as to how and in what circumstances genetic engineering might be valid points back again to the radical particularity of the incarnation. The value of all creatures is the affirmation of the incarnation. Hence creaturely existence is not simply an instrument of human ambition, but it is more than this for it reflects the intention of divine Wisdom. In working out how we are to behave toward other creatures, the Logos as Wisdom reminds us to take seriously the self-emptying of Christ on the cross. It is not, then, a matter of achieving all that can be achieved for the sake of human aggrandizement. Rather, it is through thinking how such tools might become the means of service, not just for a limited number of human beings, but for the human race in its wider context of the community of other creatures.

Postmodern critiques have persuaded many to distrust any form of constructive approach to understanding humanity and the world, including the insights of science or traditional forms of theology. Yet I suggest that while science and theology may shift through time, there is still contact with the reality to which they relate. Postmodernity can challenge arrogant claims of the all-sufficiency of any theological or scientific system. A Sophianic understanding of the way God relates to the world need not imply fixity of ordering, but is suggestive of something much more akin to metaphor. Yet, as I have argued earlier, the metaphor itself achieves its grounding in the incarnation. Suffice it to say that bringing back Sophia into our understanding of panentheism rattles any sense of complacency in the quest for relating science and religion, since she forces us to address where our wisdom is to be found, and in doing so, reaches to the heart of the moral vacuum of much secular philosophy.[37]

IV Afterword

Panentheism Today:
A Constructive Systematic Evaluation

PHILIP CLAYTON

One cannot finish reading the previous chapters without invariably finding oneself wondering, What do they share in common? Despite some clear differences and disagreements among the authors, can one discern here the makings of a recognizable school of thought concerning "God's presence in a scientific world"? Do these essays offer a platform for new constructive reflections on the nature of God's relationship to the world?

It is the view of this book's editors and most all of its authors that panentheism does in fact represent a coherent theological program today. Many explicit agreements, and a number of underlying similarities, will already have become clear to the discerning reader. The goal of this concluding chapter is to draw attention to the family resemblances that provide this volume its thematic unity.

The words "constructive" and "systematic" in this chapter's title need not entail "dominant" and "dismissive." The arguments given here are meant as an invitation to further dialogue, not as a technique to end it. Consider this chapter as another in this book's list of essays — albeit with the difference that, in place of the diverse sources of information employed by the preceding authors, this essay takes *their* work as its data.

In substance if not in name, panentheistic theologies play a role in many of the world's religious traditions. The Jewish kabbalistic traditions and the Muslim Sufi tradition have clearly identifiable panentheistic elements, and many (perhaps even most) of the Hindu philosophical traditions are panentheistic. As a matter of actual fact, however, almost all the authors in the present volume either identify themselves as Christians or stand closer to that tradition than to any other. The following comments thus primarily reflect the Christian theological context, even though a number of them may be relevant to other religious contexts as well.[1]

Generic Panentheism?

The first and most natural thing one wants to know is in what sense the contributions to this book represent variations on a single theme. Suppose one tried to formulate the various positions as varieties of panentheism; would it work? Can common principles be stated, such that the label "panentheism" really expresses a common intersection set among them?[2] I suggest beginning with this experiment, using adjectival labels to distinguish among the positions:

1. Participatory panentheism, or perhaps "logoi panentheism" (described by A. Louth)
2. "Divine energies" panentheism (K. Ware)
3. Ecclesial or communal panentheism (A. Nesteruk)
4. Eschatological panentheism, or perhaps soteriological panentheism (e.g., J. Polkinghorne, as described by several authors)
5. Sapiential panentheism (C. Deane-Drummond)
6. Emergentist panentheism (A. Peacocke, P. Clayton)
7. Sacramental panentheism (A. Peacocke, C. Knight)
8. Trinitarian panentheism (D. Edwards et al.)
9. Pan-sacramental naturalistic panentheism (C. Knight)
10. Process or dipolar panentheism (D. Griffin, J. Bracken, et al.)
11. "Body of God" panentheism (Ramanuja, via K. Ward)
12. Neopanentheism (H. Morowitz)
13. Pansyntheism (R. Page)

Let's assume for the moment that the adjectives are adequate and that the authors in question are willing to use the term "panentheism" when modified in these ways. What precisely is the intersection set that arises out of these usages?

When they met together, several of the authors attempted to give panentheism a generic description, such that it would apply to all, or at least most, of the essays above. Consider four of the proposals:

Generic Panentheism according to David Griffin

1. The world (the totality of finite things) is in some sense in God.
2. The world has a degree of independence in relation to God, whether necessarily or by grace (divine decision).
3. Besides influencing the world, God is also influenced by the world.
4. Hence, besides being unchanging in some respects, God also changes in some respect.
5. God is related to the world somewhat as the human mind is related to its body.

Generic Panentheism according to Niels Gregersen

1. God contains the world yet is also more than the world. Thus the world is (in some sense) "in God."
2. The world is (in some sense) independent from God (or: entities in the world have some causal autonomy; or: they can be viewed in some sense as causal agents).
3. As contained "in God," the world not only derives its existence from God, but also returns to God. The world is (or: will be) united with God, while yet preserving the characteristics of being created (i.e., while remaining world). Thus the relations between God and world are (in some sense) bilateral.

Generic Panentheism according to Philip Clayton

Panentheism is located as part of a continuum that runs from classical philosophical theism to pantheism. Note that end points 1 and 7 below lie outside panentheism, and some of the other theses are not distinctive to panentheism alone.

1. God created the world as a distinct substance. It is separate from God in nature and essence, although God is present to the world (classical philosophical theism in the West).
2. God is radically immanent in the world.
3. God is bringing the world to Godself.
4. The world is in God — at least metaphorically, and perhaps also in a stronger sense.

5. God's relation to the world is in some sense analogous to the relationship between mind and body.
6. The world and God are corelated (contingently for some authors, necessarily for others).
7. The world and God are "nondual" (Shankara's "Atman is Brahman"), or there is only one substance that can be called "nature" or "God" (Spinoza's *deus sive natura*).

Emphases of Panentheism according to Michael Brierley

1. The cosmos as God's body
2. Language of "in and through"
3. The cosmos as sacrament
4. Language of inextricable intertwining
5. God's dependence on the cosmos
6. The intrinsic, positive value of the cosmos
7. Divine passibility
8. Degree Christology

Clearly there are differences among these four lists. The diversity of the lists matches the diversity of adjectives with which we began; both are reminders that panentheism expresses family resemblances between related theological programs rather than a single set of theses accepted by all panentheists.

At the same time, the four attempts to formulate generic features of panentheism clearly share some common features. All speak of a location of the world "within" God, even if they vary on the degree to which the "in" is meant metaphorically (see following section). Likewise, all resist an omnideterminism by God or an obscuring of the separate identity of the world. In all cases created beings are seen as retaining a certain degree of autonomy or independence from God. Finally, what characterizes all four accounts is a sense that the world has a deeper influence on God than was generally accepted in classical Western theology. This commonality represents one of the most important common emphases in this book.

The "In" of Panentheism

Already the etymology of the term "pan-en-theism" suggests that the little pronoun "in" linking "all" and "God" must bear the brunt of the interpretive burden. Can it hold up under the pressure?

For some authors the "in" relation suggests a relationship of spatial inclusion: the world is located within the sphere of the divine, so to speak. Others employ the analogy with the human body: panentheism means that God's location within the world is in some way analogous to the way the mind is located within the body. Yet already the conjunction of these two views reveals the difficulty: the former uses "in" to locate the world within God, whereas the second "in" would locate God within the world. How can both be true?

The unity among panentheists would be greatest if the word "in" could be given a single, distinct, sharp, logical or conceptual meaning, rather than merely a locative or metaphorical sense. For example, all panentheists might accept Hegel's argument that the world must necessarily be contained within the infinite, since it is a logical entailment of any adequate definition of the infinite *(das Unendliche)* that it not be limited by a finite *(ein Endliches)* which is set over against it.

At present, unfortunately, Hegel's argument has not won such universal acceptance. What one finds instead is a sort of family-resemblance relationship between the various usages of the word "in" by panentheists. Tom Oord of Western Nazarene University has put together a list of the various meanings of "in" that seem to be entailed by the positions presented in this volume. His list is illustrative.

The world is "in" God because:

1. that is its literal location
2. God energizes the world
3. God experiences or "prehends" the world (process theology)
4. God ensouls the world
5. God plays with the world (Indic Vedantic traditions)
6. God "enfields" the world (J. Bracken)
7. God gives space to the world (J. Moltmann, drawing on the *zimzum* tradition; A. Peacocke and many of the authors in this text)
8. God encompasses or contains the world (substantive or locative notion)
9. God binds up the world by giving the divine self to the world
10. God provides the ground for emergences in, or the emergence of, the world (A. Peacocke, P. Davies, H. Morowitz, P. Clayton)
11. God befriends the world (C. Deane-Drummond)
12. all things are contained "in Christ" (from the Pauline *en Christo*)
13. God graces the world (all of the above)

In this case, as with the previous examples, one notes the diversity of approaches. Yet one also recognizes in them variations on a common theme. Indeed, the variations may even be encouraging, insofar as they reflect the theological richness of the underlying notion — one concept is expressed in more than a dozen different ways while being identical to none. The chief test of the depth, and potential significance, of the shared commitment may well lie in its application. That is, critics of Christian panentheism must look to see whether these various approaches give rise to coherent, connected responses as adherents begin to apply them across the spectrum of questions traditionally addressed by Christian doctrine (e.g., Christology, pneumatology, soteriology, ecclesiology, eschatology).

Panentheist Approaches to the God-World Relation

Michael Brierley opens this volume with a thorough overview of panentheism. His tracing of its historical antecedents and his listing of major theologians and philosophers who are panentheists offer data for evaluating the background and current scope of panentheistic theologies. Likewise, the presentation of eight "common panentheistic themes" helps to locate features that many panentheists share. Of course, one might wish to dispute one or another of these theses. Thus, for example, I have resisted his fifth theme, God's dependence on the world, if it is taken to imply that God must necessarily create a (contingent) world. Two different lines of argument support this resistance. One is drawn from the Christian theological tradition, which has maintained that God's act of creation must be completely free and unconstrained. Another comes from those process traditions (e.g., Schelling, Samuel Alexander) which defend the emergence of (at least the personal side of) God. On these views the personal God develops as the world develops; if what the world becomes is contingent, so too is God. On Brierley's side, however, are Hegel and Whitehead, who provide weighty, although not necessarily consistent, arguments for a necessary correlation of God and world.

This debate cannot be resolved here. But it is a good reminder that Brierley's eight features of panentheism should not be taken as individually necessary conditions for panentheism. Instead, his list well describes features that are generally typical of panentheistic positions. To understand the various arguments he summarizes is to obtain a good sense of the thought-world that generally motivates and permeates panentheistic theologies.

David Griffin presents panentheism as the culmination of a movement from "early modernity's supernaturalism" through "late modernity's atheism" to process panentheism. On his view process theology is not opposed to the naturalism that characterizes much of modern science — at least as long as that naturalism is not "sensationist, atheist, and materialist." Griffin is followed in this effort by several other authors in this volume, all of whom look to panentheism as a way to break free of the old *supernaturalism versus atheistic naturalism* dichotomy. Traditional theological categories are not very helpful for creating a new integration of science and theology, since they presuppose the very supernatural categories that are being contested. One of the most pressing issues facing theology today is to reconceive the activity of God within the world of natural regularities that we have come to know. The present volume provides a beautiful example of the two major strategies being employed today. One group seeks to describe a naturalized theism or "God without the supernatural."[3] Another group (to which I also belong) seeks to find a credible way to conceive the actions of a transcendent-immanent God within the natural world.[4] We return to this difficult though crucial debate in the final pages of the present chapter.

Niels Gregersen offers a helpful typology of panentheisms, placing stress on the historical antecedents and broad conceptual patterns. Although it may not be complete — there are other panentheisms available in the history of Western thought (e.g., Nicholas of Cusa) and other conceptual possibilities than those he lists — his treatment tunnels far beneath the actual statements of contemporary authors to reveal their deeper conceptual debts. As he shows, one must make a decision between the options, since it's not consistent to assert all of them at the same time.

Although the treatments of soteriological panentheism, which Gregersen presents in the greatest detail, and dipolar panentheism are beyond objection, one might have reason to be concerned about the presentation of "expressivist" panentheism. Perhaps Gregersen has been influenced in choosing this label by George Lindbeck's unfortunate but influential treatment of Schleiermacher as an "experiential-expressivist" theologian.[5] If "expressivist panentheism" is meant primarily to refer to Hegel's philosophy, it's not clear that it's the best description of absolute idealism.[6] Terminology apart, modern philosophy from (say) Spinoza to Hegel actually yields a number of distinct forms of panentheism, which it is useful to catalogue and consider, each in its own right. I am also more optimistic than Gregersen on the potential for mediating between process thought, German idealism, and trinitarian/soteriological panentheism — especially in dialogue with scholars as well informed on all three traditions as Gregersen.

Keith Ward breaks the bounds of the West by summarizing the major panentheistic systems of the East. Ward's chapter makes clear why the Eastern traditions are indispensable resources for making decisions about panentheism in Western thought. The Eastern and Western contexts are not identical, and the differences are crucial. But the similarities that nonetheless hold across the religious traditions are for that reason all the more compelling. Some might differentiate more sharply between Ramanuja and Shankara, since the two are often regarded as representing distinct philosophical viewpoints. There is another reason to do so: many regard Shankara's philosophy (and its intellectual and spiritual heirs) as the purest form of absolute nondualism ever formulated. Arguably, world philosophy is better served by distinguishing between a complete nondualism of this sort and the limited nondualism represented by panentheism, with its insistence that God is in some respect more than or transcendent of the world. If Shankara were *not* an absolute nondualist, then we would have to invent another position to represent that view.

Christopher Knight offers an interesting synthesis of naturalism with the concept of sacrament, one that may be very attractive to those looking for "naturalized" forms of Christian theism. His notion of "pan-sacramental naturalism" will be familiar to many readers from his book *Wrestling with the Divine*. Although I express my resistance to naturalism further below, I am intrigued by his fusion of "radical theistic naturalism" and "a traditional Logos cosmology."[7] However one may finally evaluate this combination, Knight offers a crucial reminder about all debates concerning panentheism: "Differences on the panentheism issue can, in fact, legitimately arise from any particular view about the causal joint of divine action. It is only from the way such a view interacts with wider theological presuppositions that conclusions about the concept can be drawn."[8] Knight rightly notes that people with widely divergent theologies can end up espousing panentheism; conversely, panentheists can be led in very different directions in developing this doctrine. As this book shows, using the word "panentheism" does not bring an end to theological reflection. Instead, it is an invitation to wrestle with some very complex historical and conceptual issues, based on the sense that the immanence of God, God's involvement with history, and the responsiveness of God to the world must at all costs be preserved.

Eastern Orthodox Perspectives on the God-World Relation

Clearly the West has a much more difficult time with panentheism than do the Eastern Orthodox traditions. Reading the Western theologians, one has the sense that we may be clawing our way back to some basic insights that the

East never lost. Thus Eastern theologians have long been critical of "externalist" models of the God-world relation. Bishop Kallistos (Timothy Ware), for example, states unambiguously, "Among all too many Christian thinkers . . . there has been . . . a widespread tendency to speak as if God the creator were somehow external to the creation. . . . All such imagery is sadly defective."[9] Orthodox theology also frequently employs "internalist" language. One thinks of the notion of participation and "hypostatic inherence" as described by Alexei Nesteruk, or Maximos's concepts of the logoi and of *theosis* as described by Andrew Louth. Ware also emphasizes the notion of God's immanent energies or operations *(energeiai)*, drawing on the work of Saint Maximus, which "are nothing else than God himself in action."[10]

But perhaps least familiar, and most significant, to Western theologians is the Orthodox idea of *theosis* or deification. Louth defines *theosis* as "the way in which the uncreated God is to share with the cosmos, through humankind, all his divine qualities, save the inalienable quality of being uncreated."[11] Louth refers to this position as panentheistic, "since it envisages a relationship between the universe and God that stresses God's immanence in the universe and sees the universe as finding its purpose or goal . . . in union with God, or more boldly in deification."[12] Western panentheists must decide: Does *theosis* correspond only with "eschatological" panentheism, or does it support the stronger claims about the God-world connection made by many of the authors in this volume? The more fruitful theological program, I believe, lies in developing the details of the latter interpretation.

It is notable that the Fathers were much less hesitant than the Latin scholastics to defend the closest of relations between God and world. Suppose, then, that we in the West take these insights to heart: that "God is *in* the world and the world is *in* God";[13] that the energies of God in the world are "the whole deity, *God in his entirety*";[14] that all that exists, exists only by participating in God; and that the ultimate destiny of the world is deification. When we do, it becomes easier to resist a certain tendency to dichotomize God and world, which is visible in certain segments of Western theology. To turn away from dichotomous approaches to the God-world relation is to take a major step toward panentheism.

I noted earlier that panentheism is generally characterized by an emphasis on the dependence of God on world, or at least the influence of the world on God. Yet this particular theme is not greatly emphasized within the Orthodox traditions. Indeed, Orthodox theologians tend to defend the opposite conclusion. Kallistos Ware, distancing himself from *each* of Gregersen's three types of panentheisms, quotes Maximus the Confessor: "God, full beyond all fullness, brought creatures into being, *not because he has need of any-*

thing, but so that they might participate in him."[15] It is as if the route the Western theologians have taken to recover the Eastern emphasis on strong immanence has now led, again, to a sometimes sharp distinction between the two traditions. Western panentheists have received impetus from (among others) feminist theologians, from process thinkers, from criticisms of the passivity of God in traditional Western thought, and from theologies of the suffering of God, such as Jürgen Moltmann's *The Crucified God.* Yet, as it turns out, each of these sources of inspiration brings with it an emphasis on the temporality, responsiveness, mutability, and even dependence of God on the creation — all themes foreign to the intellectual and religious context of the patristics. It will be interesting to see what common ground can be found between the two traditions on this topic in the coming years.

Western Theological Perspectives on the God-World Relation

At first blush there appears to be greater divergence among the four authors whose chapters appear under this heading than in any other single section of the book. All four authors espouse some form of panentheism. But Denis Edwards emphasizes evolution and communion; Joseph Bracken draws on the notion of field to defend a process panentheism; Ruth Page, in switching from *pan-en-theism* to *pan-syn-theism,* substitutes the idea of "with" for "in"; and Celia Deane-Drummond turns to the wisdom or sapiential traditions as a corrective to certain tendencies in contemporary panentheistic thought.

In the end, however, perhaps the distance between the four positions is not as great as might initially appear; and the theme that binds them is potentially of great significance to systematic theology. The dominant category in this section, one realizes, is *relation.* As Page notes, "Current theology is much more (and rightly) concerned with relationship."[16] It is for this reason that Page prioritizes the preposition "with" over the categories of "in" or "over": "A relationship is close, but not so close that one is overwhelmed by the other."[17] Edwards's focus on relationality lies at the very center of his contribution; indeed, he titles his major section "All the Entities of the Universe Are Constituted by Relationships."[18] (Note the strong parallels between this claim and process thought.) As Edwards writes, "Not only is God persons-in-relation, but each creature can be understood as a being-in-relation."[19] Although Bracken employs the notion of field as his foundational metaphor, drawing heavily from the relevant sciences, his ultimate goal is to find a richer way of conceiving society and social relations. In *Society and Spirit, The Divine Matrix,* and *The One in the Many,* Bracken has sought an approach that more deeply grasps the implications of divine community — and the community of all creation with God — than either classical theology or Whiteheadian philosophy alone could do. Bracken's attempt to understand the social nature of human existence in light of a "social ontology" points very much in the same direction as the work by Page and Edwards.

Panentheism interpreted from the standpoint of relationality goes some distance toward addressing the concerns expressed by Deane-Drummond. As she also emphasizes, "It is through a reinterpretation of transcendence that otherness and relationship become possible."[20] By introducing the resources of the sapiential traditions, Deane-Drummond hopes to return attention to the ethical (and soteriological) dimensions of the doctrine of God, to the question, What is the relationship *for?* Thus the themes of wisdom, beauty, and redemption provide her entrée into the discussion of panentheism. "Jesus as the Wisdom of God points toward understanding the relationship between God and the world in terms of friendship."[21] As friend, God participates in the world's misery and suffering, but also in its joys and creativity. This form of friendship serves as a guide for theological ethics, promoting not only the values of environmental concern but also an ethics of virtue and of community.[22]

Other authors, whose work is not represented in this volume, also emphasize the ethical, environmental, and political implications of panentheism. One thinks of Bouma-Prediger's *The Greening of Theology,* Grace Jantzen's values-based arguments for the advantages of panentheism, and above all the explicitly political agenda of Sallie McFague in *The Body of God.*[23] Perhaps these latter works offer a corrective to excessively theoretical or speculative panentheisms, and certainly to any that might pretend to be purely science-based and value-free. At the same time, one worries about selecting a theological or metaphysical position based on its political consequences.[24] Such a move would certainly cause one to worry that the resulting postulations about God had been selected not because one had reason to think them true but because of their usefulness, raising the specter of Feuerbach's "projection" critique of religious language rather dramatically.

Scientifically Motivated Responses to the God-World Relation

Part of the motivation behind this book has been to pursue theology in light of our growing scientific knowledge of the world. By closing with a word on the chapters written by scientists, I hope to show how the dialogue with science has informed the type(s) of panentheism defended in these pages.

Paul Davies argues that God could be active in the world in the traditional, "interventionist" sense only by acting contrary to the laws of physics; yet such interventions, he argues, are no longer credible today. This fact should motivate theologians to explore whether the divine could be understood as working in and through the fundamental laws of nature. Can divine action be linked to the creativity and open-endedness that we discover within the process of natural history itself? Davies sketches the revisions, on both sides, that are required if one is to link natural law and divine action. Among the existing theological options, he suggests, panentheism best supports and expresses the sort of synthesis that is needed.

Russell Stannard is drawn to panentheism through his reflections on the physics of time. Contemporary physics, he argues, supports a "block universe" consisting of (at least) four dimensions. Hence there is no "flow of history" that God could jump into and transform in midstream, as it were. Instead, we should conceive of the universe as stretched out eternally in four-dimensional space-time. To create the block universe, God constructed the entire structure all at once. Knowing (eternally) what would be the wishes of the creatures within it, God (timelessly) built benevolent responses into the four-dimensional structure in the act of creation itself. Why is this conception appropriately labeled panentheist? Here Stannard perhaps appeals implicitly to the work of the Orthodox theologians: the actions or "energies" of God cannot be external to God's own nature. Hence this work of God which is the universe must remain somehow a part of God — which is exactly the contention of panentheism.

Robert Herrmann argues similarly. He finds the panentheistic analogy — the claim that relationship of God to the world is analogous to the relationship of our minds to our bodies — helpful for interpreting the story of evolution. I take Herrmann's argument to be analogous to that of Stannard and Davies: if evolution is a lawlike process that is external to God, then given contemporary science, it would be difficult at best to interpret this process as being encompassed or influenced by divine intentions. By contrast, if the whole process of evolution is understood as internal to the divine, then evolutionary laws, regularities, and outcomes can themselves be seen as expressions of God's nature and wishes.

Harold Morowitz, more than any other author in the book, possibly including Davies, is cautious about divine transcendence. He does find himself compelled to give a theological interpretation to the emergentist structure of the natural world as described in his book *The Emergence of Everything*. Moreover, he insists that this theology is not exhausted by the uncompromising immanence of Spinoza's pantheism. Although a purely immanent theology might well be adequate to explain the laws of physics, it is not adequate to explain biological evolution. Instead, the strong emergence that typifies evolution, Morowitz argues, requires "pruning rules," laws of nature of a different kind than physical law. How should these laws of emergence be understood? "Pruning by design is a possible explanation," Morowitz suggests. A God could be acting outside the system of nature as a whole, just as the pruner comes from outside the vineyard to prune off unfruitful branches and increase the fruitfulness of the crop. With the emergence of mind, Morowitz argues, yet another aspect of transcendence becomes evident, for mind introduces actual transcendence into an otherwise immanent process. Thus Morowitz offers the intriguing speculation, "Humanity is the transcendence of the immanent, emergent God."

Although Morowitz is tempted to limit transcendence to the self-transcending human mind, he is also drawn to the possibility of a truly transcendent God (or, as I would say, a truly transcendent moment within the divine nature). He is right, it seems to me, to find himself drawn in this direction. After all, a central feature of the self-transcendence of the human mind, stretching back to the dawn of the species and the dawn of religion, is to find oneself confronted with (at least the idea of) a force that is greater than oneself and greater than the world as a whole. The theistic traditions hold this force to be genuinely transcendent — a Creator and not just the creation of our minds.

Morowitz's current epistemological commitments, however, rule out two of the three ways such a being might be known. He is skeptical of metaphysical theories about the divine, which conflict with certain Kantian assumptions that he holds, and of theological reflections within the context of specific religious traditions. Perhaps he believes that the latter are undercut by skepticism concerning the historical origins of these traditions. Both dismissals strike me as overhasty. Moreover, one would have expected Morowitz to be open to the third classic source of knowledge of the divine: knowledge through direct experience, or "intuitions of [genuine] transcendence" (to modify his phrase), which are part of the mind's experience. In any event, there is something about panentheism that rests uncomfortably under the shackles of immanence alone, that refuses to be satisfied by subordination to the strictures of the self-transcending human mind.

I have too much in common with Arthur Peacocke, whose position has greatly influenced my own, to serve effectively as critic. His reliance on a theory of "strong emergence" in explaining the natural world, his resistance to dualistic theories of mind, his espousal of "emergentist monism" in describing the universe, his acceptance of dualism only for describing the distinction of natures between created reality and its Creator, and his attraction to pan-entheism as the consequence of these positions — these are all conclusions which I also endorse.

At the same time, commentators have often noticed a slight difference in emphasis between our two articulations of panentheism. Increasingly over the years Peacocke has emphasized the naturalistic side of his position (a fact sometimes obscured by the beautiful, if sometimes dualistic-sounding, language of the Anglican liturgy that he employs). Of course, Peacocke also posits a divine creation and a christological consummation of history; he imagines a "top-down influence" by God over the course of history; and he understands the Christ event as particularly illustrative of the structure of the whole. At the same time, he insists in this volume that there are no "nonnatural causes"; it is the natural process itself that "brings forth the new"; "God is not to be found as some kind of *additional* influence or factor"; and it is (what science calls) "chance operating within the created order" that must serve as the means of divine creation. Could it be that these stipulations force his position closer to the robust naturalism of the Dutch philosopher Willem Drees than Peacocke himself intends?[25]

Stipulations like these might at first suggest that Peacocke's position is best understood as a subtle variant of classical deism. Deism generally grants the existence of a creator God but denies any subsequent causal activity of God within the natural order. Yet this interpretation can't be right: Peacocke's reason for advocating a panentheistic theology is precisely to maintain a very strong view of the immanence of God in the world. On his view God holds the universe in existence at every moment, and God is *in some sense* the source of creativity within creation. Certainly the resulting position is a far cry from the classical forms of deism advanced by his landsmen some three hundred years ago.

But the question of deism does help to raise what may be the most relevant question: Does Peacocke actually retain any place in his theology for focally intended divine actions? Consider the analogy in the human case. There are numerous actions carried out by our bodies in an autonomous fashion. Some, like the constricting of our blood vessels, are beyond our conscious control; others we can exercise some control over, such as the beating of our heart. Many actions were once consciously learned and are now carried out more or less automatically, such as walking, driving, or playing an extended sixteenth-note passage on the violin. Some of our actions, like my intention to add this sentence, are clearly focally intended. Unlike human beings, presumably a panentheistic God could *in principle* choose to alter any natural process — even those so regular in occurrence that we speak of them as "natural laws." The question is, On Peacocke's view, *does* God in fact engage in any such focally intended actions? Does God's ongoing creative involvement in fact make any difference to the way anything happens, compared to the way things would happen if God were not involved and the universe were simply allowed to run by itself? For example, when Peacocke writes of God's influence on the mind of Jesus (or anyone else), is he really thinking of a focally intended divine action rather than of the effects on human minds of God's overall action in creating and sustaining the universe?

Perhaps one can imagine a theism that dispenses with focally intended divine actions. Indeed, some clearly believe that theism *sans* such actions is the only viable metaphysical position for theists to take in an age of science. In this volume, for example, Davies, Morowitz, and Knight appear to hold this view, and others may as well. As the literature shows, the considerations that pull one in this direction are legion.

Presumably, though, Peacocke intends his proposal of God's "top-down influence" to preserve focally intended divine actions. That is, God (continuously?) provides some input to "the whole," which through "a long chain of trickle-down causes" makes "particular things happen at particular places."[26] In principle, of course, one can cause an outcome through a chain of intermediate causes, as when one knocks over the last domino in a row by knocking over the first one. But some more work is required to show how trickle-down causation would work — how, for example, an input at the level of "the whole" could cause an individual to have a particular thought at a particular time.

Thus, for better or worse, I have attempted to develop panentheism in a different direction. In part, the resources of process thought make it possible to conceive a greater degree of direct divine involvement. Process metaphysics preserves the regularities necessary for science without accepting that the physical order is metaphysically closed. As Griffin shows, process thought also supports a particular understanding of individual moments of experience ("actual occasions") that does not rule out a conscious influence on them by God.

But another line of argument also supports a panentheism with focally intended divine actions. Imagine that one begins with the "ladder of emergence" idea and uses it to help introduce the concept of a God who pervades and contains the natural history of emergence. Is the addition of theistic vocabulary only a sort of "coloring" of the whole, bracketed as it is between a divine origin and divine telos? Or does the introduction of theistic language not transform one's understanding of the entire process of natural history? To introduce the idea of a being or reality that is qualitatively distinct from the universe as a whole — infinitely greater than it, distinct from its nature as the necessary is from the contingent or the morally perfect is from the imperfect — is to reorient, rethink, and reinterpret all things.

For example, if something of God transcends the world as a whole, then the notion of pure spirit cannot be absurd, at least with regard to this element of the divine that transcends. (I assume, against Whitehead, that God is not necessarily correlated at all times with an actually existing world.) Thus one might be inclined to say that there is within us as well an element that is pure spirit, insofar as it participates in the divine essence. *Science* can never justify such language, of course; it allows only for talk of mental properties and causes, not mental essences. But if one makes theological assertions, must these assertions not at least partially *reinterpret* the world?[27]

Our struggle is to understand what the minimal conditions are for asserting divine causal influence on the world. One could not give credit to a God who created an open-ended universe and then merely *hoped* for a final consummation that would be to "his" liking. God must also "draw the world unto himself" through some sort of causal activity. The tradition has called this influence providence. If one endorses the concept of providence, must one not also leave room in one's interpretation of the world for its influence? Perhaps not at the level of macrophysics, for here all the influence that is needed can be built in *ab initio* and left to run its own course.[28] But certainly by the point that minds emerge, some influence on their creativity and comprehension could be postulated — especially if, as I think, our minds are not ultimately algorithmic or law-driven.[29] Moreover, to the extent that sentient beings of all sorts — hence most of the animal kingdom — evidence an openness and a creative striving that anticipates the virtually unconstrained creativity of mind, could there not also be some space for response to actual divine influence, even of the most limited or constrained kind, here as well?

For students of the sciences, these are difficult suggestions. But they are not absurd, and some progress has been made of late in parsing them. Panentheistic theology can undergird a research program that attempts to think the theological end point together with the sophisticated understanding of mechanisms offered by contemporary science. The project, though difficult, is not impossible. It may be that a more cautious approach to divine action will in the end prevail. But in the meantime it seems worthwhile to search for ways to think together more fully the scientific and the theological understandings of events in the natural world.[30]

Contributors

Joseph A. Bracken, S.J., is emeritus professor of theology at Xavier University in Cincinnati, Ohio, and recently retired as director of the university's Brueggeman Center for Interreligious Dialogue. He was the first occupant of Xavier's Beckman Family Chair in Roman Catholic Theology and formerly served as rector of the university's Jesuit Community. A graduate of Xavier, he earned a master's degree in philosophy at Loyola University of Chicago, a licentiate in theology from West Baden College in Indiana, and a Ph.D. in philosophy from the University of Freiburg. He has taught at St. Mary of the Lake Seminary in Illinois and at Marquette University. Dr. Bracken is the coeditor (with Marjorie Suchocki) of *Trinity in Process: Essays on the Relationality of God* (1997) and the author of six other books. His most recent study, *The One in the Many: A Contemporary Reconstruction of the God-World Relationship,* was published by Wm. B. Eerdmans in 2001.

Michael W. Brierley serves as domestic chaplain and research assistant to the Anglican bishop of Oxford. Educated at Corpus Christi College, Cambridge and Ripon College Cuddesdon, Oxford, he holds undergraduate degrees in history and in theology. He is currently studying for a doctorate in theology at the University of Birmingham. His special interest is the rise of panentheism in twentieth-century British theology.

Philip Clayton is professor of theology at Claremont School of Theology and professor of philosophy and religion at the Claremont Graduate University. A summa cum laude graduate of Westmont College, he received his M.A. at Fuller Theological Seminary and, after further graduate study at the University of Munich, earned a Ph.D. in religious studies and in philosophy at Yale University. He previously taught at Haverford and Williams colleges and at Sonoma State University in California. Dr. Clayton has been a guest professor at the Harvard Divinity School and the visiting Alexander von Humboldt Professor at the University of Munich, where he had earlier been a Fulbright Senior Research Fellow. In addition to editing a dozen books, he is the author of *The Problem of God in Modern Thought*, published in 2000 by Wm. B. Eerdmans, as well as *Explanation from Physics to Theology: An Essay in Rationality and Religion* (1989), *Das Gottesproblem: Gott und Unendlichkeit in der neuzeitlichen Philosophie* (1996), *God and Contemporary Science* (1998), and *The Emergence of the Spirit* (forthcoming).

Paul Davies is the professor of natural philosophy in the Australian Centre for Astrobiology at Macquarie University. After earning a Ph.D. in physics at University College, London, in 1970, he held academic appointments in astronomy, physics, and mathematics at the universities of Cambridge, London, Newcastle upon Tyne, and Adelaide. He has written over twenty-five books, both popular and specialist works, including *The Physics of Time Asymmetry* (1974), *Quantum Fields in Curved Space* (coauthored with Nicholas Birrell in 1981), *The Mind of God* (1992), *About Time* (1995), *How to Build a Time Machine* (2002), and most recently, *The Origin of Life* (2003). Dr. Davies also has extensive experience in television and radio. He has won numerous awards for his scientific and media work, including the 1995 Templeton Prize. He received the 2001 Kelvin Medal presented by the UK Institute of Physics and the 2002 Michael Faraday Prize of the Royal Society for his contributions to promoting science to the public. Three years ago the asteroid 1992 OG was officially named (6870) "Pauldavies" in his honor.

Celia E. Deane-Drummond is a professor of theology and biological sciences at Chester College, an affiliate of the University of Liverpool. She did her first baccalaureate degree at Girton College, Cambridge, and went on to earn a Ph.D. in plant physiology at Reading University. After postdoctoral research in botany, she later received an honors degree in theology from Trinity College, Bristol; a Ph.D. in theological studies from Manchester University; and a postgraduate certificate in education from Manchester Metropolitan University. Dr. Deane-Drummond has taught plant physiology at Durham University and theology at Manchester University. She serves as editor of *Ecotheology*. She is the author or editor of nine books, her recent publications including *Creation through Wisdom: Theology and the New Biology* (2000), *Biology and Theology Today: Exploring the Boundaries* (2001), *The Ethics of Na-*

ture (2003), and (edited with Bronislaw Szerszynski) *ReOrdering Nature: Theology, Society, and the New Genetics* (2003).

Denis Edwards is senior lecturer in systematic theology in the School of Theology at Flinders University in Australia and at the Catholic Theological College within the Adelaide School of Divinity. He was one of the founders of the Centre for Theology, Science, and Culture at Flinders and serves on the center's board of trustees. A graduate of St. Francis Xavier Seminary in Australia, Dr. Edwards received a master's degree in religious education from Fordham University and took a doctorate in sacred theology at the Catholic University of America. He is the editor of *Earth Revealing/Earth Healing* (2001) and the author of seven books, including *The God of Evolution: A Trinitarian Theology* (1999). He is currently working on a book on the theology of the Holy Spirit.

Niels Henrik Gregersen is a research professor in science and theology at the University of Aarhus in Denmark. A graduate of the University of Copenhagen, where he earned a Ph.D., he is an elected member of the Learned Society of Denmark and currently serves as its president. Dr. Gregersen is systematic theology editor of the *Danish Journal of Theology* and associate editor of the *Encyclopedia of Science and Religion* (2003). He is the author of three books and coauthor of two others in addition to editing a dozen collected works. The most recent are *The Human Person in Science and Theology*, published in the United States by Eerdmans in 2000; *Design and Disorder* (with Ulf Görman), which was published in 2002; and *From Complexity to Life* (2003).

David Ray Griffin is a professor of philosophy of religion and theology at the Claremont School of Theology and Claremont Graduate University. In the extensive body of work he has produced over the past quarter-century, he has drawn on the metaphysical system developed by Alfred North Whitehead to craft a new naturalistic theism. Dr. Griffin is a graduate of Northern Christian College in Eugene, Oregon; received a master's degree in educational counseling from the University of Oregon; and after further study at the School of Theology at Claremont and Johannes Gutenberg University in Mainz, Germany, earned a Ph.D. in religion from the Claremont Graduate School. Formerly on the faculty of the University of Dayton, he founded the Center of Process Studies at Claremont with John Cobb. Dr. Griffin is the founding editor of the SUNY Press Series in Constructive Postmodern Thought, the editor or coeditor of eleven books, the coauthor of three, and the author of nine others, including *Unsnarling the World-Knot: Conscious-*

ness, Freedom, and the Mind-Body Problem (1998), *Religion and Scientific Naturalism: Overcoming the Conflicts* (2000), and *Reenchantment without Supernaturalism: A Process Philosophy of Religion* (2001).

Robert L. Herrmann is a retired biochemist who formerly served as the executive director of the American Scientific Affiliation. A graduate of Purdue University, he earned a Ph.D. in biochemistry at Michigan State University and was a Damon Runyon Fellow at the Massachusetts Institute of Technology before joining the faculty of the Boston University School of Medicine. He also has been professor and chair of biochemistry at Oral Roberts University Schools of Medicine and Dentistry. Dr. Herrmann is the coauthor (with John Marks Templeton) of *The God Who Would Be Known* (1989) and *Is God the Only Reality?* (1994), and the author of *Sir John Templeton: From Wall Street to Humility Theology* (1998). He recently edited *Expanding Humanity's Vision of God: New Thoughts on Science and Religion* (2001).

Christopher C. Knight is a senior research associate at St. Edmund's College, Cambridge. He took first class honors in physics at the University of Exeter, earned a Ph.D. in theoretical astronomy at the University of Manchester, and subsequently received a bachelor of theology degree with distinction from the Salisbury and Wells Theological College of the University of Southampton. Dr. Knight served as chaplain of St. Mary's Cathedral in Edinburgh, rector of the Lighthorne group of parishes in the Diocese of Coventry, and then as chaplain, fellow, and director of studies in theology at Sidney Sussex College, Cambridge. His first book, *Wrestling with the Divine: Religion, Science, and Revelation*, was published in 2001.

Andrew Louth is professor of patristic and Byzantine studies at the University of Durham. A graduate of St. Catharine's College, Cambridge, where he took first class honors in mathematics and theology, he earned a master's degree in theology at the University of Edinburgh. He has taught at Oxford, where he was a fellow and tutor in theology at Worcester College and university lecturer in theology, and at Goldsmiths' College, University of London, where he was professor of cultural history. Professor Louth is a coeditor of the Oxford Early Christian Studies Series and also of the forthcoming *Cambridge History of Early Christian Literature.* He is the author of five books, including *The Origins of the Christian Mystical Tradition: From Plato to Denys* (1981), *Maximus the Confessor* (1996), and *St. John Damascene: Tradition and Originality in Byzantine Theology* (2002).

Harold J. Morowitz is the Clarence Robinson Professor of Biology and Natural Philosophy at George Mason University and a member of its Krasnow Institute for Advanced Study. A graduate of Yale University, where he earned both a baccalaureate degree and a Ph.D. in biophysics, he went on to become a professor of molecular biophysics and biochemistry at Yale and master of the university's Pierson College. Dr. Morowitz has also worked as a biophysicist at the Natural Bureau of Standards and at the National Heart Institute of the National Institutes of Health. A fellow of the American Association for the Advancement of Science, he serves as cochair of the Science Advisory Committee of the Santa Fe Institute. Dr. Morowitz is the author of fourteen books, including *Cosmic Joy and Local Pain* (1987) and *Beginnings of Cellular Life: Metabolism Recapitulates Biogenesis* (1992). His most recent volume is *The Emergence of Everything: How the World Became Complex* (2002).

Alexei V. Nesteruk is a senior lecturer in mathematics at the University of Portsmouth. He completed baccalaureate studies in St. Petersburg, received a master of science degree with honors in physics from St. Petersburg State University, and earned a Ph.D. in theoretical and mathematical physics from St. Petersburg State Technical University. He worked as a research scientist at S. I. Vavilov State Optical Institute while pursuing graduate-level studies in philosophy at St. Petersburg State University. After doing research in general relativity at the Free University of Brussels and teaching mathematics at the University of Economics and Finance of St. Petersburg, he became a Royal Society postdoctoral fellow at the Mathematical Institute at Oxford University. He studied theology at the Institute of Orthodox Christian Studies at Cambridge University, where he is currently a research associate. Dr. Nesteruk's monograph, *Light from the East: Science, Theology, and Eastern Orthodox Tradition,* was published in 2003.

Ruth Page, now retired, is the first woman to have served as principal of New College, which houses the faculty of divinity of the University of Edinburgh. A graduate of St. Andrews University, where she also took a master's degree, she subsequently earned a bachelor of divinity degree at the University of Otago in Dunedin, New Zealand, and took a D.Phil. at Oxford University. She returned to Otago as lecturer in systematic theology before joining the faculty of New College. Dr. Page served as an editor of the *Dictionary of Pastoral Concern* (2001) and is the author of four books, including *God and the Web of Creation* (1996) and *God with Us: Synergy in the Church* (2000).

Arthur Peacocke, the 2001 winner of the Templeton Prize, devoted the first twenty-five years of his career to teaching and research in the field of physical biochemistry, specializing in biological macromolecules and making significant contributions to our understanding of the structure of DNA. His principal interest during the past thirty years has been in exploring the relation of science to theology. Dr. Peacocke was the founding director of the Ian Ramsey Centre at St. Cross College, Oxford, and is the author of ten books exploring the relationship between science and religion, including *Theology for a Scientific Age* (1990 and 1993) and, most recently, *Paths from Science towards God: The End of All Our Exploring* (2001). After studying at Exeter College, Oxford, and earning a D.Phil. in physical biochemistry, he taught at the University of Birmingham and at St. Peter's College, Oxford. He also has served as Dean of Clare College, Cambridge. Dr. Peacocke was involved in founding the Science and Religion Forum in the United Kingdom, the corresponding European society (ESSSAT), and the Society of Ordained Scientists, a new dispersed religious order. He was made a member of the Order of the British Empire by Queen Elizabeth II in 1993.

Russell Stannard is an emeritus professor of physics at Open University and a longtime contributor to the science and religion dialogue not only through widely read articles and books but also through popular radio and television programs. A graduate of University College, London, where he took first class honors in physics followed by a Ph.D. in cosmic ray physics, Dr. Stannard has been a physicist at the Lawrence Radiation Laboratory in Berkeley, California, and a member of the faculty of University College, where he is now an honorary fellow. He is also a fellow of the Institute of Physics. Queen Elizabeth II made him an Officer of the Order of the British Empire in 1998. Dr. Stannard has devoted much of the past twenty years to studying the relationship between science, religion, psychology, and philosophy, as well as exploring ways of teaching modern physics to schoolchildren and incorporating modern thinking into school religious education lessons in the United Kingdom. He is the author of a dozen prize-winning books for children and the editor of *God for the Twenty-First Century* (2000).

Keith Ward, the Regius Professor of Divinity at Oxford University, is one of Britain's foremost writers on Christian belief and doctrine in the light of modern scientific discoveries and in the context of other faith traditions. A graduate of the University of Wales, where he took a first class honors degree, he holds a B.Litt. from Oxford and an M.A. and doctorate in divinity from both Oxford and Cambridge universities. He has taught at the University of

Glasgow, St. Andrews University, and King's College, London, and been dean and director of studies in philosophy and in theology at Trinity Hall, Cambridge, as well as the F. D. Maurice Professor of Moral and Social Theology at the University of London, where he was also a professor of the history and philosophy of religion. Dr. Ward is a canon of Christ Church, Oxford, and a Fellow of the British Academy. The author of fourteen books on theology and philosophy, he recently completed a four-volume comparative theology. The final volume is *Religion and Community* (2000).

Bishop Kallistos of Diokleia (Timothy Ware) was the Spalding Lecturer in Eastern Orthodox Studies at Oxford University until his retirement in 2001. Educated at Magdalen College, Oxford, where he took a double first in classics and theology, he subsequently studied at Princeton University and returned to Oxford for a D.Phil. He took monastic vows at the Monastery of St. John the Theologian in Patmos, Greece, and remains a member of that community. He is the founder of the Greek Orthodox Parish of the Holy Trinity in Oxford. In 1982 he was consecrated titular Bishop of Diokleia, the first Englishman to become a bishop within the Orthodox Church since the eleventh century. Bishop Kallistos is the cotranslator of two Orthodox service books and of *The Philokalia,* a collection of texts written between the fourth and fifteenth centuries by Orthodox spiritual masters. He is also the author of four books, including *The Orthodox Church* (1963; rev. ed., 1993) and *The Inner Kingdom* (2000), the first of six volumes of his collected works.

Endnotes

Notes to "Foreword," by Mary Ann Meyers

1. John Marks Templeton, *Worldwide Laws of Life* (Radnor, Pa.: Templeton Foundation Press, 1997), p. 465.

Notes to "Introduction," by Arthur Peacocke

1. Acts 17:28 (as in the title of this volume and, here, with emphasis and query added). The author of Luke-Acts describes Paul in his speech on the Areopagus in Athens as quoting this from a local poet (possibly Epimenides). At least this indicates that such an idea of God existed in the first-century Christian church.

2. For example, the volumes subtitled "Scientific Perspectives on Divine Action" (*Quantum Cosmology and the Laws of Nature* [1993; rev. ed., 1996], *Chaos and Complexity* [1995], *Evolutionary and Molecular Biology* [1998], *Neuroscience and the Person* [1999], *Quantum Mechanics* [2001]) published by the Vatican Observatory and the Center for Theology and the Natural Sciences over the period 1993-2001 under the editorship of R. J. Russell and others and distributed by the University of Notre Dame Press, Notre Dame, Ind., 46556.

3. *Oxford Dictionary of the Christian Church*, ed. F. L. Cross and E. A. Livingstone, 2nd ed. (Oxford: Oxford University Press, 1985), p. 1027.

4. *A New Dictionary of Christian Theology*, ed. A. Richardson and J. Bowden (London: SCM Press, 1983), p. 423. I have omitted the more explicitly "process" understanding of the term expressed in Cobb's concluding words to his article: "God's decisions in their turn profoundly influence, but do not completely determine, what happens in the world."

5. See the papers by Michael Brierley, Keith Ward, and others, passim, in this volume.

6. As recorded in the volumes mentioned in n. 2. For a recent, nontechnical over-

view, see the author's *Paths from Science towards God: The End of All Our Exploring* (Oxford: Oneworld, 2001), chap. 5.

7. Philip Clayton, *God and Contemporary Science* (Edinburgh: Edinburgh University Press, 1997), passim.

Notes to "Naming a Quiet Revolution: The Panentheistic Turn in Modern Theology," by Michael W. Brierley

1. J. Donald Neil, *God in Everything: A Layman's Guide to the New Thinking* (Sussex: Book Guild, 1984), p. x. Cf. pp. ix-x: "I believe that the doctrine of panentheism . . . holds the answer to many of the unanswered questions."

2. Claude Y. Stewart, "Naming Panentheism," *Epiphany,* winter 1987, pp. 5-6, at 6.

3. Matthew Fox, *Original Blessing: A Primer in Creation Spirituality* (Santa Fe: Bear and Co., 1983), p. 90.

4. Philip Clayton, "The Panentheistic Turn in Christian Theology," *Dialog* 38 (1999): 289-93. Cf. John Macquarrie, *Stubborn Theological Questions* (London: SCM Press, 2003), p. x: "I believe that in the past fifty years or so there has been a movement among Christian theologians to lay more stress on the closeness and immanence of God, in various forms of panentheism."

5. William M. Thompson, "A Suffering World, a Loving God? A Moderate Panentheistic View," in *Suffering and Healing in Our Day,* ed. Francis A. Eigo (Villanova: Villanova University Press, 1990), pp. 63-94, at 90, claims that panentheism is "not yet born," as its definition is still emerging.

6. J. Donald Neil, "Panentheism: A Gospel for To-Day?" (Ph.D. diss., University of Exeter, 1973).

7. Neil, *God in Everything,* p. x.

8. For modern treatments of pantheism, see Michael P. Levine, *Pantheism: A Non-Theistic Concept of Deity* (London and New York: Routledge, 1994), and at a more popular level, Paul Harrison, *The Elements of Pantheism: Understanding the Divinity in Nature and the Universe* (Shaftesbury, Boston, and Melbourne: Element, 1999).

9. Cf. M. Daphne Hampson, *Theology and Feminism* (Oxford and Cambridge, Mass.: Basil Blackwell, 1990), p. 132.

10. Two examples of this tendency are "higher pantheism" and the doctrine of the "finite God." For "higher pantheism" see the example of R. J. Campbell (below, n. 101), and also that of Edmond G. A. Holmes (who, if anything, was less "high" than Campbell): *In Quest of an Ideal: An Autobiography* (London: Richard Cobden-Sanderson, 1920); Holmes, *All Is One: A Plea for the Higher Pantheism* (London: Richard Cobden-Sanderson, 1921); and Holmes, "Two or One? A Defence of the Higher Pantheism," *Hibbert Journal* 24 (1926): 404-20. For criticism of "semi-pantheism," see Charles Harris, *First Steps in the Philosophy of Religion* (London: Student Christian Movement, 1927), pp. 98-115, and Harris, *Pro Fide: A Text-Book of Modern Apologetics for Theological Students, Ministers of Religion, and Others,* 4th ed. (London: John Murray, 1930), pp. xxiii-xxviii. Cf. the term Hartshorne used for his doctrine of God in "The New Pantheism," *Christian Register* 115 (1936): 119-20 and 141-43, cited in David H. Nikkel, *Panentheism in Hartshorne and Tillich: A Creative Synthesis*

(New York: Peter Lang, 1995), p. 7. The "finite God" was espoused during the First World War by H. G. Wells (among others) during his brief theistic phase. For an example of the discussion, see Hastings Rashdall, "Theism or Pantheism?" *Modern Churchman* 6 (1916): 395-404, reprinted in *The New Liberalism: Faith for the Third Millennium*, ed. Jonathan L. Clatworthy (London: Modern Churchpeople's Union, 1998), pp. 85-92. Arthur R. Peacocke, *God and the New Biology* (London: J. M. Dent and Sons, 1986), pp. 84-85, remarks that the "indigenous tradition" of immanentist theology in Britain may help explain why the ideas of Teilhard and Whitehead made more of an impact in the United States.

11. See Charles Hartshorne, "Panentheism," in *An Encyclopedia of Religion*, ed. Vergilius T. A. Ferm (New York: Philosophical Library, 1945), p. 557; E. Russell Naughton, "Panentheism," in *New Catholic Encyclopedia*, vol. 10 (New York: McGraw-Hill, 1967), pp. 943-45; John B. Cobb, "Panentheism," in *A New Dictionary of Christian Theology*, ed. Alan Richardson and John S. Bowden (London: SCM Press, 1983), p. 423; and Charles Hartshorne, "Pantheism and Panentheism," in *Encyclopedia of Religion*, ed. Mircea Eliade, vol. 11 (New York: Macmillan, 1987), pp. 165-71.

12. Krause used the word in a work of 1829: see Gregersen's paper in this volume; cf. Günter Meckenstock, "Some Remarks on Pantheism and Panentheism," in *Traditional Theism and Its Modern Alternatives*, ed. Svend Andersen (Aarhus: Aarhus University Press, 1994), pp. 117-29, at 121. Naughton, p. 944, claims the term was also used by Friedrich Jacobi (1743-1819); H. Maurice Relton, *Studies in Christian Doctrine* (London: Macmillan; New York: St. Martin's Press, 1960), p. 55, claims the term was also used by Baader.

13. For Krause see Arnold Zweig, "Karl Christian Friedrich Krause," in *The Encyclopedia of Philosophy*, ed. Paul Edwards, vol. 4 (New York: Macmillan and the Free Press; London: Collier Macmillan, 1967), pp. 363-65; and Teresa Rodriguez de Lecea, "Karl Christian Friedrich Krause (1781-1832)," trans. Isabel Venceslá, in *Routledge Encyclopedia of Philosophy*, ed. Edward Craig, vol. 7 (London and New York: Routledge, 1998), pp. 298-301. R. V. Orden Jiménez, *El Sistema de la Filosofía de Krause: Génesis y Desarrollo del Panenteísmo* (Madrid: Publicaciones de la Universidad Pontificia Comillas de Madrid, 1998), looks pertinent.

14. Robert C. Whittemore, "Hegel as Panentheist," *Tulane Studies in Philosophy* 9 (1960): 134-64, at 143, observes that there are no apparent references to Krause in Hegel, nor references to Hegel in the context of panentheism in Krause.

15. Hastie's preface to K. C. F. Krause, *The Ideal of Humanity and Universal Federation*, trans. William Hastie (Edinburgh: T. & T. Clark, 1900), p. x.

16. Philip Clayton, *The Problem of God in Modern Thought* (Grand Rapids and Cambridge: Eerdmans, 2000), p. 390; cf. pp. 413 and 415, and Gregory R. Peterson's claim that the roots of panentheism lie in eighteenth-century German idealism (*Minding God: Theology and the Cognitive Sciences* [Minneapolis: Fortress, 2003], p. 198).

17. Clayton, *Problem of God*, pp. 150-51; cf. p. 168.

18. Clayton, *Problem of God*, pp. 56 and 66.

19. William Ralph Inge, *Christian Mysticism: Considered in Eight Lectures Delivered before the University of Oxford*, 8th ed. (London: Methuen, 1948), p. 121; for Inge see Paul Crook, "W. R. Inge and Cultural Crisis, 1899-1920," *Journal of Religious History* 16 (1991): 410-32, and Peter J. Bowler, *Reconciling Science and Religion: The Debate in Early-*

Twentieth-Century Britain (Chicago and London: University of Chicago Press, 2001), pp. 270-77.

20. Friedrich von Hügel, "Experience and Transcendence," *Dublin Review* 138 (1906): 357-79, at 374-75; von Hügel, "The Relations between God and Man in 'The New Theology' of the Rev. R. J. Campbell," *Albany Review* 1 (1907): 650-68, at 664-65; and von Hügel, *The Mystical Element of Religion as Studied in Saint Catherine of Genoa and Her Friends*, 2nd ed. (1923; reprint, New York: Crossroad, 1999), 2:336. George Tyrrell, *Oil and Wine* (London: Longmans, Green and Co., 1907), p. ix.

21. Brigid E. Herman, *The Meaning and Value of Mysticism* (London: James Clarke, 1915), p. 304; Herman was (for a brief while) a writer for the *Church Times* (Bernard H. M. Palmer, *Gadfly for God: A History of the Church Times* [London: Hodder and Stoughton, 1991], p. 116). Other early airings of the word are Henry D. A. Major, "The Theology in the Last Lines of Emily Brontë," *Modern Churchman* 1 (1911): 458-62, at 460, and Vernon F. Storr, *The Being of God* (London: Longmans, Green and Co., 1922), p. 10.

22. Charles Hartshorne, *Man's Vision of God and the Logic of Theism* (New York: Harper and Brothers, 1941), pp. 347-52; Hartshorne, "A Mathematical Analysis of Theism," *Review of Religion* 8 (1943): 20-38, at 24 and 34; Hartshorne, "Panentheism"; and Hartshorne, *The Divine Relativity: A Social Conception of God*, 2nd ed. (New Haven and London: Yale University Press, 1964, first published in 1948).

23. Cobb, "Panentheism," p. 423.

24. Charles Hartshorne and William L. Reese, *Philosophers Speak of God* (Chicago and London: University of Chicago Press, 1953). The epilogue to this volume (pp. 499-514) is a revision of Hartshorne, "A Mathematical Analysis of Theism."

25. Robinson "first brought the word back into current use in this country" (Neil, *God in Everything*, p. 16; cf. p. 59).

26. John A. T. Robinson, *Exploration into God* (London: SCM Press, 1967) and *Honest to God* (London: SCM Press, 1963). Robinson first used the term in "God Dwelling Incognito," *New Christian*, 7 October 1965, pp. 12-13, at 12, reprinted in Robinson, *But That I Can't Believe!* (London: Collins, 1967), pp. 64-70; cf. Robinson, *Truth Is Two-Eyed* (London: SCM Press, 1979), p. 26. Robinson also used the term to describe his position in an unpublished lecture of 1967 (Lambeth Palace Library, Ms. 3544, ff. 106-7 and 121). Arthur Peacocke has advised me in personal conversation that he himself first came across the term in *Exploration into God*.

27. John Macquarrie, *In Search of Deity: An Essay in Dialectical Theism: The Gifford Lectures Delivered at the University of St. Andrews in Session, 1983-4* (London: SCM Press, 1984), is the classic textbook of twentieth-century British panentheism. I have called Macquarrie the "Grand Old Man" of British panentheism in my review of *The Grace of Being*, by Georgina Morley, *Modern Believing* 43, no. 1 (2002): 61-63, at 63.

28. Macquarrie avoids use of the term because of its similarity to "pantheism": "I am not myself intending to make much use of the term 'panentheism,' though it must be already apparent that I have a good deal of sympathy with the position for which it stands. The word 'panentheism' is too close in its formation to the word 'pantheism,' with the result that there can easily be confusion between them. I think that in the minds of many people, panentheism is assumed to be a modification of pantheism" (*In Search of Deity*, p. 54). Cf. pp. 15 and 171; Macquarrie, "God and the World: One Reality or Two?" *Theology*

75 (1972): 394-403, at 395; Macquarrie, *Principles of Christian Theology,* 2nd ed. (London: SCM Press, 1977), p. 120; Macquarrie, "Pilgrimage in Theology," *Epworth Review* 7, no. 1 (1980): 47-52, at 51; Macquarrie, "Panentheismus," *Theologische Realenzyklopädie,* vol. 25 (Berlin and New York: Walter de Gruyter, 1995), pp. 611-15, at 611; Macquarrie, *Twentieth-Century Religious Thought,* 5th ed. (London: SCM Press, 2001), p. 439; W. B. Green, "Profile: John Macquarrie," *Epworth Review* 24, no. 4 (1997): 12-20, at 17; Georgina Morley, *The Grace of Being: John Macquarrie's Natural Theology* (Bristol, Ind.: Wyndham Hall Press, 2001), p. 157 n. 12; and Douglas Pratt, *Relational Deity: Hartshorne and Macquarrie on God* (Lanham, Md.: University Press of America, 2002), p. 159.

29. Macquarrie's panentheism is recognized by his commentators Eugene T. Long, "John Macquarrie on God," *Perspectives in Religious Studies* 8 (1980): 215-26, at 222; Long, "John Macquarrie on Ultimate Reality and Meaning," *Ultimate Reality and Meaning* 6 (1983): 300-320, at 316; Long, *Existence, Being, and God: An Introduction to the Philosophical Theology of John Macquarrie* (New York: Paragon House, 1985), p. 50; Daniel W. Hardy, "Theology through Philosophy," in *The Modern Theologians: An Introduction to Christian Theology in the Twentieth Century,* ed. David F. Ford, 2nd ed. (Cambridge, Mass., and Oxford: Blackwell, 1997), pp. 252-85, at 264; and Owen F. Cummings, *John Macquarrie, a Master of Theology* (Mahwah, N.J.: Paulist, 2002), p. 37.

30. Macquarrie, *Principles of Christian Theology* (London: SCM Press, 1966), pp. 106, 151, 154, and esp. 167-70; cf. Macquarrie, "Pilgrimage in Theology," p. 50.

31. See, for example, Macquarrie, *The Scope of Demythologizing: Bultmann and His Critics* (London: SCM Press, 1960), pp. 122-29; Macquarrie, *God-Talk: An Examination of the Language and Logic of Theology* (London: SCM Press, 1967), pp. 238-48; Macquarrie, "Bultmann's Understanding of God," *Expository Times* 79 (1968): 356-60, at 360; and Macquarrie, *An Existentialist Theology: A Comparison of Heidegger and Bultmann,* 3rd ed. (Harmondsworth: Penguin Books, 1980), pp. 226-31. For retrospective assessment see Macquarrie, *On Being a Theologian: Reflections at Eighty,* ed. John H. Morgan (London: SCM Press, 1999), pp. 15-18 and 35; Georgina Morley, "Outlines of Major Works," in Macquarrie, *On Being a Theologian,* pp. 178-213, at 184; Cummings, pp. 13-14; and Pratt, pp. 83-85.

32. For example, William M. Thompson, *The Jesus Debate: A Survey and Synthesis* (Mahwah, N.J.: Paulist, 1985), pp. 370-71; Nancy Frankenberry, "Classical Theism, Panentheism and Pantheism: On the Relation between God Construction and Gender Construction," *Zygon* 28 (1993): 29-46; and Daniel A. Dombrowski, "Classical Theism, Pantheism, and Panentheism," *Cithara* 36, no. 1 (1996): 22-33.

33. See, for example, neo-Thomists who attempt to modify classical theism but stop short of panentheism as defined in this paper: William J. Hill, "The Implicate World: God's Oneness with Mankind as a Mediated Immediacy," in *Beyond Mechanism: The Universe in Recent Physics and Catholic Thought,* ed. David L. Schindler (Lanham, Md.: University Press of America, 1986), pp. 78-96; and Michael J. Langford, *A Liberal Theology for the Twenty-First Century: A Passion for Reason* (Aldershot: Ashgate, 2001). An interesting case of ambiguity between classical theism and panentheism is that of the highly influential Anglican theologian William H. Vanstone. Other cases of debate include Spinoza, often perceived as the classic pantheist (see, for example, J. B. McMinn, "A Critique on Hegel's Criticism of Spinoza's God," *Kant-Studien* 51 [1959-60]: 294-314, at 313-14), and Jon-

athan Edwards (for the claim, contra Douglas Elwood, that Edwards was not a panentheist, see Robert C. Whittemore, *The Transformation of the New England Theology* [New York: Peter Lang, 1987], pp. 50-64).

34. W. Norman Pittenger, *Rethinking the Christian Message* (Greenwich, Conn.: Seabury Press, 1956), pp. 40-41, is the earliest application by Pittenger of the term "panentheism" to his position. For the suggestion that pantheism and panentheism are "on a sliding scale," see David W. Brown, "Creation and Its Alternatives," in *Comparative Theology: Essays for Keith Ward*, ed. Timothy W. Bartel (London: SPCK, 2003), pp. 55-65, at 61.

35. L. Charles Birch, *Nature and God* (London: SCM Press, 1965), p. 112; and Birch, *A Purpose for Everything: Religion in a Postmodern Worldview* (Mystic, Conn.: Twenty-Third Publications, 1990), p. 90. Cf. Neil, *God in Everything*, p. 119.

36. Schubert M. Ogden, *The Reality of God and Other Essays* (London: SCM Press, 1967), p. 63.

37. John B. Cobb, *God and the World* (Philadelphia: Westminster, 1969), p. 80; cf. Cobb, "Hartshorne's Importance for Theology," in *The Philosophy of Charles Hartshorne*, ed. Lewis Edwin Hahn, Library of Living Philosophers 20 (La Salle, Ill.: Open Court, 1991), pp. 169-85, at 176.

38. James E. Will, "Dialectical Panentheism: Towards Relating Liberation and Process Theologies," in *Process Philosophy and Social Thought*, ed. John B. Cobb and W. Widick Schroeder (Chicago: Center for the Scientific Study of Religion, 1981), pp. 242-51; Will, "The Universality of God and the Particularity of Peace," in *Theology, Politics, and Peace*, ed. Theodore Runyon (Maryknoll, N.Y.: Orbis, 1989); and Will, *The Universal God: Justice, Love, and Peace in the Global Village* (Louisville: Westminster John Knox, 1994).

39. Jim Garrison, *The Darkness of God: Theology after Hiroshima* (London: SCM Press, 1982).

40. David A. Pailin, "God and Creation — a Process View," *Epworth Review* 9, no. 1 (1982): 72-86, at 81; Pailin, *Groundwork of Philosophy of Religion* (London: Epworth Press, 1986), pp. 127-28; Pailin, *God and the Processes of Reality: Foundations of a Credible Theism* (London and New York: Routledge, 1989), pp. 76-95; and Pailin, *Probing the Foundations: A Study in Theistic Reconstruction* (Kampen: Kok Pharos, 1994), pp. 116-32, a slightly revised version of "Panentheism," in *Traditional Theism and Its Modern Alternatives*, pp. 95-116.

41. Joseph A. Bracken, *The Triune Symbol: Persons, Process, and Community* (Lanham, Md.: University Press of America, 1985), p. 47; Bracken, *Society and Spirit: A Trinitarian Cosmology* (Cranbury: Associated University Presses, 1991), pp. 15 and 213; Bracken, "The Issue of Panentheism in the Dialogue with the Non-Believer," *Studies in Religion* 21 (1992): 207-18, at 207; Bracken, "Panentheism from a Trinitarian Perspective," *Horizons* 22 (1995): 7-28; Bracken, "Panentheism from a Process Perspective," in *Trinity in Process: A Relational Theology of God*, ed. Joseph A. Bracken and Marjorie H. Suchocki (New York: Continuum, 1997), pp. 95-113; and Bracken, *The One in the Many: A Contemporary Reconstruction of the God-World Relationship* (Grand Rapids and Cambridge: Eerdmans, 2001).

42. David R. Griffin, *God and Religion in the Postmodern World: Essays in Postmodern Theology* (Albany: State University of New York Press, 1989); Griffin, "Green Spirituality: A Postmodern Convergence of Science and Religion," *Journal of Theology* 96

(1992): 5-20, at 15 and 19; and Griffin, *Reenchantment without Supernaturalism: A Process Philosophy of Religion* (Ithaca, N.Y.: Cornell University Press, 2001), pp. 140-43 and 212-18.

43. Jay B. McDaniel, *Of Gods and Pelicans: A Theology of Reverence for Life* (Louisville: Westminster John Knox, 1989), p. 26; McDaniel, *Earth, Sky, Gods, and Mortals: A Theology of Ecology for the Twenty-First Century* (Mystic, Conn.: Twenty-Third Publications, 1990), p. 183; McDaniel, "Emerging Options in Ecological Christianity: The New Story, the Biblical Story, and Panentheism," in *Ecological Prospects: Scientific, Religious, and Aesthetic Perspectives,* ed. Christopher K. Chapple (Albany: State University of New York Press, 1994), pp. 127-53, at 137-42; and McDaniel, *With Roots and Wings: Christianity in an Age of Ecology and Dialogue* (Maryknoll, N.Y.: Orbis, 1995), pp. 97-98.

44. Daniel A. Dombrowski, "Alston and Hartshorne on the Concept of God," *International Journal for Philosophy of Religion* 36 (1994): 129-46; Dombrowski, *Analytic Theism, Hartshorne, and the Concept of God* (Albany: State University of New York Press, 1996); and Dombrowski, "Classical Theism, Pantheism, and Panentheism."

45. Anna Case-Winters, "Toward a Theology of Nature: Preliminary Intuitions," *Religiologiques* 11 (1995): 249-67.

46. C. Alan Anderson, *The Problem Is God: The Selection and Care of Your Personal God* (Walpole: Stillpoint, 1985), p. 39 and p. 268 n. 1.

47. Leonardo Boff, *Cry of the Earth, Cry of the Poor,* trans. Phillip Berryman (Maryknoll, N.Y.: Orbis, 1997), pp. 152-54.

48. Marcus J. Borg, *The God We Never Knew: Beyond Dogmatic Religion to a More Authentic Contemporary Faith* (New York: Harper Collins, 1998), pp. 11-31.

49. Philip Clayton, *God and Contemporary Science* (Edinburgh: Edinburgh University Press, 1997); Clayton, "The Case for Christian Panentheism," *Dialog* 37 (1998): 201-8; Clayton, "Panentheistic Turn"; Clayton, *Problem of God;* Clayton, "On the Value of the Panentheistic Analogy: A Response to William Drees," *Zygon* 35 (2000): 699-704; and Clayton, "Panentheist Internalism: Living within the Presence of the Trinitarian God," *Dialog* 40 (2001): 208-15.

50. Scott Cowdell, *A God for This World* (London and New York: Mowbray, 2000), pp. 37-41, 53-55, 111-13, and 123.

51. Denis Edwards, *The God of Evolution: A Trinitarian Theology* (Mahwah, N.J.: Paulist, 1999), p. 33.

52. Paul S. Fiddes, *Participating in God: A Pastoral Doctrine of the Trinity* (London: Darton, Longman and Todd), p. 292.

53. Matthew Fox, *The Coming of the Cosmic Christ: The Healing of Mother Earth and the Birth of a Global Renaissance* (New York: Harper Collins, 1988), pp. 50 and 134; and Fox, "Mystical Cosmology: Toward a Postmodern Spirituality," in *Sacred Interconnections: Postmodern Spirituality, Political Economy, and Art,* ed. David R. Griffin (Albany: State University of New York Press, 1990), pp. 15-33. For Fox's panentheism see Barbara Finan, "Panentheism and Interpersonal Presence: A Trinitarian Perspective," *Listening* 24 (1989): 73-84, and D. Runnalls, "Matthew Fox and Creation Spirituality," *Touchstone* 10, no. 2 (1992): 27-36, at 33-34.

54. Donald L. Gelpi, *The Divine Mother: A Trinitarian Theology of the Holy Spirit* (Lanham, Md.: University Press of America, 1984), pp. 95-100.

55. Peter C. Hodgson, *Christian Faith: A Brief Introduction* (Louisville: Westminster

John Knox, 2001), p. 97; cf. Sallie McFague, *The Body of God: An Ecological Theology* (London: SCM Press, 1993), p. 254.

56. See the paper by Knight in this volume; cf. Christopher C. Knight, *Wrestling with the Divine: Religion, Science, and Revelation* (Minneapolis: Fortress, 2001).

57. Paul Matthews, *The Revelation of Nature* (Aldershot: Ashgate, 2001), pp. 233-38.

58. McFague, *The Body of God*, p. 149.

59. Jürgen Moltmann, *The Crucified God: The Cross of Christ as the Foundation and Criticism of Christian Theology*, trans. Richard A. Wilson and John S. Bowden, 2nd ed. (London: SCM Press, 2001), p. 287; Moltmann, *The Trinity and the Kingdom of God: The Doctrine of God*, trans. Margaret Kohl (London: SCM Press, 1981), pp. 19 and 106; and Moltmann, *God in Creation: An Ecological Doctrine of Creation: The Gifford Lectures, 1984-1985*, trans. Margaret Kohl (London: SCM Press, 1985), pp. xi and 98.

60. Hugh W. Montefiore, *Credible Christianity: The Gospel in Contemporary Society* (London: Mowbray, 1993), pp. 126-28.

61. Helen Oppenheimer, *Incarnation and Immanence* (London: Hodder and Stoughton, 1973), pp. 38 and 198; and Oppenheimer, *Making Good: Creation, Tragedy, and Hope* (London: SCM Press, 2001), p. 79.

62. Arthur R. Peacocke, *Creation and the World of Science: The Bampton Lectures, 1978* (Oxford: Clarendon, 1979), pp. 207, 214, and 352; cf. Peacocke, *Intimations of Reality: Critical Realism in Science and Religion* (Notre Dame, Ind.: University of Notre Dame Press, 1984), p. 79; and Peacocke, *Theology for a Scientific Age: Being and Becoming — Natural, Divine, and Human*, 2nd ed. (London: SCM Press, 1993), pp. 158-60. In the latter work (p. 371), Peacocke thought the word susceptible to misconception and resolved to avoid its use (cf. Macquarrie, n. 28 above), but he had put aside these misgivings by 2001 (*Paths from Science towards God: The End of All Our Exploring* [Oxford: Oneworld, 2001], pp. xvii, 109-14, 129, 138-43, 146, 157, 159-61, 163, and 165); cf. Peacocke, "A Response to Polkinghorne," *Science and Christian Belief* 7 (1995): 109-15, at 109-10. For Peacocke's panentheism see Robert J. Russell, "A Fresh Appraisal," *Religion and Intellectual Life* 5 (1988): 64-69, at 67-69.

63. Piet J. A. M. Schoonenberg, "God as Person(al)," trans. D. Smith, in *A Personal God?* ed. Edward Schillebeeckx and Bastiaan M. F. van Iersel (New York: Seabury Press, 1977), pp. 80-93, at 89.

64. Stewart, "Naming Panentheism"; cf. Stephen Muratore, "In Response," *Epiphany*, spring 1986, pp. 4-5, at 5.

65. Kallistos Ware, *The Orthodox Way*, 2nd ed. (Crestwood, N.Y.: St. Vladimir's Seminary Press, 1995), pp. 46 and 118, and Ware, "Through the Creation to the Creator," *Ecotheology* 2 (1997): 8-30, at 12.

66. For the claim that the poets Coleridge and Wordsworth were panentheists, see (for Coleridge) Daniel A. Dombrowski, "McFarland, Pantheism and Panentheism," *History of European Ideas* 9 (1988): 569-82, which revises the interpretation of Thomas McFarland, *Coleridge and the Pantheist Tradition* (Oxford: Clarendon, 1969), and (for Wordsworth) Dombrowski, "Wordsworth's Panentheism," *Wordsworth Circle* 16 (1985): 136-42.

67. Hartshorne and Reese, pp. 285-94; Hartshorne, "Pantheism and Panentheism," p. 170; and Macquarrie, *Stubborn Theological Questions*, pp. 72-73.

68. Neil, "Panentheism," p. 233.

69. W. Norman Pittenger, *The Word Incarnate: A Study of the Doctrine of the Person of Christ* (Welwyn, England: James Nisbet, 1959), p. 200.

70. Neil, "Panentheism," p. 111; cf. p. 239.

71. Hartshorne and Reese, pp. 302-3.

72. John O'Donnell, "The Trinitarian Panentheism of Sergej Bulgakov," *Gregorianum* 76 (1995): 31-45, at 40 and 43.

73. Neil, "Panentheism," p. 12; cf. p. 103, and Neil, *God in Everything*, p. 21.

74. Macquarrie, *In Search of Deity*, pp. 153-67; cf. Charles Hartshorne, *A Natural Theology for Our Time* (La Salle, Ill.: Open Court, 1967), p. 135; and Matthews, *The Revelation of Nature*.

75. Robert C. Whittemore, "Karl Heim: Panentheism and the Space of God," *Concordia Theological Monthly* 30 (1959): 824-37, at 836.

76. Hartshorne, "Pantheism and Panentheism," p. 168.

77. Thompson, *The Jesus Debate*, p. 372.

78. Hartshorne and Reese, pp. 258-69.

79. Steven Bouma-Prediger, *The Greening of Theology: The Ecological Models of Rosemary Radford Ruether, Joseph Sittler, and Jürgen Moltmann* (Atlanta: Scholars, 1995), pp. 168 and 286.

80. Hartshorne and Reese, p. 298.

81. Ursula King, *Spirit of Fire: The Life and Vision of Teilhard de Chardin* (Maryknoll, N.Y.: Orbis, 1996), pp. 59 and 86; King, *Christ in All Things: Exploring Spirituality with Teilhard de Chardin* (London: SCM Press, 1997), p. 85; King, "Pierre Teilhard de Chardin," *Farmington Papers* PR3 (Oxford: Farmington Institute for Christian Studies, 1998); and King, "'Consumed by Fire from Within': Teilhard de Chardin's Pan-Christic Mysticism in Relation to the Catholic Tradition," *Heythrop Journal* 40 (1999): 456-77, at 471; cf. Neil, *God in Everything*, pp. 22-24.

82. Neil, *God in Everything*, p. 22; McFague, *The Body of God*, p. 254; Macquarrie, "Panentheismus," p. 614; Borg, p. 51 n. 4; and especially Nikkel, pp. 1 (where he cites other identifications of Tillich as a panentheist) and 29-82.

83. Hendrikus Berkhof, *Two Hundred Years of Theology: Report of a Personal Journey*, trans. John Vriend (Grand Rapids: Eerdmans, 1989), p. 157, and G. R. Peterson, "Whither Panentheism?" *Zygon* 36 (2001): 395-405, at 396. Sarah Coakley (*Christ without Absolutes: A Study of the Christology of Ernst Troeltsch* [Oxford: Clarendon, 1988], p. 116 n. 31) states that Troeltsch used the term "panentheism" "only once," in his *Glaubenslehre* (1925) (cf. Peter C. Hodgson, *God in History: Shapes of Freedom* [Nashville: Abingdon, 1989], p. 145), but Walter E. Wyman (*The Concept of* Glaubenslehre: *Ernst Troeltsch and the Theological Heritage of Schleiermacher* [Chico, Calif.: Scholars, 1983], p. 44; cf. pp. 191, 202, and 245) notes Troeltsch's use of the term in the second volume of his four-volume *Gesammelte Schriften* (1913).

84. Hartshorne and Reese, pp. 324-34; cf. Neil, *God in Everything*, p. 119.

85. Hartshorne and Reese, pp. 310-24.

86. Hartshorne and Reese, pp. 273-85. Cf. Peter N. Hamilton, *The Living God and the Modern World* (London: Hodder and Stoughton, 1967), p. 165; Neil, *God in Everything*, pp. 31-37; Macquarrie, *In Search of Deity*, pp. 139-52; and Griffin, *Reenchantment without Supernaturalism*, p. 141.

87. Eugene T. Long, "The Gifford Lectures and the Glasgow Hegelians," *Review of Metaphysics* 43 (1990): 357-84, at 374; cf. John Macquarrie, *Jesus Christ in Modern Thought* (London: SCM Press; Philadelphia: Trinity Press International, 1990), p. 233.

88. Huw Parri Owen, *Concepts of God* (London and Basingstoke: Macmillan, 1971), p. 94; cf. Neil, *God in Everything*, p. 19.

89. Keith W. Clements, *Friedrich Schleiermacher: Pioneer of Modern Theology* (London: Collins, 1987), p. 51.

90. Clayton, *Problem of God*, p. 445; cf. Berkhof, pp. 25-29.

91. See especially Whittemore, "Hegel as Panentheist," and Raymond Keith Williamson, *Introduction to Hegel's Philosophy of Religion* (Albany: State University of New York Press, 1984), pp. 251-94. See also Robert C. Whittemore, "Pro Hegel, Contra Kierkegaard," *Journal of Religious Thought* 13 (1956): 131-44, at 143; T. Pearl, "Dialectical Panentheism: On the Hegelian Character of Karl Rahner's Key Christological Writings," *Irish Theological Quarterly* 42 (1975): 119-37, at 119 and 134; Hans Küng, *Does God Exist? An Answer for Today,* trans. Edward Quinn (London: Collins, 1980), p. 136; Peter Singer, *Hegel* (Oxford: Oxford University Press, 1983), p. 82; Macquarrie, *In Search of Deity*, pp. 125-38; Hartshorne, "Pantheism and Panentheism," p. 169; Paul S. Fiddes, *The Creative Suffering of God* (Oxford: Clarendon, 1988), p. 231 n. 5; Hodgson, *God in History,* pp. 69 and 72; André Cloots and Jan Van der Veken, "Can the God of Process Thought Be 'Redeemed'?" in *Charles Hartshorne's Concept of God: Philosophical and Theological Responses,* ed. Santiago Sia (Dordrecht: Kluwer Academic Publishers, 1990), pp. 125-36, at 133; Clark Butler, "Hegelian Panentheism as Joachimite Christianity," in *New Perspectives on Hegel's Philosophy of Religion,* ed. David Kolb (Albany: State University of New York Press, 1992), pp. 131-42, at 138; and McFague, *The Body of God*, p. 254.

92. Hartshorne and Reese, pp. 233-34; Hartshorne, "Pantheism and Panentheism," p. 169; Robert F. Brown, "Resources in Schelling for New Directions in Theology," *Idealistic Studies* 20 (1990): 1-17, at 7-8 and 15; and Clayton, *Problem of God,* pp. 479 and 501.

93. Peter C. Hodgson, *The Formation of Historical Theology: A Study of Ferdinand Christian Baur* (New York: Harper and Row, 1966), p. 55 n. 73, and pp. 136, 140, and 269.

94. Hartshorne, "Panentheism," claims Fechner as the first clear-cut case of panentheism; cf. Hartshorne, "Pantheism and Panentheism," p. 169, and Hartshorne and Reese, pp. 243-57.

95. Hartshorne and Reese, pp. 269-70.

96. Fox, *The Coming of the Cosmic Christ*, p. 126; cf. Macquarrie, *In Search of Deity,* pp. 98-110 and n. 107 below.

97. Matthew Fox, "Meister Eckhart on the Fourfold Path of a Creation-Centered Spiritual Journey," in *Western Spirituality: Historical Roots, Ecumenical Routes,* ed. Fox (Santa Fe: Bear and Co., 1981), pp. 215-48, at 217-18, 241, and 245; and Fox, "Meister Eckhart and Karl Marx: The Mystic as Political Theologian," in *Understanding Mysticism,* ed. Richard Woods (London: Athlone Press, 1981), pp. 541-63, at 543, 553, and 557.

98. Fox, *The Coming of the Cosmic Christ*, p. 118.

99. Fox, *The Coming of the Cosmic Christ*, p. 124.

100. Larry L. Rasmussen, "Returning to Our Senses: The Theology of the Cross as a Theology for Eco-Justice," in *After Nature's Revolt: Eco-Justice and Theology,* ed. Dieter T. Hessel (Minneapolis: Fortress, 1992), pp. 40-56, at 41-46.

101. For Campbell see Alec R. Vidler, *Twentieth Century Defenders of the Faith: Some Theological Fashions Considered in the Robertson Lectures for 1964* (London: SCM Press, 1965), pp. 24-31; W. Sylvester Smith, *The London Heretics, 1870-1914* (London: Constable, 1967), pp. 207-23; B. G. Worrall, "R. J. Campbell and His New Theology," *Theology* 81 (1978): 342-48; Keith Robbins, "The Spiritual Pilgrimage of the Rev. R. J. Campbell," *Journal of Ecclesiastical History* 30 (1979): 261-76; Keith W. Clements, *Lovers of Discord: Twentieth-Century Theological Controversies in England* (London: SPCK, 1988), pp. 19-48; Peter B. Hinchliff, *God and History: Aspects of British Theology, 1875-1914* (Oxford: Clarendon, 1992), pp. 198-222; Jacqueline David, "'Under-developed and Over-exposed': R. J. Campbell," *Expository Times* 105 (1994): 140-45; Leslie McCurdy, "R. J. Campbell (1867-1956)" and "New Theology Controversy," in *The Dictionary of Historical Theology,* ed. Trevor A. Hart (Carlisle: Paternoster Press; Grand Rapids: Eerdmans, 2000), pp. 108-9 and 392-93; Paul Trudinger, "A Tale of Two Decades: R. J. Campbell and J. D. Crossan on Jesus and the Gospel," *Modern Believing* 41, no. 3 (2000): 20-32; and Bowler, pp. 224-32. Hinchliff is incorrect to see the "New Theology" as "simple pantheism," and "almost a death wish on the grandest possible scale" (p. 204). Campbell himself called it "Higher Pantheism," "the very antithesis" of pantheism (*The New Theology* [London: Chapman and Hall, 1907], p. 35; cf. Campbell, *A Spiritual Pilgrimage* [London: Williams and Norgate, 1917], pp. 190 and 194-95), in other words, what others would call panentheism; and Vidler was correct to assess that the real difficulty for Campbell was that he did not trouble to make this clear (Campbell was just "too reckless") (p. 28).

102. See Stephen B. Bevans, *John Oman and His Doctrine of God* (Cambridge: Cambridge University Press, 1992).

103. For Taylor see David G. Wood, *Poet, Priest, and Prophet: The Life and Thought of Bishop John V. Taylor* (London: Churches Together in Britain and Ireland, 2002); Trevor R. Beeson, *Rebels and Reformers: Christian Renewal in the Twentieth Century* (London: SCM Press, 1999), pp. 117-18; and William Ind, "John Vernon Taylor, Bishop and Theologian: An Appreciation," *Theology* 105 (2002): 13-21.

104. Cf. Neil, *God in Everything,* p. 98.

105. For an introduction to Lampe and Wiles, see Stephen W. Sykes, "Theology through History," in *The Modern Theologians,* pp. 229-51, at 239-43.

106. Cf. also the panentheistic tendencies of Celtic poetry suggested by A. M. Allchin, "'There Is No Resurrection Where There Is No Earth': Creation and Resurrection as Seen in Early Welsh Poetry," in *Celts and Christians: New Approaches to the Religious Traditions of Britain and Ireland,* ed. Mark Atherton (Cardiff: University of Wales Press, 2002), pp. 103-23, at 112.

107. Robert C. Whittemore, "Panentheism in Neo-Platonism," *Tulane Studies in Philosophy* 15 (1966): 47-70, at 58; cf. Macquarrie, *In Search of Deity,* pp. 59-71, and Macquarrie, "Panentheismus," p. 613. It is no coincidence that Inge was an expert on Plotinus; Clarence Edwin Rolt (for whom see my article "Introducing the Early British Passibilists," *Journal for the History of Modern Theology* 8 [2001]: 218-33, at 221-23) was a translator of Pseudo-Dionysius; Pittenger started a doctorate on Erigena ("The Christian Philosophy of John Scotus Erigena," *Journal of Religion* 2 [1944]: 246-57) and was enamored of the Cambridge Platonists ("Ralph Cudworth and the Cambridge Platonists," *Anglican Theological Review* 26 [1944]: 244-49); and Philip Clayton holds an interest in Nicholas of Cusa.

108. Soterios A. Mousalimas, "The Divine in Nature: Animism or Panentheism?" *Greek Orthodox Theological Review* 35 (1990): 367-75.

109. Neil, *God in Everything,* pp. 106-17, and Fox, *The Coming of the Cosmic Christ,* p. 57. It is no coincidence that mysticism, as noted above, was the context of the first uses of the word "panentheism" in English, by Inge, Herman, and von Hügel.

110. Alan M. G. Stephenson, *The Rise and Decline of English Modernism: The Hulsean Lectures, 1979-80* (London: SPCK, 1984), p. 7. Neil (*God in Everything,* pp. 58-59) portrays the 1938 report of the Doctrine Commission of the Church of England, which allowed modernist interpretations of doctrine after the Girton controversy of 1921, as a departure from classical theism toward panentheism.

111. Mary Roe, "Response," in *The New Liberalism,* pp. 93-98, at 94.

112. Peterson, p. 395. Cf. George L. Pattison, "We Are All Liberals Now," *Church Times,* 6 March 1998, p. 12.

113. For Barth's rejection of panentheism, see Karl Barth, *Church Dogmatics* II/1, *The Doctrine of God,* trans. T. H. L. Parker, W. B. Johnston, H. Knight, and J. L. M. Haire (Edinburgh: T. & T. Clark, 1957), pp. 312-13; cf. pp. 315 and 562.

114. John Milbank, Catherine Pickstock, and Graham J. Ward, eds., *Radical Orthodoxy: A New Theology* (London: Routledge, 1999).

115. John C. Polkinghorne, *Science and Creation: The Search for Understanding* (London: SPCK, 1988), p. 53. Polkinghorne himself, like Keith Ward in his contribution to this volume, subscribes to panentheism only in eschatological form: see John C. Polkinghorne, *Science and Christian Belief: Theological Reflections of a Bottom-Up Thinker: The Gifford Lectures for 1993-4* (London: SPCK, 1994), pp. 64 and 168; Polkinghorne, *Scientists as Theologians: A Comparison of the Writings of Ian Barbour, Arthur Peacocke, and John Polkinghorne* (London: SPCK, 1996), p. 55; Polkinghorne, *Faith, Science, and Understanding* (London: SPCK, 2000), pp. 90-91 and 94-95; and Polkinghorne, *The God of Hope and the End of the World* (London: SPCK, 2002), p. 115.

116. Macquarrie, "God and the World," p. 395; Macquarrie, *In Search of Deity,* pp. 59-124; Macquarrie, "Panentheismus," pp. 612-14; and Macquarrie, "Incarnation as Root of the Sacramental Principle," in *Christ: The Sacramental Word,* ed. David Brown and Ann Loades (London: SPCK, 1996), pp. 29-39, at 30-31. Cf. Hartshorne and Reese, pp. 36-38; Michael F. Drummy, "God and Our View of the Universe: An Uneasy Compatibility," *Studies in Religion* 25 (1996): 253-72, at 263-68; Clayton, *God and Contemporary Science,* pp. 97 and 104; and Borg, pp. 12 and 33-37.

117. Fox, *Original Blessing,* p. 90 (cf. Fox, "Mystical Cosmology," p. 25); Pailin, *Processes of Reality,* p. 76; Borg, p. 33; and Peterson, p. 397. Borg talks of his discovery of the doctrine in the language of a conversion experience.

118. "This fundamental vision of mutual coinherence in which Holy Wisdom is present throughout the universe while everything is embraced in her inclusive freedom and compassionate love is highly compatible with feminist values" (Elizabeth A. Johnson, *She Who Is: The Mystery of God in Feminist Theological Discourse* [New York: Crossroad, 1992], p. 232). Cf. Carol P. Christ, "Feminist Re-imaginings of the Divine and Hartshorne's God: One and the Same?" *Feminist Theology* 11 (2002): 99-115. For more on Johnson's doctrine of God, see Joseph A. Bracken, "The Theology of God of Elizabeth A. Johnson," in *Things New and Old: Essays in the Theology of Elizabeth A. Johnson,* ed. Phyllis Zagano and

Terence W. Tilley (New York: Crossroad, 1999), pp. 21-38, and Elizabeth A. Johnson, "Forging Theology: A Conversation with Colleagues," in *Things New and Old*, pp. 91-123, at 98-104.

119. See my article "Norman Pittenger and the Clue to Consent," *Lesbian and Gay Christians* 61 (2002): 16.

120. See Michael E. Zimmerman, "Quantum Theory, Intrinsic Value, and Panentheism," *Environmental Ethics* 10 (1988): 3-30; Griffin, "Green Spirituality"; Rasmussen, "Returning to Our Senses"; Case-Winters, "Toward a Theology of Nature"; Ivone Gebara, "Ecofeminism and Panentheism," in *Readings in Ecology and Feminist Theology*, ed. Mary Heather MacKinnon and Moni McIntyre (Kansas City: Sheed and Ward, 1995), pp. 208-13; Matthews, pp. 209-45; and the work of McDaniel and McFague.

121. See Boff, *Cry of the Earth, Cry of the Poor*, and the work of James Will.

122. Cf. Stewart, p. 6: "the panentheistic model of God and the God-world relationship provides a foundation and framework upon and within which the riches of our global religious heritage and the best in modern culture, including science, can be affirmed and conjoined with integrity." It is no coincidence that the word "panentheism" is being brought to the fore of theology by theologians connected with science, principally Arthur Peacocke and Philip Clayton.

123. Neil, *God in Everything*, pp. x and 7.

124. Peterson, pp. 396-97.

125. Drummy, p. 254.

126. Ronald Goetz, "The Suffering God: The Rise of a New Orthodoxy," *Christian Century*, 16 April 1986, pp. 385-89. Goetz calls it the "theopaschite revolution": for the correct term "passibilist," see Marcel Sarot, "Patripassianism, Theopaschitism and the Suffering of God: Some Historical and Systematic Considerations," *Religious Studies* 26 (1990): 363-75.

127. Clayton, *God and Contemporary Science*.

128. Hartshorne and Reese, pp. 1-25. Cf. Charles Hartshorne, *Creative Synthesis and Philosophic Method* (London: SCM Press, 1970), pp. 261-74.

129. Nikkel, pp. 29-82.

130. Frank L. Cross and Elizabeth A. Livingstone, eds., *The Oxford Dictionary of the Christian Church*, 3rd ed. (Oxford: Oxford University Press, 1997), p. 1213; the definition goes on to give the distinction between panentheism and pantheism as the inability of the panentheist God to be "exhausted" by the universe.

131. Polkinghorne, *Faith, Science, and Understanding*, p. 91. Cf. Thompson, "Suffering World," p. 67: "the 'en' points to this mysterious inbetween place in which panentheism wants to move."

132. On the spectrum of panentheistic positions, see Thompson, *The Jesus Debate*, p. 371, and "Suffering World," pp. 68-69, and Borg, p. 33 (cf. p. 51 n. 4).

133. One aspect of panentheistic language which replicates rather than explicates the "in" is the configuration of the poles "transcendence" and "immanence" as "transcendence in (or within) immanence": see Boff, p. 153; Peacocke, *Creation*, pp. 139-40; Robinson, *Exploration into God*, p. 118 n. 1; and John A. T. Robinson, *The Human Face of God* (London: SCM Press, 1973), p. 241 n. 141. Cf. Joseph P. Whelan, *The Spirituality of Friedrich von Hügel* (London: Collins, 1971), p. 150, and Neil, "Panentheism," p. 232. For criticism of Borg on

this point, see my review of *The God We Never Knew,* by Marcus J. Borg, *Modern Believing* 40, no. 2 (1999): 56-57.

134. These are not the only features that could be chosen: there are also, I believe, distinctive panentheistic interpretations of miracle, prayer, eschatology, etc.

135. For a thorough (but pre-McFague) discussion of divine embodiment not specifically related to the question of panentheism, see Marcel Sarot, *God, Possibility, and Corporeality* (Kampen: Kok Pharos, 1992), pp. 209-43.

136. For example, Clayton, Griffin, McDaniel, and McFague.

137. For example, Macquarrie and Pailin.

138. For example, Peacocke.

139. To compensate for this deficiency in the analogy, another model for conceiving the relationship between God and cosmos is the relationship between a mother and her unborn baby, nurtured in the womb. Clayton ("Panentheistic Turn," p. 291) has urged that in the God-cosmos relationship, the baby is never expelled, since nothing can exist "outside" of God.

140. See especially Clayton, *God and Contemporary Science,* pp. 100-101; Clayton, "Case for Christian Panentheism," pp. 205-6; Clayton, "Panentheistic Turn," p. 291; and Clayton, "On the Value," pp. 702-3.

141. Cf. his qualified acceptance of the idea in Peacocke, "Biology and a Theology of Evolution," *Zygon* 34 (1999): 695-712, at 708.

142. Peacocke, *Paths from Science,* pp. 58 and 109; cf. von Hügel, "Relations," p. 664. For a concern about ontological order from a neo-Thomist perspective, see Thomas G. Weinandy, *Does God Suffer?* (Edinburgh: T. & T. Clark, 2000), p. 154.

143. Clayton, *God and Contemporary Science,* pp. 90-92 (cf. p. 102; Clayton, "Case for Christian Panentheism," p. 206, and Clayton, "Panentheist Internalism," p. 210).

144. Griffin, *God and Religion,* p. 90 (cf. p. 79); McDaniel, *Earth, Sky,* pp. 51-52, and McDaniel, "Revisioning God and the Self: Lessons from Buddhism," in *Liberating Life: Contemporary Approaches to Ecological Theology,* ed. L. Charles Birch, William Eakin, and Jay B. McDaniel (Maryknoll, N.Y.: Orbis, 1990), pp. 228-58, at 249-51; Macquarrie, "God and the World," pp. 399-400; Pailin, *Processes of Reality,* p. 81, and Pailin, *Probing the Foundations,* p. 130 (though cf. p. 124, where Pailin does not follow McFague); and especially Sallie McFague, *Models of God: Theology for an Ecological, Nuclear Age* (London: SCM Press, 1987), pp. 69-78; McFague, "Imaging a Theology of Nature: The World as God's Body," in *Liberating Life,* pp. 201-27, at 211-19; and McFague, *The Body of God.* For Hartshorne see Sarot, *God, Possibility and Corporeality,* pp. 210-19, and Dombrowski, *Analytic Theism,* pp. 77-119. See also W. Norman Pittenger, *The Divine Triunity* (Philadelphia: United Church Press, 1977), pp. 94-96; Dombrowski, "Alston and Hartshorne," p. 134; Dombrowski, "Classical Theism," p. 30; Cowdell, pp. 41-43 and 123; and Fiddes, *Participating in God,* pp. 279-80, 285-94, and 299-302. Cf. Whittemore, "Hegel as Panentheist," p. 135.

145. Peacocke, "Biology," p. 709.

146. W. Norman Pittenger, "Paul Tillich as a Theologian: An Appreciation," *Anglican Theological Review* 43 (1961): 268-86, at 272.

147. W. Norman Pittenger, *The Christian Situation Today* (London: Epworth Press, 1969), p. 103; cf. p. 32.

148. Peacocke, *Paths from Science,* pp. 58, 129, 139, etc.; Peacocke, "The Cost of New Life," in *The Work of Love: Creation as Kenosis,* ed. John C. Polkinghorne (Grand Rapids: Eerdmans; London: SPCK, 2001), pp. 21-42, at 37; Macquarrie, "God and the World," pp. 398-99 and 403; Macquarrie, *Principles of Christian Theology,* 2nd ed., p. 115; and Macquarrie, *In Search of Deity,* p. 176. Cf. Krause, pp. 5-6; Bracken, *Society and Spirit,* p. 123; Bracken, "Issue of Panentheism," pp. 207 and 215; Bracken, "Process Perspective," pp. 97 and 100; Bracken, "Prehending God in and through the World," *Process Studies* 29 (2000): 4-15; McFague, "Theology of Nature," pp. 214 and 216; McFague, *The Body of God,* p. 150; and King, "Consumed by Fire," p. 473.

149. On the need of general implicit principles for the explicit, cf. Edward I. Bailey, *Implicit Religion in Contemporary Society* (Kampen: Kok Pharos, 1997), pp. 271-74; Bailey, "Religion and Implicit Religion: Which Is the Analogy?" *Modern Believing* 38, no. 2 (1997): 30-36; Bailey, *Implicit Religion: An Introduction* (London: Middlesex University Press, 1998), pp. 71-73; Bailey, "'Implicit Religion': What Might That Be?" *Implicit Religion* 1 (1998): 9-22; and Bailey, *The Secular Faith Controversy: Religion in Three Dimensions* (London and New York: Continuum, 2001), pp. 85-88.

150. Peacocke, "Science and the Future of Theology: Critical Issues," *Zygon* 35 (2000): 119-40, at 134, and Peacocke, *Paths from Science,* pp. 144-53. It is surprising that Macquarrie did not make more of the principle in his 1996 essay "Incarnation as Root of the Sacramental Principle," given that "the incarnational principle is extended in the sacramental principle" (Macquarrie, "God and the World," p. 395, cf. "Incarnation as Root," pp. 30-31).

151. Fiddes, *Participating in God,* pp. 280-85; Fox, *Original Blessing,* p. 90; McFague, "Theology of Nature," p. 217; McFague, *The Body of God,* p. 150; Pittenger (for example), "The Sacramental System of the Body of Christ," *Anglican Theological Review* 35 (1953): 89-97; and Ware, "Through the Creation," p. 12. Cf. Johnson, *She Who Is,* p. 231.

152. Macquarrie, "God and the World," pp. 398 and 400 (cf. p. 395), and Macquarrie, *Principles of Christian Theology,* 2nd ed., pp. 121-22.

153. Macquarrie, *In Search of Deity.*

154. Clayton, *God and Contemporary Science,* p. 91; cf. Clayton, "Case for Christian Panentheism," p. 202.

155. Boff, p. 153.

156. W. Norman Pittenger, *Picturing God* (London: SCM Press, 1982), p. 42.

157. Cf. Naughton, pp. 943-44; Neil, "Panentheism," pp. 257-58; Muratore, p. 4; Ronald H. Nash, "Process Theology and Classical Theism," in *Process Theology,* ed. Ronald H. Nash (Grand Rapids: Baker, 1987), pp. 3-29, at 14; Harris, *First Steps,* p. 98; and Harris, *Pro Fide,* p. xxv. Fiddes prefaces his defense of God's "need" with the concern that it is "theologically outrageous" (Paul S. Fiddes, "Creation out of Love," in *The Work of Love,* pp. 167-91, at 169).

158. Hartshorne and Reese, pp. 22 and 501; Griffin, *God and Religion,* pp. 139-40; and Pittenger, "Trinity and Process: Some Comments in Reply," *Theological Studies* 32 (1971): 290-96, at 293. Fiddes, "Creation out of Love," p. 182, places Keith Ward also in this category.

159. Fiddes, "Creation out of Love," p. 180.

160. Macquarrie, *In Search of Deity,* pp. 36-37; cf. pp. 178-79, and the revisions of the

more overt "need" language of his article "God and the World," in Macquarrie, *Thinking about God* (London: SCM Press, 1975), pp. 110-20, at 118. Cf. also Moltmann, who holds that God's freedom to love is axiomatic (*The Trinity*, pp. 107-8), and J. S. Keith Ward, "Cosmos and Kenosis," in *The Work of Love*, pp. 152-66, at 161.

161. Cf. Fiddes, *The Creative Suffering of God*, pp. 66-76, and Fiddes, "Creation out of Love," pp. 181-84.

162. Clayton, *God and Contemporary Science*, pp. 93-94 and 260. Cf. Clayton, "Case for Christian Panentheism," p. 207; Clayton, "Panentheistic Turn," p. 272; and Clayton, *Problem of God*, pp. 483, 490, and 498-99.

163. Clayton, personal communication with author; cf. Clayton, *Problem of God*, p. 499.

164. Clayton, personal communication.

165. For example, Clayton, "Case for Christian Panentheism," p. 205.

166. Clayton, *Problem of God*, pp. 490-93.

167. Clayton, "Panentheistic Turn," p. 293.

168. For example, Macquarrie, *In Search of Deity*, p. 182. For Macquarrie's treatment of evil, see Morley, *The Grace of Being*, pp. 153-54.

169. For a brief introduction to passibility, the arguments for it, and their connection with panentheism, see my "Early British Passibilists."

170. See n. 126 above.

171. Cf. Hartshorne's suggestion that the origin of "pan"-theology lay partly in seventeenth-century questioning of the doctrine of impassibility ("Pantheism and Panentheism," pp. 168-69).

172. Fiddes, *The Creative Suffering of God*.

173. Griffin, *God and Religion*, p. 142.

174. Hartshorne and Reese, p. 15; Charles Hartshorne, "The Kinds of Theism: A Reply," *Journal of Religion* 34 (1954): 127-31, at 130-31; and Hartshorne, *Omnipotence and Other Theological Mistakes* (Albany: State University of New York Press, 1984), pp. 27-32.

175. Macquarrie, "God and the World," p. 397, and *In Search of Deity*, pp. 41, 179-81, and 183. Cf. Cummings, pp. 41-43.

176. McDaniel, *Of Gods and Pelicans*, p. 28. Cf. McDaniel, *Earth, Sky*, pp. 51 and 183; McDaniel, "Emerging Options," p. 149; and McDaniel, *With Roots and Wings*, pp. 98 and 110.

177. McFague, "Theology of Nature," p. 216, and McFague, *The Body of God*, p. 176.

178. Moltmann, *The Crucified God*, pp. 206-303; Moltmann, *The Future of Creation*, trans. Margaret Kohl (London: SCM Press, 1979), p. 93; Moltmann, *The Trinity*, pp. 21-60; and Moltmann, *History and the Triune God: Contributions to Trinitarian Theology*, trans. John S. Bowden (London: SCM Press, 1991), pp. 122-24. Cf. Warren McWilliams, *The Passion of God: Divine Suffering in Contemporary Protestant Theology* (Macon, Ga.: Mercer University Press, 1985), pp. 27-49; Richard J. Bauckham, *The Theology of Jürgen Moltmann* (Edinburgh: T. & T. Clark, 1995), pp. 47-69; and Bauckham, preface to Moltmann, *The Crucified God*, pp. ix-xv, at xii.

179. Pailin, "God and Creation," p. 81; Pailin, *Processes of Reality*, pp. 88-89; Pailin, "God Shares in All of Man's Suffering," *Independent*, 18 November 1989, p. 17; and Pailin, *Probing the Foundations*, pp. 81 and 128-29.

180. Peacocke, *Creation,* pp. 201 and 214; Peacocke, "Biology," pp. 705-6; Peacocke, *Paths from Science,* pp. 86-88 and 142; and Peacocke, "Cost of New Life," p. 37.

181. For example, W. Norman Pittenger, *God's Way with Men: A Study of the Relationship between God and Man in Providence, "Miracle," and Prayer* (London: Hodder and Stoughton, 1969), pp. 36-37.

182. For example, Garrison, pp. 49 and 149, and MacGregor (see McWilliams, pp. 81-89, and Thompson, *The Jesus Debate,* pp. 372-75). Thompson himself subscribes only to the Hügelian view that God suffers sympathetically ("Suffering World," pp. 72-73). Cf. Neil, *God in Everything,* p. 10.

183. For degree Christology, see further Paul L. Badham, *The Contemporary Challenge of Modernist Theology* (Cardiff: University of Wales Press, 1998), pp. 95-97 and 141-42.

184. Because the doctrine of Christ's sinlessness has the effect of making Christ different in kind from other people, denial of the doctrine of Christ's sinlessness implies a degree Christology, and therefore rejection of Christ's sinlessness can also be indicative of a panentheist position. For an introduction to the doctrine of Christ's sinlessness, see Jeremy P. Sheehy, "The Sinlessness of Christ as a Problem in Modern Systematic Theology" (D.Phil. thesis, University of Oxford, 1990). Subsequent (and similarly conservative) material includes Huw Parri Owen, "The Sinlessness of Jesus," in *Religion, Reason, and the Self: Essays in Honour of Hywel D. Lewis,* ed. Stewart R. Sutherland and Tom Aerwyn Roberts (Cardiff: University of Wales Press, 1989), pp. 119-28; Trevor A. Hart, "Sinlessness and Moral Responsibility: A Problem in Christology," *Scottish Journal of Theology* 48 (1995): 37-54; and Andrew Bebb, "Was Jesus a Sinner?" *Month* 28 (1995): 323-25.

185. Robinson, *Human Face of God,* pp. 209-10.

186. Macquarrie, *Jesus Christ,* p. 346; Macquarrie, "Current Trends in Anglican Christology," *Anglican Theological Review* 79 (1997): 563-70, at 567-68; and Macquarrie, *Christology Revisited* (London: SCM Press, 1998), p. 59 (cf. p. 74). His degree Christology is recognized by Marion L. Hendrickson, *Behold the Man! An Anthropological Comparison of the Christologies of John Macquarrie and Wolfhart Pannenberg* (Lanham, Md.: University Press of America, 1998), pp. 30-31 and 93, and Cummings, p. 62.

187. Griffin, *God and Religion,* p. 10.

188. Peacocke, *Creation,* pp. 238-41.

189. McFague, *Models of God,* p. 136.

190. W. Norman Pittenger, "Some Axioms of a Catholic Christology," *Theology* 39 (1939): 106-10, at 107.

191. W. Norman Pittenger, "Degree or Kind? A Christological Essay," *Canadian Journal of Theology* 2 (1956): 189-96.

192. Pittenger, *The Word Incarnate,* pp. 189, 242-43, and 286, and *Christology Reconsidered* (London: SCM Press, 1970), pp. 111-33.

193. Peterson, p. 405.

194. Cf. the definition by William Hasker, *Metaphysics: Constructing a World View* (Downers Grove, Ill., and Leicester: InterVarsity, 1983), p. 111, which similarly condenses a number of critical points.

195. Brierley, "Early British Passibilists," pp. 229-30.

196. Brierley, "Early British Passibilists," p. 228 n. 55.

197. Clayton, "Case for Christian Panentheism," p. 203, makes the point that classical

theism has persisted in part because it was "institutionalised" in creedal statements which "silently presupposed" the substance ontology of the early Christian centuries.

198. Cf. Fox, *The Coming of the Cosmic Christ*, p. 135; Finan, p. 75; Bracken, "Issue of Panentheism," p. 209; Johnson, *She Who Is*, pp. 231-32; Will, *The Universal God*, p. 30; and Clayton, "Case for Christian Panentheism," p. 205.

199. Cf. the work of Hartshorne, which effectively establishes "relativity" as "absolute" (*Creative Synthesis*, pp. 47 and 120). "This unwarranted assumption, this metaphysical snobbery toward relativity, dependence, or passivity, toward responsiveness or sensitivity, this almost slavish (doubtless it would be too much to say knavish) worship of mere absoluteness, independence, and one-sided activity or power, this transcendentalized admiration of politico-ecclesiastical tyranny, the ideal of which is to act on all while avoiding reaction from them, this spiritual blindness and false report upon experience is, as we are about to see, the chief source of the metaphysico-theological paradoxes of which so much has been heard" (Hartshorne, *The Divine Relativity*, p. 50; cf. pp. 82-83, 86-87, and 156-57).

200. See, for example, Herbert McCabe, *God Matters* (London: Geoffrey Chapman, 1987), and Weinandy, *Does God Suffer?* Cf. W. Norris Clarke, "Charles Hartshorne's Philosophy of God: A Thomistic Critique," in *Charles Hartshorne's Concept of God*, pp. 103-23.

201. As is claimed by, for example, W. C. French, "The World as God's Body: Theological Ethics and Panentheism," in *Broken and Whole: Essays on Religion and the Body*, ed. Maureen A. Tilley and Susan A. Ross, Annual Publication of the College Theology Society, 1993, 39 (Lanham, Md.: University Press of America, 1995), pp. 135-44, at 142-44; and Thomas N. Finger, "Trinity, Ecology and Panentheism," *Christian Scholar's Review* 27 (1997): 74-98, at 75 and 98. Even Macquarrie believes retrospectively that in *In Search of Deity* he did not do sufficient justice to the dynamism in Aquinas's doctrine of God (*On Being a Theologian*, p. 74).

202. For example, Colin E. Gunton, *Becoming and Being: The Doctrine of God in Charles Hartshorne and Karl Barth*, 2nd ed. (London: SCM Press, 2001).

203. Pittenger, *Picturing God*, pp. 10-11.

204. Cf. Sterling M. McMurrin, "Hartshorne's Critique of Classical Metaphysics and Theology," in *Philosophy of Charles Hartshorne*, pp. 431-43 at 433; Fox, *The Coming of the Cosmic Christ*, p. 194; and Pailin, *Probing the Foundations*, pp. 121-22.

205. Cf. Neil, *God in Everything*, p. 16; Griffin, *God and Religion*, pp. 141 and 145; Hartshorne, *The Divine Relativity*, pp. 147-55; and Clayton, *God and Contemporary Science*, pp. 91-92.

206. "Precisely [that God loves all] is the final meaning of neoclassical theism" (Hartshorne, "Pantheism and Panentheism," p. 171). "It was, arguably, only in the 20th century that the staggering requirements which divine love places on the doctrine of God began to sink in" (Clayton, "Panentheist Internalism," p. 211). Cf. Krause, p. 117; Ursula King, *Towards a New Mysticism: Teilhard de Chardin and Eastern Religions* (London: Collins, 1980), p. 122; King, *Christ in All Things*, p. 88; and Pailin, *Probing the Foundations*, p. 117. See also above, nn. 118-23.

207. Cf. Macquarrie, "God and the World," p. 395; Johnson, *She Who Is*, p. 231; Frankenberry, p. 30; and McFague, *The Body of God*, p. 149.

208. Cf. Moltmann's connection of Rahner's rejection of passibilism with Rahner's

experience of love, cited in Weinandy, p. 157; and my review of *Does God Suffer?* by Thomas G. Weinandy, *Modern Believing* 42, no. 1 (2001): 56-58, at 57-58.

209. For the importance of naming (not specifically related to panentheism), see James A. Scherer, "Missiological Naming: 'Who Shall I Say Sent Me?'" in *Our Naming of God: Problems and Prospects of God-Talk Today,* ed. Carl E. Braaten (Minneapolis: Fortress, 1989), pp. 111-25.

210. Cf. above, n. 149.

Notes to "Three Varieties of Panentheism," by Niels Henrik Gregersen

1. See Keith Ward's contribution in this volume and my essay, "God's Public Traffic: Holist versus Physicalist Supervenience," in *The Human Person in Science and Theology,* ed. Niels Henrik Gregersen, Willem B. Drees, and Ulf Görman (Grand Rapids: Eerdmans, 2000), pp. 153-88.

2. The term "expressivism" is here used in accordance with Charles Taylor's analysis of the romanticist view of nature as striving to express itself in animal and human life. This "expressivist turn" found a correlate in the notion of a divine subjectivity which expresses itself in the world. See *Sources of the Self: The Making of Modern Identity* (Cambridge: Cambridge University Press [1989], 1992), p. 371: "God then is to be interpreted in terms of what we see striving in nature and finding a voice within ourselves. A slide to a kind of pantheism is all too easy, and this we see in the Romantic generation with the early Schelling, and later in another form with Hegel."

3. Alfred North Whitehead, *Process and Reality: An Essay in Cosmology,* ed. David Ray Griffin and Donald W. Sherburne, corrected ed. (New York: Free Press [1929], 1978), p. 348.

4. Charles Hartshorne and William L. Reese, *Philosophers Speak of God* (Chicago: University of Chicago Press, 1953), pp. vii and 17.

5. Here and below I am using the Latin text and English translation of Saint Thomas Aquinas, *Summa Theologiae* (London and New York: Blackfriars, 1964), 2:113.

6. Thomas, *Summa Theologiae,* 2:112, italics mine.

7. Vladimir Lossky, *The Mystical Theology of the Eastern Church* (Crestwood, N.Y.: St. Vladimir's Seminary Press [1944], 1998), p. 56.

8. John D. Zizioulas, *Being as Communion: Studies in Personhood and the Church* (Crestwood, N.Y.: St. Vladimir's Seminary Press [1985], 1997), p. 18. A similar community-oriented interpretation of trinitarian theology can be found among more recent Western theologians such as the Catholic Catherine Mowry LaCugna, *God for Us: The Trinity and Christian Life* (San Francisco: Harper, 1991), and the Lutheran Ted Peters, *God as Trinity: Relationality and Temporality in Divine Life* (Louisville: Westminster John Knox, 1993).

9. See, e.g., Paul S. Fiddes, *Participating in God: A Pastoral Doctrine of the Trinity* (Louisville: Westminster John Knox, 2000), pp. 11-61.

10. On the interpretation of this text, see James M. Starr, *Sharers in Divine Nature: 2 Peter 1:4 in Its Hellenistic Context* (Stockholm: Almquist & Wiksel, 2000), pp. 226-39.

11. Tertullian, *Adversus Praxean* 5, text in Migne, *Patrologia Latina,* 2:60. Cf. Theophil of Antioch, *Ad Autolycum* 2.10, text in Migne, *Patrologia Graeca,* 6:1064.

12. See the paper by Kallistos Ware in this volume. For an exposition of the soteriology of Gregory Palamas, see also Georgios I. Mantzaridis, *The Deification of Man* (New York: St. Vladimir's Seminary Press, 1984).

13. Cf. John Polkinghorne, *The Faith of a Physicist: Reflections of a Bottom-up Thinker* (Princeton: Princeton University Press, 1994), p. 64.

14. K. F. C. Krause, *Vorlesungen über die Grundwahrheiten der Wissenschaft* (Göttingen, 1829), p. 484. On Krause's life and thought, see K. M. Kodalle, "Krause, Karl Christian Friedrich," in *Biographisch-Bibliographisches Kirchenlexicon* (Herzberg: Traugott, 1988), 14:624-31.

15. K. F. C. Krause, *The Ideal of Humanity and Universal Federation*, ed. W. Hastie (Edinburgh, 1900), p. 117, quoted in David A. Pailin, "Panentheism," in *Traditional Theism and Its Modern Alternatives*, ed. Svend Andersen (Aarhus: Aarhus University Press, 1994), p. 96.

16. On the general situation, see Günther Meckenstock, "Some Remarks on Pantheism and Panentheism," in *Traditional Theism and Its Modern Alternatives*, pp. 117-29. On Schleiermacher see Julia Lamm, *The Living God: Schleiermacher's Theological Appropriation of Spinoza* (University Park: Pennsylvania State University Press, 1996); on Fichte and Schelling see Philip Clayton, *The Problem of God in Modern Thought* (Grand Rapids: Eerdmans, 2000), pp. 441-505.

17. As described by the Deist John Toland, *Adeisidaimon: Annexae sunt eiusdem Origines Iudaicae* (The Hague, 1709), p. 117: "Nullum dari Numen a materia et compage mundi huius distinctum, ipsamque naturam, sive rerum Universitatem, unicum esse et supremum Deum."

18. Baruch Spinoza, "Ethica," in Spinoza, *Opera-Werke*, ed. Konrad Blumenstock (Darmstadt: Wissenschaftliche Buchgesellschaft, 1980), vol. 2.

19. Cf. my study, "Panteismens fascination. Til forholdet mellem panteisme og skabelsestro" (The lure of pantheism: Relating pantheism and creation theology), *Dansk Teologisk Tidsskrift* 57, no. 4 (1994): 241-66.

20. See Wolfhart Pannenberg, "Fichte und die Metaphysik des Unendlichen," *Zeitschrift für philosophische Forschung* 46 (1992): 348-62.

21. G. W. F. Hegel, *Enzyklopädie der philosophischen Wissenschaften*, §564 (1830), translation from *Hegel: Theologian of the Spirit*, ed. Peter C. Hodgson (Minneapolis: Fortress, 1997), p. 144.

22. Hegel, *Enzyklopädie*, §566, translation from *Hegel*, p. 144.

23. See esp. Hegel, *Lectures on the Philosophy of Religion* (1824), translation in *Hegel*, pp. 230-39.

24. M. B. Abrams, *Natural Supernaturalism: Tradition and Revolution in Romantic Literature* (New York: Norton, 1971).

25. Revised as "The Logic of Panentheism," in Hartshorne and Reese, pp. 499-514. This book, designed as a reader in philosophical theology, probably constitutes the most extensive attempt to show the perennial roots of panentheism, while also excavating a formal structure of panentheism. If the typology proposed in this article holds true, however, panentheism is not a perennial philosophy but a rather unstable concept with different meanings which need to be respecified from one context to another.

26. Charles Hartshorne, "A Reply to My Critics," in *The Philosophy of Charles*

Hartshorne, ed. Lewis Edwin Hahn (La Salle, Ill.: Open Court, 1991), p. 614: "The creatures are also creators and the creator is also creature. Deity is the supreme form of causing and the supreme form of being caused, of activity and passivity. This is dual transcendence."

27. Hartshorne, "The Logic of Panentheism," p. 506.

28. William L. Reese comments: "It seemed to me at the time, and still seems to me, that we were successful in establishing the greater coherence of the process view of God, as well as demonstrating inconsistencies in the classical conception. But our success seemed to me to derive more from the dipolarity of the hypothesis we espoused, harmonizing polar contraries by placing them on different levels of abstraction, than from the conception of panentheism even though the latter is one way of expressing the former." See Reese, "The 'Trouble' with Panentheism — and the Divine Event," in *The Philosophy of Charles Hartshorne*, p. 188.

29. Hartshorne, "The Logic of Panentheism," pp. 506-12.

30. Charles Hartshorne, *The Divine Relativity: A Social Conception of God* (New Haven: Yale University Press, 1948), p. 20.

31. Hartshorne, "The Logic of Panentheism," p. 511.

32. This critique is also formulated by William L. Reese in *The Philosophy of Charles Hartshorne*, pp. 187-202. In his response, Hartshorne acknowledges the problem that his dipolar view may seem to presuppose a Newtonian concept of space and time for God, while he otherwise assumes a relativistic cosmology. See p. 616.

33. Whitehead, p. 343.

34. See the important study by Robert C. Neville, *Creativity and God: A Challenge of Process Theology, New Edition* (Albany: SUNY Press [1980], 1995), and the extensive discussions in *Process Studies* 10, no. 3-4 (1980); and 11, no. 1 (1981).

35. As is evident from Joseph Bracken's contribution to this volume, he is here following the classic Christian scheme rather than process thought. See also Bracken, *The Divine Matrix: Creativity as Link between East and West* (New York: Orbis, 1995).

36. Often Paul Tillich (in my typology a representative of expressivism) is placed in the camp of Hartshorne's panentheism. He was so placed by Charles Hartshorne himself in the article "Tillich's Doctrine of God," in *The Theology of Paul Tillich*, ed. Charles W. Kegley and Robert W. Bretall (New York: Macmillan, 1964), pp. 164-97. Hartshorne, however, is fair enough to acknowledge that "this interpretation is not without its difficulties" (p. 166). David H. Nikkel, *Panentheism in Hartshorne and Tillich: A Creative Synthesis* (New York: Peter Lang, 1995), likewise suggests that both Hartshorne and Tillich can be "rightly labelled panentheists" on the definition that there are both an active and a passive aspect of God, and that there is a "mutual transcendence of God and the creatures with respect to freedom" (pp. 1-3). Nikkel grants that "[r]elatively speaking, Hartshorne emphasizes the passive aspect, and Tillich the active one" (p. 9). As he proceeds, however, Nikkel is compelled to admit that just as Tillich "undermines" the passive aspect by assuming that God is beyond affectation, so does Hartshorne "undermine" the active aspect because he refuses to say that God is the source of all-that-is (pp. 113-98). It therefore seems to me that the common denominator of "panentheism" becomes somewhat fuzzy. In my view Nikkel has not shown that a synthesis between the two thinkers is possible. Tillich's ontology of God as "the power of being in everything and above every-thing" (*Systematic Theology*

[London: SCM Press (1951), 1978], p. 236) is simply not compatible with a Whiteheadian ontology.

37. In these Vedantic texts (dating from around 700-200 B.C.), we hear that Atman (who originally was the One) has entered into the very nails of the unfolded world, as a knife in the sheath or the fire in the wood (*Brihadarannyaka* 1.4.7); likewise Brahman is invisible yet everywhere, as the salt in the water (*Chandogya* 6.13); it moves and yet it moves not, it is absent and yet it is close, it is in the world and yet outside the world (*Isha* 1.5). Helmuth von Glaseknapp, *Die Philosophie der Inder* (Stuttgart: Kroner Verlag, 1985), thus employed the term "panentheism" about the Upanishads (p. 462).

38. George Lakoff and Mark Johnson, *Philosophy in the Flesh: The Embodied Mind and Its Challenge to Western Thought* (New York: Basic Books, 1999), pp. 30-36 and 544f.

Notes to "Panentheism: A Postmodern Revelation," by David Ray Griffin

1. David Ray Griffin, *Reenchantment without Supernaturalism: A Process Philosophy of Religion* (Ithaca, N.Y.: Cornell University Press, 2001).

2. Millard J. Erickson, *Christian Theology* (Grand Rapids: Baker, 1985), p. 374.

3. Erickson, p. 304.

4. Charles Hodge, *Systematic Theology*, vol. 1 (Grand Rapids: Eerdmans, 1982), p. 607.

5. Jon D. Levenson, *Creation and the Persistence of Evil: The Jewish Drama of Divine Omnipotence* (San Francisco: Harper and Row, 1988).

6. Gerhard May, *Creatio Ex Nihilo: The Doctrine of "Creation out of Nothing" in Early Christian Thought*, trans. A. S. Worrall (Edinburgh: T. & T. Clark, 1994).

7. David Ray Griffin, "Creation out of Nothing, Creation out of Chaos, and the Problem of Evil," in *Encountering Evil: Live Options in Theodicy*, ed. Stephen T. Davis, 2nd ed. (Louisville: Westminster John Knox, 2001).

8. David Ray Griffin, *Religion and Scientific Naturalism: Overcoming the Conflicts* (Albany: State University of New York Press, 2000), chap. 5.

9. I have argued this case in chapters on Augustine, Aquinas, Luther, and Calvin in my book, *God, Power, and Evil: A Process Theodicy* (Philadelphia: Westminster, 1976; reprinted with a new preface, Lanham, Md.: University Press of America, 1991).

10. Franklin I. Gamwell, *The Divine Good: Modern Moral Theory and the Necessity of God* (Dallas: Southern Methodist University Press, 1996), pp. 4-7.

11. Although it is widely said that Kant rejected any argument from the world to God, this is true only of "God" understood as a being who created this world ex nihilo. What Kant said about the "physico-theological proof" is that it can only "demonstrate the existence of an *architect of the world*, whose efforts are limited by the capabilities of the material with which he works, but not of a *creator of the world*, to which all things are subject" (see Kant, *The Critique of Pure Reason*, in *Great Books of the Western World*, ed. Robert Maynard Hutchins [Chicago: Encyclopedia Britannica, 1952], 42:188-89). Kant does not, therefore, reject the idea that the world's order points to a creator of the sort envisioned by process panentheism.

12. William James, *Some Problems of Philosophy* (London: Longman, Green, 1911), p. 194.

13. I have called the confusion of these two issues the "emergence category mistake" (Griffin, *Unsnarling the World-Knot: Consciousness, Freedom, and the Mind-Body Problem* [Berkeley: University of California Press, 1998], pp. 64-67). It seems to me, incidentally, that Arthur Peacocke's position embodies this mistake, which allows him to be sanguine about a purely materialistic view of the ultimate units of nature and thereby dismissive of the arguments for panexperientialism.

14. "It would take a supernatural magician," says Colin McGinn (*The Problem of Consciousness: Essays toward a Resolution* [Oxford: Basil Blackwell, 1991], p. 45), "to extract consciousness from matter." I have cited this and many other admissions from materialists in my *Unsnarling the World-Knot*, introduction and chap. 6, and in *Reenchantment without Supernaturalism*, chap. 6.

15. See John R. Searle, *Minds, Brains, and Science*, 1984 Reith Lectures (London: British Broadcasting Corporation, 1984), pp. 86-98; Thomas Nagel, *The View from Nowhere* (New York: Oxford University Press, 1986), pp. 110-23; Griffin, *Unsnarling the World-Knot*, pp. 38-40, 163-70.

16. David Ray Griffin, "Religious Experience, Naturalism, and the Social Scientific Study of Religion," *Journal of the American Academy of Religion* 68, no. 1 (March 2000): 99-125.

17. David Ray Griffin, "Process Philosophy of Religion," *International Journal for the Philosophy of Religion* 50 (December 2001): 131-51.

18. Griffin, *Religion and Scientific Naturalism*, chap. 8.

19. Distinguishing *me on* (relative nothingness) from *ouk on* (absolute nothingness), Berdyaev explains why God's power cannot control our activities by saying that our world was created out of "meontic freedom" (*The Destiny of Man* [New York: Harper and Row, 1960], pp. 22-35; Berdyaev, *Truth and Revelation* [New York: Collier Books, 1962], p. 124). In Whitehead's language, this primordial freedom is "creativity."

20. I have elsewhere explained process philosophy's basis for affirming that time had no beginning and for rejecting the idea that quantum and relativity physics imply a "block universe," according to which what we call past, present, and future exist simultaneously. See Griffin, "Introduction: Time and the Fallacy of Misplaced Concreteness," in *Physics and the Ultimate Significance of Time: Bohm, Prigogine, and Process Philosophy*, ed. David Ray Griffin (Albany: State University of New York Press, 1986), pp. 1-48, as well as Griffin, "Time in Process Philosophy," *KronoScope: Journal for the Study of Time* 1 (2001): 75-99.

21. In Hartshorne's last book (*The Zero Fallacy and Other Essays in Neoclassical Philosophy*, ed. Mohammed Valady [Peru, Ill.: Open Court, 1997]), he worked out a scheme of sixteen logical possibilities for understanding the relation between God and the world in terms of various polar contraries, such as necessity and contingency. Whereas traditional theism portrayed God as wholly necessary and the world as wholly contingent (N.c) and Spinoza's pantheism portrays them both as wholly necessary (N.n), process philosophy's dipolar panentheism portrays them each as having both necessary and contingent dimensions (NC.cn). Panentheism is as different from pantheism, therefore, as it is from traditional theism.

22. Charles Hartshorne, *The Divine Relativity: A Social Conception of God,* 2nd ed. (New Haven: Yale University Press, 1964; orig. published, 1948).

23. In "The Theological Analogies and the Cosmic Organism" (*Man's Vision of God and the Logic of Theism* [New York: Harper and Row, 1941]), Hartshorne adds that this analogy, which emphasizes the radical *superiority* of God to the creatures, needs to be combined with the parent-child analogy, which emphasizes the *personal* nature of the relationship.

24. Griffin, *Unsnarling the World-Knot.*

25. David Ray Griffin, *A Process Christology* (Philadelphia: Westminster, 1967).

26. Alfred North Whitehead, *Adventures of Ideas* (New York: Free Press, 1967; orig. published, 1933), p. 166.

27. See Griffin, *God, Power, and Evil;* also Griffin, *Evil Revisited: Responses and Reconsiderations* (Albany: State University of New York Press, 1991).

28. More precisely, Hartshorne has pointed out, God's responses to the world should be called God's "concrete states," with "consequent nature" referring to that which is common to all these concrete divine experiences. I have discussed this distinction in *Reenchantment without Supernaturalism,* pp. 151, 158-63.

29. Divine dipolarity is discussed in terms of this distinction between creative and responsive love in John B. Cobb, Jr., and David Ray Griffin, *Process Theology: An Introductory Exposition* (Philadelphia: Westminster, 1976), chap. 3.

30. For some of my reasons for opposing any suggestion of moral imperfection in God, see my critique of John Roth's position in *Encountering Evil.*

31. See my *Reenchantment without Supernaturalism,* chap. 5.

Notes to "Theistic Naturalism and the Word Made Flesh: Complementary Approaches to the Debate on Panentheism," by Christopher C. Knight

1. See, e.g., Philip Clayton, *God and Contemporary Science* (Edinburgh: Edinburgh University Press, 1997).

2. In this respect current debate about panentheism resembles historical debates about Christology — particularly as analyzed in John Meyendorff, *Christ in Eastern Christian Thought* (Crestwood, N.Y.: St. Vladimir's Seminary Press, 1975), and Thomas F. Torrance, *Space, Time, and Incarnation* (Oxford: Oxford University Press, 1969).

3. John Polkinghorne, *Faith and Contemporary Science* (London: SPCK, 2000), p. 95.

4. For a critique of the classic essence-energies distinction and an Orthodox response to it, see two articles in *Eastern Churches Review* 9 (1977): Rowan D. Williams, "The Philosophical Structures of Palamism," pp. 27-44; Kallistos Ware, "The Debate about Palamism," pp. 45-63.

5. See the essay by Kallistos Ware elsewhere in this volume.

6. Christopher C. Knight, *Wrestling with the Divine: Religion, Science, and Revelation* (Minneapolis: Fortress, 2001). Chap. 2 gives a fuller account of this background.

7. A. R. Peacocke, "God's Interaction with the World: The Implications of Deterministic 'Chaos' and of Interconnected and Interdependent Complexity," in *Chaos and*

Complexity: Scientific Perspectives on Divine Action, ed. R. J. Russell, N. Murphy, and A. R. Peacocke (Vatican City: Vatican Observatory, 1995).

8. John Polkinghorne, *Scientists as Theologians: A Comparison of the Writings of Ian Barbour, Arthur Peacocke, and John Polkinghorne* (London: SPCK, 1996), p. 40.

9. Clayton, *God and Contemporary Science*, p. 227.

10. Polkinghorne, *Faith and Contemporary Science*, p. 124.

11. John Polkinghorne, *Science and Christian Belief: Theological Reflections of a Bottom-up Thinker* (London: SPCK, 1994), pp. 78-79.

12. A. R. Peacocke, *Theology for a Scientific Age: Being and Becoming — Natural, Divine, and Human*, enlarged ed. (London: SCM Press, 1993), p. 65.

13. Peacocke, *Theology*, p. 119.

14. Clayton, *God and Contemporary Science*, p. xi.

15. Clayton, *God and Contemporary Science*, pp. 225-26.

16. Clayton, *God and Contemporary Science*, pp. 220-27.

17. Philip Clayton, "On the Value of the Panentheistic Analogy: A Response to Willem Drees," *Zygon: Journal of Religion and Science* 35 (2000): 699.

18. Willem Drees, "Thick Naturalism: Comments on Zygon 2000," *Zygon: Journal of Religion and Science* 35 (2000): 850.

19. Willem Drees, *Religion, Science, and Naturalism* (Cambridge: Cambridge University Press, 1996). See especially his comments on p. 251.

20. In relation to Drees's arguments, see Knight, pp. 19-20.

21. Drees, "Thick Naturalism," p. 851.

22. John Polkinghorne, *One World: The Interaction of Science and Theology* (London: SPCK, 1986), pp. 74-76.

23. Drees, "Thick Naturalism," p. 851.

24. Drees, "Thick Naturalism," p. 853.

25. Peacocke, "God's Interaction with the World."

26. For a brief discussion of the neo-Thomist position and further references, see I. G. Barbour, *Issues in Science and Religion* (London: SCM Press, 1966), pp. 425-27.

27. Maurice Wiles, *God's Action in the World* (London: SCM Press, 1986).

28. See in particular the view of divine providence outlined in Christopher Bryant, *Jung and the Christian Way* (London: Darton, Longman and Todd, 1966).

29. See Knight, p. 125 (n. 22), for a very brief account of this.

30. As noted in Knight, pp. 16 and 125 (n. 20), Peacocke and others seem to have been particularly affected in this respect by aspects of the theology of Jürgen Moltmann and W. H. Vanstone.

31. Arthur Peacocke, *God and the New Biology* (London: J. M. Dent and Sons, 1986), p. 82.

32. Peacocke, *New Biology*, p. 124.

33. The continuing relevance of this seventeenth-century Anglican tradition — embodied in the work of spiritual writers like Thomas Traherne, of poets like George Herbert and Henry Vaughan, and of theologians like Lancelot Andrewes — has been argued by A. M. Allchin. See in particular his trilogy of collected essays: *The World Is a Wedding: Explorations in Christian Spirituality* (London: Darton, Longman and Todd, 1978); *The Kingdom of Love and Knowledge: The Encounter between Orthodoxy and the West* (London:

Darton, Longman and Todd, 1979); *The Dynamic of Tradition* (London: Darton, Longman and Todd, 1981).

34. See, e.g., Alexander Schmemann, *The World as Sacrament* (London: Darton, Longman and Todd, 1966).

35. Alexander Schmemann, *The Eucharist: Sacrament of the Kingdom* (Crestwood, N.Y.: St. Vladimir's Seminary Press, 1987), pp. 33-34.

36. Knight, p. 18.

37. Knight, p. 114.

38. See, e.g., Paul Davies, "The Intelligibility of Nature," in *Chaos and Complexity*, pp. 9-13.

39. Knight, pp. 111-14.

40. See Knight, chap. 3, in which an extrapolation of Rahner's approach is attempted in order to explore the nature of Christ's resurrection appearances. A good general introduction to this aspect of Rahner's thinking is Christopher F. Schiavone, *Rationality and Revelation in Rahner* (New York: Peter Lang, 1994).

41. Knight, chaps. 3, 6, and 11.

42. See Knight, chaps. 7 and 8, for an exploration of this aspect of the character of theological language.

43. Knight, esp. chap. 11.

44. Peacocke, *Theology*, p. 30, speaks of the incarnation as "an example of that emergence-from-continuity which characterizes the whole process whereby God is creating continuously through discontinuity." He is careful, however, to stress that in his view this does not imply that the incarnation occurred without a specific divine initiative, and in this sense he repudiates the idea that his view can be labeled naturalistic or evolutionary. For a good, brief review of his approach, see David R. Copestake, "Emergent Evolution and the Incarnation of Jesus Christ," *Modern Believing* 36, no. 4 (1995): 27-33.

45. See, e.g., Polkinghorne, *Scientists as Theologians*, chap. 6, and Clayton, *God and Contemporary Science*, pp. 224-27.

46. See the essay by Andrew Louth elsewhere in this volume.

47. Lars Thunberg, *Man and the Cosmos: The Vision of St. Maximus the Confessor* (Crestwood, N.Y.: St. Vladimir's Seminary Press, 1985), p. 75.

48. Vladimir Lossky, *The Mystical Theology of the Eastern Church* (Cambridge: James Clarke, 1957), p. 101.

49. See, e.g., the comments by Archimandrite Vasileos of Stavronikita, *Hymn of Entry: Liturgy and Life in the Orthodox Church* (Crestwood, N.Y.: St. Vladimir's Seminary Press, 1984), p. 113, based in part on Pseudo-Dionysius, *On the Divine Names* 4.20 (*Patrologia Graeca*, 3:717C).

50. See the essays by Andrew Louth and Kallistos Ware elsewhere in this volume.

51. Philip Sherrard, *Christianity: Lineaments of a Sacred Tradition* (Edinburgh: T. & T. Clarke, 1998), pp. 238-39.

52. Sherrard, p. 242.

53. Sherrard, p. 58.

54. Sherrard, pp. 61-63.

Notes to "The World as the Body of God: A Panentheistic Approach," by Keith Ward

1. Ramanuja, *The Vedanta Sutras,* trans. George Thibant, in Sacred Books of the East, vol. 48, ed. F. Max Müller (Delhi: Motilal Banarsidass, 1962). Helpful expositions can be found in my *Concepts of God* (Oxford: Oxford University Press, 1998) and in Julius Lipner, *The Face of Truth* (London: Macmillan, 1986).

2. Cf. G. W. F. Hegel, *Phenomenology of Spirit,* trans. A. V. Miller (Oxford: Oxford University Press, 1977).

3. Thomas Aquinas, *Summa Theologiae* Ia, questions 2-11.

4. A. N. Whitehead, *Process and Reality* (New York: Free Press, 1978), especially part 5, chap. 2.

Notes to "Panentheism in Metaphysical and Scientific Perspective," by Philip Clayton

1. See Imre Lakatos, "The Methodology of Scientific Research Programs," in *The Methodology of Scientific Research Programs, Philosophical Papers,* ed. John Worrall and Gregory Currie, vol. 1 (Cambridge: Cambridge University Press, 1978).

2. See Charles Taylor, *Sources of the Self: The Making of the Modern Identity* (Cambridge: Harvard University Press, 1989).

3. For a book-length appeal to the biblical data, see C. John Collins, *The God of Miracles: An Exegetical Examination of God's Action in the World* (Wheaton, Ill.: Crossway, 2000).

4. Gottfried Wilhelm Leibniz, "Discourse on Metaphysics," in *Discourse on Metaphysics and Other Essays,* ed. and trans. Daniel Garber and Roger Ariew (Indianapolis: Hackett, 1991), par. 8.

5. William James, "Does 'Consciousness' Exist?" in *Essays,* republished in *William James: Writings, 1902-1910,* based on the Harvard edition of the collected works (New York: Penguin Books, 1987), p. 1141.

6. Augustine, *Confessions* 11.28.38.

7. *Friedrich Schleiermachers Dialektik,* ed. Rudolf Odebrecht (Darmstadt: Wissenschaftliche Buchgesellschaft, 1976); for a translation of the 1811 *Dialektik,* see Terrence Tice, trans., *Dialectic, or the Art of Doing Philosophy* (Atlanta: Scholars, 1996).

8. See Clayton, *The Problem of God in Modern Thought* (Grand Rapids: Eerdmans, 2000), chap. 8.

9. Descartes, *Principia* 1.51.

10. Clayton, chaps. 5, 7-9.

11. Wolfhart Pannenberg, "Fichte und die Metaphysik des Unendlichen. Dieter Henrich zum 65. Geburtstag," *Zeitschrift für philosophische Forschung* 46 (1992): 348-62.

12. I skip over a large number of subtleties and nuances that would have to be (and have been) added in a fuller treatment.

13. Many feminist theologians have argued that it has also led to a treatment of the

environment as merely "instrumental," a mistake the consequences of which are palpable in the water and air and forests around us today.

14. See Joseph A. Bracken and Marjorie Hewitt Suchocki, eds., *Trinity in Process: A Relational Theology of God* (New York: Continuum, 1997).

15. See Sallie McFague, *Metaphorical Theology* (Philadelphia: Fortress, 1982); Janet Martin Soskice, *Metaphor and Religious Language* (Oxford: Clarendon; London: Oxford University Press, 1985).

16. See Paul Davies, "Introduction: Toward an Emergentist Worldview," in *From Complexity to Life: On the Emergence of Life and Meaning,* ed. Niels Henrik Gregersen (New York: Oxford University Press, 2002), p. 10.

17. For very strong claims on behalf of the newness of this (approach to) science, see Stephen Wolfram, *A New Kind of Science* (Champaign, Ill.: Wolfram Media, 2002). Wolfram argues, for example, that "simple programs" (of the sort he writes) can provide "a basis for understanding fundamental physics"; they "are often able to capture the essence of what is going on [in physics] — even though traditional efforts have been quite unsuccessful" (p. 433). And he concludes his presentation: "all of this supports my strong belief that in the end it will turn out that every detail of our universe does indeed follow rules that can be represented by a very simple program — and that everything we see will ultimately emerge just from running this program" (p. 545).

18. See, e.g., Niels Henrik Gregersen, "From Anthropic Design to Self-Organized Complexity," in *From Complexity to Life,* pp. 206-29.

19. See Stuart A. Kauffman, *Investigations* (Oxford: Oxford University Press, 2000).

20. See Philip Clayton and Paul Davies, eds., *The Reemergence of Emergence: New Essays on the Science and Philosophy of Emergence* (forthcoming).

21. See David Chalmers, "Facing Up to the Problem of Consciousness," first published in a special issue of the *Journal of Consciousness Studies* in 1995, and now available in Stuart R. Hameroff, Alfred W. Kaszniak, and Alwyn C. Scott, eds., *Toward a Science of Consciousness* (Cambridge: MIT Press, 1996).

22. See Samuel Alexander, *Space, Time, and Deity,* Gifford Lectures at Glasgow, 1916-1918, 2 vols. (London: Macmillan, 1920). Page citations in the text are to the excellent anthology, *Philosophers Speak of God,* ed. Charles Hartshorne and William L. Reese (Amherst, N.Y.: Humanity Books, 2000).

23. "A substance or piece of Space-Time which is mental is differentiated in a portion of its mental body so as to be divine, and this deity is sustained by all the Space-Time to which it belongs" (p. 367).

24. Rabbi David Cooper, *God Is a Verb: Kabbalah and the Practice of Mystical Judaism* (New York: Riverhead Books, 1997).

25. I am grateful to Steven Knapp for a close reading and critique of this paper and for constructive discussions that influenced the formation and formulation of many of the ideas. Probing queries from Owen Thomas have improved the position.

Notes to "Teleology without Teleology: Purpose through Emergent Complexity," by Paul Davies

1. An earlier version of this essay appeared in Robert J. Russell et al., eds., *Evolutionary and Molecular Biology: Scientific Perspectives on Divine Action* (Vatican City: Vatican Observatory Press, 1998), pp. 151-62. I am grateful to Father George Coyne of the Vatican Observatory for permission to reprint it here. The connections to the theory of panentheism are new to this version.

2. These ideas are a development of previous arguments I gave in "The Intelligibility of Nature," in *Quantum Cosmology and the Laws of Nature: Scientific Perspectives on Divine Action,* ed. Robert John Russell, Nancey Murphy, and C. J. Isham (Vatican City: Vatican Observatory Press; Berkeley: Center for Theology and the Natural Sciences, 1993, 1996). See also Paul Davies, *The Mind of God: The Scientific Basis for a Rational World* (New York: Simon and Schuster, 1992).

3. See the articles by Nancey Murphy, George Ellis, Thomas Tracy, and Robert John Russell in Robert John Russell, William R. Stoeger, and Francisco Ayala, eds., *Evolutionary and Molecular Biology: Scientific Perspectives on Divine Action* (Vatican City: Vatican Observatory, 1998).

4. Ontological indeterminism is only one of several defensible interpretations of quantum physics. It is the one being adopted here, but none of these interpretations has greater predictive power than the others, leaving the choice open at this point.

5. To take a simple example, suppose a box of gas subject to Newtonian laws were in fact closed save for the influence of a single electron located at the edge of the observable universe, ten billion light years away. Furthermore, let us suppose that the electron interacted with the molecules in the box not electrically, but via the much weaker inverse square law gravitational force. Now ask the question: After how many collisions with its neighbors would the predicted and actual trajectories of a given molecule diverge to the point that continued prediction is completely compromised? The answer turns out to be about thirty, which for air molecules at room temperature would take less than a millisecond!

6. Wesley J. Wildman and Robert John Russell, "Chaos: A Mathematical Introduction with Philosophical Reflections," in *Chaos and Complexity.*

7. The question of whether the universe as a whole is closed is a subtle one, depending on the definition of "universe," but if we take it to mean the region of space within our particle horizon at any given time, then this region certainly does not constitute a closed system, because unknowable physical influences can intrude across that horizon.

8. John Polkinghorne makes a similar argument about chaos and complexity. See, for example, Polkinghorne, "The Metaphysics of Divine Action," in *Chaos and Complexity;* see also Polkinghorne, *The Faith of a Physicist: Reflections of a Bottom-up Thinker,* Gifford Lectures, 1993-94 (Princeton: Princeton University Press, 1994), p. 26. William Alston makes a similar argument about the lack of a sufficient warrant for determinism in general. See, for example, William P. Alston, "Divine Action, Human Freedom, and the Laws of Nature," in *Quantum Cosmology and the Laws of Nature;* Alston, *Divine Nature and Human Language: Essays in Philosophical Theology* (Ithaca, N.Y.: Cornell University Press, 1989).

9. See, for example, Paul Davies, *The Cosmic Blueprint: New Discoveries in Nature's*

Creative Ability to Order the Universe (New York: Touchstone, 1988); Arthur Peacocke, *Creation and the World of Science* (Oxford: Oxford University Press, 1979).

10. See, for example, Philip Clayton, *God and Contemporary Science* (Grand Rapids: Eerdmans, 2000). For the "panentheistic analogy," see in particular chap. 8.

11. See Peacocke, *Creation and the World of Science.*

12. For further discussions of design arguments, see George F. R. Ellis, "The Theology of the Anthropic Principle," and Nancey Murphy, "Evidence of Design in the Fine-Tuning of the Universe," in *Quantum Cosmology and the Laws of Nature.* See also George F. R. Ellis, *Before the Beginning: Cosmology Explained* (London: Boyars/Bowerdean, 1993); Nancey Murphy and George F. R. Ellis, *On the Moral Nature of the Universe: Theology, Cosmology, and Ethics* (Minneapolis: Fortress, 1996).

13. Davies, *The Cosmic Blueprint;* Peacocke, *Creation and the World of Science.*

14. See Peter Coveney and Roger Highfield, *Frontiers of Complexity: The Search for Order in a Chaotic World* (London: Faber and Faber, 1995), p. 89.

15. See, for example, Eugene Northrop, *Riddles in Mathematics* (Pelican, 1944), p. 33. Generally, totally rule-bound games, like the Tower of Hanoi, are tedious and pointless, soon losing their appeal, while games of *pure* chance, like the card game snap, also have limited appeal. The best games are those that combine an element of both chance and choice, for example, chess, Monopoly, whist. Wesley Wildman has suggested to me that the game Yahtzee provides the most appealing analogy to nature in its mix of order and openness.

16. John Barrow and Frank Tipler, *The Anthropic Cosmological Principle* (Oxford: Oxford University Press, 1986); P. C. W. Davies, *The Accidental Universe* (Cambridge: Cambridge University Press, 1982).

17. Richard Dawkins, *The Blind Watchmaker* (London: Norton, 1986, 1987).

18. For a helpful overview, see John Leslie, *Universes* (London: Routledge, 1989).

19. Andrei Linde, *Particle Physics and Inflationary Cosmology* (Reading, U.K.: Harwood Academic Publishers, 1990).

20. For a helpful discussion and extensive references, see Willem B. Drees, *Beyond the Big Bang: Quantum Cosmologies and God* (La Salle, Ill.: Open Court, 1990), pp. 48-51.

21. Lee Smolin, *The Life of the Cosmos* (Oxford: Oxford University Press, 1997).

22. See, for example, Gregory Chaitin, *Algorithmic Information Theory* (Cambridge: Cambridge University Press, 1987).

23. Augustine, *Confessions,* trans. F. J. Speed (London: Sheed and Ward, 1960), bk. 11.

24. The meaning of "nothing" here is highly problematic, of course. I take the concept to mean nothing existed out of which our present, visible universe arose with the exception of the eternal laws and constants of nature. If so, then the emergence of this universe may be an entirely "natural" event not requiring further special action by God. Of course, God would still have had to create the laws and choose the constants of nature. Alternatively, if our universe arose out of an eternally inflating mega-universe, as suggested by quantum cosmology, one would still need to explain why the mega-universe, its fields and laws exist. In any case, the point is that God creates from eternity, not at a moment in time. For further discussion see Paul Davies, *The Mind of God,* chap. 2. Also see Robert John Russell, "Finite Creation without a Beginning," in *Quantum Cosmology and the Laws of Nature,* esp. pp. 315-18, and articles by C. J. Isham and W. R. Stoeger in the same volume. See also C. J. Isham, "Creation of the Universe as a Quantum Process," in *Physics, Philoso-*

phy, and Theology: A Common Quest for Understanding, ed. Robert J. Russell, William R. Stoeger, and George V. Coyne (Vatican City: Vatican Observatory, 1988).

25. By "initially" I do not mean in the temporal sense, but in the sense of being logically prior in the explanatory scheme.

26. Let me give a specific example: standard quantum mechanics assigns probabilities to components of the wave function according to a well-known calculus. One might consider a world in which such assignments were made according to an alternative prescription. I conjecture that the actual calculus that pertains to the real universe is such as to optimize some information theoretic quantity, such as the mutual information between components of entangled physical systems.

27. See Paul Davies, *The Mind of God,* esp. chap. 6. See also Jack Cohen and Ian Stewart, *The Collapse of Chaos* (London: Viking, 1994).

28. See Paul Davies, *Are We Alone?* (New York: Basic Books; London: Penguin Books, 1995) and *The Fifth Miracle: The Search for the Origin of Life* (New York: Simon and Schuster; London: Allen Lane, 1998).

29. See, for example, Ilya Prigogine and Isabelle Stengers, *Order out of Chaos: Man's New Dialogue with Nature* (Toronto: Bantam Books, 1984). It might help at this point to clarify how I am using the word "self-organization" from the perspective of physics. In general, "self-organization" is often used rather loosely to describe any phenomenon in which complex organization emerges. Given this, I would want to distinguish between spontaneous and supervised self-organization. Physics provides scores of examples of spontaneous self-organization, involving just general physical laws and random variables. The famous Bénard instability in fluid mechanics involving the formation of hexagonal convection cells provides a classic example of spontaneous self-organization, a curious mix of chance and necessity. Although general mathematical principles legislate that the cells shall be hexagons, the exact size, shape, and location of the hexagons are decided by random fluctuations at the microscopic level. (In fact, the problem is even more complex. Suppose we assume that the exact pattern of the convection cells is determined by an information-bearing ingredient that could say: "A hexagon edge here, please!" How could this be achieved by an ingredient within the fluid *that is distributed homogeneously through the fluid* in its initial uniform state?)

30. Once nature discovered the value of brainpower, it seems that the encephalization quotient accelerated. The growth of brain capacity among hominids has been especially fast. See Camilo J. Cela-Conde and Gisele Marty, "Beyond Biological Evolution: Mind, Morals and Culture," in *Evolutionary and Molecular Biology: Scientific Perspectives of Divine Action,* ed. Robert John Russell, William R. Stoeger, and Francisco Ayala (Vatican City: Vatican Observatory, 1998), pp. 445-62.

31. In his earlier writings, Richard Dawkins forcefully argued that there is not only no evidence from the fossil record for "progress" or "directionality" in evolution, but also no evidence of "trends." Dawkins, p. 181.

32. See Stephen Jay Gould, "On Replacing the Idea of Progress with an Operational Notion of Directionality," in *Evolutionary Progress,* ed. Matthew H. Nitecki (Chicago: University of Chicago Press, 1988).

33. See, for example, Francisco J. Ayala, "The Distinctness of Biology," in *Laws of Na-*

ture: Essays on the Philosophical, Scientific, and Historical Dimensions, ed. Friedel Weinert (Berlin and New York: Walter de Gruyter, 1995), pp. 268-85.

Notes to "Emergence of Humans and the Neurobiology of Consciousness," by Robert L. Herrmann

1. David Wilcox, in *Is God the Only Reality?* ed. John Marks Templeton and Robert L. Herrmann (Philadelphia: Templeton Foundation Press, 1994), p. 157.

2. Philip Clayton, *God and Contemporary Science* (Grand Rapids: Eerdmans, 1997), p. 245.

3. All three of these three winning essays of the competition are accessible at www.templeton.org/pdf/creative-research.pdf (Dec. 2003).

4. Mary K. Colvin, "Awareness across Time and Brain Space: Approaches to a Scientific Understanding of Consciousness," winning essay in the Creative Research Ideas in Neurobiology Program of the John Templeton Foundation (see n. 3 above).

5. Benjamin Libet, "How Does Conscious Experience Arise? The Neural Time Factor," *Brain Research Bulletin* 50, no. 5/6 (1999): 339-40.

6. Todd C. Handy, "The Neural Basis of the Search for Meaning: A Time Scale Approach." Winning essay in the Creative Research Ideas in Neurobiology Program of the John Templeton Foundation (see n. 3 above).

7. Todd C. Handy, "Capacity Theory as a Model of Cortical Behavior," *Journal of Cognitive Neuroscience* 12 (2000): 1066-69.

8. Curt A. Paulson and Michael Persinger, "Creative Research Ideas in Neurobiology: Technologically-Assisted Spiritual Exploration." Winning essay in the Creative Research Ideas in Neurobiology Program of the John Templeton Foundation (see n. 3 above).

9. Alejandro Pienado, "Traveling Slow Waves of Neural Activity: A Novel Form of Network Activity in Developing Neocortex," *Journal of Neuroscience* 20 RC 24 (2000).

10. David Chalmers, "The Puzzle of Conscious Experience," in *Science Times Book of the Brain*, ed. Nicholas Wade (New York: Lynn Press, 1999), pp. 287-95.

11. Keith Ward, *Defending the Soul* (Oxford: OneWorld, 1992), p. 146.

Notes to "The 'Trinitarian' World of Neo-Pantheism: On Panentheism and Epistemology," by Harold J. Morowitz

1. Immanuel Kant, *Critique of Pure Reason*, trans. Norman Kemp Smith (Bedford: St. Martins, 1929).

2. Henry Margenau, *The Nature of Physical Reality* (reprint, Ox Bow Press, 1977).

3. Karl Popper, *The Logic of Scientific Discovery* (New York: Basic Books, 1959).

4. John Holland, *Emergence: From Chaos to Order* (Reading, Mass.: Addison-Wesley, 1998).

5. C. Lloyd Morgan, *Emergent Evolution* (London: Williams and Norgate, 1923).

6. Walter Elsasser, *Atom and Organism* (Princeton: Princeton University Press, 1966).

7. Donald Griffin, *Animal Minds* (Chicago: University of Chicago Press, 1992).

Notes to "Articulating God's Presence in and to the World Unveiled by the Sciences," by Arthur Peacocke

1. Thomas Traherne, *Centuries: First Century,* reflection 18 (London: Faith Press, 1963; orig. published, 1670), 1.18, p. 9.

2. J. Kim, "The Non-Reductivist's Troubles with Mental Causation," in *Mental Causation,* ed. J. Heil and A. Mele (Oxford: Clarendon, 1995), pp. 189-210.

3. H. Wheeler Robinson, "Hebrew Psychology," in *The People and the Book,* ed. A. S. Peake (Oxford: Clarendon, 1925), p. 362.

4. S. Kaufmann, *At Home in the Universe: The Search for the Laws of Complexity* (London: Penguin Books, 1996); and for wider references see A. R. Peacocke, *The Physical Chemistry of Biological Organization* (Oxford: Clarendon, 1989), chaps. 2, 4, and 5.

5. Kaufmann, passim; P. Bak, *How Nature Works: The Science of Self-Organized Criticality* (Oxford: Oxford University Press, 1997); and I. Stewart, *Life's Other Secret: The New Mathematics of the Living World* (London: Penguin Books, 1998).

6. Karl Popper, *A World of Propensities* (Bristol: Thoemmes, 1990), and Arthur Peacocke, "Biological Evolution — a Positive Theological Appraisal," in *Evolutionary and Molecular Biology: Scientific Perspectives on Divine Action,* ed. R. J. Russell, W. R. Stoeger, and F. J. Ayala (Vatican City: Vatican Observatory; Berkeley, Calif.: Center for Theology and the Natural Sciences; Notre Dame, Ind.: University of Notre Dame Press, 1998), pp. 357-76.

7. A. R. Peacocke, *Creation and the World of Science* (Oxford: Clarendon, 1979), chap. III.

8. T. W. Deacon, "Evolution and the Emergence of Spirit" (paper given at the Science and the Spiritual Quest Boston Conference, 21-23 October 2001).

9. Deacon, "Evolution and the Emergence of Spirit."

10. A. Moore, "The Christian Doctrine of God," in *Lux Mundi,* ed. C. Gore, 12th ed. (London: Murray, 1891), p. 73.

11. C. Kingsley, *The Water Babies* (London: Hodder and Stoughton, 1930; orig. published, 1863), p. 248.

12. H. Van Till, "The Creation Intelligently Designed or Optimally Equipped?" *Theology Today* 55 (1988): 349, 351.

13. See the discussion below on this divine agency being analogous to *personal* agency.

14. G. R. Peterson, "Whither Panentheism?" *Zygon* 36 (September 2001): 395-405.

15. *The Oxford Dictionary of the Christian Church,* ed. F. L. Cross and E. A. Livingstone, 2nd ed. (Oxford: Oxford University Press, 1974), p. 1027.

16. Acts 17:28 (AV and RSV).

17. J. Moltmann, *God in Creation* (London: SCM Press, 1985). The next three quotes in the text are also from this work.

18. Augustine, *Confessions* 7, trans. E. B. Pusey, in *Great Books of the Western World*, vol. 18, ed. R. M. Hutchins (Chicago: Encyclopaedia Britannica, 1952), p. 45.

19. See the series of volumes on scientific perspectives on divine action which have resulted from the biennial discussions organized by the Vatican Observatory and the Center for Theology and the Natural Sciences, Berkeley (gen. ed., R. J. Russell), and distributed through the University of Notre Dame Press, Notre Dame, Ind.

20. See the contributions by Orthodox thinkers in this volume.

21. J. G. Dunn, *Christology in the Making* (London: SCM Press, 1986), pp. 259, 262.

22. Celia Deane-Drummond, *Creation through Wisdom* (Edinburgh: T. & T. Clark, 2000), p. xv and passim.

23. John 1:1-4.

24. John 1:14.

25. W. Temple, *Nature, Man, and God* (London: Macmillan, 1934), chap. 19.

Notes to "God Immanent yet Transcendent: The Divine Energies according to Saint Gregory Palamas," by Kallistos Ware (Bishop of Diokleia)

1. Evelyn Underhill, *Worship* (London: Nisbet, 1936), p. 263.

2. See, for example, *Seed of Adam*, in Charles Williams, *Collected Plays* (London: Oxford University Press, 1963), p. 160. Williams (1886-1945) implies that this is a quotation but does not indicate a precise source. Closely similar language can certainly be found in the Hindu Upanishads.

3. Quoted in Sidney H. Griffith, "'As One Spiritual Man to Another': The Merton–Abdul Aziz Correspondence," in Rob Baker and Gray Henry, *Merton and Sufism: The Untold Story: A Complete Compendium* (Louisville: Fons Vitae, 1999), p. 114.

4. Quoted in Vladimir Lossky, *The Mystical Theology of the Eastern Church* (London: James Clarke, 1957), p. 92.

5. The outstanding monograph on Maximus in the English language is still Lars Thunberg, *Microcosm and Mediator: The Theological Anthropology of Maximus the Confessor* (Lund: C. W. K. Gleerup; Copenhagen: Ejnar Munksgaard, 1965; 2nd ed., Chicago and La Salle, Ill.: Open Court, 1995). For a brief yet excellent introduction to Maximus, consult Andrew Louth, *Maximus the Confessor* (London and New York: Routledge, 1996). On Logos and logoi, see most recently Torstein Tollefsen, *The Christocentric Cosmology of St. Maximus the Confessor — a Study of His Metaphysical Principles* (Oslo: Department of Philosophy, University of Oslo, 2000).

6. As we shall see, there is a difference in formulation here between Maximus and Palamas. The latter, when speaking of the divine energies, does not term them created, but always insists that they are uncreated and eternal.

7. Philo, *On the Posterity of Cain* 14.

8. Clement of Alexandria, *Stromateis* 2.2 (5, 3).

9. Athanasius, *On the Incarnation* 17.1.

10. Basil, *Letter* 234.1.

11. The basic work on Gregory Palamas is Jean Meyendorff, *Introduction à l'étude de Grégoire Palamas*, Patristica Sorbonensia 3 (Paris: Send, 1959); English translation, *A Study*

of Gregory Palamas (London: Faith Press, 1964). Epoch-making at the time of its first appearance, this book is now badly in need of updating. For the more recent bibliography, see the works listed in A. N. Williams, *The Ground of Union: Deification in Aquinas and Palamas* (New York and Oxford: Oxford University Press, 1999), pp. 203-11. Williams's own treatment is penetrating but often open to question. I hope that before long an English-speaking scholar will attempt a work of synthesis, similar to Meyendorff's study, but taking full account of further research in the last forty years.

12. This is a point particularly emphasized by Saint Gregory of Nyssa in his short treatise *To Ablabius: That There Are Not Three Gods.*

13. Maximus, *Ambigua* 22 (*Patrologia Graeca,* 91:1257AB). For an analysis of this obscure passage, see Lars Thunberg, *Man and the Cosmos: The Vision of St. Maximus the Confessor* (Crestwood, N.Y.: St Vladimir's Seminary Press, 1985), pp. 137-43.

14. Palamas, *One Hundred and Fifty Chapters* 78, ed. Robert E. Sinkewicz, Studies and Texts 83 (Toronto: Pontifical Institute of Mediaeval Studies, 1988), pp. 172-74. I have followed on the whole the translation in Saint Nikodimos of the Holy Mountain and Saint Makarios of Corinth, *The Philokalia: The Complete Text,* trans. G. E. H. Palmer, Philip Sherrard, and Kallistos Ware, vol. 4 (London: Faber and Faber, 1995), p. 382.

15. Palamas, *Against Akindynos* 2.14.63, ed. P. K. Christou, *Grigoriou tou Palama Syngrammata,* vol. 3 (Thessaloniki, 1970), p. 130.

16. Palamas, *On the Divine Energies and Participation in Them* 2, ed. Christou, *Syngrammata,* vol. 2 (Thessaloniki, 1966), p. 97.

17. Palamas, *Triads in Defence of the Holy Hesychasts* 1.3.23, ed. Jean Meyendorff, *Défense des saints hésychastes,* Spicilegium Sacrum Lovaniense 30-31 (Louvain: Université Catholique, 1959), p. 159.

18. Quoted in Vladimir Lossky, *Théologie négative et connaissance de Dieu chez Maître Eckhart* (Paris: Vrin, 1960), p. 255.

19. *Sermon* 18, in *Meister Eckhart: Sermons and Treatises,* trans. M. O'C. Walshe, vol. 1 (Longmead: Element Books, 1987), p. 147.

20. Palamas, *One Hundred and Fifty Chapters* 75, p. 170.

21. *The Homilies of Macarius* 15.10.

22. It has sometimes been suggested that Barlaam, like the brothers Kydones, is also influenced by Western scholastic theology; in Barlaam's case, however, so it is argued, the influence is from nominalism rather than Thomism. On the whole this seems improbable. While the Thomism of the brothers Kydones is an undoubted fact, Barlaam does not appear to have had a close knowledge of Latin theology. His starting point is Neoplatonism rather than nominalism. The debate between Barlaam and Palamas is not a dispute between the Latin West and the Greek East, but it is primarily a disagreement *within* the Greek patristic tradition. At the heart of the confrontation are two conflicting interpretations of Dionysius the Areopagite; Palamas sees Dionysius as essentially a mystical rather than a philosophical theologian. Barlaam excludes the possibility of a direct experience of the divine during this present life; Palamas insists upon its possibility and, indeed, its fundamental importance.

23. Palamas, *Letter to Gabras* 13, in *Syngrammata,* 2:340.

24. Palamas, *Triads* 3.2.7, in *Défense des saints hésychastes,* p. 657.

25. Synodical Tome of 1351, §29: ed. I. N. Karmiris, *Ta Dogmata kai Symvolika*

Mnimeia tis Orthodoxou Katholikis Ekklisias, 2nd ed., vol. 1 (Athens: Apostoliki Diakonia, 1960), p. 391.

26. See "Summaries of the Contributions to This Volume," p. xv.

27. See Niels Henrik Gregersen, "Three Varieties of Panentheism," pp. 19-35, in this volume.

28. This, of course, raises the perplexing question of what we mean by the fall, and whether — if we adopt some form of evolutionary worldview — it makes any sense whatever to speak of a "fallen" world prior to the emergence of human beings endowed with self-awareness and conscious free will (and therefore capable of sinning). At this point I would merely say that in describing the world as "fallen," I mean that the world as we at present know it — and our own human selves as we at present know them — do not express what God the creator desires the world and human nature to be. There is a tragic gap between divine intention and empirical reality; something has gone wrong.

29. Maximus, *Centuries on Love* 3.46.

30. Dionysius the Areopagite, *On the Divine Names* 4.13.

31. Julian of Norwich, *Revelations of Divine Love* 5.

Notes to "The Universe as Hypostatic Inherence in the Logos of God: Panentheism in the Eastern Orthodox Perspective," by Alexei V. Nesteruk

1. See, e.g., Georges Florovsky, "St. Athanasius' Concept of Creation," in *Aspects of Church History,* vol. 4 in the *Collected Works* (Belmont, Mass.: Nordland Publishing Co., 1975), pp. 39-62.

2. The detailed theory of the logoi of created things was developed by Saint Maximus the Confessor. See, e.g., Lars Thunberg, *Microcosm and Mediator: The Theological Anthropology of Maximus the Confessor* (Chicago and La Salle, Ill.: Open Court, 1995), pp. 72-79. An interesting discussion of the relation between the notion of uncreated energies in Gregory Palamas and logoi can be found in Thunberg's other book, *Man and the Cosmos: The Vision of St. Maximus the Confessor* (Crestwood, N.Y.: St. Vladimir's Seminary Press, 1985), pp. 137-43. See also the papers of Kallistos Ware and Andrew Louth in this volume.

3. One should point out that the distinction between substance (nature) and hypostasis made here has a specific patristic character, which is different to a certain extent from what may seem to be similar to the Aristotelian distinction between primary and secondary substances. Leontius of Byzantium articulated this distinction in words typical for his era and context: "Nature, then, that is, essence, could never exist without hypostasis. Yet nature is not hypostasis, because the terms are not convertible; hypostasis is nature, but nature is not hypostasis. For nature admits the principle of existence; hypostasis, that of existence by itself. Nature holds the principle of form; hypostasis points out an individual thing. Nature shows the distinctive mark of a universal; hypostasis divides the particular from the common." *Contra Nestorianos et Eutychianos,* in Migne, *Patrologia Graeca,* 86, i. 1277 D, quoted in H. M. Relton, *A Study of Christology: The Problem of the Relation of the Two Natures in the Person of Christ* (London: SPCK, 1917), p. 78. On further interplay between the Aristotelian philosophy and Leontius's Christology, see B. E. Daley, "Leontius of

Byzantium: A Critical Edition of His Works, with Prolegomena" (Ph.D. diss., Oxford University, 1978).

4. One can apply the distinction of nature and hypostasis to human beings. All human beings share the same nature, i.e., they have similar biology so that blood and flesh can be communicated from one human being to another. However, the different human beings are different *persons*, i.e., they have their own distinct existences, which cannot be communicated to, and imitated by, different persons. In the patristic model of a human being the body and soul are both created and have different natures, but the same hypostasis: they are *cohypostasized* by the Logos of God (Saint Maximus the Confessor). See Thunberg, *Microcosm and Mediator*, p. 106.

5. See, e.g., G. Florovsky, *The Byzantine Fathers of the Sixth to Eighth Century*, in his *Collected Works*, vol. 9 (Vaduz: Büchervertriebsanstalt, 1987), chap. 5, pp. 191-203. Fr. Florovsky refers to the terms used by Leontius by saying that *enhypostasis* points toward something which is not self-contingent, but has its being in the other and is not contemplated as it is in itself. *Enhypostasis* is the reality in the other hypostasis. See also Relton, *A Study of Christology*; Daley, "Leontius of Byzantium."

6. Maximus the Confessor, *Various Texts on Theology, the Divine Economy, and Virtue and Vice* (first century), in G. E. H. Palmer, Philip Sherrard, and Kallistos Ware, eds., *St. Nikodimos of the Holy Mountain and St. Makarios of Corinth, the "Philokalia": The Complete Text*, vol. 2 (hereafter cited in the text as *Philokalia*) (London: Faber and Faber, 1981), text 7, p. 165.

7. Olivier Clément, "L'homme dans le monde," *Verbum Caro* 12, no. 45 (1958): 11-12, quoted in Paulos Mar Gregorios, *The Human Presence: Ecological Spirituality and the Age of the Spirit* (New York: Amity House, 1987), p. 83.

8. Maximus the Confessor, *Two Hundred Texts on Theology and the Incarnate Dispensation of the Son of God. Second Century*, in *Philokalia*, vol. 2, text 3, p. 138.

9. G. Prestige in his book *God in Patristic Thought* (London: SPCK, 1955), p. 176, in order to illustrate how the apprehending knowledge becomes hypostatic existence, refers to Clement of Alexandria (*Stromata* 4.22, 136.4), who, speaking of knowledge, "observes that apprehension extends by means of study into permanent apprehension; and permanent apprehension, by becoming, through continuous fusion, the substance of the knower and perpetual contemplation, remains a living hypostasis. This appears to mean that knowledge becomes so bound up with the being of the knowing subject, as to constitute a permanent entity."

10. See, e.g., E. Levinas, *Time and the Other* (Pittsburgh: Duquesne University Press, 1987), pp. 42-43.

11. Levinas uses the verb "to contract" probably in the sense "to catch" or "to engage." He uses different wording elsewhere describing the event of hypostasis as "the apparition of a substantive" (see his *Existence and Existents* [The Hague: Martinus Nijhoff, 1978], pp. 82-83).

12. On the concept of coinherence, see Prestige, chap. 9.

13. B. J. Carr, "On the Origin, Evolution and Purpose of the Physical Universe," in *Modern Cosmology and Philosophy*, ed. J. Leslie (New York: Prometheus Books, 1998), p. 152.

14. One can find typical diagrams in many books. See, e.g., J. Barrow, *The Artful*

Universe (Penguin Books, 1995), pp. 49, 53; Barrow, *Between Inner Space and Outer Space* (Oxford: Oxford University Press, 1999), p. 20.

15. See details in A. V. Nesteruk, "Theology of Human Co-Creation and Modern Physics," in *Mémoire du XXIe Siècle*, numéro 3-4, Cahiers transdisciplinaires, *Création et Transcréation* (Paris: Editions du Rocher, 2001), pp. 163-75; also Nesteruk, "Humanity in the Universe: A Patristic Insight into Modern Cosmology," *Sourozh. A Journal of Orthodox Life and Thought*, no. 88 (2002): 1-20. The difference between natural and hypostatic in human constitution can be illustrated in terms of space and time. Indeed, is it possible for a human individual to exist at different places at the same time? If human beings are considered only as physical bodies animated by soul, it seems to be inconceivable. If, however, by its hypostatic constitution the human being is related to God, and through him to the whole world, its physical presence here and now does not exhaust its potential from being present everywhere in the universe by the power of *relation* to it, which is not so much epistemological as ontological, however, not based on the substance of nature.

16. D. Dennet, *Consciousness Explained* (Penguin Books, 1993).

17. In Greek patristic literature it was a prevailing view that the state of human being as it exists in natural environment includes body, soul (including the *dianoia* as an analytical part of the soul), and the *spirit*, which had never been dissociated from the Holy Spirit. Human spirit stands here for the *nous* (spiritual intellect, the organ of faith), linking human person to its dynamic relationship to God and to the world. But the Holy Spirit is the creator of both body and soul whose unity forms a particular human person. The presence of the Holy Spirit in human constitution thus makes the human person open upward through its calling to the divine as its destiny. Without the Spirit the human being is incomplete and imprisoned through the conditions of the created nature.

18. The acquisition of personhood can be achieved only in community. J. Zizioulas calls this the ecclesial existence; see his *Being as Communion* (Crestwood, N.Y.: St. Vladimir's Seminary Press, 1997).

19. Maximus the Confessor, *The Church's Mystagogy* 7; English trans., G. C. Berthold, *Maximus the Confessor: Selected Writings* (New York: Paulist, 1985), p. 196, italics added.

20. One should mention here that in spite of the nonscientific origin of the idea that the reality of the universe is brought into existence through the process of its apprehension by human beings, there has been an attempt to articulate this idea in modern physics by J. A. Wheeler. See, e.g., Wheeler, "World as a System Self-Synthesized by Quantum Networking," *IBM Journal of Research Development* 32 (1988): 4-15; Wheeler, *At Home in the Universe* (New York: American Institute of Physics, 1996). See our analysis of Wheeler's ideas in Nesteruk, "Theology of Human Co-Creation and Modern Physics."

21. T. F. Torrance, *Space, Time, and Incarnation* (Edinburgh: T. & T. Clark, 1997).

22. W. Pannenberg, *Jesus — God and Man* (London: SCM Press, 1968), p. 166.

23. Maximus the Confessor, *The Church's Mystagogy* 7, in Berthold, p. 188.

24. Zizioulas, pp. 119-20.

Notes to "The Cosmic Vision of Saint Maximos the Confessor," by Andrew Louth

1. For this doctrine see Bishop Kallistos's paper in the present collection.

2. For a brief introduction in English, with a selection of translated texts, see Andrew Louth, *Maximus the Confessor* (London: Routledge, 1996).

3. Dumitru Staniloae, *The Experience of God* (Brookline, Mass.: Holy Cross Orthodox Press, 1994), pp. 4f.

4. On this topic see I. H. Dalmais, "La théorie des 'logoi' des créatures chez S. Maxime le Confesseur," *Revue des Sciences Philosophiques et Théologiques* 36 (1952): 244-49; Joost Van Rossum, "The λόγοι of Creation and the Divine "Energies" in Maximus the Confessor and Gregory Palamas," *Studia Patristica* 27 (1993): 213-17; and, most recently, Torstein Tollefsen, "The Christological Cosmology of St. Maximus the Confessor — a Study of His Metaphysical Principles" (Diss., University of Oslo, 1999).

5. See Theodor Haecker, *Vergil: Vater des Abendlandes*, Fischer Bücherei (Frankfurt am Main and Hamburg, 1958), pp. 131-32.

6. Cf. Dionysius, *Divine Names* 5.8, quoted by Maximos, *Ambigua* 7 (*Patrologia Graeca*, 91:1085A).

7. Maximos, *Opusc.* 7 (*Patrologia Graeca*, 91:80A).

8. Gregory Nazianzen, *Oratio* 28.3 (ed. A. J. Mason [Cambridge: Cambridge University Press, 1899], p. 26).

9. Maximos, *Ambigua* 41 (*Patrologia Graeca*, 91:1305BC).

10. Maximos, *Ambigua* 41 (*Patrologia Graeca*, 91:1305A).

11. The most recent treatment of Saint Maximos's doctrine of deification is Jean-Claude Larchet, *La divinisation de l'homme selon saint Maxime le Confesseur*, Cogitatio Fidei 194 (Paris: Éditions du Cerf, 1996).

12. One way of putting this is to say that the arc of fall-redemption (which has dominated Western theology) is in the theology of the Orthodox East subordinated to the arc of creation-deification.

13. See, e.g., Maximos, *Ambigua* 10.31c (*Patrologia Graeca*, 91:1165D).

14. B. Pascal, *Pensées*, ed. Philippe Sellier (Paris: Mercure de France, 1976), §233 (p. 134).

15. Pascal, §231.

16. Pascal, §145.

Notes to "A Relational and Evolving Universe Unfolding within the Dynamism of the Divine Communion," by Denis Edwards

1. Augustine, *Confessions* 3.6.11.

2. Aquinas, *Summa theologiae* 1.45.3.

3. For the distinction between primary and secondary causality in Thomas Aquinas, see his *Summa theologiae* la.19.6; 19.7; 19.8; 22.2; 22.3; 23.5; 23.8; 103.7; 104.1; 104.3; 105.2.

4. Arthur Peacocke, *Theology for a Scientific Age: Being and Becoming — Natural, Divine, and Human* (Minneapolis: Fortress, 1993), p. 38.

5. William R. Stoeger, "The Mind-Brain Problem, the Laws of Nature, and Constitutive Relationships," in *Neuroscience and the Person: Scientific Perspectives on Divine Action,* ed. Robert John Russell, Nancey Murphy, Theo C. Meyering, and Michael Arbib (Vatican City: Vatican Observatory, 1999), pp. 136-37.

6. Stoeger, p. 139.

7. John Zizioulas, *Being as Communion: Studies in Personhood and the Church* (Crestwood, N.Y.: St. Vladimir's Seminary Press, 1985), p. 17.

8. Zizioulas, *Being as Communion,* p. 17. See also Zizioulas, "The Doctrine of the Holy Trinity: The Significance of the Cappadocian Contribution," in *Trinitarian Theology Today,* ed. Christoph Schwobel (Edinburgh: T. & T. Clark, 1995), pp. 44-60.

9. Walter Kasper, *The God of Jesus Christ* (New York: Paulist, 1976), p. 310. See also p. 290.

10. Catherine LaCugna, *God for Us: The Trinity and Christian Life* (San Francisco: Harper San Francisco, 1991), p. 250.

11. LaCugna, p. 310.

12. Colin E. Gunton, *The One, the Three, and the Many: God, Creation, and the Culture of Modernity* (Cambridge: Cambridge University Press, 1993), p. 230. He suggests that *perichoresis,* substantiality, and relationality can be seen as what he calls "open transcendentals," as ways creation bears the marks of its making (pp. 129-231). These bear a relation to the three characteristics of the universe that I outline here. I differ from Gunton in not wanting to separate *perichoresis* and relationality and in adding, as a third characteristic, the evolution of things in time.

13. Elizabeth Johnson, *She Who Is: The Mystery of God in Feminist Theological Discourse* (New York: Crossroad, 1992), p. 22.

14. Stoeger calls this "mereological" reducibility. See Stoeger, pp. 140-43. He points out that the claim that an entity is mereologically irreducible does not necessarily mean that something extra is needed to explain it over and beyond its constitutive relationships. Stoeger distinguishes "mereological" irreducibility from "causal" irreducibility: causal irreducibility refers to higher-level causes that are not determined solely by causes operating at a more fundamental level. Stoeger suggests that a good case can be made "that the behaviour of a water molecule, though not mereologically reducible, is causally reducible" (p. 141).

15. See, for example, Nancy Victorin-Vangerud's analysis of "poisonous pedagogy" and "poisonous pneumatology" in *The Raging Hearth: Spirit in the Household of God* (St. Louis: Chalice Press, 2000).

16. John Barrow, *The Universe That Discovered Itself* (Oxford: Oxford University Press, 2000), p. 397.

17. Ursula Goodenough, *The Sacred Depths of Nature* (New York and Oxford: Oxford University Press, 1998), p. 151. In a similar way Lynn Margulis tells us that death is the price we pay for "fancy tissues and complex life histories." See her *Symbiotic Planet: A New View of Evolution* (New York: Basic Books, 1998), p. 91.

18. The divine *"concursus"* or concurrence refers to God's ongoing cooperation, which is always needed to enable creatures to act. In the theological tradition this concurrence is understood as allowing creatures to act with their own proper autonomy.

19. Karl Rahner, "Evolution," in *Sacramentum Mundi: Volume Two*, ed. Karl Rahner, Cornelius Ernst, and Kevin Smyth (London: Burns and Oates, 1968), pp. 289-97.

20. Wolfhart Pannenberg writes of the Holy Spirit as "working in all events as the power of the future" and as "the power of the future that gives creatures their own present and their duration" (*Systematic Theology*, vol. 2 [Grand Rapids: Eerdmans, 1994], pp. 101-2). Lewis Ford often speaks of God as the power of the future. See for example his "Afterword: A Sampling of an Interpretation," in *Explorations in Whitehead's Philosophy*, ed. Lewis S. Ford and George L. Kline (New York: Fordham University Press, 1983), p. 337.

Notes to "Panentheism: A Field-Oriented Approach," by Joseph A. Bracken, S.J.

1. Cf., e.g., Sallie McFague, *Models of God: Theology for an Ecological, Nuclear Age* (Philadelphia: Fortress, 1987), pp. 59-87; also Philip Clayton, *God and Contemporary Science* (Grand Rapids: Eerdmans, 1997), pp. 82-124.

2. Cf., e.g., Max Jammer, *Einstein and Religion: Physics and Theology* (Princeton: Princeton University Press, 1999).

3. Thomas Aquinas, *Summa theologiae* I, Q. 8, a. 1.

4. Aristotle, *Metaphysics* 1040b.10-17.

5. Cf., e.g., Charles Hartshorne, *Man's Vision of God and the Logic of Theism* (Hamden, Conn.: Archon Books, 1964), pp. 230-32.

6. McFague, pp. 69-78.

7. Creation, then, is ex nihilo in the sense of proceeding from God and through the power of God rather than from some preexisting stuff or matter apart from God. For a more detailed exposition of what follows in this paper, see Bracken, *The Divine Matrix: Creativity as Link between East and West* (Maryknoll, N.Y.: Orbis, 1995); also Bracken, *The One in the Many: A Contemporary Reconstruction of the God-World Relationship* (Grand Rapids: Eerdmans, 2001).

8. Ian Barbour, *Religion and Science: Historical and Contemporary Issues* (San Francisco: Harper, 1997), p. 117.

9. Alfred North Whitehead, *Process and Reality: An Essay in Cosmology*, ed. David Ray Griffin and Donald W. Sherburne, corrected ed. (New York: Free Press, 1978), p. 18.

10. Alfred North Whitehead, *Adventures of Ideas* (New York: Free Press, 1967), p. 204.

11. Whitehead, *Process and Reality*, p. 29: "In the philosophy of organism [Whitehead's term for his own metaphysical scheme] it is not 'substance' which is permanent, but 'form.'"

12. Whitehead, *Process and Reality*, p. 90.

13. Whitehead, *Process and Reality*, p. 91: "Thus in a society, the members can only exist by reason of the laws which dominate the society, and the laws only come into being by reason of the analogous characters of the members of the society."

14. The implicit advantage to this presupposition of a collective agency at work within a Whiteheadian society rather than simply the specialized agency of a single part or member is that it better explains the minimal agency of inorganic compounds in retaining a definite character or pattern of activity over time and, even more importantly, the mani-

fest agency of supraorganic realities such as human communities or natural environments in responding to various challenges or threats to survival. Thus at all three levels of existence and activity, inorganic, organic, and supraorganic, agency is present but in a more sophisticated way than in Aristotelian metaphysics, where the notion of a soul or internal organizing principle really works well only at the organic level.

15. There is, of course, the danger of anthropomorphism in thus thinking of God as personal, indeed tripersonal, and thereby constituting a divine "community." But given Whitehead's basic understanding of a personally ordered society of actual occasions as a connected series of momentary subjects of experience with a well-defined pattern of existence and activity (Whitehead, *Process and Reality*, pp. 34-35), the resultant anthropomorphism would seem to be minimal. For even inanimate compounds as well as all nonhuman plant and animal organisms are in Whitehead's scheme personally ordered societies of actual occasions. Hence by definition the notion of personally ordered society is strictly metaphysical, applying analogously to divine persons, human persons, plant and animal organisms, inanimate compounds (even the most minimal such as electrons and protons), etc.

16. Aquinas, *Summa theologiae* I, Q. 29, art. 4 resp.

17. Whitehead, *Process and Reality*, p. 177.

18. Bracken, *The One*, pp. 132-37.

19. Cf. Ervin Laszlo, *Introduction to Systems Philosophy: Toward a New Paradigm of Contemporary Thought* (New York: Gordon and Breach, 1972), p. 23: "The new physics deals with ordered sequences of events, forming wholes, which can only arbitrarily, and usually without success in formulating exact laws, be analyzed to individual components. The general construct for those ordered wholes is *field*." In the same context Laszlo cites Albert Einstein to the effect that this shift in thinking from individual entities to fields is "'the most profound and fruitful one that has come to physics since Newton'" (cf. Albert Einstein, *The World as I See It* [New York: Covici, Friede, 1934], p. 65).

20. Josiah Royce, *The Problem of Christianity* (Chicago: University of Chicago Press, 1968), pp. 243, 312-19.

21. Laszlo, pp. 23-32.

22. Whitehead, *Process and Reality*, pp. 56-57.

23. Whitehead, *Process and Reality*, p. 244.

24. Harold J. Morowitz, "The 'Trinitarian' World of Neo-Pantheism: On Panentheism and Epistemology," p. 134, in this volume.

25. Here I consciously revise the standard Whiteheadian understanding of the divine initial aim in that I ascribe to it not only directionality from God for the self-constitution of an incipient created actual occasion but likewise the power to be, its own finite share in divine creativity. Cf. here Bracken, *Society and Spirit: A Trinitarian Cosmology* (Cranbury, N.J.: Associated University Presses, 1991), pp. 128-29.

26. All three divine persons, of course, are equally transcendent of the world, immanent within it, and operative in the progressive emergence of higher-level unities or systems within the world. But in line with the classical doctrine of the "appropriation" of different names to the divine persons (cf. Aquinas, *Summa theologiae* I, Q. 39, a. 7), I here assign differing roles in the process of cosmic evolution to different divine persons. In addition, one should recognize that if the divine persons exercised completely separate func-

tions in the cosmic process, this would be an argument for tritheism, belief in three gods in close collaboration, rather than trinitarian monotheism, belief in one God who is simultaneously three persons, three interdependent centers of activity. To maintain belief in the Trinity, therefore, the agency of the divine persons within this world must be truly collective, never individualized.

27. Arthur Peacocke, "Articulating God's Presence in and to the World Unveiled by the Sciences," p. 139, in this volume.

28. Whitehead, *Process and Reality*, p. 35.

29. Whitehead, *Process and Reality*, p. 346.

30. Further details for my understanding of human salvation within this neo-Whiteheadian scheme are provided in *The One*, pp. 175-77.

Notes to "Panentheism and Pansyntheism: God in Relation," by Ruth Page

1. *Oxford Dictionary of the Christian Church* (Oxford: Oxford University Press, 1983), p. 1027.

2. Arthur Peacocke, *Theology for a Scientific Age* (London: SCM Press, 1990), p. 61. Peacocke is aware of the ambiguities, but still represents complexity and the development of consciousness as an upward trend.

3. Peacocke, p. 245.

4. Robert Burns, "To a Mouse," in *The Poetry of Scotland*, ed. Roderick Watson (Edinburgh: Edinburgh University Press, 1995), p. 372.

5. Tracing this ambiguity and discovering what it implies for theology was the subject of Ruth Page, *Ambiguity and the Presence of God* (London: SCM Press, 1985).

6. Philip Clayton, *God and Contemporary Science* (Edinburgh: Edinburgh University Press; Grand Rapids: Eerdmans, 1997), pp. 113-14.

7. Jürgen Moltmann, *God in Creation: An Ecological Doctrine of Creation* (London: SCM Press, 1985).

8. Ruth Page, "C. H. Dodd's Use of History Critically Examined," *Theology* 79 (November 1976): 330.

9. Pieter Geyl, *Debates with Historians* (London: Fontana/Collins, 1957), p. 203.

10. Charles Birch, *On Purpose* (Kensington, N.S.W., Australia: University of New South Wales Press, 1990), p. 133.

11. Herman E. Daly and John B. Cobb, Jr., *For the Common Good: Redirecting the Economy towards Community, the Environment, and a Sustainable Future* (Boston: Beacon Press, 1989), p. 378.

12. S. Clark, "Modern Error, Ancient Virtues," in *Ethics and Biotechnology*, ed. A. Dyson and J. Harris (London: Routledge, 1994), pp. 27-29.

13. Cf. John B. Cobb, Jr., and David Ray Griffin, *Process Theology: An Introductory Exposition* (Philadelphia: Westminster, 1976), p. 53. Peacocke explicitly distances himself from this view of God's action. See Peacocke, pp. 373-74.

14. David Pailin, *God and the Processes of Reality: Foundations for a Credible Theism* (London: Routledge, 1989), p. 140.

15. Cobb and Griffin, p. 373.

16. Pailin, pp. 144-45.

17. This explanation is given at much greater length in Ruth Page, *God and the Web of Creation* (London: SCM Press, 1996).

18. Cobb and Griffin, p. 43.

19. Ruth Page, *The Incarnation of Freedom and Love* (London: SCM Press, 1991).

20. Simone Weil, *Waiting for God* (Fontana Books, 1959), p. 103, italics added.

21. Francis Thomson, "In No Strange Land," in *The Oxford Book of English Verse* (Oxford: Oxford University Press, 1949), p. 1049.

22. Simone Weil, "Are We Struggling for Justice?" in *Simone Weil: An Anthology*, ed. Sian Miles (London: Virago Press, 1986), p. 3.

23. Page, *Web of Creation*, p. 41.

Notes to "The Logos as Wisdom: A Starting Point for a Sophianic Theology of Creation," by Celia E. Deane-Drummond

1. I am capitalizing the term "Wisdom" where it refers specifically to God's Wisdom.

2. J. Martin Soskice, "Creation and Relation," in *Readings in Modern Theology*, ed. R. Gill (London: SPCK, 1995), p. 59.

3. Soskice, pp. 60-61.

4. See, for example, A. Loades, ed., *Feminist Theology: A Reader* (London: SPCK, 1990).

5. For a useful discussion of panentheism, see P. Clayton, *God and Contemporary Science* (Edinburgh: Edinburgh University Press, 1997), pp. 233-40.

6. The view that the world is God's body became more popular following the publication of Grace Jantzen's explicit *God's World, God's Body* (London: Darton, Longman and Todd, 1984) and Sallie MacFague's influential book, *Models of God* (London: SCM Press, 1987).

7. A. Peacocke, *Theology for a Scientific Age* (London: SCM Press, 1993), pp. 167-68.

8. Peacocke, pp. 371-72.

9. Soskice, pp. 58-66.

10. H. U. von Balthasar, *The Glory of the Lord: A Theological Aesthetics*, vol. 1, *Seeing the Form* (Edinburgh: T. & T. Clark, 1982), p. 449. Parenthetical page numbers in the following text refer to this work.

11. C. Deane-Drummond, *Creation through Wisdom: Theology and the New Biology* (Edinburgh: T. & T. Clark, 2000), chap. 2, pp. 35-71.

12. G. O'Collins, *Christology: A Biblical, Historical, and Systematic Study of Jesus* (Oxford: Oxford University Press, 1995), p. 40.

13. O'Collins, p. 41.

14. E. Schüssler Fiorenza, *Jesus: Miriam's Child; Sophia's Prophet* (London: SCM Press, 1994), p. 153. I have discussed the significance of Sophia as feminine elsewhere. See Deane-Drummond, *Creation through Wisdom*, chap. 4, pp. 131-37.

15. This view is taken by Martin Scott, who has pointed to the particular significance of Sophia as a female category. M. Scott, *Sophia and the Johannine Jesus* (Sheffield: JSOT Press, 1992).

16. O'Collins, p. 42.

17. J. D. G. Dunn, *Christology, the Christ, and the Spirit,* vol. 1 (Grand Rapids and Cambridge: Eerdmans, 1998), p. 329.

18. Dunn, p. 330.

19. For a discussion of Solovyov's Sophiology, see Deane-Drummond, *Creation through Wisdom,* esp. pp. 79-82.

20. 1 Cor. 8:6; Col. 1:16.

21. Dunn, p. 339.

22. Irenaeus, *Demonstration of the Apostolic Teaching,* trans. J. A. Robinson (London: SPCK, 1920), chap. 5; see also Deane-Drummond, *Creation through Wisdom,* pp. 124-26.

23. Deane-Drummond, *Creation through Wisdom,* pp. 126-31.

24. Von Balthasar, p. 457.

25. Deane-Drummond, *Creation through Wisdom,* p. 149.

26. Luke 24:40.

27. J. Ray, *The Wisdom of God Manifested in the Works of Creation* (New York: Arno Press, 1977).

28. S. J. Gould, *Hen's Teeth and Horse's Toes* (London: Penguin Books, 1983), pp. 32-45.

29. For an excellent historical discussion see P. Harrison, *The Bible, Protestantism, and the Rise of Natural Science* (Cambridge: Cambridge University Press, 1998), pp. 161-76.

30. R. Bauckham, *James: Wisdom of James, Disciple of Jesus the Sage* (London: Routledge, 1999), p. 34.

31. For a discussion of the cross as the wisdom of God, see Deane-Drummond, *Creation through Wisdom,* chap. 2, esp. pp. 52-56.

32. R. Page, *God and the Web of Creation* (London: SCM Press, 1996), pp. 40-52.

33. For a discussion about Jesus as the Wisdom of God and the implications for an ecological theology, see D. Edwards, *Jesus: The Wisdom of God: An Ecological Theology* (Homebush: St. Paul's, 1995), esp. pp. 133-52.

34. See Stanley Hauerwas, *Character and the Christian Life: A Study in Theological Ethics* (San Antonio: Trinity University Press, 1975).

35. J. Porter, *The Recovery of Virtue* (London: SPCK, 1990), pp. 156-62.

36. For further discussion see C. Deane-Drummond, *Biology and Theology Today: Exploring the Boundaries* (London: SCM Press, 2001), pp. 39-46.

37. Alastair MacIntyre has put this pointedly in *After Virtue: A Study in Moral Theology* (London: Duckworth, 1985).

Notes to "Panentheism Today: A Constructive Systematic Evaluation," by Philip Clayton

1. I hope soon with colleagues to produce a volume on panentheism across the world's religions, which, we hope, will rectify this limitation.

2. The following exercise is not meant to imply that every one of the authors would agree that "panentheism" is the best label for the position he or she presents, though in fact most have agreed that this label is indeed appropriate to their work.

3. See Peter Forrest, *God without the Supernatural: A Defense of Scientific Theism* (Ithaca, N.Y.: Cornell University Press, 1996).

4. Of course, there are other options as well, for example, to understand all of cosmic history as a single, sustained act of God. See Maurice Wiles, *God's Action in the World*, 1986 Bampton Lectures (London: SCM Press, 1986); see also the article by Wiles and ensuing discussion in Thomas F. Tracy, ed., *The God Who Acts: Philosophical and Theological Explorations* (University Park: Pennsylvania State University Press, 1994).

5. See George Lindbeck, *The Nature of Doctrine: Religion and Theology in a Postliberal Age* (Philadelphia: Westminster, 1984).

6. In fact, Gregersen's presentation might give the impression that Hegel's philosophy is actually a variant of trinitarian soteriological panentheism.

7. Christopher C. Knight, "Theistic Naturalism and the Word Made Flesh," pp. 60-61, in this volume.

8. Knight, p. 50.

9. Kallistos Ware, "God Immanent yet Transcendent: The Divine Energies according to Saint Gregory Palamas," p. 159, in this volume.

10. Ware, p. 160.

11. Andrew Louth, "The Cosmic Vision of Saint Maximos the Confessor," pp. 192-93, in this volume.

12. Louth, p. 184.

13. Ware, p. 166, referencing Palamas.

14. Ware, p. 165.

15. Ware, p. 167.

16. Ruth Page, "Panentheism and Pansyntheism: God in Relation," p. 228, in this volume.

17. Page, p. 231.

18. Denis Edwards, "A Relational and Evolving Universe Unfolding within the Dynamism of the Divine Communion," p. 202 in this volume.

19. Edwards, p. 204.

20. Celia E. Deane-Drummond, "The Logos as Wisdom: A Starting Point for a Sophianic Theology of Creation," p. 241, in this volume.

21. Deane-Drummond, p. 242.

22. Deane-Drummond, p. 243.

23. See Steven Bouma-Prediger, *The Greening of Theology: The Ecological Models of Rosemary Radford Ruether, Joseph Sittler, and Jürgen Moltmann* (Atlanta: Scholars, 1995); Grace Jantzen, *God's World, God's Body* (Philadelphia: Westminster, 1984), and even more clearly in her *Becoming Divine: Towards a Feminist Philosophy of Religion* (Bloomington: Indiana University Press, 1999); and Sallie McFague, *The Body of God: An Ecological Theology* (Minneapolis: Fortress, 1993).

24. Note that this is *not* a move Celia Deane-Drummond advocates.

25. See Willem B. Drees, *Beyond the Big Bang: Quantum Cosmologies and God* (La Salle, Ill.: Open Court, 1990); Drees, *Religion, Science, and Naturalism* (New York: Cambridge University Press, 1996); and Drees, *Creation: From Nothing until Now* (New York: Routledge, 2002).

26. Arthur Peacocke, personal communication.

27. Peacocke has responded: "I agree that if God transcends the world then we can use a special word about God's ontology and describe God as pure 'spirit.' But that does not justify using the same word of human beings in whom the capacity to relate to God (as 'spirit') emerges as the fruition of human personhood. We do not have to share God's ontology in order to relate to God" (personal communication).

28. There are difficulties here as well, it turns out. See the essays in Robert J. Russell, Nancey Murphy, and Arthur Peacocke, eds., *Chaos and Complexity: Scientific Perspectives on Divine Action* (Vatican City: Vatican Observatory, 1995).

29. Donald Davidson calls this view of mind "anomalous monism"; see Davidson, "Thinking Causes," in *Mental Causation,* ed. John Heil and Alfred Mele (Oxford: Clarendon, 1995), pp. 3-17.

30. I am grateful to Arthur Peacocke and Mary Ann Meyers for helpful criticisms of earlier drafts, and to Steven Knapp for detailed discussions of the problem of divine action, which have influenced the position, and in some cases also the formulations, in this chapter, particularly in the final section.

Index